THE
UNCOLLECTED POETRY AND PROSE
OF
WALT WHITMAN

THE
UNCOLLECTED POETRY
AND PROSE OF
WALT WHITMAN

MUCH OF WHICH HAS BEEN
BUT RECENTLY DISCOVERED
WITH
VARIOUS EARLY MANUSCRIPTS
NOW FIRST PUBLISHED

COLLECTED AND EDITED BY
EMORY HOLLOWAY
PROFESSOR OF ENGLISH IN ADELPHI COLLEGE

ILLUSTRATED

—

IN TWO VOLUMES
VOLUME
ONE

GARDEN CITY, N. Y., AND TORONTO
DOUBLEDAY, PAGE & COMPANY
1921

WHITMAN AT SEVENTY

From a remarkably lifelike Gutekunst proof given by the poet to
Mr. Thomas B. Harned, through whose courtesy it is here first
reproduced.

TO

MY MOTHER AND MY WIFE

A vast batch left to oblivion.
—WHITMAN

PREFACE

SINCE 1914, when I began work on this book, I have often hoped that its appearance might coincide with the centennial of the poet's birth, and that it might thus serve as my stone to cast upon his cairn, which, I knew, would then swell under the contributions of many hands. But the World War—strange fulfilment of the prophecy in Whitman's "Years of the Modern"—taking me overseas for a year, delayed the completion of the work by so much, and more. Now that it is ready to print, I trust the poet will not find the peace of his rest diminished that I have added my stone to his grave. And yet I have been warned by some who claim special information in the matter that Whitman himself would hardly approve of such a work as this that I have done. However that may be, Whitman has already had his ample say. The autobiographical "Leaves of Grass" is, at least for those who have the clue to its meaning, his best interpretation; but he has also laid a shaping hand upon the biographies of Burroughs, and Bucke, and Traubel, and (through these and his own often-quoted "Specimen Days") indirectly upon all others. There is a sphere for autobiography and another sphere for biography. The present volumes, though in no sense authorized by Whitman, are indeed far more autobiographical than biographical. In fact, they are autobiographical in the Whitman sense to a degree greater than the writings which he himself preserved. Somewhere—in one of the conversations with Horace Traubel—he registered an objection to autobiographies which, like Rousseau's "Confessions," are deliberately planned in retrospect; such books should grow unconsciously, he said, like a diary. Now, from 1855 on, Whitman's autobiography did grow in this manner, keeping tally of his unfolding life; that was the principle on which he steadfastly retained in it the expression of certain phases of his life even when he had happily outgrown the passions which gave them meaning. But so far as the real evolution of the man who published the First Edition in 1855 is concerned, the record was never collected in any adequate way by himself; thus his autobiography is of two sorts, part retrospective and part introspective. I have compiled these volumes in the belief that, however a poet may elect to write about himself, the serious student should approach his life and work historically, examining both in accurate relation to the age in which he lived and wrote.

For some reason Whitman seems to have preferred that his past, particularly the period before 1855 and certain later periods, should remain secret except in so far as he himself might be willing to illuminate it. That was, of course, the privilege of the living poet; but it is as clearly the duty of the biographer who writes long after his death to seek in that past, and especially in the literary records of that past, the true evolution of the man and the writer. There were two probable reasons why Whitman thus did his part in intensifying the shadow cast upon his youth and young manhood by the disproportionately brilliant light of those minute chronicles written by friends who had known him only in old age: (a) the early work of his pen was decidedly inferior and uninspired, and (b) Whitman found it congenial and convenient, as have most prophets, not only to cast in his lot with the future, but also rather sedulously to cultivate the obscurity of his own past. Moses must emerge from the desert and Mahomet from his mountain in order to obtain a hearing; Whitman followed a similar prophetic instinct in his efforts to make a picturesque and romantic wilderness of his own early environment. To that extent his autobiography as hitherto known is unrealistic.

But it is more strange that among all the books that have been written about Whitman few have approached the study of his unique genius in a manner and with a method at once sympathetic and thorough. The great bulk of the writings preserved in this sourcebook appears never to have been examined by Whitman's biographers at all, though such writings were obviously the place in which to discover the crescent poet, philosopher, and reformer. None of his biographers seems to know that he contributed to the Hempstead *Inquirer*, the *Long Island Democrat*, or the *Long Island Farmer*. I cannot discover that any but a few essayists, and they most cursorily, has made a personal examination of his contributions, chiefly during his most formative years, to the Brooklyn *Eagle*, *Times*, or *Union*, or to the New Orleans *Crescent*, or to the New York *Tribune*, *Evening Post*, or *Daily Graphic*. It would seem that not many hours have been spent in searching for his war correspondence in the New

York *Times*, and students of Whitman have, one and all, been
unaware that during the early years of the Civil War he
contributed to the Brooklyn *Standard* a specially copyrighted
series of articles on local history that would itself fill a fair-
sized volume.   Most biographers pay their passing respects to
"Franklin Evans," Whitman's dime novelette, and yet the tales
"Little Jane" and "The Death of Wind-Foot" have always
been given erroneous dates of composition notwithstanding
the fact that they lie imbedded in this much-talked-of, but little-
read, "tendency" novel.   To point out these hiatuses in Whit-
man biography is not to disparage the work of his biographers
nor to minimize the importance of the light they have cast upon
the problems involved.   Few, perhaps none, of them have had
opportunities for examining all the material contained in these
volumes.   And yet it seems to me that the time has come for a
more thorough study of Whitman origins than any yet recorded.
It is the attempt of the present publication to assist in the study
of Whitman through an examination of his earlier and less-
known writings, unguided by any preconceived notions of his
youth drawn from his own maturer work or from the familiar
character of the Camden sage, kindly and dignified but young
no longer.   Whatever value the book may have will therefore
appear, not when tested by previous conceptions of Whitman's
growth and character, but when employed as a test of those
conceptions.   If the work that I have done corrects old errors
or if it substitutes facts for old guesses, my object will, in either
case, have been accomplished.

Specifically, my purpose has been to collect all of Whitman's
magazine publications not found in his "Complete Prose" and
to select from his countless newspaper stories, book reviews,
editorials, criticisms of art, music, drama, etc., such as have
particular biographical or literary value, with such others as
may be needed fairly to indicate his thought and style of com-
position in each stage of his pre-poetic career.   The volumes
contain also the first publication of a considerable number of
Whitman manuscripts which possess unusual value in the study
of the genesis of his poetry.   The Whitman notebooks are too
numerous, and in some cases too illegible, to be presented here
in their entirety; I have, however, included without omission
or abridgment those which are the most important from the
point of view of the present collection, *i.e.*, those antedating
1855, and from the later ones I have extracted whatever seemed

to throw new or important light on Whitman problems, biographical or critical. The complete set of these notebooks is now available to the student in the Library of Congress. . . . The only Whitman compositions known to me which, though falling under the principle of selection just stated, are not here included are his contributions to certain newspapers, like the Brooklyn *Freeman*, of which diligent search has as yet failed in locating any files or numbers, and a few manuscripts (such as "An American Primer," "Diary in Canada," "Lafayette in Brooklyn," and "Criticism: An Essay") which have been published in fairly accessible booklets since the poet's death.

The authenticity of the writings given in this collection is established by Whitman's signature (in a few cases that of his known *nom de plume*), by the direct transmission of the manuscripts through his literary executors or other responsible persons, or by such other evidence as is set forth in the footnotes to the various selections. In the case of newspapers for which Whitman was the sole editorial writer, the dates that bounded his editorship have been established beyond peradventure and selections made only from issues comprehended between those dates. A careful study has also been made, by way of verification, of all the internal evidence afforded by the selections themselves.

With the exception of the excerpts from the Brooklyn *Times*, to the files of which I had only a limited access, and the digest of his book reviews in the *Eagle*, nearly all the quotations have been made without any abridgment whatever. Nothing has been "expurgated" or altered in its meaning, and wherever a word or a passage has been omitted or inserted the fact has been indicated, omissions by asterisks and additions by brackets. But it has seemed to me that it would be unjust to Whitman and inconvenient for the reader should I preserve the punctuation exactly as it stands in the columns of the very inexpert journals of half a century and more ago, or that I should retain obvious typographical errors. Some commas which were not only superfluous but obstructive I have omitted, and in a few cases I have modernized other marks of punctuation where to do so would not alter the meaning except to make it clearer. But, believing that punctuation and spelling no less than phraseology and grammar have their place in revealing mental processes, I have preserved Whitman's eccentricities in regard to these except where I judged that they would be particularly baffling or irritating to the modern reader. All verse and manuscripts have been given in faithful copy even to the point of retaining meaningless punctuation and fragments of sentences.

To facilitate the use of the volumes by the Whitman student, I have added numerous footnotes, giving places and dates of publication, cross references, and such other information or interpretation as was deemed helpful toward an understanding of the text. In a few cases several Whitman utterances on a given subject, or in a series, have been placed in juxtaposition (out of their strict chronological order) that one might throw light upon another. The manuscripts which antedate the 1855 edition of the "Leaves of Grass" have been collated both with that edition and with the current authorized edition. Furthermore, I have attempted, in two introductory essays, to evaluate all this heterogenous material and to render it accessible to various types of students, such as psychologists, genealogists, historians, students of American life, manners, journalism, and literature, and students of Whitman in particular. Space has been wanting, of course, to give a complete story of Whitman's life or to essay a comprehensive estimate of his work, but I have tried to point out the relation of this new material to the outstanding problems of Whitman biography and criticism. The definitive biography of Whitman, when it comes to be written, will make use of this material only in its just relation to what has hitherto been known; but here there is opportunity to do little more than to index the material in the volumes in the form of two essays.

The student who desires to examine in chronological order all the early writings of Whitman, including those preserved in the "Complete Prose," is referred also to the bibliography which, in collaboration with Mr. Henry S. Saunders, I prepared to accompany my chapter on this poet in the "Cambridge History of American Literature," Volume II.

In collecting material for such a sourcebook as this I have naturally been placed under manifold obligations both to libraries and to individuals. Of the former I desire to thank, in particular, the Queens Borough Public Library, of Jamaica, Long Island, which repeatedly opened for me its rare files of the *Long Island Democrat* and of the *Long Island Farmer;* the Long Island Historical Society, of Brooklyn, for innumerable courtesies during several years, including the supplying of files of the Brooklyn *Star, Eagle, Advertiser, Standard,* and *Patriot,* as well

as many other rare and serviceable volumes; the Howard Me-
morial Library and the Louisiana State Historical Society, of
New Orleans, for giving me access to their files of the New Or-
leans *Crescent* and for other services; the Brooklyn Public
Library, the Pratt Library (Brooklyn), the Columbia Univer-
sity Library, the library of Mr. J. Pierpont Morgan, the Li-
brary of Congress, and especially the New York Public Library,
without whose united assistance I could never have brought the
present work to a state of even approximate completion. My
indebtedness to individuals is likewise great. Not to mention
by name the officials of the institutions just enumerated, I have
been placed under obligation by the following persons: Mr.
William Kernan Dart, of New Orleans, who kindly permitted
me to read his article "Walt Whitman in New Orleans" while
it was still in manuscript and who otherwise assisted me in iden-
tifying some of Whitman's contributions to the *Crescent;* Mr.
Herbert F. Gunnison, Mr. William H. Sutton, and Mr. A. J.
Aubrey, of the Brooklyn *Eagle*, for the highly appreciated court-
esy of having unsealed for me many volumes of their journal
which were not to be duplicated elsewhere, and for other ser-
vices; Mr. Richard C. Ellsworth and Mr. George R. Rothwell,
of the Brooklyn *Times*, for a similar kindness; Mrs. M. L. Val-
entine, of New York, for permission to examine her large col-
lection of Whitman manuscripts and to make use of one of them
here; Mr. Louis I. Haber and Mr. Alfred L. Goldsmith, also
of New York, for permission to publish Whitman manuscripts
which they own; Mr. Frank Hopkins, Mr. Max Breslow, Mr.
Oscar Lion, the late Horace Traubel, Mrs. Orvetta Hall Bren-
ton, Miss Rica Brenner, Mr. Edgar P. Holloway, and Miss
Mary Holloway, for varied assistance; Mrs. Ina M. Seaborn, of
London, Ontario, who placed me deeply in her debt by allowing
me to make an extended examination of the great collection of
Whitmaniana left by her father, Dr. Richard Maurice Bucke;
Mr. Thomas B. Harned, a close friend and now the only sur-
viving literary executor of Whitman, who generously placed in
my hands, for use here and elsewhere, all the Whitman material
that came to him under the poet's will, including the extremely
interesting and valuable manuscript notebooks to which refer-
ence has already been made, and who has offered me, for use as
a frontispiece, the last unreproduced Gutekunst photograph
of Whitman; Mr. Henry S. Saunders, of Toronto, who placed
at my service his uncommonly large collection of Whitman

writings and who has rendered important and enthusiastic assistance in tracing some of the poet's very fugitive publications; Mr. G. G. Wyant and a certain anonymous reader, sometime connected with the Yale University Press, for helpful criticism; Professors John Erskine and Ashley H. Thorndike, of Columbia University; Professor Bliss Perry, of Harvard; and Professor Killis Campbell, of the University of Texas, and my colleague, Professor Edgar A. Hall, a suggestion from the first of whom was largely responsible for my undertaking, in a different form, the present research. Nor can one publish a collection similar to this without being made the debtor, in sundry ways, to that genial fraternity, the dealers in old and rare books.

To no one, however, am I so much indebted as to my wife, who has prepared the Subject Index and who by years of varied assistance and encouraging faith has lightened a laborious task.

Brooklyn, 1920.

Emory Holloway

POSTSCRIPTUM

The manuscript of the present work was already in the hands of its publishers when a selection from Whitman's writings in the Brooklyn *Daily Eagle*, entitled "The Gathering of the Forces," appeared. Since the announcement of my intention to publish the results of the research offered to the reader herewith had antedated by some years the work of Messrs. Rodgers and Black, there was no occasion, as there was little opportunity, for me to alter the principle on which I had included or excluded material. A very few minor changes have been made, however, as the book went through the press. Wherever possible I have consulted the reader's convenience by referring him to "The Gathering of the Forces," rather than to the rare files of the *Eagle*, for some material not reproduced here.

E. H.

CONTENTS

VOLUME I

*A redaction of an earlier poem.
†Date of composition. Other dates are those of publication.

ILLUSTRATIONS

INTRODUCTION: BIOGRAPHICAL

I. ANCESTRY AND EARLY LIFE (1819–1836)

OUR knowledge of Whitman's ancestry comes largely from the poet himself. The blood of English, Dutch, and Welsh forbears blended in his veins, but it is obvious that he was proudest of his Hollandic stock. In his historical sketches of Brooklyn and Long Island[1] he has much to say in praise of the physical soundness, the cleanliness, intelligence, and religion of the Dutch colonists in New Amsterdam,[2] but very little to say about the English. Yet if the common sense, the sound judgment, the enterprise and patience, the slowness of movement and of thought, and the religious toleration of his Dutch (and Quaker) forbears were all to appear in the man and in his work, hardly less apparent were to be the tenacity of purpose and the mystical idealism of his English (New England) stock. As one reads the present volumes, these two ancestral strains will be found contending together for the mastery, or else, in moments of greatest achievement, uniting to create the "Leaves of Grass."

Whitman's maternal grandfather, Major Cornelius Van Velsor, a prosperous farmer at Cold Spring, he describes as "jovial, red, stout, with sonorous voice and characteristic physiognomy,"[3] while his wife is pictured as being "of sweet, sensible character, housewifely proclivities, and deeply intuitive and spiritual."[4] It is pleasant to see this wholesome couple in the simple country setting of the ghost story which Whitman, as editor of the Brooklyn *Eagle*, culls for his readers from the stores of family legend.[5] Both the Major and his sweet-tempered wife were

[1] The "Brooklyniana," II, pp. 222–321, *passim*.

[2] See II, pp. 5, 224–227, 300.

[3] Walt Whitman's "Complete Prose," 1914, p. 5. Hereafter this volume will be referred to by its title alone.

[4] Quoted from John Burroughs in "Complete Prose," p. 6.

[5] "An Incident on Long Island Forty Years Ago," I, pp. 149–151.

of the Quaker persuasion, a fact which—chiefly through the
poet's mother—came to influence his own character and writings.
Major Van Velsor, like Walt's father, was a personal friend of
Elias Hicks, whose home was at Jericho,[1] not far from Cold
Spring; and any anecdote concerning the Quaker leader was
carefully preserved by Whitman.[2] It would seem, however,
that the younger Whitman never went the whole way with the
disciples of Fox; he did not believe, for instance, that the doc-
trine of non-resistance could ever dominate the lives of men.[3]
But he was at times powerfully influenced by what these reli-
gious mystics call the "inner light."[4] He even interpreted the
Scriptures so much in the manner of the Friends as once to
conceive of the spirit which inspires his own poetry as a rein-
carnation of the soul of Jesus.[5] To him "the divine Jew" was
the supreme character of the ages, but unique only in the degree
of his divinity.[6] As to the genuine Quaker, so to him outward
show and ceremonialism meant little,[7] creed and dogma no
more.[8] He detested the doctrinal bickering of the sects,[9]
since to him religion was always the simple spirit of reverence
and direct communion with an immanent deity that it was to
the Hicksite Quaker; he looked upon religion as a mode of living
rather than as a phase of life.[10] If we may judge by the great
number of his allusions and quotations, the Bible[11] was one of
the chief sources of his inspiration, Shakespeare[12] being its only
close rival. Whatever strictures Whitman may have laid
upon the churches[13] and whatever lapses there may have been
in his conduct from the idealism of his best moments, one
need not go beyond the pages of the present work to be con-
vinced that his nature was spiritually sensitive to a high degree[14]
and that his sympathy and love for his fellow men was pro-
foundly Christian.[15]

[1]See II, p. 311.   [2]See II, pp. 3–4; also "Complete Prose," pp. 457–473.

[3]See I, p. 197.   [4]See I, pp. 38, 42–44; II, pp. 66–67, 71, 72, 80–81, 89.

[5]See II, p. 74; cf. the poem "To Him That Was Crucified."

[6]See II, pp. 83, 91–92.   [7]See I, p. 94–96, 145.   [8]See I, pp. 39 ff.; II,p. 13, note 4.

[9]See I, pp. 39 ff.   [10]See I, pp. 95–96, 186.

[11] Page references to these allusions will be found in the Subject Index. The aim of the
footnotes in this Introduction is to illustrate and substantiate the various points made,
not to exhaust the evidence contained in the volumes.

[12] It seems that Whitman knew a good deal of Shakespeare by heart. See II, p. 318,
and Subject Index.

[13]See II, pp. 74, 84–85, 90.   [14]See II, pp. 61, 69–70, 79–80, 82–83, 159, 163, 166.

[15]See I, pp. 46–48, II, pp. 69–71, 74, 81, 84, 146–147, 160, 173.

Whitman's memory for dates is seldom worthy of implicit trust, but when he says[1] that his father moved the family to Brooklyn in May, 1823, he is at least approximately correct.[2] Except for summer excursions to the Island, the poet spent his boyhood in Brooklyn, then a village small and primitive enough[3] for his curious eyes to have explored all its picturesque corners[4] and to have been familiar with all its leading personages.[5] As a sturdy lad of six, he stood in line among his schoolfellows to await the arrival of that hero of the Revolution who was by chance to lay upon him the "sacred hands"[6] of a patriot.[7] This act of Lafayette's can scarcely be said, in the light of the original story (told in 1857),[8] to have had any reference to the boy's character or appearance; nevertheless it seems to have lingered in the latter's mind with the significance of a prophetic symbol. At any rate, it was several times repeated by him[9]—not, it must be admitted, without a natural increment of sentimental detail. We next see the idle and mischievous boy[10] throwing brickbats into the mulberry trees in Nassau Street, unafraid of being driven away by the good-natured ladies who owned them and unmindful how near his missiles might fall to the heads of unwary pedestrians.[11] And doubtless he was with the rest of the village urchins when they went, equipped with bent pin and tow string, to angle for "killy-fish" in the stagnant marshes of the Wallabout, long since obliterated by the construction of the City Park.[12]

On Sundays he attended the Dutch Reformed Sunday School in the old-fashioned, gray stone church on Joralemon Street[13] as later he was to study human nature from his vantage-point in the galleries of the Sands Street Methodist Church during the hey-day of the old-time revivals.[14] The fervour with which the revival hymns were sung may have given him some early ideas of the power of song to fuse the sentiments of a people.[15] Whether

[1] See II, p. 86.

[2] Whitman's references to this date vary from 1822–3 to 1825. The earliest record in the city directory (Spooner) is 1825.

[3] See II, p. 292 ff.   [4] *Cf.* I, pp. 141–144, 168–171, 174 ff.; II, pp. 2–5, 222–321, *passim.*

[5] See I, pp. 234–235, II, 293–296.   [6] See II, p. 288.

[7] See II, pp. 3, 256–257, 284–288; *cf.* I, p. 77, 118.   [8] See II, p. 2–3.

[9] See *infra*, note 7; also "Complete Prose," pp. 9, 510–511, and "Lafayette in Brooklyn," New York, 1905.

[10] *Cf.* "Complete Prose," p. 465; *post*, II, pp. 3, 255.

[11] See II, p. 295.   [12] See II, p. 269.   [13] See II, p. 262, *cf* "Complete Prose," p. 10.

[14] See II, p. 293.   [15] *Ibidem.*

he included himself among the third of the young apprentices and mechanics of Brooklyn who "experienced religion" in those revivals,[1] we do not know; but his later emotional and mystical experiences render such a supposition tenable.[2]   In any case, he remembered the beauty of the girls he saw there—the more beautiful to him, perhaps, for being sensitive to spiritual impressions.   In the latter half of his life Whitman seldom went to church, but it would seem that he had no deep prejudice against the institution when he was younger.   He was on good terms with the ministers[3] and not infrequently surrendered the editorial columns of the *Eagle* for long reports of their sermons,[4] and as editor advised the building of more houses of worship[5] and recommended attendance upon divine service.[6]   At times he even looked upon himself, in inspired moments, as the founder of a new religion or cultus,[7] though not, to be sure, of an institutionalized church.[8]

On week days the boy attended the public school in Sands Street,[9] where, however, the only incident that impressed him as worthy of later record was his hearing the explosion that wrecked the Frigate *Fulton* (June, 1829) in the Navy Yard

[1] See II, p. 293.

[2] If so, it was probably not the type of conversion in which a sense of sin predominates for he once said to Horace Traubel: "I never, never was troubled to know whether I would be saved or lost: what was that to me?"   ("With Walt Whitman in Camden," III, p. 494.)

[3] See I, p. 176, pp. 255, 313.   Whitman was a friend of Beecher, whom he thought indebted to the "Leaves of Grass."   ("With Walt Whitman in Camden," I, pp. 137–138; III, *passim*; also *post*, I, pp. 234–235.)

[4] *E. g.*, in the Brooklyn *Daily Eagle*, March 30, November 23, 1846.   Whitman also introduced in the *Eagle* (December 19, 1846) a column called "Sunday Reading."

[5] See I, p. 141.   [6] See I, pp. 221–222.   [7] See II, pp. 91–92.   [8] See II, pp. 66–67.

[9] Most of Whitman's prose writings betray his want of the formal and disciplinary training more often found in the schoolroom than in the newspaper office.   In the 1830's the schools, like the newspapers, were, of course, far below modern standards. When Whitman studied the public school as teacher and as a self-appointed editorial inspector, he came to realize how poor they often were.   Possibly he had sensed this even as a pupil.   Apparently he had not made much use, however, of what educational opportunities he had at school.   A granddaughter of his Brooklyn schoolmaster, Miss Theodora Goldsmith, Lady Principal of the Adelphi Academy, writes me: "He [Whitman] was a boy in Sands Street school, now called Public School No. 1, some time during the thirties.   My grandfather, Benjamin Buel Halleck, was a teacher for ten or a dozen years in that school and for a part of the time principal as well.   He remembered Walt Whitman as a big, good-natured lad, clumsy and slovenly in appearance, but not otherwise remarkable.   My grandfather was surprised when Walt proved, long afterwards, to be a poet, saying: 'We need never be discouraged over anyone.'"   Whitman had his own method of self-education, as will appear in this essay and in the one which follows; but he always exerted as much influence as he possessed in securing a higher standard of schools for others, whether secondary or higher, in city or country.   See I, pp. 144–146, 220–221; II, 13–15.

close by.[1] A few days later he followed, boy-like, the funeral procession of an officer slain on the *Fulton*, only to have his sensitive nature offended when the band, which had approached the cemetery with all the impressive solemnity of a naval funeral, marched off to the tune of a lively jig.[2] Whitman seems to have spent much of his time, both as boy and as man, in loitering in burial grounds, whether in the city or in the country, meditating much, as from the first he was to write much, on the problems of death and the grave.[3] It would be far from accurate, however, to describe him as a moody lad, obsessed with gloomy thoughts. It was doubtless first-hand knowledge that he had of the village entertainments which he recalled in the "Brooklyniana" sketches thirty years later— the balls, parties, sleigh rides, lectures, concerts, itinerant shows, singing schools,[4] or special celebrations.[5]

Either Whitman had left school by 1830, at the age of eleven,[6] or else he began work as office and errand boy to "Lawyer Clarke" during a vacation period. Neither this employment nor that in the office of the unnamed doctor mentioned by Bucke[7] could have been of very long duration, for in the next summer the office boy was to become printer's devil for the *Long Island Patriot*, in the office of which he was to learn from that venerable printer, William Hartshorne, "the craft preservative of all crafts."[8] It has not been sufficiently emphasized that during his more formative years Whitman's vantage point for looking at life was nearly always a newspaper office,[9] except when it was some favourite spot in nature. It

[1]See II, p. 265.   [2]II, p. 266.
[3]See I, pp. 1–2, 4–5, 5–6, 7, 8–9, 9–10, 10–11, 12, 13–15, 18, 20, 28–30, 32, 35–37, 38–39, 60–67, 84–89, 97–103, 107–108, 218–219, 243–244; II, pp. 15–16, 22, 89, 148–150, 178–181, also "A Brooklynite in N. Y. Churchyards," Brooklyn *Daily Eagle*, July 7, 1846, and "The Gathering of the Forces," II, pp. 105–113.
[4]See II, p. 257.   [5]See II, pp. 255–257.   [6]See II, p. 86.
[7]In the "Chronological Forecast" which Whitman wrote for Bucke's "Walt Whitman," p. 8.
[8]See II, pp. 86, 245–249.
[9]Whitman is known to have been directly connected with the press in the following years, as well as to have written for many other newspapers concerning his connection with which we know almost nothing (see "Complete Prose," p. 188): *Long Island Patriot*, 1831–32; *Long Island Star*, 1832–33; *Long Islander*, 1838–39; *Long Island Democrat*, 1839–1841; *New World*, 1841–42; *Aurora, Sun, Tattler*, 1842; *Statesman*, 1843; *Democrat*, 1844; Brooklyn *Eagle*, 1846–48; New Orleans *Crescent*, 1848; Brooklyn *Freeman*, 1848–49; Brooklyn *Daily Advertizer*, 1850, 1851; New York *Evening Post*, 1851; Brooklyn *Times*, 1857–58 (?); Brooklyn *Standard*, 1861–62; New York *Herald*, 1888. This leaves out of account his lifelong habit of contributing to magazines. For a list of these see the Whitman bibliography in the "Cambridge History of American Literature," Vol. II

was fortunate for him that his initiation into the journalistic world should have been given in a building closely associated with Revolutionary heroism[1] and under the influence of a man so able to fire his patriotic imagination with stories of Washington, Jefferson, and other makers of the nation.[2] The reverence thus engendered for Washington, in particular, was in the boy and young man little less than religious.[3] His own prophetic mission, when it should be announced to him, was thus predestined to take on a patriotic significance. With the proprietor of the *Patriot*, Samuel E. Clements,[4] a "hawk-nosed Southerner," the young apprentice was on good terms and was taken riding by him on Sundays.[5] From Clements Whitman doubtless received his first ideas of the South, and perhaps from him adopted the arguments in defence of slavery which he was to introduce into his hastily written "Franklin Evans"[6] (1842). In the *Patriot* office he also became acquainted with Henry C. Murphy, later to prove influential in local politics, to be elected repeatedly to Congress, and to be sent as minister to The Hague.[7] The law firm of Murphy, Lott, and Vanderbilt, it is said, shaped very largely the policies of the *Eagle;* it may have been therefore that Whitman's early friendship for Murphy in the *Patriot* office had something to do with the former's selection, in 1846, as editor of the *Eagle*. His loss of that editorship, in any case, was due to his opposition to the conservative Murphy faction of the Democratic Party[8]—to this and to some dissatisfaction on the part of the *Eagle's* proprietor, Isaac Van Anden, with Whitman's irregularity in performing his editorial duties. Though Murphy had been a cause of his losing so comfortable a berth,[9] Whitman was willing to write a very laudatory sketch of the politician for the Brooklyn *Times* in 1857.[10] Precisely what Whitman did after leaving the *Patriot* is not clear. "I was at Worthington's in the summer of '32," he records.[11] This

[1] See II, p. 247.   [2] See II, pp. 246–247.

[3] See I, pp. 22, 72–78, 95, 118, 197, 246; *cf.* II, pp. 2–3, 284–288.

[4] See I, p. 234, note, II, pp. 3–4, 9, note 3, 86, 248–249, 294.

[5] See "Complete Prose," p. 10.   [6] See II, pp. 183–184.

[7] See I, pp. 165; II, 1–2, 5, 225.

[8] See "Complete Prose," p. 188; *post,* II, p. 1 and note.   [9] *Ibidem.*

[10] See II, pp. 1–2, 5.

According to the testimony of a friend of Van Anden. At the time of Whitman's dismissal, the charge was made and denied that there had been a personal encounter in which the young editor had kicked a prominent political personage down the editorial stairs. This is not the place to sift the evidence, but probably a difference of politics was at the root of the matter.

[11] See II, p. 86.

Worthington was probably another printer, and perhaps at the time postmaster as well.[1] With him, however, Whitman remained only a few months, for in the fall he went to work as printer's devil on Col. Alden Spooner's *Long Island Star*, a Whig organ published weekly.[2] He was still doing odd jobs for the *Star* when his family returned to the Island to live, in 1833.[3] He joined the family for a short period in 1836,[4] but where he was and what he was doing in the three intervening years we can only surmise. Perhaps he remained with Spooner later than 1833. But this, rather than the date he gives[5] (1836–7), must have been the period in which he wandered as a journeyman compositor to the larger and more fascinating city across the East River. In that case it is not unlikely that he himself had at that time the difficulties in finding a boarding-house which are reflected in the experience of Franklin Evans.[6] In 1835 it was not easy, it seems, to discover an inexpensive room in the home of a family that was clean, that had young children about, and that did not make attendance upon family worship obligatory. Much of the poet's life was to be spent in boarding-houses and hotels,[7] a fact which doubtless had its influence in shaping his rather detached attitude toward the family as an institution. At this time he was making the acquaintance of the theatre and the opera,[8] both of which were to have much to do in his education. A naïvely condescending exposition of the latter forms the theme of one of his earliest manuscripts.[9] Of the theatre and the opera he made a serious study however impressionistic it may have been, and prepared himself by reading the play or libretto in advance.[10]

[1] See II, p. 296, note.   [2] See II, pp. 86, 246.   [3] See II, p. 86.   [4] *Ibidem*.

[5] "Complete Prose," p. 10. From the middle of 1836 till the middle of 1841 Whitman lived in the country. (See *post*, II, pp. 86–87.) Even before 1836 he probably spent his summers on the Island. (See "Complete Prose," p. 10.)

[6] See II, pp. 126–127; *cf.* also p. 218.

[7] See I, pp. XLV, 61, 223, 224, 248, 249, II, pp. 23–24, 58, 59, 87–88.

[8] See "Complete Prose," p. 514; I, pp. 255–259, II, pp. 148, 253–255. In the course of an acrimonious editorial tilt with the Brooklyn *Advertizer* (January, 1847) Whitman provoked the ire of certain Brooklyn "counterjumpers" by his casual allusion to their complete want of critical ability. One of them replied in an open letter (*Advertizer*, January 18), in which I find a suggestion that Whitman once had some function in the theatre other than that of newspaper critic: "Now whether or not he thinks the station of printer's 'devil' or a prompter's 'devil,' as he has been, or somebody else's 'devil,' as he now is—an intellectually super [*sic*] to that of a clerk we know not," etc.

[9] "A Visit to the Opera," II, pp. 97–101.

[10] As to the latter, see p. II, 100.

2. LONG ISLAND (1836–1841)

We can only guess the reason which influenced Whitman, in 1836, to turn his back on the city which had fascinated him with its varied sights and which, through its opportunities for self-education in newspaper office, theatre, opera, amateur theatricals, and multitudinous human contacts, had generated in him a deep but ill-defined ambition.   If, as I believe, "The Shadow and the Light of a Young Man's Soul"[1] be largely autobiographical, perhaps it suggests the cause of Whitman's five-year absence from New York; he may have been, like Archie Dean, simply out of employment.[2]   For it was unemployment, he tells us, that drove most of the country school-teachers to their unremunerative if not uncongenial tasks.[3]   Or he may have made his customary summer visit to his relatives, intending to enjoy such natural beauties as the season and the Island afforded, and from this he may have drifted into school-teaching in the same casual manner in which he seemed to drift from newspaper to newspaper.   A glance at his photograph of this period[4] is sufficient to discover in him that "want of energy and resolution"[5] which he ascribed to Archie Dean.   He was ambitious, as I have said, but not wholesomely or happily so, for he was proud, disinclined to steady work, and prone to feel that the labour dictated by necessity was somehow beneath his capacity.[6]

> Each has his care; old age fears death;
> The young man's ills are pride, desire,
> And heart-sickness, and in his breast
> The heat of passion's fire.[7]

It was natural for him to shift from district to district, seeking novelty where advancement was impossible.   Within five years he had taught seven schools, besides editing one paper for eight or ten months and writing for others.[8]   These frequent changes

[1] See I, pp. 229–234.   [2] See I, pp. 229–231.   [3] See II, p. 13.

[4] *Frontispiece*, Vol. II.   [5] See I, p. 230; *cf.* II, p. 194.   [6] *Ibidem.*   [7] See I, p. 10.

[8] Manuscript Notebook—4 gives us our most complete record of these changes: Norwich, beginning in June, 1836; school west of Babylon, winter, 1836–37; Long Swamp, spring, 1837; Smithtown, fall and winter, 1837; the *Long Islander* edited at Huntington, June, 1838—spring, 1839; school between Jamaica and Flushing (Little Bay Side?), winter, 1839–40; Woodbury, summer, 1840; Whitestone, winter, 1840–41; return to New York, May, 1841.   See II, pp. 86–87.

may argue his incapacity,[1] on which point there is a difference of testimony,[2] or they may merely indicate his roving disposition. On the whole they were fortunate, for they not only brought him into contact with the various phases of life on the Island,[3] but likewise taught him the solid worth and common sense of the self-reliant country folk and of the middle classes,[4] a lesson which he had scarcely learned, or was likely to learn, in the eastern cities.[5]   In celebrating the "divine average" the poet began with the small farmer rather than with the industrial proletariat.   But in electing to spend the years from seventeen to twenty-two in the country, this sensitive, inclusive, mystical bard derived another benefit.   It meant that he would develop more slowly but more sanely.   A Walt Whitman without poise,[6] balance, would be inconsequential indeed.   The chief significance of his "boarding round" among the rather illiterate Islanders, of his attendance upon country frolics[7], clam bakes,[8] fishing and sailing parties,[9] of his solitary walks by day or night, and of his long rides,[10] is therefore to be sought in the whole spirit and conception of the "Leaves of Grass" no less than in the pages of reminiscent prose in the "Brooklyniana" sketches or in the "Letters from Paumanok."[11]

What merits Whitman's experimental *Long Islander* may have had we cannot know, for, though the paper still flourishes, there seems to exist no file running back to the days of his connection with it.   A contemporary sheet, however, chanced to preserve for us mere samples of his prose[12] and verse[13] quoted from the Huntington weekly.   They are nothing of which a nineteen- or twenty-year-old boy without appreciable schooling needed to be ashamed, yet they constitute no unanswerable argument why their author should not have been replaced by another editor when he grew hopelessly irregular in mounting his

---

[1] In point of information Whitman was probably as well equipped as the average country teacher of his day, for the small salary paid—twenty years later, it was only forty or fifty dollars a quarter, exclusive of board—could not command the masters of a pretentious curriculum. See I, p. 46, note, II, pp. 13–14, 124.

[2] *Cf.* Charles A. Roe in "Brooklyniana," *passim.* "Walt Whitman Fellowship Paper," No. 14, and J. Johnston's and J. W. Wallace's "Visits to Walt Whitman in 1890–1891," pp. 70–71.

[3] See I, pp. 119–120, 124–125, 146–147, 247–254; "Brooklyniana," *passim.*

[4] See I, pp. 120–121, 232–233, 248–254, II, p. 14, 59.

[5] See I, pp. 151–152, 185, 231.   [6] See II, p. 61.   [7] *Cf.* I, pp. 48–51.

[8] *Cf.* I, pp. 164–166; II, pp. 319–320.   [9] See I, pp. 48–51, 248.

[10] See I, p. 232; "Complete Prose," pp. 8, 188.

[11] See I, pp. 247–254.   [12] See I, p. 32.   [13] See I, pp. 1–2.

good horse Nina[1] in order to deliver its ostensibly weekly issues. It is likely that the *Long Islander* experience was helpful in securing for Whitman the first, impermanent editorial positions in the city after his return.[2]

By the fall of 1839, as we have seen, he found it necessary to return to school-teaching, that stand-by of budding American genius. But as his ambition for a journalistic, if not a literary, career was growing more definite, he this time effected a compromise which permitted him to oscillate between the school-house and the printing-office. Whitman lived in the family of James J. Brenton, in the village of Jamaica, who edited and published the weekly *Long Island Democrat*, for which the young journalist worked as typesetter and as contributor at such times as he was not occupied at his school a short distance down the Flushing road. The combination of teaching and journalism, however, seems to have had little influence upon his writing while at Jamaica other than to have suggested the caption for a series of very immature essays. Not one of the "Sun-Down Papers from the Desk of a Schoolmaster"[3] refers to school matters, but all are frankly didactic in manner. Though only seven of these have come to light,[4] there were apparently eleven in all.[5] Ten poems complete the publications of the Jamaica period. The connection with Mr. Brenton was on the whole very beneficial to Whitman. The older journalist had faith in him as a writer and encouraged him, both then and through the varying fortunes of later years.[6] In the *Democrat* office Whitman doubtless learned something about the management of a newspaper, he had an opportunity to publish his juvenilia pretty regularly,[7] and he had access to a circulating library of four hundred volumes.[8] It appears that the youth also knew at that time Henry Onderdonck, Jr.,[9] the

[1] See II, p. 87; *cf.* "Complete Prose," p. 188.

[2] See II, pp. 87–88.   [3] See I, pp. 32–51.

[4] Including one copied from the Hempstead *Inquirer* and one published in the other Jamaica weekly, the *Long Island Farmer*.

[5] The series was numbered.

[6] Brenton included Whitman's sentimental sketch, "Tomb-Blossoms," in the "Voices from the Press," which he published in 1850, and through the *Democrat* congratulated Whitman whenever the latter obtained a new editorial position. See also the letter quoted in the note on p. xxxiii.

[7] See footnote 1, to pp. 1, 2, 4, 5, 8, 9, 10, 12, 13, 15, 32, 35, 37, 39, 44, 46.

[8] See the *Long Island Democrat*, January 17, 1838.

[9] See II, p. 309, note 3.

antiquarian, who could tell him as many tales about Long Island's past as William Hartshorne had related of Revolutionary heroes.

Concerning Whitman's domestic life at this period, little is known,[1] but clearly he was already going his own strange, self-

---

[1] New and welcome light is thrown upon this period of Whitman's life by a letter to me from Mrs. Orvetta Hall Brenton, daughter-in-law of Whitman's Jamaica employer. Some allowance will have to be made, in reading it, for inaccuracy in detail, since it was based on conversations that took place about forty years ago, but it preserves at least the household tradition of Whitman and doubtless gives a fairly true picture. I omit only the general introductory paragraph.

"Whitman was a very young man when he became a member of the Brenton household at Jamaica to learn the printing trade from my father-in-law at the office of the *Long Island Democrat*. It is not possible, however, for me to verify your dates of 1839 or 1840. This definite information might be found in the files of the *Long Island Democrat* at Jamaica. My husband's parents died some thirty-five years ago, and my husband was too young when Whitman lived at the house to remember much about him.

"My mother-in-law, Mrs. Brenton, was a practical, busy, New England woman, and very obviously, from her remarks about Whitman, cared very little for him and held him in scant respect. He was at that time a dreamy, impracticable youth, who did very little work and who was always 'under foot' and in the way. Except that he was always in evidence physically, he lived his life very much to himself. One thing that impressed Mrs. Brenton unfavorably was his disregard of the two children of the household—two small boys—who seemed very much to annoy him when they were with him in the house.

"Mrs. Brenton always emphasized, when speaking of Whitman, that he was inordinately indolent and lazy and had a very pronounced disinclination to work! During some of the time he was in the household, the apple trees in the garden were in bloom. When Whitman would come from the printing office and finish the mid-day dinner, he would go out into the garden, lie on his back under the apple tree, and forget everything about going back to work as he gazed up at the blossoms and the sky. Frequently, at such times, Mr. Brenner would wait for him at the office for an hour or two and then send the 'printer's devil' up to the house to see what had become of him. He would invariably be found still lying on his back on the grass looking into the tree entirely oblivious of the fact that he was expected to be at work. When spoken to, he would get up reluctantly and go slowly back to the shop. At the end of such a day, Mr. Brenton would come home and say, 'Walt has been of very little help to me to-day. I wonder what I can do to make him realize that he must work for a living?' and Mrs. Brenton would remark, 'I don't see why he doesn't catch his death of cold lying there on the ground under that apple tree!'

"Whitman was such an annoyance in the household that Mrs. Brenton was overjoyed when he finally decided to leave the office of the *Democrat*. Mr. Brenton, however, was sorry to have him go, for, even in those early days, he showed marked ability as a writer and was of great value to the 'literary' end of the newspaper work. How long he was in Jamaica, or what salary he received, I do not know. Of course, in those days, a considerable part of the salary consisted in 'board and lodgings.'

"I do not think he attended school at all at Jamaica, and I do not know where he first taught school, but I have always been under the impression that it was at, or near, Huntington.

"Another detail comes to mind in regard to his behavior in the house. He cared nothing at all about clothes or his personal appearance, and was actually untidy about his person. He would annoy Mrs. Brenton exceedingly by 'sitting around' in his shirt sleeves, and seemed much abused when she insisted on his putting on his coat to come to the family table. While she would be setting the table for meals, Whitman was always in her way in the dining room. His favourite seat was in the dining room near the closet

guided way, with none to understand the dreams which filled
him with somewhat more than the ordinary unrest and un-
happiness of adolescence.   Ultimately he found a way to recon-
cile the world of his fancy with the equally wondrous world of
his senses—a "path between reality and the soul"; but his
Jamaica days knew the distraction of dwelling in two discon-
nected realms at once.   His fondness for loafing and inviting his
soul,[1] already becoming pronounced, accounts for what success
he was to attain both as seer and poet, as well as for what nu-
merous failures he was to experience as a professional writer.
But he was as yet less a "kosmos" than a chaos.   Though his
nature was never to conform to a really simple character type,
certain later experiences, mystical or practical, were to charge
him with a dominating purpose, single and powerful enough to
impel, to fortify, and to encourage;[2] but at twenty he was un-
able to fuse and focalize his desires on any of the ordinary ob-
jects of human endeavour, whereas the extraordinary end of his
singular existence was still but a tantalizing adumbration.[3]

During a part of Whitman's residence at Jamaica he had
taken an active interest in politics.   The warfare of political
parties was still a new and exciting game in America, and Walt's
patriotic upbringing and his fondness for addressing himself
directly to the people[4] insured his participation in it sooner or
later.   Webster's oratory never left much impression on his
memory,[5] yet it may have been the speech which the eloquent
senator delivered in Jamaica on September 24, 1840, that stimu-

door where Mrs. Brenton had to pass him every time she wished to get the dishes and
stumble continually over his feet.   He would never think to remove his feet from the
pathway until requested definitely to do so, nor would he move at all out of the way
unless he was told to.

"I am sorry I cannot tell you more.   My impression has always been of a dreamy,
quiet, morose young man, evidently not at all in tune with his surroundings and feeling,
somehow, that fate had dealt hard blows to him.   I never heard him spoken of as being
in any way bright or cheerful.   I cannot see how he could have been an interesting or suc-
cessful teacher because of his apparent dislike of children at the time we knew him.   I
never heard a word against his habits.   He spent most of the time off duty reading by
the fire in the winter or out of doors dreaming in the summer.   He was a genius who lived
apparently, in a world of his own.   He certainly was detached enough from the Brenton
household at Jamaica."

[1] See I, pp. 44–46; II, p. 314.

[2] See "A Backward Glance O'er Travel'd Roads," "Leaves of Grass," 1917, III, 44.
See also II, p. 60.

[3] *Ibidem* (first reference).   [4] See I, p. 115.

[5] See "With Walt Whitman in Camden," III, pp. 175–176.

lated him to active political enthusiasm, for he was himself electioneering in Queens County that fall.[1] By July 29, 1841, he had so far ingratiated himself with the Tammany organization as to be selected as one of the speakers to address a mass meeting of some ten thousand persons in the Park (now City Hall Park) in New York;[2] and by 1848 he was politically important enough to be appointed one of Brooklyn's fifteen delegates to the Free-soil Convention which met that year in Buffalo.[3] But in time his interest, though always enlisted in political causes, ceased to be attracted (if indeed there had ever been any serious attraction) to a political career. Even had he chosen to deliver his "Leaves of Grass" message through the spoken instead of the written word, it is improbable that Whitman could ever have become a great orator. He thought too slowly to adapt himself to the exigencies of impromptu eloquence.[4] But if he did not have the talents of an orator, he nevertheless had the instincts of one. His most successful prose is vibrant with declamatory periods,[5] while all his serious writing is an effort to address himself more or less personally to his reader.[6] That his patriotism was idealistic rather than time-serving is sufficiently indicated by the single fragmentary speech that has come down to us[7] and by the occasional patriotic odes published in his youth.[8] His political power lay in his sound and disinterested judgment[9] and in his fearless public spirit.

The sentimental eagle-screaming of the odes just mentioned was nothing novel in that platitudinous age, but Whitman fell into it the more readily, no doubt, because his personal sentiment had found inadequate means of expression. That strong amative nature which was to get itself recorded fifteen years later

[1] See II, p. 87.

[2] See I, p. 51 note. In the *Eagle* of January 4, 1847, appears the following: "Our answer to the Tammany Committee: Yes, Messrs. of the Tammany Society of New York, the Brooklyn *Eagle* will be happy to attend the 8th of January ball—not forgetting to thank you for your politeness and consideration."

[3] See the Brooklyn *Daily Eagle*, August 7, 1848. Whitman was one of the speakers who addressed the meeting at which nominations were made, introducing a resolution instructing the delegates for Martin Van Buren. (See the New York *Evening Post*, August 7, 1848.)

[4] *Cf.* "With Walt Whitman in Camden," I, p. 249.

[5] *E. g.*, I, pp. 154–155, 160–162, 172–174, 255–259.   [6] See I, pp. 115; II, 104–105.

[7] See I, p. 51.   [8] See I, pp. 15–16, 22–23.

[9] In turning the pages of Whitman's early prose, especially the editorials written sixty or seventy-five years ago, one is impressed by the fact that he nearly always was on the side that was to be espoused by history. (See I, pp. 30–31, 51, 158, 174, 175, 263; *cf.* II, pp. 57, 79, 83, 201, 252, 274, 276, 292.)

in the outspoken pages of "Children of Adam" and "Calamus" must also have been growing during adolescence with the development of his large but sensitive body and mind. He seems to have found no one at this period, however, who could understand or respond satisfyingly to his mystical hunger for affection. Archie Dean had a confidant in his mother, but Whitman's mother, though doubtless the best friend of his youth, found him as much a mystery as did the rest, and could only ponder in her heart the strange nature of her son.[1] As we have seen, he was too much of a dreamer to fit comfortably into the practical New England household of the Brentons, while his Quaker liberality of religious views sometimes caused him to be looked at askance by the orthodox Long Islanders.[2] His life must have been devoid even of any intimate friendship with the young of either sex, for his verse insistently complains that

> Luckless love pines on unknown.[3]

Despairing of ever finding a lover on earth, he at times longs, as the unrequited affection of youth has taught many a poet to long, for death, that in another world a spirit may perchance be found to mate with his.[4] Thus he who was to become the poet of joy and of absorbing affection began his singing with melancholy chants of despair and the grave.[5] The dream of death as a release from an unhappy life persisted with him for years.[6] Often it is tragic death that he describes,[7] sometimes the death of youth and innocence, fit for flowers and sentimentalizing.[8] He dallies with the idea in the introverted luxury of his loneliness, even going so far as to imagine an ideal death scene for himself amidst the nature that he loved.[9] It is well not to take these poems too seriously, however, for, profoundly self-revealing though they be, Whitman's native caution probably reminded him from the first that they were only idle dreams.[10]

This unreciprocated affection did more than to make the poet moody; it made him humanitarian. Had the youth met a Mrs. Stannard or a Miss Royster, like Poe, his later celebration of affection might have been more often personal and less often

[1] See "In Re Walt Whitman" (Traubel, Horace, ed.), p. 34; also "With Walt Whitman in Camden," III, p. 538.

[2] See "Walt Whitman Fellowship Paper," No. 14.

[3] See I, p. 10.   [4] See I, pp. 9–10.   [5] See *infra*, p. xxvii, note 3.   [6] *Ibidem*.

[7] *E. g.*, I, pp. 8–9, 12–13, 52–60.   [8] *E. g.*, I, pp. 35–37.   [9] See I, pp. 5–7.

[10] *Cf.* II, pp. 53–54.

scientific or philanthropic. But as it was, his affection was to
become most characteristic when most indefinite, atmospheric,
impersonal.[1] He professed to take no stock in the romantic
sentiments as described by Byron and Bulwer,[2] and when he
urged upon mankind the duty of brotherly love he meant simply
"that healthy, cheerful feeling of kindness and good will, an
affectionate tenderness, a warm-heartedness, the germs of which
are plentifully sown by God in each human heart."[3] Thus
ungratified desire finds a temporary relief in sublimated ex-
pression, and the youthful writer naïvely follows a deep instinct
in preaching against impulses which he subconsciously fears.
Whitman the reformer sometimes had himself for his most
interested and susceptible audience.[4] When he plunged with
extravagant zeal into the various reform movements that were
sweeping over the country in the 1840's, and excoriated the users
of even tea, coffee, and tobacco[5]—as later he was to speak out
against less venial sins—he probably did not realize it, so blame-
less were his own habits at the time, but it was the puritan in him
challenging to a long and tragic struggle the "caresser of life."[6]

Growing out of the causes of unrest which I have mentioned,
itself perhaps a greater cause of unrest than any other, was
Whitman's fermenting literary ambition. It became the
stronger because it promised to satisfy his other desires. The
political idealist, the dogmatic teacher, the priest of brotherly
love, the social reformer, the dreaming poet, and the original
artist might conceivably combine in the writer, though the
world would have to wait fifteen years to learn just what unique
sort of book such a writer would bring forth. At first the pros-
pect of a career entered upon from motives of worldly ambition
seemed vain and unworthy.[7] But when the literary life came to
appear, not as an enticement to personal ambition, but as an

[1] See I, pp. 46–48; II, pp. 69–71, 74, 81, 84, 146, 160, 173.

[2] See I, p. 48. But Whitman later quoted Byron freely (see I, p. 48, note 1).

[3] *Ibidem.*

[4] Witness the story of his writing "Franklin Evans," a temperance novelette, while im-
bibing his inspiration, much against his conscience, from gin punch. (See Bliss Perry's
"Walt Whitman," p. 28.) Contrast, also, his editorial on honest book reviews (I. pp.
125–126) with his habit of anonymous self-criticism, or his advice to young men to
avoid the bar-rooms (I, pp. 148–149) with his New Orleans sketches.

[5] See p. 34.

[6] "A Legend of Life and Love" (I, pp. 78–83), written in 1842, seems to indicate that
Whitman soon came to realize that the issue was joined between a cautious asceticism
and a generous trust in natural instincts.

[7] See I, pp. 4–5, 19–20.

opportunity to extend to mankind (instead of a mere roomful
of country youths) the benefit of his inspired tutelage, Whitman
felt that the wilderness temptation would bear reconsideration.
He began to dream of a book which was one day to make him
famous.[1] It is interesting to note that originally the intent of
the book is philosophical (perhaps religious) rather than artistic,
that no novelty of form is mentioned, and that in it the treat-
ment of romance and sex, which later came to have such import-
ance in the plan of the "Leaves of Grass," was to be definitely
and totally excluded because of complete ignorance on the part
of the prospective author.[2] The plan of the book was as yet
very hazy in Whitman's mind,[3] but he intends its burden to be a
caution against what he afterward called "the mania of owning
things." In this he was probably too sincere to realize that by
adding the vow of poverty to those of chastity and charity he
was justifying to himself, not only his absorption in a mystical
contemplation of the universe, but also his constitutional anti-
pathy to the sort of routine application which accumulates the
goods of this world. Anyway, this child certainly was father
of the Brooklyn carpenter who is said to have turned his back
on fairly profitable house-building in order to publish, again
and again, a volume of poems that would not sell. This early
announcement that, if the world would but have patience,
Nazareth should yet produce her prophet affords, in its amusing
mixture of modesty and naïve egotism, a suggestive glimpse of
the process whereby the affection of a gifted man, turned inward
upon himself for want of other object, produces the artist and
benefactor of mankind. It also warrants us in tracing the con-
scious genesis of the "Leaves of Grass" farther back in the life
of its author than has commonly been done. It would seem, in-
deed, that Whitman's conception of truth was already trans-
cendental and that he was acquainted with some simpler type
of mystical ecstasy.[5]

But to suppose that the young man was always inditing in
his heart such weighty matters would be to neglect that other
side of his nature which took uncommon delight in physical sen-
sations and personal experiences as such. He attended coun-
try celebrations,[6] entered with zest into the spirit of picnic

[1] See I, pp. 37–39.   [2] Ibidem.
[3] See "A Backward Glance O'er Travel'd Roads," in "Leaves of Grass," 1917, III, p. 44.
[4] See I, pp. 37–39.   Cf. "Leaves of Grass," 1855, p. 34.
[5] See I, pp. 38, 39–44.   [6] See I, pp. 73–74.

excursions to the Great South Bay,[1] occasionally visited New York,[2] and mingled with every class of people. Once he wrote a bit of absurd doggerel, perhaps descriptive of himself.[3] Again, he preceded Stevenson by a generation in writing a frank and unabashed apology for idlers—philosophic idlers—like himself.[4] Clearly his feet were already set on the Open Road, and henceforth neither man nor woman would be able long to detain him in his journey through These States as a vagabond prophet of art, religion, and democracy. If in these Jamaica sketches he appears to lack reverence for man and for man-made conventions, it cannot be said that he was deficient in that sense of religious awe which Carlyle always discovered in his heroes, whether men of letters or founders of religions.[5]

3. NEW YORK AND BROOKLYN (1841–1848)

If it was fortunate that the nascent poet could spend the years between seventeen and twenty-two amidst the simple, wholesome conditions of country life, where, under the influence of work and play, of human contact and mystical meditation, he might with Dutch thoroughness lay the foundation of his future health and character, perhaps it was equally to be desired that the coming bard of democracy should spend the following years of his protracted youth in the heart of the metropolis. Concerning the next seven years of his life we know little except what Whitman has seen fit to tell us in his own writings or what has cautiously been entrusted to his biographers. Some of these writings have only recently come to light, and the mass of them —particularly the newspaper editorials—have never been given a really thorough examination by any competent person. Such neglect can no longer be excused by blanket allusions to the banality of his early prose; for whether a poet begin his successful singing at twenty or at thirty-five, the third decade of his life is always biographically important.

The elements of Whitman's nature which were beginning to emerge into consciousness during the last period now assume more definiteness of expression. There he had dreamed of reforming the world; now he seriously tries his hand at it. On the Island he had prayed for love, but prayed in vain; in the city he appears to have learned the language of love and friendship,

[1]See I, pp. 48–51.   [2]See II, p. 87.   [3]See I, pp. 2–4.
[4]See I, pp. 44–46.   [5]See I, pp. 40–44.

though it is not known that at this time he found any lasting lover or friend. His transcendental faith in the goodness and trustworthiness of nature now begins to lead him into spheres of indulgence that were in marked contrast to the asceticism of the previous period—spheres from which he later withdrew with aversion if not regret.[1] But all these experiences were the education of the poet, and they help to explain the *weltschmerz* and the discernment in his verse. In the preceding period he had slowly realized that his calling was literature; now he begins that intimate connection with newspapers, magazines, and books which one must look upon as constituting his chief apprenticeship as a writer. Of course Whitman's tenure of office in the newspaper world was likely to be no more permanent than in the less exacting realm of country schools. According to his own record he was connected—as compositor, contributor, or editor—with nine newspapers or literary journals in eight years,[2] besides writing a novelette and contributing to four magazines. If the ordinary criteria of success be applied, this was, without doubt, a bad record; but if Whitman's peculiar mission was, first, to be in himself a synthesis of life in America during the turbulent nineteenth century and, second, to express that life in a book more or less suggestive of its youth, its energy, its flowing picturesqueness, and its crude democracy, then the constant shifts whereby he was enabled to study life and nature from a multiplex viewpoint were, in the main, not only beneficial but absolutely necessary. During this period the youthful bigotry evidenced in his fondness for lecturing the world is gradually qualified by an increasing receptiveness to new and diverse impressions, until the time for his first true oracular expression comes in 1847–1848. No conventional duty is allowed to interrupt his lifelong habit of strolling amidst his kind—observing, sympathizing, "absorbing"—and thus forming, against the day of his authentic poetic utterance, the subconscious mystical synthesis to which I have referred. Thus his famous "catalogues," which appeared in his prose before they were incorporated in his verse,[3] assume a significance that is biographical as well as artistic. He missed nothing that was to be seen. He attended the theatre and the opera;[4] he studied the fairs and

[1] See Bliss Perry, *loc. cit.*, pp. 151–152.

[2] See *infra*, p. xxvii, note 9.   [3] See *post*, pp. lxii–lxiii.

[4] See I, pp. 143–144, 152–154, 156–158, 255–259; II, pp. 97–101, 148; also "The Gathering of the Forces," II, pp. 349–351, 359.

exhibitions;[1] he patronized the public baths;[2] he was familiar with all the police courts and the slums;[3] he wrote crude special articles on Sing Sing,[4] on the hospitals,[5] the asylums,[6] the schools;[7] he attended picnics,[8] went on steamboat and railway excursions,[9] and was present to take part in political meetings and celebrations.[10]   He attended lectures[11] and concerts,[12] gazed in awe at the great city fires,[13] and loitered amidst the shipping[14] and on the ferries.[15]   Wherever human life was "magnificently moving in vast masses," there was he to feel and absorb it.   It was no accident, therefore, that he should have found much to attract and inspire him in the "average man" of the city, even as he had discovered the more obvious virtues of the countryman.

His own life is still, as always, fundamentally complex.   He can resist anything better than his own "diversity," which has as yet prevented any blending of his sentimental dreams of the past with his heroic prophecies of the future.   He still broods on death and the grave;[16] he continues his puerile moralizing about children;[17] his imagination still consorts with angelic beings, as fanciful as those which called Poe father;[18] he vene-

---

[1] See I, pp. 142–143; Brooklyn *Daily Eagle*, July 2, November 21, 1846; also "The Gathering of the Forces," II, pp. 113–117, 363–365.

[2] See Brooklyn *Daily Eagle*, May 3, 1847; also "The Gathering of the Forces," II, pp. 201–207, which is apparently in error in stating that Whitman remained in the bath twenty minutes, for in the *Eagle* of July 30, 1846, he advises bathers to remain in the water at Gray's Baths not more than five or six minutes.

[3] *Cf.* II, pp. 10–12.

[4] See Brooklyn *Daily Eagle*, June 30, 1846.

[5] *Cf.* II, pp. 27–28, 291.

[6] See Brooklyn *Daily Eagle*, June, 3, 9, 24, 1846; July 17, 1846.

[7] See I, pp. 144–146; Brooklyn *Daily Eagle*, June 4, September 5, 1846; also "The Gathering of the Forces," I, pp. 121–133, 136–145.

[8] See I, pp. 164–166; Brooklyn *Daily Eagle*, June 25, 1846.

[9] See I, pp. 118–121; Brooklyn *Daily Eagle*, June 25, August 1, 1846.

[10] See I, pp. 22–23; Brooklyn *Daily Eagle*, July 1, 2, 6, 1846, June 2, 1847, August 7, 1848.

[11] See Brooklyn *Daily Eagle*, March 5, 6, 7, 1846; *cf.* p. 000.

[12] See I, pp. 104–106 and notes; Brooklyn *Daily Eagle*, November 20, 1846; also "The Gathering of the Forces," II, pp. 351–359.

[13] See I, pp. 154–156.

[14] See Brooklyn *Daily Eagle*, March 9, June 27, 1846.

[15] See I, pp. 142, 168–171.

[16] See I, pp. 60–67, 91–92, 108–110, 146–147; Brooklyn *Daily Eagle*, September 10, 1846.

[17] See I, pp. 21, 91–92, 138–139; "The Gathering of the Forces," I, pp. 145–147.

[18] See I, pp. 83–86, 86–89.

rates more than ever the fathers of freedom;[1] and he resents
the architectural reforms which would molest the ancient
churches and other building sacred to his memories.[2] But, on
the other hand, he cries out for progress along various lines and
himself seeks to lead the way. Thus he was learning to be, not
only a voice of the present complexity, but a link between the
past achievement and the future hope. At the same time that
he was growing to be a reformer without a party, an artist with-
out a school, and a prophet without a cult, he was also translat-
ing into the "American" language wisdom as old as the world.

Not one of Whitman's contributions to the *Aurora*, the *Sun*,
the *Tattler*, the *Statesman*, or the *Democrat* (all of New York)has
as yet been unearthed; but fortunately we have complete files of
the Brooklyn *Eagle* during the two years of his editorship.
These old numbers of the *Eagle* make it clear that here as else-
where Whitman was himself first and newspaper functionary
afterward. And yet—perhaps for that very reason—it can be
said that, like Greeley and Bennett, he went beyond the cur-
rent conception of editorial opportunity and responsibility.[3]
Had his training fitted him for such a hearing as Greeley
or Bryant obtained through the *Tribune* and the *Evening
Post*, his influence upon journalism might have been as wide
as his policy was far-sighted and individual. For to him a
newspaper was a living thing, its readers individual human
beings.[4] Sometimes his journal is the scourge of reform, purg-
ing the temple of democracy;[5] sometimes it is an Athenian
forum, resounding with discussions of the basic principles of
good government;[6] at other times it is a humanitarian pulpit,
defending the ignorant, the weak, the helpless;[7] now it is a
college class-room, in which books are sifted and appraised,
and their treasures disclosed;[8] now it is itself a miniature li-
brary, stocked with poems, tales, novelettes, extracts, or "Sab-
bath reading";[9] again it is a political stump, from which the
editor urges the claims of candidate or party with a vehemence

[1] See I, pp. 22–23, 72–78, 95–96, 117–118.   [2] See I, pp. 92–97.
[3] See I, pp. 115–117, 137; Brooklyn *Daily Eagle*, September 29, 1846.
[4] See I, p. 115.
[5] See I, pp. 106–108, 108–110, 121–123, 125–126, 137, 152–154, 156, 162–163, 168–170.
[6] See I, pp. 159–160, 166–168; Brooklyn *Daily Eagle*, December 14, 1846; also"The
Gathering of the Forces," I, pp. 57–74.
[7] See I, pp. 106–108, 108–110, 138–139, 144–146; cf. II, pp. 9–12.
[8] See I, pp. 121–123, 125–126, 126–137, 139–141, 163–164; cf. II, pp. 19–21.
[9] See I, pp. 129–130, note.

that passed with the youth of the nation;[1] finally, it at times becomes a man talking to other men, of the life he sees about him or of the life he foresees in the more or less distant future.[2] No paper in the city, I think, attempted to cultivate so large a field of usefulness. If Whitman was often out of the editorial office, it was to become his own reporter, for he had none. If he neglected or ignored party politics at times, he was acting as his own musical or dramatic critic. If he occasionally broke away from the confinement of the city and had a loiter over the Island, he was at once renewing his youth and awakening his self-interested city readers with country correspondence.[3] His style often left much to be desired, but certainly it was fresher and dealt with more important journalistic matter than was to be found in the pages of any Brooklyn contemporary. If the circulation of the *Eagle* really decreased during his editorship, as it is said to have done,[4] that fact no more disproves the value of Whitman's innovations than the popular neglect of the 1855 edition of the "Leaves of Grass" accurately rates the worth of that highly original book. However, the employer watched the "ninepences"[5] and laid store by them even if the editor did not, and so the time came when Whitman's intractability, when he swung the paper vigorously in line with the radical Barnburner or Free-soil wing of the party, gave Mr. Van Anden and the conservative bosses of the party a welcome opportunity to replace him with S. G. Arnold,[6] a more correct, conventional,[7] and docile editor.[8] The doggedness with which Whitman later issued his "Leaves," refusing to be persuaded, either by Emerson or by the Attorney General of Massachusetts,

[1] See I, pp. 160–162,171–174; also "The Gathering of the Forces," II, pp. 2-45.

[2] See I, pp. 114–115, 141–144, 151–152, etc.; also "The Gathering of the Forces," I, pp. 25–26, 27–28.

[3] See I, pp. 174–181.

[4] By W. A. Chandos-Fulton in "The Local Press" (Brooklyn *Standard*, October 22, 1864).

[5] See I, p. 115.

[6] A friend of Van Anden.

[7] Readers who approach Whitman's *Eagle* writings with the typical current conception of the man and the poet in mind are likely to find them more conventional than did the readers of 1846. Yet there were plenty of sentiments expressed by the editor of the *Eagle*, even on such subjects as sex, education, and literature, which might as well have appeared in the pages of his contemporaries. This very conventionality, however, shows his later radicalism to have been deliberate, vision-inspired, rather than temperamental.

[8] For a somewhat fuller, but hardly a new, account of this episode see "The Gathering of the Forces," I,xxiv–xxxvi; II,pp. 179–186, 191–200, 203–208, 214–228. *Cf. infra*, p. xxviii.

to modify it in deference to what he considered the low tone of
public morals and taste, will be the occasion of no surprise to
those who have followed his editorial history. Here he was
right on nearly every question of public interest, he conscien-
tiously strove to elevate the standards and to enlarge the whole-
some influence of the press, he was public-spirited and fearless,
and he knew not how to turn back from a course deliberately
chosen. But when, in his casual, self-confident way, he se-
cured his next employment, in New Orleans, it was to be in an
environment as strange to the puritan in him as it was congenial
to the indolent if wide-awake caresser of life.

4. NEW ORLEANS (MARCH—MAY, 1848)

Few indeed were the facts known concerning Whitman's
journey to New Orleans until very recent years. Whitman
wrote for the New Orleans *Crescent*, but failed otherwise to
preserve an interesting account of this trip, made by rail,
mountain stagecoach, and river steamboat[1]; but like other
accounts born of novelty and child-wonder, it shrinks in size as
its inspiration wanes, until, when the Father of Waters is
reached, the prose ceases entirely, giving way to only an impres-
sionistic little poem in conventional measures.[2] The narrative
is entertaining, however, because of the light it throws upon
the means of transportation common at the time, on the ap-
pearance of the towns and rivers, on the incredible cheapness
of living costs, the character of the inland inhabitants, and the
promise the young poet saw in the West.[3]

Walt had left Brooklyn, with his fifteen-year-old brother
Jeff, on February 11; they arrived in New Orleans about
ten o'clock on the night of February 25. The two weeks of
varied travel were doubtless crammed with experiences of inter-
est and enlargement for the virile and receptive child of New
York. As for New Orleans, we know that it remained in Whit-
man's memory as one of his three "cities of romance."[4]

[1] See I, pp. 181–190.

[2] "The Mississippi at Midnight," the original version of which is to be found in the
Yale Review, October, 1915, p. 173. The six original stanzas are given also by Doctor
R. M. Bucke in his "Notes and Fragments," pp. 41–42, where he adds two more. Still
others are to be seen in "Complete Prose," pp. 373–374.

[3] See I, p. 185; *cf.* pp. 151–152.

[4] See "With Walt Whitman in Camden," II, p. 29.

The day after their arrival the Whitmans found a boarding house at the corner of Poydras and St. Charles streets, but to youths accustomed to the Dutch spotlessness of Madam Whitman's housekeeping, the place seemed dirty beyond endurance.[1] More comfortable quarters were soon found in the "Fremont house, next door to the theatre and directly opposite the office."[2] It appears that a month later they were not living in New Orleans proper, but in Lafayette, then a suburb.[3] Walt found the Fremont House convenient because there one might go to his meals as irregularly as one liked.[4] Occasionally, at least, his breakfasts were taken in the French market.[5] If any of his adolescent asceticism with reference to the use of coffee remained in 1848, it was to vanish before the delicious beverage he found in this market.[6] Many years afterward he recalled the superior wines of which the city had boasted,[7] but he either did not drink much in the spacious bar-rooms he loved to frequent[8] or else he concealed the fact from his brother.[9] His dress was simple, but immaculate.[10] He was trying to save money, for he hoped to be able to send home enough to pay the interest on a loan;[11] and by the last of April he had, according to Jeff, "quite a sum."[12] His salary is unknown, but it must have been a very fair one for that time, for the amount saved would be in addition to all or a part of the two hundred dollars advanced to him in New York to cover travelling expenses and to bind the bargain.[13] Possibly, however, misunderstanding this as "expense money" instead of a loan (the agreement had been made in fifteen minutes),[14] he thought he had more to his credit than the

[1] Manuscript letter from Jefferson Whitman to his mother, in the Bucke collection.

[2] *Ibidem. Cf.* II, p. 77.   [3] See I, p. 223.   [4] See II, p. 77.

[5] See "Complete Prose," p. 440.

[6] *Ibidem;* see also I, p. 204.

[7] See "Complete Prose," p. 440. Whitman had learned to like champagne before going to New Orleans (I, p. 165), though his brother George said "I do not suppose, Walt drank at all till he was thirty." ("In Re Walt Whitman," p. 36.)

[8] See "Complete Prose," p. 440; I, pp. 199, title.

[9] In a letter to his mother written on March 27, Jeff assures her that she need have no fear that they will fall victims to the then prevalent yellow fever, inasmuch as he attributes it largely to intemperance, and adds: "You know that Walter is averse to such habits."

[10] See I, pp. 204, 208–209, 226; see also the 1849–1850 photograph in the Camden Edition of his works.

[11] Walt Whitman manuscript, dated March 28, in the Bucke collection.

[12] Jefferson Whitman manuscript, dated April 23, in the Bucke collection.

[13] See "Complete Prose," p. 188.   [14] *Ibidem.*

accounting office would allow. At any rate, though pleasantly situated, he intended to return north as soon as he had saved a thousand dollars.[1] New Orleans interested him, but apparently it was no rival to his affection for his home.[2]

Whitman's work was in the editorial department of the *Crescent*, but, in contrast to much of his earlier experience, he was not sole editor nor even editor-in-chief. Besides him there were an editorial writer, a city editor, and a translator, his own principal duty being to "make up the news" with pen and scissors, though he also wrote some editorials and sketches.[3] He went to work about nine in the morning and got away from the office before eleven at night.[4] But he must have had his usual stroll about town within these hours—between the time for "copy" and that for "proofs" perhaps—for he sometimes covered the recorders' courts (police courts) and collected material for his "Sketches of the Sidewalks and Levees."[5] Notwithstanding the pleasantness of his situation, it is difficult to see how a man of Whitman's habits, temperament, and training could have long continued to work harmoniously, even with affable co-labourers, in an office where his independence was left so unprotected by the indefinite division of labour. However, the break, when it came, was with his employers, and was occasioned by a difference over money matters and a (to Whitman) inexplicable estrangement between himself and the owners of the paper, Messrs. Hayes and McClure.[6] This difficulty, taken with the fact of Jeff's homesickness and indisposition and of Walt's own unrooted nature, sufficiently accounts for their departure homeward, only three months after their arrival in New Orleans.[7]

Whitman's writings of this period will be criticized in the following essay, but some of them, having biographical implications, must also be mentioned here. With the exception of the single poem before mentioned,[8] Whitman wrote no verse on this Southern "jaunt," unless some of the "Leaves of Grass"

[1] See note 12, p. xlv, *infra*.

[2] On March 28 he wrote to his mother: "My prospects in the money line are bright. O how I long for the day when we can have our own quiet little farm, and be together again—and have Mary and her children come to pay us long visits." (Manuscript letter in the Bucke collection.)

[3] See II, p. 78.

[4] See I, p. 224; II, p. 77, note; also manuscript letter of Jefferson Whitman, dated March 14, in the Bucke collection.

[5] See I, pp. 199–218.   [6] See II, pp. 77–78; *cf.* pp. 165, 187.   [7] See II, pp. 77–78.

[8] See *infra*, p. xliv, note 2.

passages descriptive of the South were written at that time and
preserved many years only in manuscript.[1]   And even his prose,
with a few exceptions, was uncommonly slipshod and inartistic.
Perhaps he had never before been so typically a *journalist* as in
these hasty and crude expressions of what he was seeing and
feeling in New Orleans, impressions not crystallized but held a
moment in solution ere they should be gone forever.   It is
therefore instructive to compare the anonymous record of his
New Orleans life written at the time for a newspaper which
could have been read by very few who knew him at the North
—written with little expectation that it could ever be used to
throw light on the evolution of a great poet—with his later
culled reminiscences of that life published by that poet grown
famous.[2]   In these earlier sketches we recognize the Whitman
familiar to the pilot-houses of the New York ferries and to the
drivers' boxes of the Broadway stages.   He roams among the
cemeteries,[3] visits the old St. Louis Cathedral,[4] converses with
the returning heroes of the Mexican War,[5] lounges in the
spacious bar-rooms of the hotels, studying the picturesque
cosmopolitanism of the types to be found there,[6] exposes the
frauds of fake auctioneers,[7] strolls about the levee and con-
verses with the river-men,[8] or satirizes human folly and drops,
like Irving, a sympathetic tear upon misfortune.[9]   But do these
contributions to the *Crescent* reveal a romance of his own?

Biographers who believe that there was a very significant
Whitman romance in New Orleans in 1848 have based their
conjecture largely on the following evidence:[10]

(1) In reply to persistent and disconcerting inquiries from his Eng-
lish admirer, John Addington Symonds, concerning the inner meaning
of some of Whitman's poems of affection, the poet wrote, on August 19,
1890, the following rather cryptic sentences: "My life, young man-
hood, mid-age, times South, etc., have been jolly bodily, and doubt-
less open to criticism.   Tho' unmarried I have had six children—two

---

[1] See Bucke's "Walt Whitman," 1883, p. 136.

[2] "Complete Prose," pp. 439–441.

[3] See manuscript letter of Jefferson Whitman, dated March 14, in the Bucke collection.

[4] See I, pp. 221–222.   [5] See I, p. 225, and note.   [6] See I, pp. 193–195.

[7] See I, pp. 199–202.

[8] See I, pp. 213–216, 223–224; "Complete Prose," p. 440.

[9] See I, pp. 199–218, 223, 225–228.

[10] Most of the passages in the present essay dealing with Whitman's love affairs are
reprinted from an article which I published in the *Dial* (November, 1920), by whose
courteous permission the reprint is made.

are dead—one living, Southern grandchild, fine boy, writes to me oc-
casionally—circumstances (connected with their fortune and benefit)
have separated me from intimate relations." Horace Traubel re-
corded a number of rather hazy allusions to the subject made in his
presence by Whitman during the closing years of the latter's life,[1]
and both he and Mr. Thomas B. Harned have mentioned the old poet's
promise to give them, his literary executors, a deposition concerning
the facts of his "secret"—a promise which he never found the right
mood for keeping.[2]

(2) Whitman's departure from this congenial Southern city, in
which he had pleasant employment and good health, was so sudden,
and the reasons which he gave for it seemed so inadequate, that some
biographers have concluded that the real cause was to be found in a
romance which threatened his prophetic and artistic independence.

(3) Until recently none of Whitman's characteristic verse could be
traced back beyond the 1848 journey to New Orleans, so that the ex-
periences of this journey are sometimes taken to have been the inspira-
tion that liberated his song.

(4) A poem, "Once I Pass'd through a Populous City," seems to de-
scribe a transitory residence in some large and picturesque city of
which the reminiscent poet recalls only the passionate attachment of a
woman who was broken-hearted at his parting.

From these facts Mr. H. B. Binns, M. Léon Bazalgette, and
others have elaborated a fairly complete story, with the result
that it is now quite commonly assumed that Whitman did have a
liaison in New Orleans in 1848. A young man of fine personal
presence—so the story goes—he was seen by a Southern woman
of high social standing, for whom to see him was to love him.
This attachment, the chief responsibility for which (despite
Whitman's confession to Symonds of his own culpability) is
usually placed at the lady's door, in time bore fruit; but an ob-
stacle to an open marriage with the middle-class Northern jour-
nalist had been encountered in the pride of her family. Ac-
cordingly some versions of the story suppose that there was a
secret marriage (again despite the evidence of Whitman's
letter to Symonds), and that the young husband was bound for
life by a pledge of secrecy concerning the whole affair. Then,
having learned in three months the mysteries of true love, and

---

[1] See "With Walt Whitman in Camden," II, pp. 316, 328, 425, 510–511, 543; III, pp. 80,
119-120, 140, 253, 364.

[2] Horace Traubel has also told me of Whitman's surprise and confusion when the former
one day called on the poet almost immediately after the departure of a visitor who, he
was told, was Whitman's grandson (or son?).

having learned to forswear them, he returned north and began composing the "Leaves of Grass."

Now, Whitman may indeed have had an *affaire de cœur* in New Orleans, but in the light of new evidence we shall have to modify this explanation of how it all occurred and perhaps assign its date to a later journey to the South, even if we do not abandon the common theory altogether. First let us re-examine the evidence used by the biographers. As we have seen, the suddenness and the unlooked-for earliness of Whitman's departure from New Orleans is adequately accounted for without supposing that a woman or her family had anything to do with it. As to the *a posteriori* evidence found in the maturer and more poetic verse which followed, it may be true that the first rhythmical lines of the "Leaves" were written shortly after the return North rather than just before;[1] but they appear in a notebook containing the date 1847, to which year we must assign Whitman's first definite efforts[2] to compose the novel volume which was to see the light of print in 1855. The latter part of this notebook contains,[3] it is true, the first draft of the description of sexual ecstasy to be incorporated in "Song of Myself" (Sections 28–30); but as to that, Whitman's letter to Symonds, in its studied indefiniteness, implies that the period of his "body-jolliness" included his earlier manhood as well.[4] There remains the evidence of the poem, "Once I Pass'd through a Populous City." This lyric probably refers to New Orleans, but its original form[5] proves that it was first intended, not for a "Children of Adam" poem descriptive of the love between the sexes, but for a "Calamus" poem descriptive of that "adhesiveness," or attachment of man to man, which Whitman preached as a complement to his gospel of individuality, in his religion of sentimental democracy.[6] I suppose his reason for disguising the emotion which gave birth to this poem was the poet-prophet's desire to avoid a charge of effeminacy. But the important fact made clear by it is that a Whitman poem of tenderness addressed to a "rude and ignorant man" (doubtless a counterpart to the Pete Doyle of the Washington period) could, through slight emendations, become

[1] See II, p. 63, note 1.
[2] Unless still earlier notebooks have been lost.
[3] See II, pp. 72–73.
[4] See also John Burroughs's "Notes on Walt Whitman as Poet and Person," 1867, p. 81.
[5] See II, pp. 102–103. [6] See II, p. 96, note 4.

a lyric of man-and-woman love on which biographers might unsuspectingly build a romantic story. The history of the poem goes far, I think, toward showing that Whitman retained in manhood some of the characteristics of the sexually indiscriminate affection of a child. And his ability to direct his romantic sentiments toward man as well as toward woman accounts, perhaps, for a certain indefinable attraction which healthy-minded men like Doctor Bucke no less than healthy-minded women like Mrs. Gilchrist have felt in his verse. The artist is expected to pass in his imagination from the man's point of view to the woman's, and back again, at will; Whitman is almost solitary among the major poets of the world—unless Shakespeare be an exception—in his tendency to do this with his heart. This peculiarity, he seems to have thought, was what made him akin to the great religious teachers of the past. But he also knew that such a nature would be misunderstood, and that it might even prove dangerous.[1]

But let us return to the problem of the New Orleans romance. It is now plain that if a woman entered Whitman's life between March and May, 1848, the fact, as well as her character and social position, must be established by other evidence. The letter to Symonds is apparently competent testimony, though it has at times been discounted as being either a fabrication or the result of hallucination; but it is not definite as to dates.[2] However, some of Whitman's prose pieces written for the *Crescent* show how far he was from being insensible to womanly beauty in the social capital of the South.[3] Nine days before he left for home he published anonymously a humorous skit[4] describing his experiences at a masked ball where he met, and instantly fell in love with, a charming and cultivated lady, who, to his sudden discomfiture and chagrin, soon proved to be already married. Who, or what manner of woman, she was, it is of course impossible to determine. She may have been one of the accom-

[1] See II, pp. 96–97.

[2] If the parent of the "Southern grandchild" were the offspring from a union which took place in 1848, then his or her birth must naturally have occurred by 1849. But an examination, extending down to 1850, both of the records of the Health Department of the city and of the archives of the St. Louis Cathedral, gives no clue to it. However, though all births were legally required to be entered in the former and though the baptismal records of the latter at that time included the majority of both legitimate and natural births in the city, neither record is at all complete.

[3] See I, pp. 202–205, 222, 225–228.

[4] "A Night at the Terpsichore Ball," I, pp. 225–228.

plished vampires who infested the New Orleans of that day,[1] who, finding that he had less wealth than his correct evening apparel[2] might have led her to believe, gave the wink to her accomplice-husband and thus shook him off. Or she may have been a married woman of social standing who sought in a ball-room flirtation momentary diversion from a domestic life which bored her. Or, on the other hand, the chance meeting may have proved more serious to her and to him than Whitman's light treatment of it would indicate.[3] It would be safer to pass the sketch by as merely an exaggerated, if indeed not a fictitious, account of the ludicrous mistake of an impulsive youth who, in printing it, could screen himself behind a *nom de plume;* but the testimony of one of Whitman's intimate friends[4] curiously corroborates this story if the latter be taken as the narrative of a real and serious attachment. In any case, something drew Whitman from his Northland again,[5] whether it was the "magnet South" itself, or the "rude and ignorant man" celebrated in the hitherto misinterpreted poem (and presumably also in "I Saw in Louisiana a Live-Oak Growing"), or the original of the photograph of the "sweetheart long ago" which hung in his den in Camden.[6]

[1] See "New Orleans as It Is," by a Resident (New Orleans), printed for the publisher, 1850, pp. 38–39.

[2] See I, p. 226.   [3] See I, p. 216, note.

[4] Mr. Francis Howard Williams, who is reported (Philadelphia *Record*, August 12, 1917) as saying: "Walt was sensitive when people asked him why he never married. He talked pretty freely to me about his personal affairs. There was one woman whom he would have married had she been free; that was the married woman he met in his sojourn in New Orleans when a young man. Her husband knew of their love, too, I believe." It is possible that this woman has been confused with a lover whom Whitman had in Washington. See I, p. lviii.

[5] See II, p. 59, where Whitman mentions having visited other Gulf states than Louisiana. *Cf.* Bucke's list of states visited (*loc, cit.*, p. 136), which includes Texas. But the 1848 journey is accounted for in detail, and did not include Texas (see II, pp. 77–79, and also Herbert Harlakenden Gilchrist's "Anne Gilchrist, Her Life and Writings," London, 1887, p. 253). On the whole it seems probable that Whitman had visited Texas on a later journey to the South. In the list of newspapers to which he had contributed, Whitman included one in Colorado which he thought was the *Jimple-cute* ("Complete Prose," pp. 188–189). In "Slang in America" he alludes to "*The Jimp-lecute*, of Texas" (*Ibidem*, p. 409). Now, there is not, and so far as I can discover never was, a paper by that title in Colorado; whereas there has been, since 1865, a *Jimplecute* published at Jefferson, Texas. Another hint that Whitman had made journeys of which we have no definite record is to be found in a casual allusion to the fact of his having explored the Mammoth Cave in Kentucky (Brooklyn *Times*, February 4, 1858), which he could hardly have done on the 1848 journey to New Orleans. See also "Complete Prose," p. 251.

[6] See II, p. 60.

Whether this journey brought an entanglement into his life or not, it was important in that it opened his eyes to the spirit and the prospects of the great West and of the South; it helped to make of him, even during reconstruction times, the poet of the whole people; and it introduced him to experiences until then strange to his eye and soul.

The return journey was, naturally, a little longer in point of time than the journey southward had been. A week was spent on a Mississippi steamboat in reaching St. Louis.[1] Chicago was given a cursory inspection.[2] Lakes Michigan and Huron were traversed and the Niagara Falls were gazed upon in unrestrained awe.[3] The scenery along the banks of the Hudson, south of Albany, he pronounced the grandest he had ever beheld.[4] At five o'clock on Wednesday, June 15, he was at home again—four months after his departure, one month of which had been spent in travelling.[5]

5. BROOKLYN (1848–1862)

Whitman had been in Brooklyn but a week when, in the Whig press, appeared rumors of a Barnburner paper to be started in that city, with Whitman as editor.[6] The *Eagle* had refused to open its columns to reports of the proceedings of the radical Democrats, and this had determined Judge Samuel E. Johnson[7] and other Brooklyn Free-soilers to start a paper of their own. This weekly[8] paper, the *Freeman*, was burned out in a great fire which swept the business section of the city on the night after its very first issue.[9] There was no insurance, but the paper was revived after two months.[10] On April 25, 1849, it was changed to a daily, its staff was apparently in-

---

[1] See "Complete Prose," p. 441.   [2] *Ibidem.*   [3] See II, p. 79.   [4] *Ibidem.*

[5] *Ibidem,* and *cf.* "Complete Prose," pp. 442–443.

[6] See Brooklyn *Daily Advertiser*, June 23, 24, 1848.

[7] See Henry R. Stiles's "History of the City of Brooklyn," 1870, III, p. 938; also Chandos-Fulton's "The Local Press," Brooklyn *Standard*, November 5, 1864.

[8] The *Freeman* was first published at 110 Orange Street, later at 96 Myrtle Avenue, at Fulton and Middagh, and on Fulton near Myrtle. See II, p. 3, note 1.

[9] September 9, 1848. See Brooklyn *Evening Star*, of that date, also II, p. 254.

[10] When the paper was again commenced, on November 1, Whitman said in it: "The fire which burnt us clean out, as we began at our former place, completely deranged the arrangements previously made. We had not much to lose; but of what we had not a shred was saved—no insurance. This time we are determined to go ahead. Smiles or frowns, thick or thin, we shall establish a Radical Newspaper in Kings County. Will it remain to be said that the friends of Liberal Principles here give it a meagre and lukewarm aid?" (Quoted in the Brooklyn *Evening Star*, November 1.)

creased,[1] and its circulation extended. However, Whitman's valedictory, full of bitter defiance toward his enemies, appeared within the year (September 11, 1849).[2] Persistent search has failed to bring to light a single copy of this short-lived sheet. Had we a file of it, perhaps we should discover evidences of Whitman's growing hatred of the spread of slavery, such as we do not expect to find in the *Crescent*. Possibly, too, we should discover some lost verse.

For during this period Whitman was experimenting with new forms of verse. The "Isle of La Belle Riviére,"[3] what would now be called an imagist poem, was written on Blennerhasset Island, in the Ohio, in 1849 or 1850,[4] possibly on a second journey to the South. The political lampoon, "Song for Certain Congressmen,"[5] appeared in Bryant's *Evening Post* on March 2, 1850, over the pseudonym "Paumanok." This was an unpoetic thing, but not because of unconventionality in form. In the same month, however, Whitman published his first free verse, "Blood-Money," republished it after a few weeks,[6] and two months later followed it with other poems in the same form: "The House of Friends,"[7] and "Resurgemus."[8] All of these poems, it should be noted, were inspired by indignation at political injustice or treachery, the "Song for Certain Congressmen" being occasioned by rumours of Webster's coming defection from Free-soil principles, and "Blood-Money" by his Seventh of March speech[9] and the Fugitive Slave Law. Thus political rather than personal events seem to have been

[1] Mr. Daniel M. Tredwell, in his "Personal Reminiscences of Men and Things on Long Island" (Brooklyn, 1912, II, p. 212), says that on March 12, 1848, he engaged to take a position on the *Freeman* under Whitman, and that on April 25, the new sheet came out and was much complimented. He confuses the daily with the weekly, and so his dates are just a year too early. Mr. Tredwell was then a law student, and was engaged to write up the court-house news for the new daily, at ten dollars a week.

[2] Quoted in the *Eagle*, September 11: "After the present date, I withdraw entirely from the Brooklyn *Daily Freeman*. To those who have been my friends, I take occasion to proffer the warmest thanks of a grateful heart. My enemies—and old Hunkers generally—I disdain and defy the same as ever. Walter Whitman."

[3] See I, pp. 24–25.

[4] See I, p. 24, note. Since Whitman's whereabouts can now be stated definitely for the period before September, 1849, and for that after June, 1850, whereas we know nothing of his movements between those dates (unless the publication of "Blood-Money" on March 22 be significant) it seems to me very likely that a second trip South was made in the fall of 1849.

[5] Title changed to "Dough-Face Song," "Complete Prose," pp. 334–335.

[6] In the New York *Evening Post*, April 30.

[7] I, pp. 25–27.   [8] I, pp. 27–30.

[9] Whittier's "Ichabod," similarly inspired, appeared a few days later.

hurrying Whitman toward his destined career as a reformatory poet. "Resurgemus" is the earliest separate and complete poem of the "Leaves of Grass" known to have been previously published. It indicates that Whitman's poetic ambition, which for two or three years had been "hovering on the flanks," as he said, is now leading him into unconventional publications and straight toward the versification of 1855.

Concerning Whitman's employment in 1850–1851, biographies have never agreed. Some of them, following Whitman himself, have placed the *Freeman* venture in these years; others have supposed this to have been the period of his house-building. Neither statement is correct. Apparently Whitman was as much a journalist as ever; but now, instead of being in charge of a paper, he had to resort to what odd jobs he could get. In May and June, 1850—perhaps for a longer period—he had some anonymous connection with the Brooklyn *Daily Advertizer*, a Whig sheet, for which he wrote a series of "Paragraph Sketches of Brooklynites,"[1] much of which was to be worked over in the "Brooklyniana" of 1861–1862. Just how much he wrote for the *Advertizer* is unknown, but mention should be made of a signed editorial in it[2] which he published to urge the city to build a system of water works, an improvement which came within a few years. During 1851 he wrote five prose contributions for the New York *Evening Post*, most of them signed "Paumanok."[3] I think it likely that it was Whitman also who contributed the Brooklyn notes to the "City Intelligence " column of the *Post* in 1851–1852. At any rate, the indications are that the pen, rather than carpenter's tools, was yet his chief source of income. The making of an income, however, was far from the dominant concern of this crescent poet, whose first-born song was soon to be delivered in a world unprepared to receive it. He took an increased interest in art and in artists,[4] entered familiarly into the hopeful Bohemia of his day,[5] and, in pleading at once for art in life and life in art,[6] he took a definite step toward his own authentic career. A fortunately preserved specimen of Whitman's operatic criticism—of Bettini in "*La Favorita*"[7]—not only reveals his ecstatic sensitiveness to the

[1]See I, pp. 234–235.

[2]"A Plea for Water," I, pp. 254–255.

[3]See I, pp. 236–238, 239–241, 247–249, 250–254, 255–259.   [4]See I, pp. 236–238, 241–247.   [5]See I, p. 237.

[6]See I, pp. 236–237, 241–247.   [7]See I, pp. 255–259.

charm of this tenor, whose singing was gratefully remembered
for forty years,[1] but also the mystical exaltation he felt in
contemplating the grandeur of nature, both of which con-
tributed, perhaps, to the profound mystical experience which
by biographers has commonly been assigned to Whitman's
early thirties.   It is only natural that his style should gradually
become more serious, tempered, mature, and attractive.[2]   But
one is not to conclude that Whitman was merely an artist
engrossed with his art or a mystic withdrawn from life.   Even
in an address to an "art union" he deliberately takes occasion
to satirize the want of taste displayed in American fashions[3] and
the want of poise and dignity in American manners,[4] while in the
"Letters from Paumanok"[5] he describes with appropriate sim-
plicity the "powerful uneducated persons" he encounters while
summering on east Long Island.   Nor was Whitman's contact
with the real world—so imperatively demanded as a counter
influence to his artistic and religious subjectivity—limited to
mere observation or to sympathetic "absorption."   He was a
public-spirited citizen, proud of his American birthright and
determined to exercise it, in a day of half-achieved democracy,
in shaping his city more to his liberty-loving heart's desire.
When, in 1854, the Common Council and the Mayor of Brook-
lyn undertook to forbid the running of street cars or the open-
ing of restaurants, and otherwise to enforce by law the strict
observance of the Sabbath, Whitman, the individualist, ad-
dressed a memorial[6] to the city fathers protesting in no slavish
tones against prohibitory and meddling puritanism in the city
administration in general, and against the restrictions imposed
upon street railways, bakeries, and restaurants in particular.

The year 1855 was, of course, a turning point, or rather a
date of metamorphosis, in the life of Whitman.   Through a
long development, brought to a climax by mystical experience,
he had attained the immortal youth of spirit which one associ-
ates with the creative artist.   He still dreamed, but his dreams
were thenceforth no longer mere rapturous observation; instead
they were the pregnant dreams of a seer.   He continued to
preach, but now with an authority unlearned of the scribes.

[1] See "Complete Prose," pp. 427, 499, 514–515.
[2] See I, pp. 234–235, 236–239, 241–247, 255–259, 259–264.   [3] See I, pp. 246–247.
[4] See I, p. 245; cf. pp. 168–170.   [5] See I, pp. 247–249, 250–254.
[6] See I, pp. 259–264.

The new poetry, however, made no popular headway, and was absolutely unremunerative. As a result the poet was forced to remain a journalist as well.

At some date not later than June, 1857,[1] he became editor of the Brooklyn *Daily Times*,[2] a position which he retained as late as January, 1859.[3] He continued to be interested in his poetry and in its dissemination, seeking even to have it translated into the German.[4] This divided interest accounts, at least in part, for the fact that his *Times* editorials were more detached, reminiscent, judicial than had been his compositions for the *Eagle*. Occasionally his editorials throw light on his poetry. His discussion of the evils of prostitution,[5] for example, not only reveals an advanced interest in sociology, but it gives also a hint as to why, in the 1860 edition of his "Leaves of Grass," he was to emphasize what he considered the normal and healthy physiology of sex. That his motive in this was to combat the unclean prudery to which he traced much of the shockingly prevalent vice of the day, and not to celebrate free-love, is indicated by his strictures on free-love in another editorial.[6] His sociological interest often took him, as previously in Brooklyn and New Orleans, to the police courts, in his reports of which he mingles a motherly tenderness with his satire.[7] Such sketches place the stamp of utter sincerity upon poems like "You Felons on Trial in Courts" (1860).[8] . . . This is the period in his life when, if ever, Whitman might be expected to feel the need of a home of his own. Perhaps he did, momentarily at least;[9] but the most congenial atmosphere that he found was that of Pfaff's bohemian restaurant,[10] where he discussed politics, art, and literature with a group of young writers as ambitious as he, but less gifted. Believing (like Longfellow and Lowell) that no other poet in America was attempting to perform the task assigned to himself,[11] he uncovered his heart more and more unreservedly in his verse, in comparison to which the man he exhibits in the cafés and on the streets is but a shadow.[12] As

---

[1] See II, p. 1, note.

[2] Then published at 145 Grand Street, Williamsburg.

[3] See II, p. 1, note.   [4] *Ibidem.*   [5] See II, pp. 5–8.

[6] See II, p. 7, note. But *cf.* "With Walt Whitman in Camden," III, pp. 438–439.

[7] See II, pp. 10–12.

[8] "Leaves of Grass," 1917, II, p. 160.

[9] See II, p. 19.   [10] See II, pp. 92–93.   [11] See II, p. 91.   [12] See II, p. 93.

his peculiar mission becomes clearer to him, its religious nature grows in importance, until he regards himself as the prospective founder of a religion comparable to Christianity itself, though humbly acknowledging his indebtedness to both the Hebrew and the Greek.[1] By this time Whitman is a full-fledged Hegelian—pragmatic, transcendental, evolutionary.

During 1860 Whitman was engrossed in the publication of the first Boston edition of his poems; but when the outbreak of the war stopped the sales of his book, he turned again to the newspapers for a livelihood. While editing the Brooklyn *Times*, he had written an article reminiscent of the early days in Brooklyn,[2] which showed that he was drawing inspiration from the past as well as from the future.[3] Now he proposes to elaborate the idea by publishing, in the Brooklyn weekly *Standard*, a series of articles on the history of the city. This claimed to be something of an innovation for the press,[4] but Whitman was nothing if not an innovator. The "Brooklyniana" papers[5] were copyrighted and eulogistically advertized by the *Standard*,[6] and, if we may take the word of the editor for it, they were well paid for. Their publication was interrupted, however, while Whitman took one of his characteristic rambling journeys to his old haunts on Long Island[7]—fishing at Montauk Point,[8] living with idyllic unceremoniousness among the country and fisher folk,[9] making himself a boon companion,[10] and studying with a poet's eye the beauties of nature.[11] Nor was this really out of character in the man who was soon to be so closely connected with the horrors of the war that was already raging. I think Whitman had a prophetic sense of the fact that his own life, like that of his country, was near a historic turning; and he was here taking a lingering farewell of beloved scenes which, after the war, he should never be able to look upon with the same eyes again. . . . He had barely concluded the twenty-five articles in the series when an accident—the wounding of his brother George, erroneously reported as serious—called him to the war front, and so introduced him to his life of composite service as a "welfare worker" and surgeon's helper, on the battlefield and in the Washington hospitals.[12]

[1] See II, pp. 91–92.   [2] See II, pp. 1–5.   [3] See I, pp. 246–247.
[4] See II, p. 223, note.
[5] See II, pp. 222–321.   [6] See II, p. 223, note.   [7] See II, p. 222, note, 306–321.
[8] See II, p. 313.   [9] See II, pp. 313–321; *cf.* I, pp. 247–254.   [10] *Ibidem.*
[11] See II, pp. 314, 317–318, 320.
[12] See II, pp. 21–22, 27–29, 33–34, 93.

6. WASHINGTON (1863–1873)

In camp and on the battlefield Whitman not only received impressions which were later to be coined into the incomparable little poems of "Drum-Taps,"[1] but he formed associations which developed his sensitiveness to manly friendship.[2]   In the presence of death he learned a new lesson in immortality,[3] and saw, as before he had only dreamed of, the spiritual resources of the painfully unifying nation.[4]   Returning to Washington with the wounded, he devoted a moiety of his time to supporting himself by contributions to the New York and Brooklyn papers[5] and by copying for Major Hapgood, an army paymaster[6]; but his real interest lay in the pathetic and heroic sights of the hospitals[7] and in the picturesque spectacles of the capital in wartime.[8]   His realistic descriptions of these will not be lost on a generation of readers who have themselves just emerged from an unromantic conflict.   To Whitman the Civil War was not a mediæval adventure, its tragedy obscured by chivalric glamour, but a great spiritual struggle for national ideals, in the light of which alone its inhuman horror was endurable.[9]   At times he doubted the success of the Union cause,[10] as he at times doubted the success of his own poetic mission;[11] but when the forces of nationalism finally brought the war to a victorious close, he had deep cause for rejoicing, inasmuch as he loved the South as he loved the North.[12]   These war-time letters and the descriptive articles sent in 1873 to the New York *Daily Graphic*[13] throw much light upon the passing show that attracted his outward eye. But underneath his entertaining exterior Whitman was suffering a private disappointment, if not indeed a tragedy.[14]   He passionately loved a woman who was, like Thackeray's inamorata, married to another.[15]   This attachment (possibly but not

[1] See II, p. 93.   [2] See II, pp. 21, 93, 96 and note.   [3] See II, p. 22.
[4] See II, pp. 23, 30–31, 102; *cf.* I, p. 156.   [5] See II, pp. 23, 26–29, 29–36, 37–42.
[6] See II, pp. 23, 25.   Later he had a clerkship, first in the Interior, and later in the Attorney-General's, Department.
[7] See II, pp. 22–23, 27–29, 31.   [8] See II, pp. 22–23, 25, 26–36, *passim.*
[9] See II, pp. 22, 30–31; *cf.* p. 43.   [10] See II, pp. 26, 101.
[11] See II, p. 101.   [12] See II, pp. 21, 102.   [13] See II, pp. 42–49, 49–53.
[14] See "With Walt Whitman in Camden," II, p. 543.
[15] In the original draft of the article, "Personal Recollections of Walt Whitman," which Mrs. Ellen M. Calder (formerly Mrs. William D. O'Connor) wrote for the *Atlantic Monthly* (June, 1907) appears a very important but for some reason unpublished passage. The manuscript from which I quote is in the Bucke collection.
"He [Whitman] had met a certain lady, and by some mischance a letter revealing

probably a continuation of the one commonly associated with New Orleans) ended unhappily,[1] but it seems to have given birth to a considerable amount of Whitman's poetry dating from this period.[2] Moreover, during the latter part of his residence in Washington his emotional attachment to his own sex threatened to destroy the poise and aplomb of his life.[3] But disappointment, physical affliction, and struggles with himself finally brought peace to his passion-torn heart and serenity to his poems.[4]

7. CAMDEN (1873–1892)

The war over and recorded in the 1867 volume of poems, the hospitals closed and summed up in the "Calamus" and "Wound

---

her friendship for him fell into her husband's hands, which made this gentleman very indignant and jealous, and thereupon, in the presence of his wife and another lady, he abused Walt. All that excited Walt's sympathy for the lady, over and above the admiration and affection he felt for her, so that in telling about it, he said 'I would marry that woman to-night if she were free.' Correspondence was kept up between them for some time after that, and he was very strongly attracted to this lady. This is the only instance I have known where he was strongly attracted toward any woman in this way. It was this lady for whom he wrote the little poem in 'Children of Adam' beginning: 'Out of the rolling ocean, the crowd,' etc.

"Describing this lady to me he said that she was quite fair, with brown hair and eyes, and rather plump and womanly and sweet and gentle, and he said that she bore herself with so much dignity and was so keenly hurt by what her husband said, that I think that drew her to him more. It was in '64 (?).

"In connection with the above:—The idea that he conveyed to me was that he did not think it would have been well for him to have formed that closest of ties, he was so fond of his freedom, it would have been a great mistake if he had ever married. He said to me many times that he did not envy men their wives but that he did envy them their children. He often used this expression, 'Well, if I had been caught young I might have done certain things or formed certain habits.'"

It will not escape the reader that practically all our trustworthy evidence on Whitman's romance points to a married woman as his paramour. If by such a woman, or women, he actually had offspring, then the enigmatic language of his confession to Symonds would grow clearer. It would mean that, on the birth of the child, the three principals in the tragic triangle agreed to keep the matter quiet, sacrificing their own individual feelings in the interest of the legal, social, and financial "benefit" of the innocent child. Yet it should be remembered that the very existence of these children rests entirely upon the testimony of Whitman himself.

[1] See II, pp. 94–96.

[2] See second note above; cf. also "To a Certain Civilian" (1865), "Not Youth Pertains to Me" (1865), "O Me! O Life!" (1865), "Ah, Poverties, Wincings, and Sulky Retreats" (1865), and "I Heard You, Solemn-Sweet Pipes of the Organ" (1865–1866). See also II, p. 93.

[3] See II, p. 96.

[4] See, in particular, "Give Me the Splendid Silent Sun" (1865), "Passage to India" (1871; Part 5, at least, was written before January 20, 1869), "Pioneers! O Pioneers!" (1865), "Darest Thou Now O Soul" (1868), and "Prayer of Columbus" (1874).

Dresser" letters and in the notes for "Specimen Days," Whitman was, in 1873, stricken with paralysis. He removed to Camden, New Jersey, in which his sun, that had witnessed such an expansive, tragic, hopeful half-century, was to set twenty years later. From his invalid's chair he wrote down scraps of ideas for friendly New York journals like the *Daily Graphic*, discussing art, poetry, the drama, culture, politics, democracy.[1] A few years before his death he indulged in one of the anonymous self-criticisms[2] with which he had earlier sought to extend the knowledge of the inner meaning of his life and work. These reminiscences review the whole of his varied life.

Thus, in the writings brought together for preservation in the present volumes, one can trace Whitman's personal and literary growth from his youth up, revealed all the more candidly in publications and manuscripts which he never wrote for preservation over his own name. In particular, the collection increases our knowledge of the following hitherto obscure periods in his biography: (1) his youth and apprenticeship, (2) his residence at Jamaica in 1839–1841, (3) his single attempt at fiction, (4) his connection with the Brooklyn *Eagle*, 1846–1848, (5) his trip to, and his life in, New Orleans, together with his romances, there or elsewhere, (6) his connection with the Brooklyn *Advertizer*, the New York *Tribune*, the New York *Evening Post*, the Brooklyn *Times*, and the Brooklyn *Standard*, and (7), most important of all, the growth of the First Edition of the "Leaves of Grass."

[1] See II, pp. 53–58.
[2] See II, pp. 95–62.

INTRODUCTION: CRITICAL

I. WHITMAN'S PROSE

1. RELATION OF HIS PROSE TO HIS VERSE

IT WAS not by publishing the "Leaves of Grass," at the age of thirty-six, that Whitman began to be either original or eccentric. Though in varying degrees, his prose is as truly individual as his verse. One finds it possible, indeed, to trace many of the faults and virtues of his poetry back to his earlier prose. As much was to have been expected, though as yet nobody has inquired particularly into the matter. Whatever unanalyzable influx of vision, of taste, or of power may have come to Whitman through the mystical experiences of mid-life, the utterance of his enlarged being was conditioned by what he had previously been. For when it introduces genius as a veritable *deus ex machina*, biography degenerates into superstitious hero-worship. Genius there is, else there would be fewer occasions for biography; but we can make no progress by asserting that genius is superior to the laws of causation, albeit their operation may lie deeply hidden from the eyes of even the man of genius himself. The critic, no less than the biographer, needs to be familiar with the writings of Whitman's youth, regardless of their intrinsic interest or value.

2. DIFFICULTIES IN STUDYING WHITMAN'S EARLY PROSE

In tracing Whitman's poetic peculiarities to his earlier prose, difficulty is encountered in determining the precise limits of his responsibility. Most of the prose included in the present collection comes to us either in the form of manuscript or in the form of magazine and newspaper writing. But since the manuscript was seldom, if ever, used in its present form for publishing copy, it is unfair to suppose that it represents Whitman's ideal; and though he himself read the proofs of most of the newspaper writing here reprinted,[1] there was still abundant opportunity for typographical variation from his copy or proofs. Moreover, we must keep in mind the haste in which newspaper writing was done in the day of small editorial staffs.[2] The frequency and the uniformity of some of the peculiarities of his prose, however, are enough to convince us that Whitman tolerated them, if indeed he did not insist upon them.

3. The Mechanics of Writing

His system of punctuation, for instance, was unique. Neither his contemporaries nor the newspapers on which he had served his apprenticeship punctuated just as he did. There was a meticulousness about it which sometimes defeated its own object. A parenthesis seldom sufficed, but it must be reinforced with commas.[3] . . . Throughout his entire career as a prose writer Whitman relied as much upon the dash as Poe did in his verse, and that without Poe's excuse for overworking the careless and ineffective mark. This abuse of the dash (sometimes to emphasize the period) appears in one of his earliest manuscripts as prepared for the printer.[4] It occurs in his editorials,[5] and in his formal memorial to the City Council.[6] From his mystical notebooks[7] it passes naturally into his free verse.[8] It agrees so well with his habit of panoramic observation,[9] with his style of rapid, terse, suggestive description,[10] and with his emotional periods[11] that it must be taken to have been characteristic of his mental processes. Sometimes the dash is employed at the beginning of the paragraph, as if to accentuate the break in the thought.[12] Frequently the period and dash is abandoned in favour of the French series of points,[13] indicating a feeling for precision of form—even where the general effect is so deliberately indefinite!—which I have not observed in the

[1] In some cases he did the composing himself, though not often. He was his own compositor on the *Long Islander* and his one-time office boy, Mr. William S. Sutton, has told me that when editor of the *Eagle* Whitman was very particular about his proofs.
[2] See I, p. 116.
[3] See I, pp. 174, 176, 179, 181. This style of punctuation was more common in the eighteenth century than in the nineteenth, and might have been taught Whitman by much older men, like William Hartshorne.
[4] See II, pp. 97–101.   [5] See I, pp. 117–118, 121–125, 144–146..
[6] See I, pp. 263–264.   [7] See II, pp. 63–68.
[8] See II, pp. 91–93.   [9] See I, pp. 141–144, 193–195, 223–224; II, pp. 25, 47–48.
[10] See I, pp. 107, 140.   [11] See I, pp. 72–73, 172–174, 242, 245, 256–257, 263–264.
[12] See I, pp. 110–113, 114–117, 174–177.
[13] See I, pp. 126, 137, 139, 140–144, 147, 155–157, 159–160, 223–224; cf. pp. 27–30.

contemporary press.   This habit of expression led naturally to
the mystical synthesis of his poetic "catalogues"[1] wherein he
attempts to suggest a unifying principle by a rapid sketching of
its variant manifestations, very much as the effect of motion is
produced, in the cinema, by the rapid sequence of a multitude of
photographs.   Too frequent use of the dash, however, tended to
confirm in Whitman the habits of carelessness and incoherence
which his lack of any thorough apprenticeship in writing made
inevitable.   His punctuation at times really obscures his mean-
ing, as in the following sentence:

Which of those friends or relatives can say—I have, on my conscience,
none of the responsibility of that man's intemperance and death?[2]

Like Poe again, Whitman was fond of using italics for the sake
of emphasis, both in passages that are serious[3] and in others
that are humorous,[4] satirical,[5] or facetious.[6]

4. GRAMMAR

The poet, says Whitman, is a man gifted with the divine
power of using words; and by that definition he was himself cer-
tainly often a poet.   But such divinity became articulate in him
only after a long struggle with a devilish liability to misuse the
language.   Sometimes he is not even grammatical.[7]   The
verbs lie and lay give him constant trouble.[8]   In a leader on
the opportunity of the editorial writer, he allows "it don't."[9]
Elsewhere he says, "myself and Colby sprang,"[10] "with I and my
companion,"[11] "learning him to read,"[12] "as if our world was
weak,"[13] "some of ye,"[14] "all the hitherto experience of The
States,"[15] "ain't,"[16] "the then time,"[17] "most all,"[18] "plen-
tier,"[19] "the persons largest engaged in whaling."[20]   Many of
these crochets Whitman was slow in outgrowing.   An early
manuscript concludes:

[1] See I, pp. 223–224, 242, 263–264; II, p. 42.   [2] See II, p. 164.
[3] See I, pp. 4, 66, 73, 117, 126, 149, 159–162, 180.   [4] See I, pp. 174–177.
[5] See I, pp. 178, 205.   [6] See I, pp. 33, 177, 201, 203.
[7] Whitman was once called upon to defend his grammar in the *Eagle*. See "The Gath-
ering of the Forces," II, pp. 7–12.
[8] See I, pp. 6, 47, 66, 187.   [9] See I, p. 116.   [10] See II, p. 121.   [11] See I, p. 253.
[12] See I, p. 145.   [13] See I, p. 110.   [14] See II, p. 94.   [15] See II, p. 58.
[16] See I, p. 115.   [17] See I, p. 75.   [18] See II, p. 41.   [19] See I, p. 154.
[20] See I, p. 120.

So, friendly reader, we have filled our column, more or less, with a visit, us two, to the Italian opera with you, etc.[1]

But as late as 1862, when he was forty-three, he could commit to print so slovenly a sentence as this:

Ah, if these occurrences, and the foregoing names are perused by any of the remaining old folks, their contemporaries, we (then a boy of twelve years), have jotted down, above, they will surely have some curious, perhaps melancholy reflections.[2]

Reflections shared, no doubt, with a difference, by the twentieth-century admirer of Whitman. . . . Sometimes Whitman was careless of the idiom of the language, as in such expressions as "inculcate on,"[3] and "akin with."[4] Many of these solecisms can be accounted for, I think, by the fact that, since he was a slow thinker,[5] Whitman did not have time in his journalistic prose for the painstaking revision which was given to his verse.

5. Diction

The besetting sin of Whitman's early prose is its lack of restraint. Readers of his "Slang in America" and his "American Primer" know how eagerly he quested about for words, and how successful he was in his etymological predictions.[6] But in the period to which belong most of the selections in these volumes, he collected and employed words and phrases, including colloquialisms and slang, with very little judicial discrimination. Particularly when he is attempting to be "funny," slang comes natural to his pen,[7] sometimes but not always enclosed between apologetic quotation marks. The following will illustrate: "His arm must have ached some,"[8] "used to did,"[9] "he went it with a rush,"[10] "loaded down to the guards,"[11] "a great place and *no* mistake,"[12] "the thing,"[13] "b'hoys,"[14] "whaler,"[15] "they do say,"[16] "doff my beaver,"[17] "tympanums" (ears),[18] "to go" (to risk),[19] "bones" (money),[20] "conceited spark,"[21] "not to be

[1] See II, p. 101.   [2] See II, p. 296.   [3] See I, p. 220.   [4] See I, p. 284.
[5] See "With Walt Whitman in Camden," I, p. 249.
[6] See Mr. H. L. Mencken's "The American Language," New York, 1919, pp. 73, 320.
[7] "Slang was one of my specialties," said Whitman to Traubel. ("With Walt Whitman in Camden," I, p. 462.)
[8] See I, p. 118.   [9] See I, p. 205.   [10] *Ibidem.*   [11] See I, p. 206.
[12] See I, p. 224; *cf.* p. 193.   [13] See I, p. 208.   [14] See I, pp. 194, 195.
[15] See I, p. 50.   [16] See I, p. 215.   [17] See I, p. 44.   [18] See I, p. 45.
[19] See I, p. 201.   [20] See I, p. 223.   [21] See I, p. 33.

beat,"[1] "some pumpkins,"[2] "diggins,"[3] "her Irish gets up,"[4] "passes" (mesmeric).[5] Rarely Whitman combines slang with a pun, as in "It is doubtful whether Cairo will ever be any 'great shakes,' except in the way of ague."[6]

Foreign terms had for Whitman the fascination they often possess for young writers unacquainted with any but their mother tongue. Most of these borrowed expressions are from the French and occur in the New Orleans sketches. Occasionally his pseudo-learnedness becomes mere barbarism, as when *ecaille* is used for *écaillers*.[7] Sometimes these borrowed words and phrases are employed as slang in English; sometimes they are introduced to give a superior air to the page. Such diction, of course, becomes infinitely tedious, as in this sentence from the unspeakably affected "Samuel Sensitive":

> It was a present to Julia, that Sam had, with due consideration of the consequences, resolved to abstract forty dollars and upward from his oyster and billiard account, and bestow it in a beautiful, enameled, filagree, morceau of *bijouterie*, whose value, intrinsically, *per se*, was perhaps about six bits.[8]

But at times he has difficulty with the diction of his own tongue as well. Not infrequently he falls into malapropisms as nonchalant as they are naïve. He says "unpretensive" for "unpretentious,"[9] "locale" for "location,"[10] "peril" for "imperil,"[11] "vocable" for "vocal,"[12] "deathly" for "deadly,"[13] "fixings" or "fitments" for "fixtures,"[14] "merchantable" for "mercantile,"[15] and he declares "obfusticated" to be an expressive word.[16]

Whitman's later fear of "stock poetical touches" is to be matched by his avoidance of conventionality in his early prose diction, an avoidance which betrayed him into an excess of colloquialism. Perhaps it is an indication of his desire to keep near "the people"[17] as distinguished from the colleges and the

---

[1] See I, p. 119.   [2] See I, p. 183.   [3] See I, p. 177.
[4] See I, p. 216.   [5] See I, p. 216.   [6] See I, p. 189.
[7] See I, p. 211. Unlike most printers, Whitman was not a very accurate speller when young. This is so obvious that I have not called particular attention to it here; yet it had a bearing on his use of malapropisms, and may have awakened his interest in simplified spelling later in life.
[8] See I, p. 216.   [9] See II, p. 49.   [10] See II, p. 35.   [11] See I, p. 97.
[12] See I, p. 201.
[13] See II, p. 119.   [14] See I, p. 170; II, p. 46.   [15] See I, p. 218.   [16] See II, p. 187.
[17] See II, p. 105.

critics. Whatever his motive, such expressions as "without these follow,"[1] "bless their stars,"[2] "considerable of a trading town,"[3] "we will e'en just have to give the go-by,"[4] and "genteel squirts"[5] are sufficiently removed from literary conventionality. The following sentence flows so naturally from Whitman's pen, and so negligently, as to create a presumption that he spoke very much after this fashion:

> Every person attached to the road jumps on from the ground or some of the various platforms, after the train starts—which (so imitative an animal is man) sets a fine example for greenhorns and careless people at some future time to fix themselves off with broken legs or perhaps mangled bodies.[6]

Nearly all these colloquialisms have been quoted from writings belonging to the period of Whitman's maturity; in youth he was, both as poet and as prose man, at times ridiculously conventional and affected in diction.   Sooner than did his Victorian ancestor, the modern reader wearies of such expressions as "I bethink me,"[7] "certes,"[8] "ycleped,"[9] "wended,"[10] "he remembered him of,"[11] "pale emblems of decay,"[12] "the gentle orbs of benevolence and philosophy,"[13] "we trow,"[14] "aneath,"[15] "haply,"[16] "it wonders me,"[17] and "whilome."[18]

It would thus be easy to make game of Whitman's early diction, were that my purpose. He himself found fault with it, and omitted the present writings from his collected editions. These faults are pointed out rather to show from what limitations Whitman, in his best work, freed himself, and also to make it clear that if crudities and blemishes are discoverable in his more ambitious work they should furnish no cause for wonder, no occasion for strained justification. Considering his opportunities, Whitman possessed, even in his younger days, a very comprehensive vocabulary. All of life was language to him, and he saw life from many angles. The faults, like the virtues, of his diction are largely traceable to the unlimited range of his interest. A vocabulary adequate to the needs of the many types of prose with which he experimented was in itself an achievement in self-education. What Whit-

---

[1] See I, p. 145.   [2] See I, pp. 149, 164.   [3] See I, p. 176.   [4] See II, p. 52.
[5] See II, p. 68.   [6] See II, p. 307.   [7] See I, p. 103.   [8] See I, pp. 119, 174
[9] See I, p. 211.   [10] See I, pp. 48, 90.   [11] See I, p. 84.   [12] See I, p. 80.
[13] See I, p. 125.   [14] See I, p. 116.   [15] See I, pp. 93, 160.   [16] See I, p. 73.
[17] See I, p. 80.   [18] See I, p. 183.

man needed was a strong inspiration to awaken the slumbering fires of his soul. When he had it, his diction became clear, picturesque, and forceful, sometimes even beautiful,[1] but when it was lacking—when he did hack work or wrote in a dreamy, undisciplined manner—his diction frayed off most immorally.[2]

7. TYPES OF PROSE

a. The News-Story

In attempting to classify roughly the varied prose compositions contained in the present volumes, it will be convenient to begin with the news-story. But the use of the modern terminology must not be taken to imply that in Whitman's day the news-story had been influenced by the technique of the short-story; indeed it can scarcely be said to have had any recognized technique of its own. The reporter had to rely upon his wit to see something picturesque or important in the doings of the day; or, if this were lacking, something on which he might witticize, moralize, or sentimentalize. Such writing tended greatly to develop Whitman's sense of individual freedom, but it did not afford him, on the other hand, the rigid discipline whereby a modern newspaper office sometimes supplies the want of a college education. His own reports vary greatly in interest and significance. The earliest we have,[3] which belongs in his twentieth year, is in no way indicative of promise or power. As he grew older he was inclined to moralize on the passing events he recorded.[4] His purpose in visiting the police courts, for instance, was to hold a mirror up to lowly life and to play Rhadamanthus to culprit and court alike.[5] Except in the form of the news-editorial, the news-story gave Whitman, however, little opportunity to display his best prose. Fortunately, therefore, he was (so far as we know) never a mere reporter;[6] and when, in New Orleans, he was the "scissors editor,"[7] he was inclined to write an editorial on an event[8] or else to let the exchanges do the work for him.[9] And so ardent a reformer was he that no chance was missed to cull

[1] E. g., I, pp. 102–103, 107–108, 154–156, 168–170, 171–174, 181–186, 220–221, 236–238, 241–247, 255–259; II, pp. 112–120, 320.

[2] E. g., I, pp. 44–46, 117, 211–213, 216–218; II, pp. 53–58, 97–101.   [3] See I, p. 32.

[4] See I, pp. 141–144, 221–222, 223–224, 236–238.   [5] See II, pp. 10–12.

[6] Unless such was his position on the Brooklyn *Advertiser* or the New York *Evening Post*, 195–198, 218–219, 220–221. See *infra*, p. liv.

[7] See II, p. 78.   [8] See I, pp. 195–198, 218–219, 220–221.   [9] See I, p. 229.

from the exchanges news-stories that would keep before his readers the brutality of the slave trade, the inhumanity of capital punishment, the excesses of Abolitionism, the dangers of intemperance, or the absurdity of Fourierism.[1] But occasionally, as if by way of compensation, he writes of a picnic[2] or excursion[3] in a chatty, colloquial vein no longer possible to the reporters for the metropolitan press. In these stories, as in his editorial correspondence[4] and his war reporting,[5] the perennial boyishness in him refuses to abase itself before the dignity of the editorial tripod.

Now and then Whitman would attempt something a little more pretentious—a sort of special article before the day of the special article. He would visit a prison,[6] a hospital,[7] an asylum,[8] the Navy Yard,[9] or a school[10] and write a long description of it from the point of view of a curious-minded rambler about town or that of a public-spirited guardian of the welfare of the state. Once he described a great fire in New York,[11] with a vividness that suggests his treatment of the same theme in verse.[12]

b. Essays and Sketches

More or less similar to his news articles are his essays and sketches of various types. The earliest of these are the puerile "Sun-Down Papers"[13] which Whitman contributed to the Jamaica weeklies in 1839–1841. It is to be hoped that the five missing numbers of this series will yet be discovered, but the seven anonymous essays in this volume throw most welcome light on their author's development. Had we a file of the *Long Islander* running back to the period of Whitman's editorship, or could we identify the "piece or two" which he declared himself to have contributed to George P. Morris's *Mirror*,[14] the "Sun-Down Papers" would be slightly less important than they are; as it is, they are practically the earliest of his publications extant, and they illuminate a most interesting stage in

---

[1] See I, p. 229. [2] See I, pp. 48–51, 164–166. [3] See I, pp. 118–121.
[4] See I, pp. 174–181, 247–254. [5] See II, pp. 26–41; *cf.* pp. 21–26.
[6] See Brooklyn *Daily Eagle*, June 30, 1846; *cf.* also II, p. 274.
[7] *Cf.* II, pp. 288–292.
[8] See Brooklyn *Daily Eagle*, June 3, 9, July 17, 1846.
[9] *Ibidem*, June 27, 1846, January 30, 1847; *cf.* March 9, 1846.
[10] See *infra*, p. xli, note 7. [11] See I, pp. 154–156. [12] See I, p. 154, note 1.
[13] See I, pp. 32–51. [14] See "Complete Prose," p. 187.

his growth. The style is very uneven. At times it is slip-
shod,[1] defiant,[2] sentimental,[3] or given to moralizing and to
"castigating the age," like the "Salmagundi Papers" but without
their grace and good humour.[4]   But at other times it is rhyth-
mical though not restrained, and once, at least, the young
author is inspired and achieves an allegorical "dream,"[5] done
partly in the eighteenth century and partly in the Biblical
manner, a device which Whitman was to employ repeatedly in
his prose[6] and which may have had some connection with his
dream and trance passages of his verse.[7] Attention has already
been called to the fact that these early sketches give us our first
intimation of Whitman's life-long ambitions for authorship.

When this dreamy, kind-hearted, sensitive young man goes
to the city in 1841, his writing continues to express the senti-
mentality of the "Sun-Down Papers," but it also displays an
increasing amount of, as yet, unharmonized realism. The
combination is significant in that it persists, in more artistic
form, in his "Leaves of Grass" itself. In "The Tomb-Blos-
soms"[8] the full sentimentality of that tearful age expends itself
over the unhappy lot of an immigrant widow mourning beside a
grave. In "The Little Sleighers"[9] the mood is more natural
and healthy, but even here the spirited description of a cold
morning on the Battery cannot end without a most inappro-
priate (and, considering the temperature, a most unconvincing)
fit of moralizing on the threadbare themes of youth and inno-
cence. "Tear Down and Build Over Again,"[10] a sentimental
plea for the preservation of historic old buildings, reminds us
that, though Whitman as philosopher and patriot was radical
enough, as poet he was deeply rooted in the past and its mani-
fold associations. "A Dialogue"[11] passionately arraigns the
institution of capital punishment, particularly the justification
of it on Biblical grounds. In this argumentative essay Whitman
employs the method of an imaginary dialogue between a con-
demned murderer and society, somewhat in the Socratic man-
ner; and it is not without its effectiveness,[12] despite the author's
obvious prejudice. In this reform, however, Whitman cannot

[1]See I, pp. 44–46, 46–48.   [2]*Ibidem.*   [3]See I, pp. 35–37.   [4]See I, pp. 32–34.
[5]See I, pp. 39–44.   [6]See I, pp. 74–78; II, pp. 200–204.
[7]See II, pp. 70, 71, 74; "The Sleepers" and "Song of Myself," *passim.*
[8]See I, pp. 60–67.   [9]See I, pp. 90–92.   [10]See I, pp. 92–97.   [11]See I, pp. 97–103.
[12]Another good example of Whitman's impassioned argument is "American Working-
men *versus* Slavery," I, pp. 171–174.

be credited with originality or leadership, for he was but follow-
ing such men as Bryant, Whittier, Greeley, Hawthorne, and
others who were making of it a crusade in the 1840's.[1] Another
essay of the sentimental-disputatious type is that entitled
"Boz and Democracy."[2] In it he acknowledges his obligation
to Dickens, an indebtedness which perhaps appears in the pica-
resque elements of "Franklin Evans,"[3] though one hesitates to
lay "Franklin Evans" in any measure at Dickens's door. The
influence of "Boz" consisted chiefly in his exhibition of the
humanitarian opportunities of the "democratic writer," whose
pages tend to "destroy the old land-marks which pride and
fashion have set up, making impassable distinctions between
the brethren of the Great Family."[4] Here we have, also, the
earliest expression of Whitman's conception of the "average
man" and of that "philosophy which teaches to pull down the
high and bring up the low."[5] By insisting upon human sympa-
thy in the literature of a democracy, Whitman was, of course,
holding a brief for the future. Another essay looking in the
same direction was the "Art-Singing and Heart-Singing"[6] which
he wrote in 1845 for Poe's *Broadway Journal*. The naïve
manner in which he here writes on the subject of America's
need for a native style of music, even while confessing his entire
ignorance of music as an art, indicates that no lack of special
or detailed information is to restrain the coming prophet from
delivering his message, addressed to the spirit, rather than to
the lower intelligence, of his people.[7]

Still another sort of essay is found in the "Sketches of the
Sidewalks and Levees,"[8] which portray the motley types of
humanity that filled the romantic city of New Orleans in 1848.
In general plan they appear to be imitations of the Addisonian
"characters," but they make no pretentions to grace or elegance
of expression, even degenerating at times into a careless and silly

[1] See II, p. 15. In August, 1846, Whitman ran serially a story of circumstantial evi-
dence by Robert Treat Irving ("John Quod, Esq.").

[2] See I, pp. 67–72.

[3] To be published in the latter part of the same year (1842).

[4] See I, p. 68–69.   [5] *Ibidem*. See also II, p. 10.   [6] See I, pp. 104–106.

[7] The conclusion—"These hints we throw out rather as suggestive of a train of thought
to other and more deliberate thinkers than we"—gives us, no doubt, the *psychological*
reason for his complacent declaration, "Let others finish specimens—I never finish
specimens."

[8] See I, pp. 199–218.

facetiousness unworthy of detailed study.[1]   But these sketches show Whitman's tendency at the time to substitute humorous satire for his earlier preachments, and they reveal also his powers of shrewd, if unselective, observation.   He is beginning to study life in a more objective way; he is seeing men as types.   When he discovers in himself a typical, though not an "average," man, subjective and objective treatment will blend in one of the most strangely composite books of modern times.

The essays written from Washington, descriptive of the army, the city, the Capitol, and the Congress,[2] are naturally the most mature, picturesque, and lifelike in our collection.   One finds an unusual delight in observing the nation's capital through the eyes of the nation's poet,[3] and one enjoys, as he evidently enjoyed, the contrast between the functions of the legislator and those of what he would have called the *littérateur*.[4]   But in "The Christmas Garland" (1874)[5] we have only hasty patchwork, suggestive in detail but all too evidently the work of a hand which illness has robbed of its cunning.   That Whitman himself recognized this is shown by his determination to select only a few passages for preservation.   The last essay, "Walt Whitman in Camden,"[6] and the curtain speech, "The Old Man Himself,"[7] reveal how little the poet had altered in his fundamental conception of himself as he approached old age and death.   The same self-confident spirit which, forty years before, had announced, anonymously, "Yes; I *would* write a book! And who shall say that it might not be a very pretty book?"[8] here looks back upon a life guided by one imperious ambition and concludes, as it were, "So, you see, I *did* write a book; and who shall say that it isn't a very pretty book?"   There is something of childlike naïveté in such detachment as this in so subjective a poet as Whitman—perhaps it was but a compensatory result of his deep subjectivity.   And yet there is in it just a suggestion of secretiveness where one looks for candour, a sort of harmless but private joke at the reader's expense.   There is in the essay one significant sentence, which throws emphasis upon the need for such a study of Whitman's early newspaper work as

---

[1] See especially I, pp. 211–213, 216–218.

[2] See II, pp. 26–29, 29–36, 37–41, 42–49, 49–53.   [3] See II, pp. 29–36.

[4] See II, pp. 42–53.   [5] See II, pp. 53–58.

[6] See II, pp. 58–62. This appeared over a pseudonym.

[7] See II, pp. 62–63.   [8] *Cf.* p. 37.

the present volumes make possible: "It is perhaps only be-
cause he was brought up as a printer, and worked during his
early years as a newspaper and magazine writer, that he has put
his expression in typographical form, and made a regular book
of it, with lines, leaves, and binding."[1] The distinctly dotage-
like self-importance of "The Old Man Himself" causes the
reader to hesitate between regret that Whitman's illness should
have spared him to write such pitiable prose and, on the other
hand, wonder that he should have had courage to play the
game to its realistic end, he who had determined to express in
writing a complete life, not merely its best and happiest mo-
ments.

c. Narrative

In fiction and other narrative Whitman was rather less
successful than he was in the essay or sketch form. He could
make a rough drawing of a type, but he could not delineate a
character. Moreover, the incubus of a puritan purpose marred
nearly every bit of fiction he ever wrote. This betrayed him
into neglecting his plots and the dramatic qualities of his
story, even though he did sometimes imitate Poe to the
extent of seeking unity of impression. The artist could
never emancipate himself completely from the preacher and
propagandist. This is true of "Bervance,"[2] a tale of paternal
aversion and enforced insanity, as well as of "The Last of the
Sacred Army,"[3] a legend designed to inculcate a sentimental
sort of hero-worship. In "Franklin Evans"[4] the moral not only
kills the story, but it is not even justified by the argument of the
story, wherein a youth who is an ingrate, a drunkard, a criminal,
an unfaithful spouse, and all but a murderer succeeds in shuffling
off the coil of his intemperance through no particular effort of
his own, in time to inherit a fortune he in no wise deserves. The
same insistent didacticism lays its blight upon each part of the
narrative—even upon episodes or imbedded tales which, like
"The Death of Wind-Foot,"[5] had enough interest in themselves
to tempt Whitman to republish them,[6] and which, but for the
young author's riding the Washingtonian crusade too hard,
might have afforded momentary relief from the unrelenting
melodrama of the novelette. Whitman professed to believe

[1] See II, p. 62. [2] See I, pp. 52–60. [3] See I, pp. 72–78.
[4] See II, pp. 103–221. [5] See pp. 112–120. [6] See II, pp. 111, note 2, 181, note 1.

that in this blending of morality with art, preachments with fiction, he was discovering a new field for the novel! Or perhaps he meant that he was the first fictionist to employ the novel in this particular propaganda. In reality what he was doing was to serve a low grade of diluted fiction to a provincial people unaccustomed as yet to take it straight. Whitman himself was too honest a writer, however, not to outgrow such a conception of art,[1] and he lived to write satirically of melodrama like this.[2] Nevertheless his capacious philosophy refused to condemn it entirely, finding a function for it as the strong diet of the uneducated masses.[3] . . . Despite its autobiographical interest, "The Shadow and the Light of a Young Man's Soul"[4] is difficult reading, so full is it of puerile moralizing, while "A Legend of Life and Love,"[5] a plea for the wholehearted acceptance of life notwithstanding its manifold risks, is without a single artistic touch to ameliorate its platitudes. Even stories so deliberately fanciful as "The Angel of Tears"[6] and "Eris; A Spirit Record,"[7] for any intrinsic value, deserved to die in the age of sighs that gave them birth.

In simple narratives without such specific moral intent Whitman makes a closer approach to readable prose. "An Incident on Long Island Forty Years Ago,"[8] "A Fact Romance of Long Island,"[9] "Excerpts from a Traveller's Note Book,"[10] the second "Letter from Paumanok,"[11] and certain passages in the "Brooklyniana" are homely but interesting stories, told with zest and a degree of skill. "A Night at the Terpsichore Ball"[12] is marred by cheap attempts at humour, but it has a genuine, if crude, feeling for definiteness of effect.

It would be inaccurate to describe the "Brooklyniana"

[1] Whitman is reported by Traubel as having said to him, in 1888: "Parke Godwin and another somebody (who was it?) came to see me about writing it. Their offer of cash payment was so tempting (seventy-five dollars down and fifty more when the book had an unexpectedly large sale)—I was so hard up at the time—that I set to work at once ardently on it (with the help of a bottle of port or what not). In three days of constant work I finished the book. Finished the book? Finished myself. It was damned rot— rot of the worst sort—not insincere, perhaps, but rot, nevertheless: it was not the business for me to be up to. I stopped right there: I never cut a chip of that kind of timber again." ("With Walt Whitman in Camden," I, p. 93.) The fact remains, however, that Whitman reprinted the story four years later in the *Eagle*, with editorial endorsement. There is also some evidence that Whitman was the "Brooklynite" who wrote a tragic Indian story dealing with summary punishment, called "The Half-Breed," for the *Eagle*, beginning with June 1, 1846.

[2] See I, pp. 122, 140; II, pp. 19–21.   [3] See II, p. 20.   [4] See I, pp. 229–234.
[5] See I, pp. 78–83.   [6] See I, pp. 83–86.   [7] See I, pp. 86–89.   [8] See I, pp. 149–151.
[9] See I, pp. 146–147.   [10] See I, pp. 181–190.   [11] See pp. 250–254.
[12] See I, pp. 225–229.

as a serial history of Brooklyn. It was full of "personal chronicles and gossip" concerning matters of local interest written in an easy, chatty style; but after all it was news-writing and not history. As has been intimated, Whitman had been collecting his material for years,[1] but his thinking was comprehensive rather than systematic or thorough, he wrote without adequate plan, his information was drawn from various but limited sources, and his style was that of the journalist whose ears ring with the cries for more "copy." Hence he repeats, rambles, pads his narrative with statistics[2] and with quotations which (particularly the very lengthy one from Mary L. Booth's "History of New York")[3] emphasize both the limitations to his knowledge of his field and the weaknesses of his style. The methods of securing "suggestion, atmosphere, reminder, the native and common spirit of all"[4] which he employed more or less successfully in his verse would hardly serve in prose history. This relative impotency in prose doubtless had exerted a strong, even if unconscious, influence in causing him to adopt prose-verse as his main vehicle of expression; for, though he had begun to write verses by his twentieth year, he never looked upon himself as a born poet in the sense that Poe and Longfellow and Lowell regarded themselves, and, as we have seen, he once said the fact that he had expressed his message in print of any sort was due to an accident of training.[5] But the "Brooklyniana" articles are far from worthless, notwithstanding their deficiencies as conventional history. They are largely memoirs, given at first and at second hand, and pretend to be little more. As such they give competent testimony on many points of local history; they breathe the spirit of the city in which Whitman passed his youth, and reveal what that city meant to the maturing man; they supply the earliest account we have of certain events in his life, and do this with a freedom possible only to the anonymous writer; and, in many passages, they possess an antiquarian interest which, like the pleasantness of good wine, will increase with age.

d. Speeches

The present collection contains the text of one of Whitman's speeches and the peroration of another. With such scanty

---

[1] See *infra*, p. lvii, and I, 234, note; II, p. 223, note. [2] See II, pp. 250–251, 291–292.
[3] See II, pp. 301–306.   [4] See II, p. 63.   [5] See II, p. 62.

evidence one cannot draw dogmatic conclusions as to his ability as a public speaker. Much of his early prose is declamatory, however, some of it to such a degree as to create a presumption that it was composed aloud even if it were not at some time intended for a speech.[1] If we may judge from the Art Union address, Whitman did not rely on impromptu inspiration or any native ability to "think on his feet" or even to adapt his thinking to the conditions of delivery. His lectures would have been orations rather, or perhaps public readings of essays.[2]

The speech in the Park[3] indicates the young orator's personal independence, his devotion to the cause of his party, his interest in ideal issues, and his faith in the outcome of those issues. His style is amateurish, his employment of periods and vision sophomoric. His appeal is not to self-interest, to shrewd common sense, but to that American idealism concerning which he was to express his doubts in the Art Union address[4] and of which his "Leaves of Grass" was to be perhaps our best exponent.

In the "Art and Artists" speech he has a more promising theme—too broad, no doubt, but handled so as to produce a certain unity of impression. In this address he shows a command of a variety of moods, passing from satire to anecdotes, from burlesque to eloquent and inspiring appeals to heroic action. Perhaps the most noteworthy fact about the address is its natural combination of prose with a specimen of the free verse on which he was then experimenting and which he had already begun to publish. Some devices, such as alliteration, the parallel construction, and aphorisms, are common to both. But the careful reader will observe that there is a rhythm peculiar to the verse; the difference is not an accident of printing. And he will also observe that even in quoting from Bryant's blank verse Whitman manages to extort a movement of syllables not unlike his own. There is a close kinship between Whitman's prose intended for oral delivery and his free

---

[1] See, e. g., II, pp. 102–103, 172–174, 263–264.

[2] I think there can be no doubt that the text of this Art Union address was furnished the *Advertizer* by Whitman himself. It is also known that when, in the later 1850's, Whitman contemplated a lecture tour, he intended to sell the lectures in pamphlet form for a nominal price.

[3] See I, p. 51.

[4] See I, pp. 241–247.

verse; but, as will presently be shown, the one is not the real origin of the other as Professor Carpenter surmised.[1]

e. Memorial

The tone of Whitman's memorial to the Mayor and the City Council[2] is dignified and public-spirited; but it savours too much of his contempt for the whole race of office-holders[3] and is too overtly a sermon to them in public to have had any effect in constructive legislation.[4] His democratic jealousy of government as a rival to individual liberty in the realm of personal morals (and, *pari passu*, of the general as opposed to the local government) had root, no doubt, in his own independent nature and in his early political training; but it may have been intensified by reading Emerson and by his brief residence in the South. Whitman never allowed his abstract attitude of sympathy for the slave to drive him into a denial of the minority rights of the several states,[5] though he could hardly go all the way with Calhoun.[6] In the special issue involved in the memorial Whitman, in seeking to preserve the Sabbath for man rather than man for the Sabbath, took a position which the history of municipal government in America as increasingly strengthened.

f. Editorials

More important than any or all of the forms of prose composition we have noted in shaping Whitman's prose style, were his newspaper editorials, both because for twenty years they were his most common form of communication with his public and also because they afforded him his best opportunity to address that public in his personal, hortatory, or didactic manner. He conceived of his readers as his personal, if anonymous, friends, in whose physical, intellectual, æsthetic, and moral education

---

[1] In his "Walt Whitman," English Men of Letters Series, 1909, pp. 43–44.

[2] See I, pp. 259–264.

[3] *Cf.* "Complete Prose," pp. 204, 217, 252.

[4] See I, p. 259, note.   [5] See I, pp. 156, 162; II, pp. 10, 57.

[6] See I, p. 162. *Cf.* "Complete Prose," p. 69. In 1846, however, Whitman admired Calhoun very much. On May 14 of that year he said editorially in the *Eagle*: "We like a bold honest *morally* heroic man! We therefore like John C. Calhoun * * * We believe that a higher souled patriot never trod on American soil* * *." (See "The Gathering of the Forces," II, pp. 191–192.)

he was more concerned than he was in their financial support.[1]
Of course the editor of a party organ in those days was re-
quired to furnish a considerable amount of "grave political dis-
quisition," particularly about election time; but Whitman
frankly states that for this more "dignified" part of his editorial
labours he has little relish.[2] Whatever his accomplishments as an
editor, he had definite ideals for the editorial function.[3] The
true editor, he says, must possess a free and untrammeled spirit,
unbiased by fear or convention. His mission is to reform
and to enlighten, to inspire and to guide. He must not set too
high a value upon patience, poise, deliberation. In shaping
his style he must seek polish and elegance less than earnestness,
spontaneity, terseness—the vital fluidity of impromptu oratory.
So Whitman thought in 1846; but some years later, after the
appearance of the second edition of his "Leaves of Grass," and
when he had learned to place a proper emphasis upon poise
as well as upon youthful fervour, upon literary style as well as
upon mere sincerity of purpose, he gratefully acknowledged
the leadership of Bryant in improving the tone of journalistic
prose.[4] At last he had come to perceive the relation between
style and morals, and this perception had helped to harmonize
in him the preacher and the artist. But in 1846 Whitman re-
garded content more than form. He thought that the editor
should have an inexhaustible fund of general information, par-
ticularly concerning his own country.[5] This editorial necessity
must not be underrated as an influence not only in Whitman's
painstaking, if rather unsystematic, self-education, but also
in his unusually wide familiarity with the life of his fellow men.
   Thus Whitman's editorials naturally covered a wide range of
topics; but there were certain subjects that recurred so fre-
quently in his leaders and elsewhere as to indicate a predilec-
tion for them. One of these was education, concerning which
he had three fixed opinions: (a) education should be more
generously supported and more carefully supervised,[6] (b)
moral suasion and inspirational methods should supplant the
time-honoured flogging system,[7] as they had done in his own
school-room and in those of Transcendental teachers like Alcott

[1]See I, pp. 114–117.   [2]See I, p. 115.   [3]See I, pp. 114–117.
[4]See I, p. 115, note.   [5]See I, p. 115.
[6]See II, pp. 13–15; Brooklyn *Daily Eagle*, April 16, 1846; "The Gathering of the
Forces," I, pp. 121–145, *passim.*
[7]See Brooklyn *Daily Eagle*, June 12, September 3, 1846; also "The Gathering of the
Forces," I, pp. 144–145.

and Thoreau, and (c) the curriculum should not be based upon the custom or authority of the past alone, but should be adapted to the largest needs of the future citizen of a democracy.[1] His hatred for sham in education was matched by his disgust at sham everywhere.[2] Another subject of frequent recurrence was America's tendency to ape the Old World in music,[3] art,[4] literature,[5] manners[6], and the drama[7]. Another was the dangers of materialism, whether in the form of African slavery[8] or in the more alluring guise of ordinary money-making.[9] Other favourite themes were: the abolition of capital punishment,[10] the evils of intemperance,[11] sympathy for the unfortunate and the criminal,[12] a living wage for working women,[13] the ennobling influence of the gentler sex,[14] the beauty and educative function of nature,[15] the greatness and the origin and destiny of America,[16] the free spirit of the West,[17] the necessity of the Union,[18] the need of personal cleanliness and of æsthetic surroundings,[19] the opportunities for civic improvement,[20] the absurdities of fashion,[21] the mission of democracy,[22] and the blessing of good books.[23]

g. Reviews and Criticism

The comprehensive duties of an editor, as understood by Whitman, brought him into touch not only with the best plays, operas, concerts, lectures, and sermons that the two cities afforded, but also with the publications of the New York press

[1] See I, pp. 144–146, 220–221.

[2] See I, pp. 126, 193–195, 199–202, 257; II, pp. 68–69, 83, 84, 90, 134.

[3] See I, pp. 104–106.   [4] See I, pp. 185–186, 236–238.   [5] See I, pp. 121–123.

[6] See I, pp. 104–106.   [7] See I, pp. 152–154, 158.

[8] See I, pp. 106–108, 160–162; 171–174; II, pp. 8–10.

[9] See I, pp. 37–39, 123–125, 236–237.   [10] See I, pp. 97–103, 108–110; II, pp. 15–16.

[11] See I, pp. 149, 223; II, pp, 6, 11–12, 103–221.

[12] See I, pp. 60–67, 83–86, 138–139, 154–156, 212–213, 223, 232–234; II, pp. 10–13.

[13] See I, p. 137; Brooklyn *Daily Eagle*, August 19, 1846; also "The Gathering of the Forces," I, pp. 148–151, 157–158.

[14] See I, pp. 65–66, 138–139, 216–217; Brooklyn *Daily Eagle*, March 17, 1846.

[15] See I, pp. 113–114, 164–166, 181–186, 248–249, 255–256.

[16] See I, pp. 153, 156, 158, 171–174; and "The Gathering of the Forces," I, pp. 229–234, 235–239.

[17] See I, pp. 151–152, 185.   [18] See I, p. 156; II, pp. 30–31, 57.

[19] See I, pp. 190, 208–209, 249, 254–255; II, pp. 90, 127; Brooklyn *Daily Eagle*, March 11, 23, 24, April 15, June 30, 1846; "The Gathering of the Forces," II, pp. 201–207.

[20] See I, pp. 141–142, 169, 190, 239–241, 259–264.

[21] See I, pp. 162–163, 208–210, 245–246, 249.

[22] See I, pp. 159–160, 160–162, 166–168.

[23] See I, pp. 125–126, 126–137, 188–189; cf. II, pp. 22, 23, 26–41, 76.

and the periodicals of the country. Probably his most en-
joyable work was to attend the play or opera and to criticize
the production in his paper. Certainly he is seldom more
eloquent or enthusiastic than when so engaged.[1] His critical
standards were his own, formulated in a long and regular at-
tendance at the opera and theatre.[2] Mere technique never sat-
isfied him;[3] the artist must touch his deeper feelings, and when
he did Whitman was the most responsive man in the audience.[4]

If space permitted, a detailed study should be made of
Whitman's book criticisms in his formative years. They cor-
respond more nearly than anything else to the reports, criti-
ques, and examination papers whereby we try to estimate the
intellectual progress of college students. They furnish hints, at
least, as to the influence of various authors on his growing mind,
and are proof enough that his effort to educate himself was
comprehensive, intelligent, and serious. I have brought to-
gether (I, pp. 126-137) Whitman's critical opinions on some
thirty-five American and European authors, and have listed
the titles of a hundred other books reviewed or "noticed"
in the *Eagle*. It is unnecessary here to summarize these
opinions, but a few conclusions may be drawn from them.
There can no longer be any question as to whether Whitman
knew Emerson's writings before 1855.[5] As poets Longfellow[6]
and Bryant[7] apparently had more influence on him, the one
because of his sentiment and the other because of his dignified
poems on nature and freedom. Similarities to "Sartor Resartus"
have been pointed out in the " Leaves of Grass," but now we
know that Carlyle was making a gradual but strong impression
on Whitman's mind as early as 1846.[8] Perhaps Goethe's "Auto-
biography" gave him his most definite hint for the plan of his
own volume.[9] Martin Tupper has been mentioned by one biog-
rapher as a possible "influence" on Whitman; that influence
was, I think, a limited one, but now we know that at least Whit-
man had read Tupper with admiration.[10] Indeed he read all
kinds of books, but seems to have preferred the profounder
sort. To each, whether written on this or on the other side of
the Atlantic, he applies the standard of modern democracy.[11]
One regrets that Whitman attempted so many things that his

---

[1] See especially I, pp. 143–144, 255–259.   [2] See I, p. 257.   [3] *Ibidem.*
[4] See I, pp. 143–144, 256–259.   [5] See I, p. 132; *cf.* p. 243, note.
[6] See I, pp. 133–134.   [7] See I, pp. 128–129.   [8] See I, pp. 129–130.
[9] See I, pp. 132, 139–141.   [10] See I, p. 136.
[11] See I, pp. 121–123, 133–134, 163–164.

book reviews are for the most part hastily written or incomplete; for they reveal the same shrewd judgment and quick intuition that in later life rendered his discussion of literature so pleasantly stimulating.

8. Summary of Journalistic Prose

It happens that all this journalistic work, though it was Whitman's method of earning his daily bread, was also his only apprenticeship in letters. Are there, then, in this early magazine and newspaper writing any hints of the unfolding of his own artistic spirit and of the plan of the "Leaves?" In a general way we can trace the development of that spirit in him as, first, he dreams of writing a great book for the good of mankind, the nature of the book being as hazy as the dream in which it was born; second, as he grows temporarily but genuinely enthusiastic over his discovery of what he mistakenly believes to be a new field for the novel; third, as he strives to elevate the newspaper to a plane on which a great man might put forth his full greatness for the good of his country; and finally, as he stumbles upon the unpredictable poetic rôle for which he was foreordained. And what were the steps leading blindly but inevitably to that rôle? When he urged upon American concert singers the necessity of being natural, unaffected Americans instead of imitating the here exogenous graces of courtly Europeans, he was unconsciously announcing what was to be a fundamental differentium between his own art and that, say, of Spenser and Shakespeare. When he called the attention of American painters to the wealth of *genre* studies afforded by their own country,[1] he was in reality awakening the word-painter in himself, who was one day to write poems worthy to be likened to the canvases of Millet. When he demanded vision, originality, and reformatory fervour of the editor, he was shaping his composite ideal of that poet-prophet who was within a few months to hear the voice of the Future, bidding him lead his people to the promised land of a vital, if somewhat sentimental, democracy. Dreaming of the coming of an artist great enough to create a true, indigenous American drama,[2] he expressed a longing which, like that of Ernest in "The Great Stone Face," was to be satisfied in a doubly unexpected manner. It is worth

[1] *Cf.* I, pp. 185–186.   [2] See I, pp. 152–154.

noting that even in his dreams of what the American stage might be, he emphasized its educative function rather than its æsthetic: "The drama of this country *can* be the mouthpiece of freedom, refinement, liberal philosophy, beautiful love for all our brethren, polished manners and good taste."[1] And finally when, in a book review, he shouted "Eureka" over the discovery, in Goethe's "Autobiography," of a man's life-story full and intimate and true enough to satisfy his exorbitant longings,[2] his own unborn volume stirred with excitement within him. . . . Yet the closest connection between Whitman's early prose and his characteristic verse is to be found in the manuscript note-books, to which I shall presently advert.

On the whole, one is disposed to pronounce Whitman's connection with newspapers and magazines beneficial to the poet. It brought him into contact with hasty and mediocre writers, to be sure, and it forced upon him a habit of writing without revision that could but be detrimental to his prose style. Moreover, a distinctly literary manner was hardly in place in the newspaper columns of his day. But, on the other hand, it developed in him a deep sense of the responsibility of the writer; it brought to him the best books issuing from the press, books which he might not otherwise have had the opportunity or the incentive to read; it gave him the entrée to the art of the metropolis; and it afforded him a vantage point from which he could learn to look at the growing young country as a whole. The breadth of view, the tolerance of opinion, the interest in the eternal present with its consequent sense of progress, and the quick judgment of values which make his "Leaves of Grass" so nearly what it attempted to be—a picture of the average man in the midst of the maelstrom America of the nineteenth century—could hardly have been obtained in any other way. Certainly the colleges of his time, whatever they might have done in "correcting" or in restraining his style, would never have developed in him that ability to derive an Antæan power from his contact with humanity which it was, after all, that made him a great writer. In this respect the American newspaper office may be said to have done for Whitman very much what it did for Mark Twain, if we make allowance for the difference between the humour and the romance of the one and the sentiment and idealism of the other.

[1] See I, p. 152. [2] See I, pp. 139-141.

9. MANUSCRIPT NOTE BOOKS

About 1847, as we have seen, Whitman began the composition which was to grow, through seven or eight years, into the First Edition of the "Leaves of Grass." Now, that edition contains approximately one fourth as much prose as it does verse— oracular, incoherent, picturesque prose so closely akin to the verse it was designed to introduce to the reading public that much of it could later be incorporated in the poem "By Blue Ontario's Shore." This fact supplies a hint as to the origin of the whole book, a hint which is confirmed by a study of the manuscript note books printed in the second volume of the present work.

The first of these begins with a sense of suppressed, half-articulate power, in the language of a novel ecstasy. Some mystical experience, some great if not sudden access of intellectual power, some enlargement and clarifying of vision, some selfless throb of cosmic sympathy, has come to Walt Whitman. At first he can only ejaculate his wonder, and pray for the advent of a perfect man who will be worthy to communicate to the world this new vision of humanity.[1] Then, like the prophet Isaiah, whose great book he is wont to carry in his pocket to Coney Island, he suddenly realizes that a vision is itself a commission; and from this moment he dedicates himself to a life task as audacious as it seems divine.[2] At last he has the courage and feels the mystic authority to assume the rôle that he has, somewhat indefinitely, been calling upon others to assume. The burden of his message, as in his dream of seven years before, is the future good of man, but as yet he can only hint it in imperfect prose, the only language he has learned in the newspaper offices. He announces the tokens of the true American character—health,[3] liberty,[4] independence,[5] haughty pride,[6] self-reliance,[7] prudence,[8] tolerance,[9] equality;[10] he marvels at that miracle of the mystic's imagination by which the soul is enabled to dissolve and to comprehend the solid things of the earth;[11] he is drunk with the limitless dilation of the liberated spirit;[12] he divines the dual but harmonious mystery which others know only as mind and matter, soul and body, and thus

---

[1] See II, p. 68.   [2] See II, p. 69.   [3] See II, pp. 64, 65.   [4] *Ibidem.*
[5] See II, pp. 63, 64.   [6] See II, pp. 63–64.   [7] See II, p. 67.   [8] See II, p. 63.
[9] See p. 64.   [10] See II, pp. 63, 64, 65.   [11] See II, pp. 64–66.   [12] See II, p. 66.

he arrives at Emerson's conception of an evil which is merely privative;[1] he discovers that true nobility has no relation to wealth or rank, but is to be sought even among "drivers and boatmen or men that catch fish or work in the field";[2] he feels his kinship with all flesh.[3]   Stated in unemotional prose, as I have stated them, these ideas seem platitudinous indeed; but the genius of the mystic is that he can make a platitude throb with life, and even in Whitman's prose there is an indefinable promise of the inspiration which was in time to set the seal of genius upon the book here struggling to its birth.   Presently he comes to realize that he must have a new language, capable of manifold suggestion, appropriate for multiform effects, plastic as his own personality.   The poet alone can master such a language,[4] and so, relying for guidance upon the Spirit which has bidden him write, he sets about the stupendous task of creating a new sort of poetry for America.   It is hardly surprising that the form of the new poetry should have borne a striking resemblance to Hebraic verse, particularly when one remembers how familiar Whitman was with the Scriptures.[5] But it is important to observe that his book is, originally, not a song singing itself, but the utterance of mystical inspiration, often first expressed in prose and later rendered into long and rhythmical lines.   First in his mind came the message or suggestion, then the "making it more rhythmical."   This is shown by the fact that Whitman passes almost indifferently from prose to verse, or from verse to prose, without noticeable change of mood.   It is further shown by comparing these note-book specimens with the First Edition of the "Leaves of Grass" and noting the great increase of terseness and rhythm in the latter.   There, as an artist, he has begun to think more of *im*pression; whereas here, as a seer, he is chiefly engrossed in the difficult task of *ex*pression.

It is reassuring to the lay mind to know that all the beauty and the invigorating freshness of the "Leaves of Grass" were thus fully earned by the sweat of the poet's brow, and that the divine fire did not descend upon the altar of a lazy man who had accumulated no goods for the sacrifice.   Here we have the rare privilege of attending what its author would have called the *accouchement* of the greatest single volume America has yet

[1]See II, pp. 65, 68.   [2]See II, p. 69.   [3]See II, pp. 66–69.   [4]See II, p. 65.

[5]See I, p. 127, and also the list of quotations from the Bible given in the Subject Index.

produced. The reader is not often permitted to see a "bible of democracy," or a bible of any sort, in the making.

II. WHITMAN'S VERSE

Our study of Whitman's prose led us to its culmination in his free verse. But though Whitman wrote comparatively little verse previous to 1847, or before 1855 for that matter, his new departure in literary form resulted also from a gradual evolution of his poetry.[1] That when these two lines of development met they should have produced a form of expression that broke down the distinction between prose and poetry as commonly understood, was perhaps inevitable. A rapid review of these youthful compositions in verse will make this evolution clear.

"Our Future Lot"[2] reveals how seriously the nineteen-year-old poet was taking the great mysteries of human life and death. The dignity of the theme lends a kind of sad simplicity to the treatment, finally relieving it of the morbid subjectivity with which it opens. Whitman naturally begins his versifying with a simple ballad stanza (4, 4, 4, 3; *abcb*,) despite its inappropriateness, for he had not yet mastered even the elementary rhyme scheme of the ballad. He allows such crude rhymes as *fear-wear, torn-burn, mystery-to die,* and *majesty-eye.* The cæsura slides about to accommodate the thought, in prophecy, perhaps, that the substance of his verse will ever mean more to Whitman than its form. At this stage he takes full advantage of poetic license and conventional diction.

"Young Grimes,"[3] published the next year, is serious neither in theme nor in treatment; and yet it illustrates how difficult it was for Whitman to be entirely trivial or objective with a pen in his hand. He opens the poem in a spirit of genial satire not unsuited to the popular ballad, but before he concludes he has read a sermon on the rewards of virtue and has (apparently)

---

[1] At one time critics attempted to dispose of Whitman's claims as a poet by charging that he had invented a new form only because he could not compete with others in conventional measures. In reply more friendly critics have sometimes cited the few bits of conventional verse hitherto known to be Whitman's, to prove that he could manipulate rhyme and metre when he chose. The contention of the latter critics is considerably strengthened with the new poems here preserved, but their argument does not seem to me the strongest by which to defend the poetry of the "Leaves of Grass"—if, indeed, defense be necessary at this late day. The fair test of his poetic ability is to inquire, not whether he could write in rhyme, but whether he could make poetry of what he chose to write.

[2] See I, p. 1.   [3] See I, pp. 2–4.

with gentle irony described himself! These stanzas appear in the *Long Island Democrat* amid a number of other mock-heroic ballads, from anonymous contributors, on the fortunes of Father Grimes and his posterity, as if Whitman had fallen a victim to a passing epidemic of doggerel. The stanza is that of the ancient ballad (4, 3, 4, 3; *abcb*),[1] employed somewhat loosely. In one verse the rhyme, being double, produces hypercatalectic lines.[2] The rhyming shows improvement, on the whole, for in a poem nearly twice as long as "Our Future Lot" the number of defective rhymes is scarcely greater: *fourteen-pain, board-yard, son-town, men-pain,* and *prove-love.* The author personifies abstract ideas, as Plenty, Benevolence, Happiness, and Content, and he makes use of a few poetic contractions; but diction and imagery are neither oppressively conventional nor noticeably original. A fact worthy of note, however, is that Whitman at this period contrasts life in the country with life in the city to the disadvantage of the latter; yet within two years he was to go to the city—to live in it and to become its poet. For once in his early verse, he here seeks, by means of unexpected variations, a humorous effect.

"Fame's Vanity,"[3] also written in 1839, reverts to the stanza form of "Our Future Lot," but it evinces a marked increase of imagination and a decided improvement in phrasing. The rhyming is still imperfect, allowing *store-power* and *know-brow,* while a few lines are wanting in regularity of metre and even in rhythm; but the emotional effect of the stanzas is more sustained than in the previous poems. Here the heart of the young man is debating whether his ambition be not a vain and selfish thing in the presence of man's inescapable mortality. The affirmative answer he reaches does not satisfy him for long, for three years later the poem is altered and republished.[4] Abstractions are again personified, such as Glory and Oblivion, and such poetic diction as "viewless air" is utilized. But the concluding stanza is more imaginative than anything he has yet written. It may have been suggested by the conclusion of "Thanatopsis."

In the next preserved poem, "My Departure,"[5] Whitman

---

[1] With this stanza Whitman had early become familiar in Scott's "Border Minstrelsy."
[2] The second and fourth lines of the second stanza.
[3] See I, pp. 4–5.
[4] Under the caption "Ambition"; see I, pp. 19–20.
[5] See I, pp. 5–6.

resumes his meditations on death. Here, however, death appears as a dream rather than a passionate desire, as in "The Love That Is Hereafter."[1] The influence of nature has made the thought of death pleasant, whereas in the first of his poems Whitman had invoked the consolations of religion to make the thought endurable. The stanza form is the tetrameter quatrain, rhyming *abcb*. The rhymes are faulty, as *cloud-blood, come-bloom, have-wave, overhead-shade*, and *sun-alone*; and the metre is at times irregular if not actually pedestrian. On the other hand, due to the influence of nature, which will in the end prove Whitman's poetic salvation, there is an increased unity of tone and a more concrete and objective treatment. In 1843 Whitman published a redaction of the poem, improving it enough to earn the qualified praise of the editor of the *Brother Jonathan*, in which it appeared.[2] That the young poet was inexperienced rather than careless in his early poetizing is indicated not only by his frequent revisions but also by the increasing skill with which he handles simple measures and by the relative success of his attempts to employ more and more complicated forms. In the redaction of "My Departure," the improvement is sometimes due to alterations in diction or phrasing, sometimes to the elimination of redundancy, but especially to the substitution of the third person for the first. There is, however, no improvement in the rhyming.

"The Inca's Daughter,"[3] which follows, is a little ballad of eight regular stanzas. It conforms to the early-ballad type much more closely than anything Whitman has yet written, not only in the management of the stanza, but also in the selection of a theme—the self-destruction of a proud captive maiden —and in the impersonality of treatment. I have been unable to discover where Whitman got the idea for this poem—not, of course, from the "Border Minstrelsy," though Scott's collection probably gave him the method.

A fortnight later Whitman published "The Love That Is Hereafter,"[1] in quintets of four iambic tetrameters closed by an Iambic trimeter, the stanza rhyming *aabbc*. Either he or the compositor forgot to count the verses in the third stanza, which is only a quatrain, but the remaining eight stanzas are regular. The new stanza form, being more difficult, is not always employed without uncouthness, and the rhymes include *man-vain, rest-least, care-bier, then-pain*, and *wove-above*. However,

[1]See I, pp. 9–10.   [2]See I, p. 7.   [3]See I, pp. 8–9.

the poem is carefully constructed so as to accentuate the effect of the prayer uttered in the final stanzas. The poet contrasts the peace and harmony of nature with the vexatious and futile strife, the unsatisfied hope, of mankind; and then, despairing of finding real affection on earth, he prays that this boon may at least be granted in heaven.

After two months he again sang of death as a release from a troubled life. The conclusion to "We All Shall Rest at Last"[1] almost certainly was written with "Thanatopsis" in mind.[2] The stanza, the same as that in "Our Future Lot" and "Fame's Vanity," is here handled well enough to demand no revision at Whitman's hands when he republished a poem about a year later. The rhyme is almost faultless.

Shortly after the publication of the last-mentioned poem, appeared a second little ballad dealing with a tragic story, "The Spanish Lady."[3] Its stanza may be described as a ballad stanza the first line of which is catalectic and feminine and in which anapæsts are freely but ineffectively substituted for the regular iambs. In one instance[4] an iambic tetrameter replaces the regular trimeter composed of one anapæst and two iambs. The poem is far from successful. Whitman never possessed skill in telling a story in verse. Not only is the phrasing prosaic, but the narrative is without motivation, suspense, or climax.

In "The End of All,"[5] published in September, 1840, Whitman turns to a favourite theme of the period, the vanity of human ambitions when compared to the achievements of Creation. But here he attempts a less subjective treatment—a more didactic method, in fact—and a new verse form. The stanza is a sestet composed of five iambic tetrameters and one iambic trimeter, rhyming *abcbdb*. There are two imperfect rhymes (*destiny-eye* and *brow-slow*), but there are no glaring irregularities in the metre. When the poem was republished as

[1] See I, pp. 10–11.

[2] For Whitman's indebtedness to Bryant see also I, p. 115, note. Attention has been called to the similarity between a section of "My Departure," and "Thanatopsis." Perhaps a more striking similarity exists between "The End of All" (I, pp. 13–15) and Bryant's "The Flood of Years," published long afterward. Whitman, like Bryant, frequently poetized about man in the mass, but he learned to do so with a warmth of affection unknown to the older poet's eighteenth-century verse. *Cf.* "With Walt Whitman in Camden," III, p. 515.

[3] See I, pp. 12–13.

[4] The second line in the last stanza.

[5] See I, pp. 13–15.

"The Winding-Up"[1] in the same paper in 1841, a few changes
were made in the diction, and one in the arrangement of the
stanzas, while one stanza was completely rewritten, each
alteration being an improvement.

The tendency to experiment with more intricate verse forms
was carried still further in the following month, when Whitman
published "The Columbian's Song"[2] in four stanzas irregular in
length, rhyme scheme, and construction. Since only two
stanzas have the same number of lines, it is improbable that
Whitman was following a model. Whether the "song" was
ever sung, as was the author's Fourth of July "Ode,"[3] I do not
know; but if sung it could hardly have aroused much patriotic
emotion. Nevertheless, it has its place as an experiment in
versification and among the "glory of America" poems that had
been common enough since the days of Philip Freneau. The
national pride which inspires this prophetic outburst was to
become even more prominent as an element of Whitman's
maturer singing than was the celebration of death.

The next poem to be published, though it had been written a
year or so earlier, was an allegory on "The Punishment of
Pride,"[4] which appeared in December, 1841. The poet still
dreams of the realm of spirits, but now much more poetically.
This imaginative composition belongs in a class with such bits of
poetic prose as "The Angel of Tears"[5] and "Eris,"[6] which
seem to show the influence of Edgar Allan Poe. This allegory
teaches how charity and pity grow from actual knowledge of
human weakness and sorrow, and indicates the abandonment
of the youthful pharisaism of some of the earlier pieces. The
stanza used is a new one for Whitman—seven lines, all iambic
tetrameters except the third and fifth (which are usually iambic
trimeters), rhyming *aabcbdd*. The diction, phrasing, and
versifying are now more mature and modulated, but the un-
accustomed rhyme scheme, taken with the length of the poem,
results in a large number of poor endings: *throne-one, come-
doom, worn-scorn, messenger-fair, heard-scared, high-majesty,
shone-one,* and *charity-eye.* The poet's vocabulary is still very
conventional and limited, and it may have been that the
absence of more than a single poem in which he was rhyme-
perfect indicted a conscious or unconscious reason for his final
creation of a verse form in which rhyme was unnecessary. That

[1]See I, p. 13, note,   [2]See I, pp. 15–16.   [3]See I, pp. 22–23.
[4]See I, pp. 17–19.   [5]See I, pp. 83–86.   [6]See I, pp. 86–89.

in itself, however, was manifestly not Whitman's only, or principal, reason for inventing a new prosody, for he could write correct, smooth blank verse when he chose, as will appear in the next poem that he published.

This was "Ambition,"[1] the redaction of "Fame's Vanity" previously mentioned. The alterations in form and content are noteworthy. The original stanzas are enveloped between a prologue and an epilogue of blank verse. The prologue describes a youth tormented with the desire for fame, in whom, without much difficulty, the reader recognizes the author himself. To him a mystical voice speaks in the language of the original poem, declaring human ambition to be vanity of vanities. This part of the poem displays marked improvement over the original draft. In the epilogue we are informed that the youth, though silenced by the words of the unseen visitor, does not take his rebuke very meekly. So far as we know, his poetic attempts were, however, limited to two publications in the next five years. But in 1847 or soon afterwards he received a very different visit from the Muse.

One of the remaining poems of the conventional sort is "The Play-Ground."[2] This mawkishly sentimental verse gets nowhere, either as a description or as a bit of dreamy moralizing. The form is the simplest that Whitman knew and the diction is particularly conventional.

The last poem written before the beginning of Whitman's experiments in free verse was an ode composed to be sung to the tune of the national hymn on the Fourth of July, 1846.[3] The stanza was perhaps the most exacting that he had attempted, and yet in it his success is noteworthy for an occasional poem. The rhyming is, for once, without fault, and the patriotic sentiment is not only disencumbered of the weakening braggadocio of "The Columbian's Song," but it is particularly well adapted to the time and place.

Then came the irregular, undecided attempts in what has come to be called *vers libre*, preserved in the manuscript notebooks to which reference has already been made in the preceding section of this essay. The slow, eventful growth of the First Edition is nowhere more clearly indicated than in the fact that, though these note books contain many of the very lines to be employed in that edition, the great experiment was not committed to type until after many years of careful revision.

[1] See I, pp. 19–20.   [2] See I, p. 21.   [3] See I, pp. 22–23.

Remembering that these note-book essays were in Whitman's mind during these years, we shall continue to trace the rest of the poems known to have been written before 1855.

At the very beginning of 1848 he wrote, it must have been impromptu, a little poem[1] comparing the weather changes of New Year's day and the shifting fortunes of human life. It would be unjustifiable, perhaps, to seek to discover a subconscious meaning in his prayer to be guarded from "caprices and all foolish ways" recorded only a few weeks before he was to provoke the ire of his employer and so to lose his "comfortable berth" in the *Eagle* office, but the coincidence is at least interesting. In form the poem is neither fish, flesh, nor fowl; for though it opens, apparently, with the intention of being blank verse, the second line is iambic tetrameter, others are hexameters, and the last three rhyme together! Possibly this is what the first drafts of all Whitman's early poems looked like, for we know his habit of carefully revising his verse before publication; but, in part, at least, it must have been due to his then novel ideas of rhythm.[2] Of course, one does not expect in a poem written impromptu in an album the sort of inspiration that gives the note-books their freshness and dynamic power. Accordingly, knowing that Whitman was neither an improvisator nor a master of society verse, one is not surprised to find in the poem verses which regard neither rhythm nor metre, but are simply prose.

That, although Whitman did not at once determine to abandon rhyme and metre, he was nevertheless hampered in his composition of conventional verse by a divided mind, is shown, I think, by the unusual roughness in the metre of "The Mississippi at Midnight"[3] as originally printed in the New Orleans *Crescent* early in March, 1848.[4] This poem betrays a consciousness, not only of mysterious emotional depths within himself, but also of a new mission in life. As has been stated, New Orleans inspired Whitman with no poetry at the time of his first visit, though it gave him hints for numerous passages in his later verse. The caresser of life, the saunterer in bar-

[1] See I, pp. 23–24.

[2] If the poetic parts of the first note-book were written in 1848 or 1849 (see II, p. 63, note) then of course this poem belongs before them in strict chronology.

[3] Not included in this collection.

[4] Another conventional poem published after the date of the note-book specimens is the Dough-Face Song."

rooms and along the levees, the student of humanity is for the time engrossed in the luscious enjoyment of what is to him a new and romantic world, quite foreign to the one in which had been born the mystic and the prophet bent on creating a new national poetry. But, as has been shown in the foregoing essay, Whitman went south more than once, and it is possible that he was on his way thither, in the fall of 1849,[1] when he wrote his next poem, "Isle of La Belle Rivière,"[2] and gave it to his host on Blennerhasset Island. It is interesting to note that this poem, written in what is now called imagist verse, was not a development of, but a step toward, the rhythms of the "Leaves of Grass." It has rhythm, but it is bare in diction and smacks much more of wit than of emotion. The title, it will be observed, makes use of the French which had caught Whitman's fancy while in New Orleans. And the somewhat peculiar images employed, though obviously only figures of speech, may have had some psychological connection with the poet's errand southward if we are entitled to surmise that errand to have had anything to do with his paternity of children by a married woman.[3]

Three poems approximating much more closely than did this imagist verse the style of 1855 were published in the summer of 1850. One of these, "The House of Friends,"[4] contains so much about the South,[5] said almost as a Southerner might have said it, as to strengthen the belief that there had been a southern journey in the spring or fall preceding. It is plain that what differentiates these poems—"Blood-Money,"[6] "The House of Friends," and "Resurgemus"[7]—from the imagist verse just mentioned is the charge of passionate indignation which gives them a freer swing of rhythm, as of eloquence born of deep and sudden feeling. Just what is wanting to make true "Leaves of Grass" verse of these early contributions to Horace Greeley's New York *Tribune* can be discovered by comparing the original text of "Resurgemus" with the version of that poem in the 1855 edition of the "Leaves," which is reproduced in the present volumes.[8] A few "stock poetical touches" remain to be eliminated, but the chief alteration to be made is not in the diction or phrasing, but in the line length. The style in the later ver-

---

[1] See *infra*, p. li, note 5. [2] See I, p. 24, note; also, p. 216, note.

[3] See *infra*, p. lviii, note 15. [4] See I, pp. 25–27. [5] See p. 25, note 2.

[6] See "Complete Prose," p. 372. [7] See I, pp. 27–30. [8] *Ibidem.*

sion is rendered more coherent, and there is an increased parallelism within the line and between the lines. The whole is given a more impressive dignity by doubling the length of most of the lines, which yet can be accommodated on a large octavo page, the distinction between the original verses being preserved by means of a series of points in the middle of each line. In tone the later version is equally impassioned, but more restrained, less defiant. Most important of all, as giving us the working principle which Whitman next evolved, the line is now based on an idea, stated with or without explication, and a free rhythm, rather than upon any predetermined standard of measurement.

To recapitulate: Whitman began versifying with the simplest of forms, the ballad measure, employing it with certain variations and with increasing skill; then he made use of more difficult stanza forms, but limiting himself to trimeter and tetrameter iambic lines; next he wrote a little blank verse, though he did not abandon rhyme at once, but rather increased his mastery of it; then he made private experiments with some of the very material he was to work over, through several years, for the 1855 edition of the "Leaves of Grass," experiments dictated by some new and powerful mystical experience; after that the verse he gave to the world was either hybrid or otherwise irregular; then came hard and objective imagist verse, as though in working out a new vehicle of expressson the mind had come unduly to dominate his usual emotion; next, fired by cowardice and injustice on the part of the leaders of the nation, he published some of his new verse, charged with passion, but it was passion timed for the moment rather than for eternity, and hence was ejaculatory and unrhythmical; and, finally, this was disciplined, poise and sweeping rhythm were added, and a standard of line length was adopted which would fit the bold but delicate burden of his song. Thenceforth there was a new poetry in America.

THE
UNCOLLECTED POETRY AND PROSE
OF
WALT WHITMAN

POEMS
—

OUR FUTURE LOT[1]

This breast which now alternate burns
    With flashing hope, and gloomy fear,
Where beats a heart that knows the hue
    Which aching bosoms wear;

This curious frame of human mold,
    Where craving wants unceasing play—
The troubled heart and wondrous form
    Must both alike decay.

The cold wet earth will close around
    Dull senseless limbs, and ashy face,
But where, O Nature! where will be
    My mind's abiding place?

Will it ev'n live?   For though its light
    Must shine till from the body torn;
Then, when the oil of life is spent,
    Still shall the taper burn?

O, powerless is this struggling brain
    To pierce the mighty mystery;
In dark, uncertain awe it waits,
    The common doom—to die!

.   .   .   .

[1] From the *Long Island Democrat* (Jamaica, L. I.), October 31, 1838, into which it had been copied, in whole or in part, "from the *Long Islander.*"   This latter paper was the first that Whitman edited.   It was a weekly issued at the little town of Huntington near Whitman's birthplace, beginning in June, 1838.   On this sheet Whitman did practically all the work, being editor, reporter, printer, publisher, and news-carrier all in one.   This fact, taken with the obvious Whitman manner of treatment both as to theme and as to style, seems to establish his authorship, although the poem was not signed in the *Democrat.*

Mortal! and can thy swelling soul
   Live with the thought that all its life
Is centered in this earthy cage
   Of care, and tears, and strife?

Not so; that sorrowing heart of thine
   Ere long will find a house of rest;
Thy form, re-purified, shall rise,
   In robes of beauty drest.

The flickering taper's glow shall change
   To bright and starlike majesty,
Radiant with pure and piercing light
   From the Eternal's eye!

———

YOUNG GRIMES[1]

WHEN old Grimes died, he left a son—
   The graft of worthy stock;
In deed and word he shows himself
   A chip of the old block.

In youth, 'tis said, he liked not school—
   Of tasks he was no lover;
He wrote sums in a ciphering book,
   Which had a pasteboard cover.

Young Grimes ne'er went to see the girls
   Before he was fourteen;
Nor smoked, nor swore, for that he knew
   Gave Mrs. Grimes much pain.

He never was extravagant
   In pleasure, dress, or board;
His Sunday suit was of blue cloth,
   At six and eight a yard.

[1] From the *Long Island Democrat*, January 1, 1839.

But still there is, to tell the truth,
   No stinginess in him;
And in July he wears an old
   Straw hat with a broad brim.

No devotee in fashion's train
   Is good old Grimes's son;
He sports no cane—no whiskers wears,
   Nor lounges o'er the town.[1]

He does not spend more than he earns
   In dissipation's round;
But shuns with care those dangerous rooms
   Where vice and sin abound.

It now is eight and twenty years
   Since young Grimes saw the light;
And no house in the land can show
   A fairer, prouder sight.

For there his wife, prudent and chaste,
   His mother's age made sweet,
His children trained in virtue's path,
   The gazer's eye will meet.

Upon a hill, just off the road
   That winds the village side,
His farm house stands, within whose door
   Ne'er entered Hate or Pride.

But Plenty and Benevolence
   And Happiness are there—
And underneath that lowly roof
   Content smiles calm and fair.

[1] The subjectivity which permeates nearly all of Whitman's early verse here appears. perhaps, as a description of himself. (*Cf.* "Habitants of Hotels," *post,* I, pp. 194–195 which, as Mr. W. K. Dart suggests, may belong in the same category.) But such details as are given in this stanza contradict the evidence of his only extant photograph of the period (see frontispiece, Vol. II) which shows both cane and beard, while his avowed fondness for loafing was to be recorded, within the year, by the poet himself. (See *post,* I, pp. 44–46.)

Reader, go view the cheerful scene—
By it how poor must prove
The pomp, and tinsel, and parade,
Which pleasure's followers love.

Leave the wide city's noisy din—
The busy haunts of men—
And here enjoy a tranquil life,
Unvexed by guilt or pain.

———

FAME'S VANITY[1]

O, MANY a panting, noble heart
Cherishes in its deep recess
The hope to win renown o'er earth
From Glory's prized caress.

And some will reach that envied goal,
And have their fame known far and wide;
And some will sink unnoted down
In dark Oblivion's tide.

But I, who many a pleasant scheme
Do sometimes cull from Fancy's store,
With dreams, such as the youthful dream,
Of grandeur, love, and power—

Shall I build up a lofty name,
And seek to have the nations know
What conscious might dwells in the brain
That throbs aneath this brow?

And have thick countless ranks of men
Fix upon *me* their reverent gaze,
And listen to the deafening shouts,
To *me* that thousands raise?

[1] From the *Long Island Democrat*, October 23, 1839.
The poem was later incorporated in "Ambition" (see *post*, I, pp. 19–20) with a number of significant alterations.

Thou foolish soul! the very place
   That pride has made for folly's rest;
What thoughts with vanity all rife,
   Fill up this heaving breast!

Fame, O what happiness is lost
   In hot pursuit of thy false glare!
Thou, whose drunk votaries die to gain
   A puff of viewless air.

So, never let me more repine,
   Though I live on obscure, unknown,
Though after death unsought may be
   My markless resting stone.[1]

For mighty one and lowly wretch,
   Dull, idiot mind, or teeming sense,
Must sleep on the same earthy couch,
   A hundred seasons hence.

MY DEPARTURE[2]

Not in a gorgeous hall of pride,
   Mid tears of grief and friendship's sigh,
Would I, when the last hour has come,
   Shake off this crumbling flesh and die.

---

[1] This early passage has a peculiar interest in view of the fact that the poet saved money for several years previous to his death to build the massive granite tomb bearing the simple legend "Walt Whitman" in which, with other members of his family, his body now rests.

Cf. also *post*, I, pp. 230-231; II, pp. 125, 152.

[2] From the *Long Island Democrat*, November 27, 1839.

The poem was reprinted in the *Brother Jonathan* (New York), Vol. IV, No. 10, March 11, 1843. As the later version shows many alterations and improvements, it is given on p. 7, *post*. The editor of the *Brother Jonathan* introduced the poem with the remark, "The following wants but a half-hour's polish to make of it an effusion of very uncommon beauty.—*Ed.*"

In this latter version the poem was reprinted again, after Whitman's death, in the *Conservator*, Vol. XII, p. 189, January, 1905.

My bed I would not care to have
  With rich and costly stuffs hung round;
Nor watched with an officious zeal,
  To keep away each jarring sound.

Amid the thunder crash of war,
  Where hovers Death's ensanguined cloud,
And bright swords flash, and banners fly,
  Above the sickening sight of blood:

Not there—not there, would I lay down
  To sleep with all the firm and brave;
For death in such a scene of strife,
  Is not the death that I do crave.

But when the time for my last look
  Upon this glorious earth should come,
I'd wish the season warm and mild,
  The sun to shine, and flowers bloom.

Just ere the closing of the day,
  My dying couch I then would have
Borne out in the refreshing air,
  Where sweet shrubs grow and proud trees wave.

The still repose would calm my mind,
  And lofty branches overhead,
Would throw around this grassy bank,
  A cooling and a lovely shade.

At distance through the opening trees,
  A bay by misty vapours curled,
I'd gaze upon, and think the haven
  For which to leave this fleeting world.

To the wide winds I'd yield my soul,
  And die there in that pleasant place,
Looking on water, sun, and hill,
  As on their Maker's very face.

I'd want no human being near;
  But at the setting of the sun,
I'd bid adieu to earth, and step
  Down to the Unknown World—alone.

THE DEATH OF THE NATURE LOVER

Not in a gorgeous hall of pride
  Where tears fall thick, and loved ones sigh,
Wisht he, when the dark hour approached
  To drop his veil of flesh, and die.

Amid the thundercrash of strife,
  Where hovers War's ensanguined cloud,
And bright swords flash and banners fly
  Above the wounds, and groans, and blood.

Not there—not there! Death's look he'd cast
  Around a furious tiger's den,
Rather than in the monstrous sight
  Of the red butcheries of men.

Days speed: the time for that last look
  Upon this glorious earth has come:
The Power he serves so well vouchsafes
  The sun to shine, the flowers to bloom.

Just ere the closing of the day,
  His fainting limbs he needs have
Borne out into the fresh free air,
  Where sweet shrubs grow, and proud trees wave.

At distance, o'er the pleasant fields,
  A bay of misty vapors curled,
He gazes on, and thinks the haven
  For which to leave a grosser world.

He sorrows not, but smiles content,
  Dying there in that fragrant place,
Gazing on blossom, field and bay,
  As on their Maker's very face.

The cloud-arch bending overhead
  There, at the setting of the sun
He bids adieu to earth, and steps
  Down to the World Unknown.

THE INCA'S DAUGHTER[1]

BEFORE the dark-brow'd sons of Spain,
   A captive Indian maiden stood;
Imprison'd where the moon before
   Her race as princes trod.

The rack had riven her frame that day—
   But not a sigh or murmur broke
Forth from her breast; calmly she stood,
   And sternly thus she spoke:—

"The glory of Peru is gone;
   Her proudest warriors in the fight—
Her armies, and her Inca's power
   Bend to the Spaniard's might.

"And I—a Daughter of the Sun—
   Shall I ingloriously still live?
Shall a Peruvian monarch's child
   Become the white lord's slave?

"No: I'd not meet my father's frown
   In the free spirit's place of rest,
Nor seem a stranger midst the bands
   Whom Manitou has blest."

Her snake-like eye, her cheek of fire,
   Glowed with intenser, deeper hue;
She smiled in scorn, and from her robe
   A poisoned arrow drew.

"Now, paleface see! The Indian girl
   Can teach thee how to bravely die:
Hail! spirits of my kindred slain,
   A sister ghost is nigh!"

[1]From the *Long Island Democrat*, May 5, 1840.

Her hand was clenched and lifted high—
  Each breath, and pulse, and limb was still'd;
An instant more the arrow fell:
  Thus died the Inca's child.

———————

THE LOVE THAT IS HEREAFTER[1]

O, BEAUTEOUS is the earth! and fair
The splendors of Creation are:
Nature's green robe, the shining sky,
The winds that through the tree-tops sigh,
        All speak a bounteous God.

The noble trees, the sweet young flowers,
The birds that sing in forest bowers,
The rivers grand that murmuring roll,
And all which joys or calms the soul
        Are made by gracious might.

The flocks and droves happy and free,
The dwellers of the boundless sea,
Each living thing on air or land,
        Is formed for joy and peace.

But man—weak, proud, and erring man,
Of truth ashamed, of folly vain—
Seems singled out to know no rest
And of all things that move, feels least
        The sweets of happiness.

Yet he it is whose little life
Is past in useless, vexing strife.
And all the glorious earth to him
Is rendered dull, and poor, and dim,
        From hope unsatisfied.

He faints with grief—he toils through care—
And from the cradle to the bier
He wearily plods on—till Death
Cuts short his transient, panting breath,
        And sends him to his sleep.

[1] From the *Long Island Democrat*, May 19, 1840.

O, mighty powers of Destiny!
When from this coil of flesh I'm free—
When through my second life I rove,
Let me but find *one* heart to love,
          As I would wish to love:

Let me but meet a single breast,
Where this tired soul its hope may rest,
In never-dying faith: ah, then,
That would be bliss all free from pain,
          And sickness of the heart.

For vainly through this world below
We seek affection.   Nought but wo
Is with our earthly journey wove;
And so the heart must look above,
          Or die in dull despair.

———

WE ALL SHALL REST AT LAST[1]

On EARTH are many sights of woe,
     And many sounds of agony,
And many a sorrow-withered cheek,
     And many a pain-dulled eye.

The wretched weep, the poor complain,
     And luckless love pines on unknown,
And faintly from the midnight couch
     Sounds out the sick child's moan.

Each has his care: old age fears death;
     The young man's ills are pride, desire,
And heart-sickness, and in his breast
     The heat of passion's fire.

[1] From the *Long Island Democrat*, July 14, 1840.   This poem was republished under the
title "Each Has His Grief" and over the initials "W. W." in the *New World* (New York),
Vol. III, p. 1, November 20, 1841.   The only alterations are in the punctuation and
capitalization, which are uniformly improved, in the substitution of *grief* for *care* in
the first line of the fourth stanza, and in the insertion, after the third stanza, of the
following lines:
          And he who runs the race of fame,
               Oft feels within a feverish dread,
          Lest others snatch the laurel crown
               He bears upon his head.

All, all know grief; and at the close,
　All lie earth's spreading arms within,
The pure, the black-souled, proud and low,
　Virtue, despair, and sin.

O, foolish, then, with pain to shrink
　From the sure doom we each must meet.
Is earth so fair or heaven so dark?
　Or life so passing sweet?

No: dread ye not the fearful hour;
　The coffin, and the pall's dark gloom;
For there's a calm to throbbing hearts,
　And rest, down in the tomb.

Then our long journey will be o'er,
　And throwing off this load of woes,
The pallid brow, the feebled limbs,
　Will sink in soft repose.

Not only this; for wise men say
　That when we leave our land of care,
We float to a mysterious shore,
　Peaceful, and pure, and fair.

So, welcome, death; whene'er the time
　That the dread summons must be met,
I'll yield without one pang of awe,
　Or sigh, or vain regret;

But like unto a wearied child,
　That over field and wood all day
Has ranged and struggled, and at last,
　Worn out with toil and play—

Goes up at evening to his home,
　And throws him, sleepy, tired, and sore,
Upon his bed, and rests him there,
　His pain and trouble o'er.

THE SPANISH LADY[1]

On a low couch reclining,
  When slowly waned the day,
Wrapt in gentle slumber,
  A Spanish maiden lay.

O beauteous was that lady;
  And the splendor of the place
Matched well her form so graceful,
  And her sweet, angelic face.

But what doth she lonely,
  Who ought in courts to reign?
For the form that there lies sleeping
  ·Owns the proudest name in Spain.

Tis the lovely Lady Inez,
  De Castro's daughter fair,
Who in the castle chamber,
  Slumbers so sweetly there.

O, better had she laid her
  Mid the couches of the dead;
O, better had she slumbered
  Where the poisonous snake lay hid.

For worse than deadly serpent,
  Or mouldering skeleton,
Are the fierce bloody hands of men,
  By hate and fear urged on.

O Lady Inez, pleasant
  Be the thoughts that now have birth
In thy visions; they are last of all
  That thou shalt dream on earth.

[1] From the *Long Island Democrat*, August 4, 1840.
   This legend-incrusted story of fourteenth-century Spain was the inspiration for much drama, fiction, and poetry in Spanish, French, Italian, and English. The narrative, of which Whitman makes use of only the climax, can be read in concise form in Mrs. Alphra Behn's "Agnes de Castro," pp. 209–256, of Vol. 5 of the Summers edition of her works, London and Stratford, 1915.

Now noiseless on its hinges
  Opens the chamber door,
And one whose trade is blood and crime
  Steals slow across the floor.

High gleams the assassin's dagger;
  And by the road that it has riven,
The soul of that fair lady
  Has passed from earth to heaven.

————

THE END OF ALL[1]

BEHOLD around us pomp and pride;
  The rich, the lofty, and the gay,
Glitter before our dazzled eyes,
   Live out their brief but brilliant day;
Then, when the hour for fame is o'er,
  Unheeded pass away.

[1] From the *Long Island Democrat*, September 22, 1840.
This poem was worked over and republished under the rather inelegant title "The Winding-Up" by "W. Whitman" in the same paper, June 22, 1841. In the later version stanzas three and four are reversed, while for the sixth stanza of the earlier form the later poem substitutes the following:

      Children of folly, here behold
        How soon the fame of man is gone:
      Time levels all. Trophies and names
        Inscription that the proud have drawn
      Surpassing strength—pillars and thrones
      Sink as the waves roll on.

The redaction has also the following minor changes:
  Ll. 3, 21, 39—dashes substituted for commas.
  L 19—hyphen omitted.
  L. 25—comma omitted.
  L. 26—colon substituted for comma.
  L. 38—semicolon substituted for interrogation point.
  L. 39—*High though you stand—tho' on your breast.*
  L. 40—*Pride* substituted for *rank.*
  L. 37—*Nor think* substituted for *Think not.*
  Ll. 44, 46—dashes substituted for commas.
  L. 45—*world* substituted for *worlds.*
  L. 47—*this strife* substituted for the *silly strife.*
  L. 48—*Fame* substituted for *fame.*

The warrior builds a mighty name,
   The object of his hopes and fears,
That future times may see it where
   Her tower aspiring glory rears.
Desist, O fool!   Think what thou'lt[1] be
     In a few fleeting years.

The statesman's sleepless plodding brain
   Schemes out a nation's destiny;
His is the voice that awes the crowd,
   And his the bold, commanding eye:[2]
But transient is his high renown;
     He, like the rest, must die.

Beside his ponderous, age-worn book,
   A student shades his weary brow;
He walks philosophy's dark path,
   A journey difficult and slow:
But vain is all that teeming mind,
     He, too, to earth must go.

And beauty, sweet, and all the fair
   That sail on fortune's sunniest wave,
The poor, with him of countless gold,
   Owner of all that mortals crave,
Alike are fated soon to lie
     Down in the silent grave.

Why, then, O, insects of an hour![3]
   Why, then, with struggling toil, contend
For honors you so soon must yield,
   When Death shall his stern summons send?
For honor, glory, fortune, wit,
     This is, to all, the end.

---

[1] The original has *thou'l't.*

[2] Possibly this was suggested by the fact that Webster was to deliver an address at Jamaica two days after the appearance of the poem.

[3] *Cf. post,* I, p. 47.

Think not, when you attain your wish,
 Content will banish grief and care!
High though you stand, though round you thrown
 The robes that rank and splendor wear,
A secret poison in the heart
  Will stick and rankle there.

In night go view the solemn stars,[1]
 Ever in majesty the same;
Creation's worlds: how poor must seem
 The mightiest honors earth can name;
And, most of all, this silly strife
  After the bubble, fame!

———

THE COLUMBIAN'S SONG[2]

WHAT a fair and happy place
 Is the one where Freedom lives,
And the knowledge that our arm is strong,
 A haughty bearing gives!
For each sun that gilds the east,
When at dawn it first doth rise,
  Sets at night,
  Red and bright,
On a people where the prize
Which millions in the battle fight
Have sought with hope forlorn,
 Grows brighter every hour,
 In strength, and grace, and power,
 And the sun this land doth leave
 Mightier at filmy eve,
Than when it first arose, in the morn.

Beat the sounding note of joy!
 Let it echo o'er the hills,
Till shore and forest hear the pride,
 That a bondless bosom fills.

[1] *Cf. post*, I, p. 186.

[2] From the *Long Island Democrat*, October 27, 1840.

And on the plain where patriot sires
  Rest underneath the sod,
Where the stern resolve for liberty
  Was writ in gushing blood,
    Freemen go,
      With upright brow,
And render thanks to God.

O, my soul is drunk with joy,
  And my inmost heart is glad,
To think my country's star will not
  Through endless ages fade,
That on its upward glorious course
  Our red-eyed eagle leaps,
While with the ever moving winds,
  Our dawn-striped banner sweeps:
That here at length is found
  A wide extending shore,
Where Freedom's starry gleam,
Shines with unvarying beam;
  Not as it did of yore,
With flickering flash, when CÆSAR fell,
Or haughty GESLER heard his knell,
  Or STUART rolled in gore.

Nor let our foes presume
  That this heart-prized union band,
Will e'er be severed by the stroke
  Of a fraternal hand.
Though parties sometimes rage,
  And Faction rears its form,
Its jealous eye, its scheming brain,
  To revel in the storm:
Yet should a danger threaten,
  Or enemy draw nigh,
Then scattered to the winds of heaven,
  All civil strife would fly;
And north and south, and east and west,
  Would rally at the cry—
"Brethren, arise! to battle come,
For Truth, for Freedom, and for Home,
  And for our Fathers' Memory!"

THE PUNISHMENT OF PRIDE[1]

ONCE on his star-gemmed, dazzling throne,
Sat an all bright and lofty One,
                 Unto whom God had given
To be the mightiest Angel-Lord
                 Within the range of Heaven;
With power of knowing things to come,
To judge o'er man, and speak his doom.

O, he was pure! the fleecy snow,
Falling through air to earth below,
                 Was not more undefiled:
Sinless he was as the wreathed smile
                 On lip of sleeping child.
Haply, more like the snow was he,
Freezing—with all its purity.

Upon his forehead beamed a star,
Bright as the lamps of evening are;
                 And his pale robe was worn
About him with a look of pride,
                 A high, majestic scorn,
Which showed he felt his glorious might,
His favor with the Lord of Light.

Years, thus he swayed the things of earth—
O'er human crime and human worth—
                 Haughty, and high, and stern;
Nor ever, at sweet Mercy's call,
                 His white neck would turn;
But listening not to frailty's plea,
Launched forth each just yet stern decree.

---

[1] From the *New World* (New York), III, p. 394, December 18, 1841. Although "For the *New World*" was printed above this poem, it is certain that it was written, if not printed, as early as Whitman's school-teaching days, for one of his pupils refers to it, under the title of "The Fallen Angel," as one of the poems that Whitman gave his students to recite. See the interview with Charles A. Roe in the "Walt Whitman Fellowship Papers," No. 14, where Mr. Roe gives proof of the early composition by quoting from the poem.

Perhaps the poem was suggested by the following quotation from "Sir W. Raleigh" which immediately follows it upon the printed page: "Pity.—He that hath pity on another man's sorrow shall be free from it himself; but he that delighteth in, and scorneth the misery of another, shall one time or other fall into it himself."

These verses were reprinted in the *Conservator*, February, 1902, XII, p. 189.

At last, our Father who above
Sits enthroned with Might, and Truth, and Love,
      And knows our weakness blind,
Beheld him—proud, and pitying not
      The errors of mankind;
And doomed him, for a punishment,
To be forth from his birth-place sent.

So down this angel from on high
Came from his sphere, to live and die
      As mortal men have done;
That he might know the tempting snares
      Which lure each human son;
And dwell as all on earth have dwelt,
And feel the grief we all have felt.

Then he knew Guilt, while round him weaved
Their spells, pale Sickness, Love deceived,
      And Fear, and Hate, and Wrath;
And all the blighting ills of Fate
      Were cast athwart his path;
He stood upon the grave's dread brink,
And felt his soul with terror sink.

He learned why men to sin gave way,
And how we live our passing day
      In indolence and crime;
But yet his eye with awe looked on,
      To see in all his prime
That godlike thing, the human mind,
A gem in black decay enshrined.

Long years in pennance thus he spent,
Until the Mighty Parent sent
      His loveliest messenger—
Who came with step so noiselessly,
      And features passing fair;
Death was his name; the angel heard
The call, and swift to heaven he soared.

There in his former glory placed,
The star again his forehead graced;

But never more that brow
Was lifted up in scorn of sin;
        His wings were folded now—
But not in pride: his port, though high,
No more spoke conscious majesty.

And O, what double light now shone
About that pure and heavenly one:
        For in the clouds which made
The veil around his seat of power,
        In silvery robes arrayed,
Hovered the seraph Charity,
And Pity with her melting eye.

———

AMBITION[1]

ONE day an obscure youth, a wanderer,
Known but to few, lay musing with himself
About the chances of his future life.
In that youth's heart, there dwelt the coal Ambition,
Burning and glowing; and he asked himself,
"Shall I, in time to come, be great and famed?"
Now soon an answer wild and mystical
Seemed to sound forth from out the depths of air;
And to the gazer's eye appeared a shape
Like one as of a cloud—and thus it spoke:

        "O, many a panting, noble heart
            Cherishes in its deep recess
        The hope to win renown o'er earth
            From Glory's prized caress.

        "And some will win that envied goal,
            And have their deeds known far and wide;
        And some—by far the most—will sink
            Down in oblivion's tide.

[1] From the *Brother Jonathan* (New York), Vol. I, No. 5, January 29, 1842. This is an elaboration of "Fame's Vanity" (see *infra*, pp. 4–5). All the changes have been improvements, while the opening and closing lines constitute Whitman's first, and almost only, blank verse.

Cf. post, I, pp. 230; II, pp. 125, 152.

"But *thou*, who visions bright dost cull
    From the imagination's store,
With dreams, such as the youthful dream
    Of grandeur, love, and power,

"Fanciest that thou shalt build a name
    And come to have the nations know
What conscious might dwells in the brain
    That throbs beneath that brow?

"And see thick countless ranks of men
    Fix upon *thee* their reverent gaze—
And listen to the plaudits loud
    To *thee* that thousands raise?

"Weak, childish soul! the very place
    That pride has made for folly's rest;
What thoughts, with vanity all rife,
    Fill up thy heaving breast!

"At night, go view the solemn stars
    Those wheeling worlds through time the same—
How puny seem the widest power,
    The proudest mortal name!

"Think too, that all, lowly and rich,
    Dull idiot mind and teeming sense,
Alike must sleep the endless sleep,
    A hundred seasons hence.

"So, frail one, never more repine,
    Though thou livest on obscure, unknown;
Though after death unsought may be
    Thy markless resting stone."

And as these accents dropped in the youth's ears,
He felt him sick at heart; for many a month
His fancy had amused and charmed itself
With lofty aspirations, visions fair
Of what he *might be*. And it pierced him sore
To have his airy castles thus dashed down.

THE PLAY-GROUND[1]

WHEN painfully athwart my brain
    Dark thoughts come crowding on,
And, sick of worldly hollowness,
    My heart feels sad and lone—

Then out upon the green I walk
    Just ere the close of day,
And swift I ween the sight I view
    Clears all my gloom away.

For there I see young children—
    The cheeriest things on earth—
I see them play—I hear their tones
    Of loud and reckless mirth.

And many a clear and flute-like laugh
    Comes ringing through the air;
And many a roguish, flashing eye,
    And rich red cheek, are there.

O, lovely, happy children!
    I am with you in my soul;
I shout—I strike the ball with you—
    With you I race and roll.—

Methinks white-winged angels,
    Floating unseen the while,
Hover around this village green,
    And pleasantly they smile.

O, angels! guard these children!
    Keep grief and guilt away:
From earthly harm—from evil thoughts
    O, shield them night and day!

[1]Printed as an "original" poem in the Brooklyn *Daily Eagle*, June 1, 1846 (during Whitman's editorship of the paper), and signed "W."

ODE[1]

To be sung on Fort Greene; 4th of July, 1846
Tune " Star Spangled Banner"

I.

O, God of Columbia!   O, Shield of the Free!
    More grateful to you than the fames of old story,
Must the blood-bedewed soil, the red battle-ground, be
    Where our fore-fathers championed America's glory!
Then how priceless the worth of the sanctified earth[2]
We are standing on now.   Lo! the slopes of its girth
    Where the martyrs were buried: Nor prayers, tears, or stones,
    Marked their crumbled-in coffins, their white holy bones!

2.

Say! sons of Long-Island! in legend or song,
    Keep ye aught of its record, that day dark and cheerless—
That cruel of days—when, hope weak, the foe strong,
    Was seen the Serene One—still faithful, still fearless,
Defending the worth of the sanctified earth
We are standing on now, etc.

3.

Oh, yes! be the answer.   In memory still
    We have placed in our hearts, and embalmed there forever!
The battle, the prison-ship, martyrs, and hill,
    —O, may *it* be preserved till those hearts death shall sever!
For how priceless the worth, &c.

[1]From the Brooklyn *Daily Eagle*, July 2, 1846. This song was reprinted in the *Daily Eagle* on June 15, 1900, and in the *Eagle's* "Walt Whitman Centenary Number," May 31, 1919; it was also used as a motto in Peter Ross's "A History of Long Island" (Chicago and New York, 1902), where it is given the title "Sons of Long Island," and is credited to "Walt Whitman."   The poem was likewise reprinted in the New York *Times Magazine*, September 16, 1916, and in "The Gathering of the Forces," I, pp. 75–76.
    The song was duly sung in the patriotic demonstration at Fort Greene on the Fourth of July. (See also *post*, II, p. 255, note.) Whitman's interest in the prison-ship martyrs and in their burial-ground appears frequently in his writings, both prose and verse. *Cf.* "Brooklyniana," Chapter 5, *post*, II, pp. 236-245, 266-267; "The Centenarian's Story" and "The Wallabout Martyrs" (in "Leaves of Grass," II, 58, and II, 296, respectively).

[2]The *Eagle* text has a comma after *earth*.

4.

And shall not the years, as they sweep o'er and o'er,
  Shall they not, even *here*, bring the children of ages—
To exult as their fathers exulted before,
  In the freedom achieved by our ancestral sages?
And the prayer rise to heaven, with pure gratitude given
And the sky by the thunder of cannon be riven?
  Yea! Yea! let the echo responsively roll
  The echo that starts from the patriot's soul!

———

NEW YEAR'S DAY, 1848[1]

A MORNING fair: A noontide dubious:
Then gathering clouds obscure the Sun:
Then rain in torrents falls, subsiding soon
Into a gentle dropping. By eve the sun ·
Sinks into a cloudless west; and a mild breeze
With pleasant motion stirs the atmosphere.
Next in the blue vault above do moon and stars
Vie in bright emulation to destroy the gloom of night.

Such was our New Year's Day, and eventide!
Was it not an index of each passing Year,
Within whose seasons circumstance and change
Ever with Hope and Happiness war?
One now superior: anon the other:
And as succeeds pleasure or pain or joy or sorrow,
Clouding the firmament of each heart,
Raindrops of melancholy dim the eyes,
To shortly dry, hiding the Past and Present
'Neath bright starry thoughts—
Suggestive of a Future aye serene.

[1] From the *Home Journal* (N. Y.), March 30, 1892, where it is preceded by the following explanation: "The following verses were written by Walt Whitman in 1848, in the album of a lady, from which a friend of the *Home Journal* copied them. They do not appear in any of the poet's published collections, but are interesting as a specimen of his early essays in verse."
  The poem was prophetic, so far as Whitman was concerned, for within the month he lost his position as editor of the Brooklyn *Eagle*, but immediately found an opening in New Orleans, whither he took his famous journey in February.

Day of a coming year promising change,
Yet full of promises, we need but watch
And pray for guardianship to come
Over caprices and all foolish ways!
So shall bright sunshine in advancing days
And starry invitations lead to Heavenly praise.

———

ISLE OF LA BELLE RIVIÈRE[1]

BRIDE of the swart Ohio;
Nude, yet fair to look upon,
Clothed only with the leaf,
As was innocent Eve of Eden.
The son of grim old Alleghany,
And white-breasted Monongahela
Is wedded to thee, and it is well.

---

[1] From the Cincinnati *Post*, April 30, 1892. The poem is explained in the *Post* as follows:

"Parkersburg, W. Va.—April 30.—(Special)—It is well known that the late Walt Whitman made a pilgrimage down the Ohio Valley in the year 1849; that he stopped on Blennerhassett Island for a brief season (a spot almost world-famous in song, story and history as the home of the exiled Blennerhassett, and as the scene of Aaron Burr's machinations for the destruction of this Republic); that he drank from the historic old well of Blennerhassett, and that he retained pleasant recollections of his pilgrimage long afterward.

" But it is not so well-known, in fact, it is scarcely known at all, that he composed a characteristic poem while on the visit to the old island which appears in the *Post* for the first time. The original draft of the poem was left at the home of Whitman's entertainer, old Farmer Johnson, who then lived on the island. The poet took a copy, and the *Post* representative has a copy of the original, so that these three are the only known copies of the poem in existence, if indeed the copy which Whitman took exists anywhere.

"The original draft of the poem has lain unnoticed all these years between the leaves of an old Bible. It is written in the irregular, scrawling hand of the much-abused poet on a sheet of old-fashioned foolscap paper. It is just such a piece of venerable chirography as would set a Browning student clean daft and throw a Concord blue-stocking into a fit of hysterics.

"The death of Whitman recalled the fact of his visit to the island, and the present proprietor of Blennerhassett, Mr. Amos Gordon, having heard something about Whitman and his poem on the island, began a search for it, and finally found it. As an old friend, the *Post* representative was the only person permitted to copy it, and here it is."

But Whitman's famous pilgrimage was made in 1848, not 1849. If therefore the date ("aged 30") be not a mere reckoning by some misinformed person, but Whitman's own, it is likely that this poem gives us a hint as to the date of one of Whitman's little-known visits to the South. (*Cf. post*, II, p. 59.) He would not have made a mistake of more than a year in his own age at the time. The imagery of the poem suggests the autumn, and in September, 1849, Whitman gave up the *Freeman*, which he had been editing for about a year, and so was free to travel. The conclusion that this poem was actually written when Whitman was thirty (1849–50) is strengthened by the fact that no mention is made of the Island in the account of his first journey down the Ohio. (See "Excerpts of a Traveller's Note Book," *post*, II, pp. 181-190.)

His tawny thighs cover thee
In the vernal time of spring,
And lo! in the autumn is the fruitage.
Virgin of Nature, the holy spirit of the waters enshrouds thee
And thou art pregnant with the fruits
Of the field and the vine.
But like the Sabine maid of old,
The lust of man hath ravished thee
And compelled thee to pay tribute to the
Carnal wants of earth.
Truth and romance make up thy
Strange, eventful, history,
From the cycle of the red man,
Who bowed at thy shrine and worshipped thee,
To the dark days of that traitor[1]
Who linked thine innocent name to infamy.
Farewell, Queen of the waters,
I have slept upon thy breast in the innocence of a babe,
But now I leave thee
To the embraces of thine acknowledged lord.

At Blennerhassett—Aged 30.

———

THE HOUSE OF FRIENDS[2]

"And one shall say unto him, What are these wounds in thy
hands? Then he shall answer, Those with which I was wounded
in the house of my friends."—Zechariah, xiii. 6.

If thou art balked, O Freedom,
The victory is not to thy manlier foes;
From the house of friends comes the death stab.

Vaunters of the Free,

[1] Aaron Burr.

[2] From the New York *Tribune*, June 14, 1850.
Whitman preserved this poem in the "Collect" under the title "Wounded in the House
of Friends." But since about one third of the original version was rejected in the re-
vision, it is deemed useful to include the complete original poem here.
The Brooklyn *Daily Advertizer*, the Whig daily with which Whitman had an anony-
mous connection during the summer of 1850 (see *post*, I, p. 234, note) in quoting the third
stanza of this poem, in order to confute Democrats generally, gives the composition a
local and a personal interpretation:
"When our friends the locofocos fall out, they occasionally amuse themselves by

Why do you strain your lungs off southward?
Why be going to Alabama?
Sweep first before your own door;
Stop this squalling and this scorn
Over the mote there in the distance;
Look well to your own eye, Massachusetts—
Yours, New-York and Pennsylvania;
—I would say yours too, Michigan,
But all the salve, all the surgery
Of the great wide world were powerless there.

Virginia, mother of greatness,
Blush not for being also the mother of slaves.
You might have borne deeper slaves—
Doughfaces, Crawlers, Lice of Humanity—
Terrific screamers of Freedom,
Who roar and bawl, and get hot i' the face,
But, were they not incapable of august crime,
Would quelch the hopes of ages for a drink—
Muck-worms, creeping flat to the ground,
A dollar dearer to them than Christ's blessing;
All loves, all hopes, less than the thought of gain,
In life walking in that as in a shroud:
Men whom the throes of heroes,
Great deeds at which the gods might stand appalled
The shriek of a drowned world, the appeal of women,

drawing portraits of each other. The schism of the Hunkers and Barnburners has been especially prolific of these interesting specimens of descriptive literature. The fun of it is, that a great deal of what each side says about the other is true.

"Here, now, is a specimen of the way one of the young democracy, Master Walter Whitman, lays it on to the members of 'the party' whom he has had the pleasure of knowing:—Master Walter has evidently a very poor opinion of his old cronies; but who can wonder at that, after he was in the Brooklyn *Eagle* so long, and saw the operations of the Brooklyn 'democracy'? See now how he talks to 'em; we extract from a queer little poem in one of the New York papers. [Here followed the third stanza above.]

"Well, upon the whole, and considering the opportunities Master Walter has 'enjoyed' for taking a full and fair survey of the cautious old leader of 'the party' it is every way likely that he has hit the nail very near the head. But then, Master W., it is very naughty of you to expose the brethren—very naughty." (June 22, 1850.)

Whitman and Henry A. Lees, the editor of the *Advertiser*, had often locked horns and even indulged in personal remarks in their respective papers, but Lees never lost an opportunity to play Whitman off against the conservative Democrats, and professed a liking for the man. He may have known the author's own reasons for the composition of this poem. Perhaps Whitman had in mind the turn of fortune which soon transferred the Free-soil paper which he had started (the *Freeman*) into a Hunker journal. But the poem itself seems to imply a somewhat broader view of the whole slavery situation.

The exulting laugh of untied empires,
Would touch them never in the heart,
But only in the pocket.

Hot-headed Carolina,
Well may you curl your lip;
With all your bondsmen, bless the destiny
Which brings you no such breed as this.

Arise, young North!
Our elder blood flows in the veins of cowards—
The gray-haired sneak, the blanched poltroon,
The feigned or real shiverer at tongues
That nursing babes need hardly cry the less for—
Are they to be our tokens always?

Fight on, band braver than warriors,
Faithful and few as Spartans;
But fear not most the angriest, loudest, malice—
Fear most the still and forked fang
That starts from the grass at your feet.

RESURGEMUS[1]

SUDDENLY, out of its state[2] and drowsy air,[3] the air[3] of slaves,
Like lightning Europe le'pt forth,
Sombre, superb and terrible,
As Ahimoth, brother of Death.

THE 1855 VERSION

SUDDENLY out of its stale and drowsy lair, the lair of slaves,
Like lightning Europe le'pt forth . . . half startled at itself,
Its feet upon the ashes and the rags. . . . Its hands tight on the throats of kings.

[1] From the New York *Daily Tribune*, June 21, 1850. Whitman preserved the poem in altered form, in the 1855 edition of "Leaves of Grass," pp. 87–88. Here it had no title, but in the 1917 edition (II, pp. 27–29), it bears the title "Europe, the 72d and 73d Years of These States," as in editions since 1860. For variorum readings and alteration in title see the 1917 edition, III, pp. 192–193. This is the only poem in the 1855 edition known to have been previously published. A comparison of its 1850 version with that of 1855, therefore, is of great importance. That the reader may the more easily make this comparison I quote the 1855 version here (see also comment in the Critical Introduction, p. xci.

[2] Apparently a typographical error for *stale*. *Cf.* 1855 version and all later versions.

[3] Apparently a typographical error for *lair*. *Cf.* 1855 version and all later versions; also "Complete Prose," p. 207.

God, 'twas delicious!
That brief, tight, glorious grip
Upon the throats of kings.
You liars paid to defile the People,

Mark you now:
Not for numberless agonies, murders, lusts,
For court thieving in its manifold mean forms,
Worming from his simplicity the poor man's wages;
For many a promise sworn by royal lips
And broken, and laughed at in the breaking;
Then, in their power, not for all these,
Did a blow fall in personal revenge,
Or a hair draggle in blood:
The People scorned the ferocity of kings.

But the sweetness of mercy brewed bitter destruction,
And frightened rulers come back:
Each comes in state, with his train,
Hangman, priest, and tax-gatherer,
Soldier, lawyer, and sycophant;
As appalling procession of locusts,
And the king struts grandly again.

Yet behind all, lo, a Shape
Vague as the night, draped interminably,
Head, front and form, in scarlet folds,

O hope and faith! O aching close of lives! O many a sickened heart!
Turn back unto this day, and make yourselves afresh.

And you, paid to defile the People . . . you liars mark:
Not for numberless agonies, murders, lusts,
For court thieving in its manifold mean forms,
Worming from his simplicity the poor man's wages;
For many a promise sworn by royal lips, And broken, and laughed at in the breaking,
Then in their power not for all these did the blows strike of personal revenge . . . or
    the heads of the noble fall;
The People scorn the ferocity of kings.

But the sweetness of mercy brewed bitter destruction, and the frightened rulers come
    back:
Each comes in state with his train . . . hangman, priest and tax-gatherer . . .
    soldier, lawyer, jailer and sycophant.

Yet behind all, lo, a Shape,
Vague as the night, draped interminably, head front and form in scarlet folds,

Whose face and eyes none may see,
Out of its robes only this,
The red robes, lifted by the arm,
One finger pointed high over the top,
Like the head of a snake appears.

Meanwhile, corpses lie in new-made graves,
Bloody corpses of young men;
The rope of the gibbet hangs heavily,
The bullets of tyrants are flying,
The creatures of power laugh aloud:
And all these things bear fruits, and they are good.

Those corpses of young men,
Those martyrs that hang from the gibbets,
Those hearts pierced by the grey lead,
Cold and motionless as they seem,
Live elsewhere with undying vitality;
They live in other young men, O, kings,
They live in brothers, again ready to defy you;
They were purified by death,
They were taught and exalted.
Not a grave of those slaughtered ones,
But is growing its seed of freedom,
In its turn to bear seed,
Which the winds shall carry afar and resow,
And the rain nourish.

Whose face and eyes none may see,
Out of its robes only this . . . the red robes, lifted by the arm,
One finger pointed high over the top, like the head of a snake appears.

Meanwhile corpses lie in new-made graves . . . bloody corpses of young men:
The rope of the gibbet hangs heavily . . . the bullets of princes are flying . . .
   the creatures of power laugh aloud,
And all these things bear fruits . . . and they are good.

Those corpses of young men,
Those martyrs that hang from the gibbets . . . those hearts pierced by the gray
   lead,
Cold and motionless as they seem . . . live elsewhere with unslaughter'd vitality.

They live in other young men, O kings,
They live in brothers, again ready to defy you:
They were purified by death. . . . They were taught and exalted.

Not a grave of the murdered for freedom but grows seed for freedom . . . in its
   turn to bear seed,
Which the winds carry afar and re-sow, and the rains and the snows nourish.

Not a disembodied spirit
Can the weapon of tyrants let loose,
But it shall stalk invisibly over the earth,
Whispering, counselling, cautioning.

Liberty, let others despair of thee,[1]
But I will never despair of thee:
Is the house shut?   Is the master away?
Nevertheless, be ready, be not weary of watching,
He will surely return; his messengers come anon.[2]

———

[ON DULUTH, MINNESOTA][3]

The nations hear thy message;
A fateful word; oh, momentous
Audition!   The murmur of waves
Bearing heavy freighted argosies; the sigh
Of gently stirring life in the birth-beds
Of not o'er distant grain fields; the

———

Not a disembodied spirit can the weapons of tyrants let loose,
But it stalks invisibly over the earth . . . whispering counseling cautioning.

Liberty let others despair of you . . . I never despair of you.

Is the house shut?   Is the master away?
Nevertheless be ready . . . be not weary of watching,
He will soon return . . . his messengers come anon.

[1] This *thee* giving place to the *you* of the 1855 and later editions is an illustration of Whitman's "getting rid of the stock poetical touches" which appeared in the first drafts of his "Leaves of Grass."   Observe also the omission of the reference to Ahimoth (l.4) in the 1855 edition.

[2] *Cf.* "Matthew," xxiv: 48–50.

[3] From the New Orleans *Item*, April 2, 1892, where it is prefaced by the following dispatch:
"Duluth, Minn.   April 4.—(Special).—A fragment of a poem by the late Walt Whitman, written while in this city a year ago, is published here to-day.   The good gray poet was quite impressed with Duluth, whose interests were shown him by a friend, and after leaving he sent his friend the following, which has remained unprinted until now."
But the only time that Whitman is known to have been at all near Duluth was on the return from his 1848 visit to New Orleans.   If this poem were written by him then, it would be a companion, though a poor one, to "Isle of La Belle Rivière."   It is possible that the outrageous division of the lines is due to a careless reading of the manuscript.   It is more likely that the whole is a puerile attempt at burlesque.   It is given here only because, since it is ascribed to Whitman on its first publication, the reader should judge for himself how authentic the authorship is likely to be.

Solemn plaint of pines whose limbs
Quite feel the bite of men's
Omnivorous axe; the roar,
Like old Enceladus's of furnaces volcanic
And Hell-like; the thunderous and
Reverberant iteration
Of hammers striking the uncomplaining anvil.
These are all in thy voice.
To what end?   Because thou singest
Of empire and the great To Come,
General good, Democracy, the
Return at length to things primeval,
And, therefore, real and true,
And worth returning unto.
Then sing, Duluth, thy
Song, and listen,
Nations!
Or it will repent ye,
When the bridegroom cometh.

SHORTER PROSE PUBLICATIONS

EFFECTS OF LIGHTNING[1]

At Northport, on Sunday, 28th ultimo, an unfortunate and somewhat singular accident occurred from the lightning. Mr. Abraham Miller, of that place, had been in the fields, engaged in some farm work, and was returning home, as a storm commenced in the afternoon, carrying in his hands a pitchfork. A friend of his who was with him advised him not to carry it, as he considered it dangerous. Mr. Miller, however, did not put down the fork, but continued walking with it; he had gone some distance on his way home, and had just put up the bars of a fence he passed through when a violent clap of thunder occurred, followed by a sharp flash. The acquaintance of Mr. Miller was slightly stunned by the shock and turning round to look at his companion he saw him lying on his face motionless. He went to him and found him dead, the lightning, having been attracted by the steel tines of the fork, had torn his hand slightly, and killed him on the instant.

SUN–DOWN PAPERS—[No. 5][2]

From the Desk of a Schoolmaster

Amidst the universal excitement which appears to have been created of late years, with regard to the evils created by ardent

[1] From the *Long Island Democrat*, August 8, 1838, where it is copied from the *Long Islander*, then being edited by Whitman. (See *infra*, I, p. 1, note.) This is the earliest extant prose from Whitman's pen.

[2] From the *Long Island Democrat*, April 28, 1840, where it is copied from the Hempstead *Inquirer*. This paper is unnumbered, but apparently should be Number 5 of the series. Whitman's authorship of these sketches is established by both internal and external evidence. The internal evidence consists not only in the celebration of ideas which Whitman was to make famous later on but in the utilization of practically a whole sentence,

spirits, it seems to have been forgotten that there are other, and almost as injurious, kinds of intemperance. The practice of using tobacco, in any shape, is one of these. Not only does the custom contribute to the discomfort of company, but it is, in itself, a fruitful source of ill to those that use it.

This is sufficiently proved by the fact, that the first taste of it almost invariably causes sickness and nausea. Our young men, however, entertain an idea that there is something very manly in having a segar stuck in the corner of their lips; or a round ball of sickening weed that a dog would not touch, rolling in their mouths. Boys, like monkeys, are generally ambitious of apeing their superiors; and many a young fellow has voluntarily undergone hours of misery in learning how to smoke or chew, in order that he might perfectly acquire this noble accomplishment, and assume the attributes of manhood. There is something very majestic, truly, in seeing a human being with a long roll of black leaves held between his teeth, and projecting eight or ten inches before him. It has been said by some satirical individual, that a fishing-rod is a thing with a hook at one extremity, and a fool at the other: it may with much more truth be affirmed, that a segar, generally has a *smoky fire* at one end, & a *conceited spark* at the other. Weak, and silly indeed, must be that youth, who thinks that these are the characteristics of manhood, they are much oftener the proofs of empty brains, and a loaferish disposition.[1]

---

the first in "Sun-Down Paper, No. 6," in a signed Whitman sketch, "The Little Sleighers" (see the last paragraph on I, p. 91, *post*). The external evidence is to be found in an editorial by E. B. Spooner (son of the Aldin Spooner for whom Whitman had as a boy set type on the *Long Island Star*) in the *Star* (now the Brooklyn *Evening Star*) for July 30, 1841, anent Whitman's speech in the Park and his apparent entry into politics: "He [Maj. Davezac] was followed by Walter Whitman, of Long Island. Heaven save the mark. Shall not we have some more small scraps from the desk of a school-master? We feel ourselves bound to look after Long Islanders, and this is a great joke! Come back young man, come back and finish your apprenticeship. Teaching very small children may be an easy life, but teaching those big children of Tammany Hall may look big but it seems very farcical." It will be observed that this comes just after the last "Sun-Down Paper" was published, and from a man who knew Whitman well. It is also known, through the family of James J. Brenton, who owned and edited the *Long Island Democrat*, that Whitman was a valued contributor to the pages of the paper, which could hardly have been said of his verse alone. (See Introduction, p. xxxiii, note.)

Diligent search has been made for the missing numbers of the series, but I have been unable to locate a file of the Hempstead *Inquirer* that goes back to the required date, and even the various files of the *Long Island Democrat* and the *Long Island Farmer* that I have examined are somewhat incomplete.

[1] *Cf. post*, I, pp. 44-46.

Custom may, and does, enable some people to become so habituated to these things, that they produce no very evident evil. But it is still not less the cause [case] that they *do* produce evil. They weaken the strength of the nervous system; they alternately excite & depress the powers of the brain; and they act with constant and insidious attacks upon the health. There may be instances where these effects do not follow; for there are some men who have such horselike constitutions, that if they were to eat the shovel and tongs, these would not sit heavily on their stomachs; nor would a blacksmith's hammer be able to shatter their nerves. These are exceptions to the correctness of my assertions with regard to the evils of tobacco; but facts and the experience of medical men will bear me out in saying that they are generally true.

The excessive use of tea and coffee, too, is a species of intemperance much to be condemned. It is astonishing that people can consent to take twice a day, three or four gills of a hot liquid into their stomachs to destroy its tone and impair its legitimate powers. And not only this; for it would not be so bad if it was pure water merely; but it must be infused with a bitter and unpleasant shrub—and to crown the climax of absurdity, it must have a lump of sugar to take away the bitter taste, and a spoonful of milk to destroy its insupportable hotness.

Into what ridiculous lengths can people be led by fashion! Hot drinks of this kind are fatal to the teeth, deleterious to physical strength, the cause of impure blood, and the means of producing many a head ache, many a pale face, and many an emaciated body.

In conclusion, I would remark, that I am not one of those who would deny people any sensual delights because I think it a sin to be happy and to take pleasure in the good things of this life. On the contrary, I am disposed to allow every rational gratification, both to the palate, and the other senses. I consider that we were placed here [by the Creator] for two beneficent purposes; to fulfil our duty, and to enjoy the almost innumerable comforts and delights which he has provided for us.[1] But the pernicious things I have mentioned are not worthy the name of comforts: long habit may have caused them to be regarded as such by some people; but nature, and experience, and enlightened reason, all go to prove their injurious effect.

[1] *Cf. post*, II, p. 146.

SUN–DOWN PAPERS—[No. 6][1]

FROM THE DESK OF A SCHOOLMASTER

I KNOW not a prettier custom than that, said to have been prevalent among several nations, of strewing the coffins of young people with flowers.   When persons of middle or old age die, the work of the Pale Mower seems connected with something of roughness: it creates what I would call a coarse kind of grief, often overpowering, and always without any aid from very refined associations.   But when we see an infant laid away to a quiet slumber in the bosom of the great mother of men—when we behold a young girl departed to those mysterious regions which we are fond of believing to be filled with resplendent innocence and beauty—or when we look on a boy, shrouded in the cerements of death, his hair parted on his forehead, and those features and limbs that we have known as so joyous and active now without motion, and all prepared for that fearful ceremony, the burying—then our painful sensations have much about them of gentleness and poetic melancholy.   In the last cases, our grief is not gross, but delicate, like the just perceptible fragrance of the lily: in the former, it more resembles the scent of a thick and full blown rose.

One reason, probably, of this different mode of view is this: we are well aware that men who have lived a length of time in the world, must have committed many little meannesses—must have done wrong on various occasions—must have had the fine bloom of simplicity and nature nearly rubbed off—and must have been connected with much that would sully that healthiness and freshness of character, which almost every body has for the first few years of life—while with the quite young none of these things have happened: they are taken away, like blossoms with the dew upon them, in all their sweetness and modesty: time has not seared up the delightful spring of spirits; the course of years has not withered that susceptibility and pliancy which might be turned to so much account, but is so often misdirected by the carelessness of the old; nor have Guilt and Wretchedness yet had dominion over them.—The contrast between the two cases is, therefore, the contrast between the drying up of some clear and narrow brook, and the extinction of an inland river: the latter stronger, to be sure, and of more importance than the other, but not so pure, transparent, and resigned. The last would leave a greater vacuum also; but on its dry bed would remain signs of its having done evil—traces of its fury, its remorselessness, and its treacherous wrecking of what had been trusted to its bosom.

When a man dies, who can say what deep stains may have rested, at one time or another, upon his soul? what crimes (untouchable, perhaps, by the laws of men or the rules of society) he has committed, either in evil wishes or in reality? How many persons go down to the grave, praised by the world and pointed to as examples, who were still far, very far, from good men! They may have respected custom, honored the government, followed the fashion, paid to public charity every cent which the law demanded, kept clear of glaring transgressions, stood up or bowed down their heads in houses of worship just at the due time, and still, if we could open their hearts and see what went on there we should be sickened and amazed! It is a true saying, that we can never, in the great drama of life, pronounce judgment upon the good or ill performance of his part by a fellow creature, until the last act and the last scene are over, the bell rung, and the curtain dropped.—With the dead girl or boy, the transient play *is* finished: we know that the worst deeds they ever committed were but children's follies; and one great balm, on such occasions, is the knowledge, that for them the future has no terrors, the time to come no temptations or miseries.

Perhaps I may as well relate, in conclusion, the incident that has given rise to these reflections. I have just received, through a newspaper, intelligence of the death of one whom I knew slightly, and whose gentleness and brightness of intellect could not help endearing him to all who love the young. His age was fourteen or fifteen years: he died at a place some distance from home, where he had been sent for his education. The last time I saw him, we walked a mile or two together. It was in the country, and the season was Autumn. How little did I think that ere the grain or fruits would ripen again he would be blighted!—that *his* Autumn would arrive ere the Spring had passed. Rest in peace, young boy! Your silver thread of life is cut soon; but there are ills on earth to make men envy your fate. Your sleep is calm and quiet. Oh, when the pulse grows faint with its last throbbing—when the cold sweat has dried upon the brow—when the pantings of "life's fitful fever"[1] have

1"Macbeth," III, 2, 23.

ceased—then let us hope to meet you in that far off land of mystery which passes the imagination of man to conceive or the utmost stretch of his intellect to trace.

SUN-DOWN PAPERS—[No. 7][1]

FROM THE DESK OF A SCHOOLMASTER

I THINK that if I should make pretensions to be a philosopher, and should determine to edify the world with what would add to the number of those sage and ingenious theories which do already so much abound, I would compose a wonderful and ponderous book. Therein should be treated on, the nature and peculiarities of men, the diversity of their characters, the means of improving their state, and the proper mode of governing nations; with divers other points whereon I could no doubt throw quite as much light as do many of those worthy gentlemen, who, to the delight and instruction of our citizens, occasionally treat upon these subjects in printed periodicals, in books, and in publick discourses.[2]   At the same time that I would do all this, I would carefully avoid saying any thing of woman; because it behoves a modest personage like myself not to speak upon a class of beings of whose nature, habits, notions, and ways he has not been able to gather any knowledge, either by experience or observation.

Nobody, I hope, will accuse me of conceit in these opinions of mine own capacity for doing great things. In good truth, I think the world suffers from this much-bepraised modesty.[3] Who should be a better judge of a man's talents than the man himself? I see no reason why we should let our lights shine under bushels. Yes: I *would* write a book! And who shall say that it might not be a very pretty book? Who knows but that I might do something very respectable?

And one principal claim to a place among men of profound sagacity, by means of the work I allude to, would be on account of a wondrous and important discovery, a treatise upon which would fill up the principal part of my compilation. I have found out that it is a very dangerous thing to be rich.[4] For a considerable time past this idea has been pressing upon

[1]From the *Long Island Democrat*, September 29, 1840.
[2]*Cf. post*, II, p. 76. [3]*Cf. post*, II, p. 89. [4]*Cf. infra*, pp. 111, 123-125 II, pp. 63, 67.

me; and I am now fully and unalterably convinced of its truth. Some years ago, when my judgement was in the bud, I thought riches were very desirable things. But I have altered my mind. Light has flowed in upon me. I am not quite so green as I was. The mists and clouds have cleared away, and I can now behold things as they really are. Do you want to know some of the causes of this change of opinion? Look yonder. See the sweat pouring down that man's face. See the wrinkles on his narrow forehead. He is a poor, miserable, rich man. He has been up since an hour before sunrise, fussing, and mussing, and toiling and wearying, as if there were no safety for his life, except in uninterrupted motion. He is worried from day to day to preserve and take care of his possessions. He keeps horses; and one of them is by him. Look at the miserable brute (the horse, I mean). See how his sides pant. I warrant me, the animal has no rest for the soles of his feet.

I don't know when I have been more pleased than I was the other day by an illustration which a friend of mine gave of the trouble of great wealth. Life, said he, is a long journey by steamboat, stagecoach, and railroad. We hardly get fairly and comfortably adjusted in the vehicle that carries us for the time being, when we are obliged to stop and get into another conveyance, and go a different road. We are continually on the move. We may sometimes flatter ourselves in the idea of making a comfortable stop, with time enough to eat our dinner and lounge about a little; but the bell rings, the steam puffs, the horn blows, the waiters run about half mad, every thing is hurry-scurry for a moment, and whiz! we are off again. What wise man thinks of cumbering up this journey with an immense mass of luggage? Who, that makes pretensions to common sense, will carry with him a dozen trunks, and bandboxes, hatboxes, valises, chests, umbrellas, and canes innumerable, besides two dirty shirts in the crown of his hat, and a heavy brass watch that won't keep time, in his waistcoat pocket?

This is, in all sincerity, a true picture of the case. People groan, and grieve, and work, to no other purpose than merely their own inconvenience. And when at last they arrive at the grand stopping place for their travels here, and start on that mysterious train we all go with sooner or later, they find that the Grand Engineer admits no luggage therein. There is no freight car to the Hidden Land. Money and property must be left behind. The noiseless and strange attendants gather from every passenger his ticket, and heed not whether he be dark or fair, clad in homespun or fine apparel. Happy he whose wisdom has purchased beforehand a token of his having settled satisfactorily for the journey!

SUN–DOWN PAPERS—[No. 8][1]

FROM THE DESK OF A SCHOOLMASTER

ON A pleasant, still, summer evening, I once took a walk down a lane that borders our village. The moon was shining with a luscious brightness; I gazed on the glorious evidences of divinity hanging above me, and as l gazed strange and fitful thoughts occupied my brain. I reflected on the folly and vanity of those objects with which most men occupy their lives; and the awe and dread with which they approach its close. I remembered the strife for temporary and puerile distinctions—the seeking after useless and cumbersome wealth—the yielding up the diseased mind to be a prey to constant melancholy and discontent; all which may be daily seen by those who have intercourse with the sons of men. But, most of all, I thought on the troubles caused under the name of Truth and Religion—the dissentions which have arisen between those of opposing creeds—and the quarrels and bickerings that even now prevail among men upon the slightest and most trivial points of opinion in these things. While such imaginings possessed my mind, I unconsciously seated myself upon a grassy bank; weariness, induced by the fatigues of the day, overpowered me; I sank into a tranquil sleep, and the spirit of dreams threw his misty veil about my soul.

I was wandering over the earth in search of TRUTH.[2] Cities were explored by my enterprise; and the mouldy volumes which for years had lain undisturbed, were eagerly scanned to discover the object of my labours. Among the pale and attenuated votaries of science, I mixed as with kindred spirits; and the proudest of the learned were my familiars. My piercing gaze penetrated far down into the mines of knowledge, endeavouring to reach that jewel fairer, and brighter, and more precious than earthly jewels; but in vain, for it eluded my sight. Through the crowded ranks of men who swarm in thickly peopled

[1] From the *Long Island Democrat*, October 20, 1840.
[2] *Cf.* "Complete Prose," pp. 232-333.

places, I took my way, silent and unobserved, but ever on the alert for a clew to guide me toward the attainment of that which was the hope of my soul.   I entered the gorgeous temples where pride, dressed in rich robes, preaches the doctrine of the holy and just Nazarene: I waited at the courts of powerful princes, where pomp, and grandeur, and adoration combined to make a frail mortal think himself mighty: I stood in the presence of the youthful and the gay—beauty, flashing in its bloom—strength, rearing itself in pride—revellers, and dancers, and feasters. But my heart turned comfortless from them all, for it had not attained its desire, and disappointment was heavy upon it.   I then travelled to distant and uncivilized regions.   Far in the north, among mountains of snow and rivers of ice, I sought what alone could gratify me.   I lived, too, with the rude Tartar in his tent, and installed myself in all the mysteries which are known to the Lamas of Thibet.   I wandered to a more southern clime, and disputed with the Brahmins, who profess to believe in a religion that has existed for more centuries than any other one has years.   The swarthy worshipper of fire made known to me his belief; and the devotee of the camel-driver of Mecca strived for my conversion to his faith.   But useless was all my toil, and valueless were all the immense stores of learning I had acquired.   I was baffled in all my attempts, and only began new projects to find them meet with as little success as the former.

Sick and disheartened, I retired far from the inhabited portions of earth, and lived in solitude amid a wild and mountainous country.   I there spent my time in reflection, and the pursuit of the various branches of learning, and lived upon the frugal produce of the neighboring fields.   I had one day travelled to some distance from my usual retreat, and kept insensibly wandering onward and onward, till I found myself suddenly brought to a stand by an immense ledge of rocks which rose almost perpendicularly in front of me, and, reaching far away on each side, effectually closed up my advance.   The top of this stupendous pile was hidden in the clouds, and so steep was it that it seemed impossible to ascend.   I stood perplexed and wondering, incited by curiosity to explore its heights and warned by prudence to return to my cell, when I heard a low but clear and silvery voice pronounce these words, as if from the cloud over my head:

"Mortal, thou hast now an opportunity of seeing what has been the search of thy life.   From the top of the mountain

which rises before thee, thou mayest behold on the opposite side
the holy altar of Truth.   Ascend, and refresh thine eyes with the
picture of its loveliness."

Amazed and transported with this assurance, I immediately
began to climb the precipice.   The ascent was rugged and dif-
ficult, but perseverance and incessant vigour enabled me to
surmount every bar.   I succeeded in reaching the top, and
threw myself, panting and covered with sweat, on the stony sand.
When weariness had at length given way before the power of
repose, I walked onwards over the mountain, which was com-
posed of sterile black rocks and sand, with not a spot of verdure
to relieve its gloomy appearance, and at length arrived at the
brow of the precipice.   On this side, the mountain appeared
still more steep, and to advance to the edge was evidently
attended with great danger.   I did so, however, and my dazzled
eyes fell on a sight more beautiful than was ever before re-
vealed to mortals.   Far below stretched a country exceeding
the imagination of the seeker after pleasure, and more lovely
than the dreams which benignant spirits sometimes weave
around the couch of youth and innocence.   The surface of the
land was covered with soft grass, and with fragrant trees, and
shrubs, and flowers, far fresher and fairer than those of our
world.   Here and there it was decked with sparkling streams of
water, sweet as the tear which falls in behalf of sorrow from
the eye of virtue, and fair as snow-drops in the tresses of
beauty.   These brooks broke occasionally into little cascades,
which gushed forth joyously, and seemed to murmur their
happiness in sounds of thankful gratitude to heaven.

But it was not the flowers, or the rich verdure, or the bubbling
waters that attracted my attention.   The scene was delight-
fully variegated with rolls and slight elevations of land: on the
highest of these I beheld a white marble base, on which were
raised several columns, and over the whole was thrown a roof
of the same material, presenting an edifice of singular appear-
ance, but of the most exquisite finish.   I could not at once make
out its proportions, for there appeared around it something like
a mist, which was the more singular, as in every other place the
light was of a radiant clearness.   In fact, when I first viewed
the spot, though I was on the alert, this temple, if so it may be
called, did not strike my eye at all; but now, by dint of the
most intent gazing, I could perceive its various parts with tol-
erable accuracy.   While I was communing with myself in what

manner I should endeavour to reach the ground below, and ex-
plore the very recesses of the marble temple, the silence around
me was suddenly broken, and I heard the voice which had once
before addressed me at the foot of the mountain, speaking in
tones which sounded like the notes of a flute breathed through
groves of spicy flowers:

"Seek not, O child of clay," it said, "to discover that which is
hidden by an allseeing God, from the knowledge of mortals!
Wert thou to attain thy desire, thou wouldst still be impotent,
for thine eyes, covered as they are with the dark web of mortal-
ity, would be unable to comprehend the awful mysteries which
Nature veils from thy mind.   But turn thy gaze to the left,
below the hill on which the temple stands, and learn a lesson of
instruction which will repay all thy fatigue."

The voice ceased, and, struck with awe, I looked in the direc-
tion it had pointed out to me.   I beheld a country different en-
tirely from the one I have just described, and in almost every
respect like that earth on which we live.   It was not far from
the temple of Truth, which could be perceived from it, but the
two were divided by an impassable vacuum.   Upon the small
spot of ground which resembled our native planet, I beheld
many people, of all classes, and nations, and tongues and dresses,
constantly passing, with their attention directed toward the
temple.   Each one seemed to view it with the utmost care, and
to wish to penetrate the veil of surrounding mist that dimmed
its clearness.   There was one thing, however, which astonished
and at first somewhat bewildered me.   I observed that each one
of these inquirers after Truth held in his hand an optical glass
and never gazed at the temple but through its medium.   Upon
observing closely, I saw that these glasses were of the most in-
congruous shapes and forms, and exercised singular and amaz-
ing power over the appearance of whatever was beheld through
them.   With some they were narrow and contracted, making
the temple appear insignificant and mean.   Some had them of
one colour, and others of a different.   Many of the glasses were of
so gross a texture, that the temple was completely hid from view.
Some of them distorted it into the most grotesque shapes and
forms: others again would make it appear an ordinary edifice;
and few were so true as to give a view of the temple nigh to its
correct representation.   But if whatever correctness were these
glasses, each individual persisted in looking at the object of his
attention through their aid.   No one, or at least very few, was

seen to examine the temple with the clear and undistorted organs which nature had given him: and that few, I found, were scoffed at and persecuted by all the others, who, though they differed to the utmost in their manner of viewing Truth among themselves, yet united to a man in condemning those who endeavoured to see what little could be perceived of the temple without the false assistance of some glass or other.

I stood gazing on these things, perplexed, and hardly knowing what to think of them, when I once more heard the voice which had twice addressed me. It had lost none of its sweetness, but there was now in it an admonishing tone which sank into my soul as the rich stores of learning penetrate the open ears of attention:

"Behold!" thus it spoke, "and learn wisdom from the spectacles which have been this day unfolded to thine eyes. Thou hast gazed upon the altar of Nature; but hast seen how impossible it is to penetrate the knowledge which is stored within it. Let pride therefore depart from thy soul, and let a sense of the littleness of all earthly acquirements bow down thy head in awe before the mighty Creator of a million worlds. Thou hadst seen that whatever of the great light of Truth it has been deemed expedient to show to mortals can be most truly and usefully contemplated by the plain eye of simplicity, unaccompanied by the clogs and notions which dim the gaze of most men—and hast with wonder seen how all will still continue to view the noblest objects of desire through the distorted medium of their own prejudices and bigotry. The altar of Truth is immutable, unchangeable and firm, ever the same bright emanation from God, and ever consistent with its founder. Though worlds shoot out of existence—though stars grow dim, and whole systems are blotted out of being by the hand of the mighty conqueror, Change—yet will Nature and Truth, for they two in [are] one, stand up in everlasting youth and bloom and power. Thou seest, then, how miserable are all the creeds and doctrines prevailing among men, which profess to bring down these awful mysteries, [as] things which they can fathom and search out. Kneel, then, oh! insect of an hour, whose every formation is subject enough for an eternity of wonder—and whose fate is wrapped in a black shroud of uncertainty—kneel on that earth which thou makest the scene of thy wretched strife after corruptible honors—of thy own little schemes for happiness—and of thy crimes and guilt—kneel, bend thy face to the sand, spread out the puny arms with which thy pride would win so much glory —and adore with a voiceless awe, that Unknown Power, the very minutest idea of whose abode and strength, and formation, and intentions, it would be more difficult for thee to comprehend than for a stroke of thy hand to push out of their orbits the suns and systems which make the slightest evidence of his strength."

Speechless and trembling, I listened to the sounds of this awful voice. I had sunk to the earth in fear, for a strange and pervading terror had filled my frame, while the unseen spirit had given utterance to his words. But at length I arose, and endeavored to return the gratitude of my soul for the priceless treasures which had been showered upon my mind.

The agitations of my thoughts, however, broke my slumbers. I awoke and found that the moon had long raised her radiant face, and was throwing down floods of light to illuminate the earth. The cold mists of night had stiffened my limbs, and were falling heavy around on the wet grass. I slowly wended my way homeward, my soul improved in knowledge, and determined to treasure during life the instruction I had gained from the vision that night.

SUN–DOWN PAPERS—[No. 9][1]

FROM THE DESK OF A SCHOOLMASTER

How I do love a loafer! Of all human beings, none equals your genuine, inbred, unvarying loafer. Now when I say loafer, I *mean* loafer; not a fellow who is lazy by fits and starts—who to-day will work his twelve or fourteen hours, and to-morrow doze and idle. I stand up for no such half-way business. Give me your calm, steady, philosophick son of indolence; one that does n't swerve from the beaten track; a man who goes the undivided beast. To such an one will I doff my beaver. No matter whether he be a street loafer or a dock loafer—whether his hat be rimless, and his boots slouched, and his coat out at the elbows: he belongs to that ancient and honourable fraternity, whom I venerate above all your upstarts, your dandies, and your political oracles.

All the old philosophers were loafers. Take Diogenes for instance. He lived in a tub, and demeaned himself like a

[1] From the *Long Island Democrat*, November 28, 1840.
Cf. post, II, p. 314.

true child of the great loafer family. Or go back farther, if you like, even to the very beginning. What was Adam, I should like to know, but a loafer? Did he do any thing but loaf? Who is foolish enough to say that Adam was a working man? Who dare aver that he dealt in stocks, or was busy in the sugar line?

I hope you will not so far expose yourself as to ask, who was the founder of loafers. Know you not, ignorance, that there never was such a thing as the *origin* of loaferism? We don't acknowledge any founder. There have always been loafers as they were in the beginning, are now, and ever shall be—having no material difference. Without any doubt, when Chaos had his acquaintance cut, and the morning stars sang together, and the little rivers danced a cotillion for pure fun—there were loafers somewhere about, enjoying the scene in all their accustomed philosophick quietude.

When I have been in a dreamy, musing mood, I have sometimes amused myself with picturing out a nation of loafers. Only think of it! an entire loafer kingdom! How sweet it sounds! Repose,—quietude,—roast duck,—loafer. Smooth and soft are the terms to our jarred tympanums.

Imagine some distant isle inhabited altogether by loafers. Of course there is a good deal of sunshine, for sunshine is the loafer's natural element. All breathes peace and harmony. No hurry, or bustle, or banging, or clanging. Your ears ache no more with the din of carts; the noisy politician offends you not, no wrangling, no quarreling, no loco focos, no British whigs.

Talk about your commercial countries, and your national industry, indeed! Give us the facilities of loafing, and you are welcome to all the benefits of your tariff system, your manufacturing privileges, and your cotton trade. For my part, I have had serious thoughts of getting up a regular ticket for President and Congress and Governor and so on, for the loafer community in general. I think we loafers should organize. We want somebody to carry out "our principles." It is my impression, too, that we should poll a pretty strong vote. We number largely in the land. At all events our strength would enable us to hold the balance of power, and we should be courted and coaxed by all the rival factions. And there is no telling but what we might elect our men. Stranger things than that have come to pass.

These last hints I throw out darkly, as it were. I by no means assert that we positively *will* get up and vote for, a regu-

lar ticket to support the "great measures of our party." I am
only telling what *may* be done, in case we are provoked. Myster-
ious intimations have been thrown out—dark sayings uttered,
by those high in society, that the grand institution of loaferism
was to be abolished. People have talked of us sneeringly and
frowningly. Cold eyes have been turned upon us. Over-
bearing men have spoken in derogatory terms about our rights
and our dignity.[1] You had better be careful, gentlemen.
You had better look out how you irritate us. It would make
you look sneaking enough, if we were to come out at the next
election, and carry away the palm before both your political
parties.

———

SUN–DOWN PAPERS—[No. 9, *bis*][2]

FROM THE DESK OF A SCHOOLMASTER

As I was taking a solitary walk the other evening, the moon
and stars shining over me with a beautiful brightness, I came
suddenly upon a man with whom I was bitterly at variance.
The philosophic meditation which the balmy coolness and the
voluptuousness of the scene had led me into, being thus broken
in upon, my thoughts took a different channel. I considered
within myself, how evil a thing it is to be at enmity. I thought
of the surpassing folly of a man in allowing his disposition to
hate, whether in a great or little degree, to be cherished in his
mind.—This individual, my enemy, and I, had differed upon a
matter of opinion; a sharp word had passed, and after that
there was an impassable gulf between us. Miserable childish-

---

[1]The editorial in the column adjoining the above paper deals with "School Matters."
Criticizing the inspectors of schools, it says: "Half the time they allow certificates to men
ignorant and stupid, of shattered characters, of questionable morality, of intemperate
habits, of blasphemous tongues, or of raw and illiterate minds. Two thirds of the
common school teachers are unfit for the office. As a class, they are by no means of the
highest order. They seem to be made up, in the main, of persons who have broken
down in other business, who are too ignorant or too lazy to do *anything else*, and who
take up the profession, because they can't get any other way to make a living. Passing
about here and there, they acquire irregular habits, and fall into dissolute trains of
thinking and acting. Most of them are far more proper subjects for feeling the rod than
wielding the rod. They begin and go through the accustomed routine of the school
room, and at the end of the week it is fortunate for the young tribe, if they are as far
ahead as they were when they began." *Cf. post*, II, pp. 13–15, 124.

[2]From the *Long Island Democrat*, July 6, 1841.

ness! that man, the insect of an hour,[1] whose life is but a passing breath, must have his mighty quarrels with his brother, and for something of a feather's value, entrench himself upon his dignity, and meet his fancied foe with a scowl or a contemptuous lip-curl.

He to whom many persons are hateful is a very unhappy being. It is far better to love than to hate. But even he who leans neither upon one side or the other, but jogs through the world with no stronger feeling for his fellows than indifference, loses all the rich bloom and flavor of life. Down in every human heart there are many sweet fountains, which require only to be touched in order to gush forth. Yet there are hundreds and thousands of men who go on from year to year with their pitiful schemes of business and profit, and wrapped up and narrowed down in those schemes, they never think of the pleasant and beautiful capacities that God has given them. Affection, that delicate but most fragrant flower of Paradise, sits folded up within them, but never blossoms there.—Love and charity, twin angels of ineffable grace, and favorites of the great Source of Glory, lock their arms around each other, and lie themselves to slumber, in those souls—slumber but wake not.[2] I pity such people. I pity them for that they enjoy no true pleasure; for that they are all gross, sensual, and low; for that they do so little honor to their Maker, and let such costly and glorious treasures lie undigged in the mine.

I would have men cultivate their disposition for kindness to all around. I would have them foster and cherish the faculty of love. To be sure, it may not bring in a percentage like bank stock, or corporation scrip, or bonds and mortgages, but it is very valuable, and will pay many fold. It is a faculty given to every human soul, though in most it is dormant and used not. It prompts us to be affectionate and gentle to all men. It leads us to scorn the cold and heartless limits of custom, but moves our souls to swell up with pure and glowing love for persons or for communities. It makes us disdain to be hemmed in by the formal mummeries of fashion, but at the kiss of a sister or a brother, or when our arms clasp the form of a friend, or when our lips touch the cheek of a boy or girl whom we love, it proves to us that all pleasures of dollars and cents are dross to those of loving and being beloved.

Ere I close this paper, I will add a sentence or two, lest I

[1] *Cf. infra*, I, p. 14. [2] *Cf. post*, p. 86, II, p. 71.

be misunderstood. By "love" as I have used the term in the preceding essay, I do not mean the sickly sentimentality which is so favorite a theme with novelists and magazine writers. What I would inculcate is that healthy, cheerful feeling of kindness and good will, an affectionate tenderness, a warm-heartedness, the germs of which are plentifully sown by God in each human breast; and which contribute to form a state of feeling very different from the puerile, moping love, painted by such trashy writers as Byron and Bulwer, and their more trashy imitators.[1]

———

SUN–DOWN PAPERS—[No. 10][2]

From the Desk of a Schoolmaster

We had all made up our minds to take a jaunt in the South Bay; and accordingly at the appointed morning, about sunrise, might have been seen wending their way toward the place of rendezvous, the various members of our party. The wise

[1] Whitman's supposition that only sexual affection was in danger of becoming sickly in its sentimentality is, in the light of the present sketch, not to mention many another, rather naïve. It was natural enough, however, to the elevated and exacting idealism of a poet's adolescence. He seems never to have cared much for Bulwer (see *post*, pp. 122, 157), but he quoted Byron freely while in New Orleans and found that there was a rebel in the fiery Englishman as well as a lady-killer (see *post*, II, pp. 179, 203, 212, 218). In time he was to celebrate sex quite as much as Byron or Bulwer, though, for the most part, in a different way. Compare this early deliverance on romantic affection with the following passage from John Burroughs's "Walt Whitman, A Study" (pp. 194–195): "It is charged against Whitman that he does not celebrate love at all, and very justly. He has no purpose to celebrate the sentiment of love. . . . Of that veiled prurient suggestion which readers so delight in—of 'bosoms mutinously fair,' and 'the soul-lingering loops of perfumed hair,' as one of our latest poets puts it—there is no hint in his volume. He would have fallen from grace the moment he attempted such a thing. . . . From Whitman's point of view, it would have been positively immoral for him either to have vied with the lascivious poets in painting it as the forbidden, or with the sentimental poets in depicting it as a charm. . . . Whitman is seldom or never the poet of a sentiment, at least of the domestic and social sentiments. . . . The cosmic takes the place of the idyllic; the begetter, the Adamic man, takes the place of the lover; patriotism takes the place of family affection; charity takes the place of piety; love of kind is more than love of neighbour; the poet and the artist are swallowed up in the seer and the prophet." This is a better statement of the fact than Whitman himself ever achieved in prose; but it remains to inquire whether there were a psychical or a physiological necessity in the poet's equipment such as to compel him to omit from the expression of the complete life of an "average man" elements which the average man hitherto has felt to be both beautiful and essential. (See I, pp. xlix–l, 112, note 2, II, pp. 94–97.) The present sketch, while indicating his capacity for affection, betrays also, I think, the bifurcation of his sexual nature which was to give us, in the same volume, "Children of Adam" and "Calamus."

[2] From the *Long Island Farmer* (Jamaica), July 20, 1841.

Bromero, with his clam-rake, and narrow-brimmed straw hat; Señor Cabinet, with sedate face, and an enormous basket, containing a towel, fishing tackle, and incalculable quantities of provisions; Captain Sears, with his usual pleasant look; one of the Smith family with a never-failing fund of good humor; Kirbus, with his gun, breathing destruction to snipe and seafowl generally; and other personages whose number will prevent their being immortalized in this veracious history.

Having first stowed our persons away in the wagons provided for that purpose, we started for the shore, fifteen precious souls in all; not forgetting to place in safe situations various baskets, kettles, jugs, bottles, and nondescript vessels, of whose contents we knew not as yet. We hoisted the American flag on a clam-rake handle, and elevated it in the air, very much to our own pleasure and the edification no doubt of all patriotic beholders. Thus riding along it was discovered by an inquisitive member of our party that one of us, a married man, had come from home without his breakfast; whereupon an inquiry was instituted that resulted in bringing out the astounding fact that every married man in the company was in the like predicament. An evil-disposed character among us was ungallant enough to say that the fact was a fair commentary on matrimonial comfort.

When we arrived at the point of embarkation, we found a tight clean boat, all ready for us, with Sailor Bight to superintend the navigation of the same. Having perfectly ensconced ourselves therein, by no means forgetting the baskets, jugs, &c., afore-mentioned, we boldly put forth into the stream and committed our lives to the mercy of the wind and waves. We reached the mouth of the creek with no adventures of any importance, except that Kirbus came very near getting a wild duck who was seen foraging on the waves not far from us; it would have been very easy to have got him—if Kirbus had shot him. I had liked to have forgot mentioning that Señor Cabinet got the tail of his black coat quite wet by dragging it in the salt water, as he was seated on the gunwale of the boat.

We had brought a musical instrument with us, and accordingly in due time we proceeded to give some very scientific specimens of the concord of sweet sounds.[1] The popular melodies of "Auld Lang Syne" and "Home, Sweet Home," were sung with great taste and effect. Thus the time passed away very pleas-

[1]"The Merchant of Venice," V, 1, 82.

antly until we arrived at the beach; when some of us dashing
boldly through the water to dry land—and the more effeminate
being carried thither on the back of Sailor Bight—we started
forth to visit the other side, whereon the surf comes tumbling,
like lots of little white pigs playing upon clean white straw.
Before we went thither, I must not forget to record, we were
entertained with some highly exquisite specimens of Shakes-
pearian eloquence by one of our company, formerly a member of
the "Spouting Club" and, therefore entitled to be called a *whaler*.

Having arrived at the surf, a portion of our party indulged
themselves in the luxury of a bath therein.   The rest returned to
the boat, and forthwith each, arming himself with a clam-rake,
did valorously set to work a-scratching up the sand at no small
rate.   After a while, the individual before spoken of as belong-
ing to the Smith family, not feeling contented with his luck
where he was, did, in company with another discontented per-
sonage, betake himself off in the little skiff which had accom-
panied our little vessel.   He rowed most manfully, for half a
mile, to a place where he thought he could better himself.   By
dint of pulling and hauling there nearly an hour, he managed to
catch one clam, and then was content to return from whence he
came.   Thus was exemplified in the fortunes of this Smith in-
dividual, the truth of the old maxim: "Let well enough alone."

But my limits will not allow me to expatiate upon the events
of this interesting voyage.   I shall therefore not say a word about
the astonishing appetite of Señor Cabinet; or the fun we had in
Bromero's stories; or how a hat belonging to one of our chaps
blew off into the wide waters and was recovered again by the
Smith individual, but with the loss of a sort of a short-necked pipe,
which had for many days before been safely kept therein.   Nor
shall I tell how we cut up divers clams into small bits, and thrust
the said bits upon fish-hooks, and let down the said hooks by long
lines into the water, and then sat patiently holding the lines, in
the vain hope of nabbing some stray members of the finny tribe.

Passing over all these, and other like important matters, I
shall wind up this most accurate account by saying that we re-
turned home perfectly safe in body, sound in limb, much re-
freshed in soul, and in perfect good humor and satisfaction
one with another.

P.S.—I came very near forgetting to say, that some of us
had our faces highly improved in color, and that Kirbus, and
others of the married men, after we came ashore, bought

several shillings' worth of eels and clams, probably in order to ward off the danger that would inevitably have followed their return empty-handed.

———

[REPORT OF WALTER WHITMAN'S SPEECH, IN THE PARK, IN NEW YORK CITY, JULY 29, 1841][1]

AFTER touching upon various points of democratic doctrine and policy, Mr. Whitman concluded as follows: Meetings have been held by our people in various sections, to nominate a candidate for the next presidency. My fellow citizens: let this be an afterthought. I beseech you to entertain a noble and more elevated idea of our aim and struggles as a party than to suppose that we are striving [to raise] this or that man to power. We are battling for great principles—for mighty and glorious truths. I would scorn to exert even my humble efforts for the best democratic candidate that ever was nominated, in himself alone. It is our creed—our doctrine, not a man or set of men, that we seek to build up. Let us attend then, in the meantime, to measures, policy and doctrine, and leave to future consideration the selection of the agent to carry our plans into effect.[2] My firm conviction is that the next democratic candidate, whoever he may be, will be carried into power on the wings of a mighty re-action. The guardian spirit, the good genius who has attended us ever since the days of Jefferson, has not now forsaken us. I can almost fancy myself able to pierce the darkness of the future and behold her looking down upon us with those benignant smiles she wore in 1828, '32, and '36.[3] Again will she hover over us, amid the smoke and din of battle, and leading us to our wonted victory, through "the sober second thought of the people."[4]

---

[1] From the Brooklyn *Daily Eagle*, April 6, 1847, where it is quoted from the *New Era* of July 30, 1841, to refute the charge made by the Brooklyn *Advertizer*, that in the summer of 1841 Whitman had been a Whig. (See "The Gathering of the Forces," II, pp. 3–7.)

The *New Era* estimated that 15,000 persons had attended the meeting; the *Evening Post* put it at 8,000 to 12,000. There were several speakers.

[2] *Cf. post*, I, p. 260.

[3] This prophecy was fulfilled in the election three years later, in which Polk, who in 1840 had received but a single vote in the electoral college, defeated Henry Clay by a vote of 170–105.

[4] "I consider biennial elections as a security that the sober second thought of the people shall be law."—Fisher Ames: "On Biennial Elections," 1788. (Bartlett's "Familiar Quotations," 10th edition, p. 288.) The phrase was particularly common in the 1840's.

BERVANCE: OR, FATHER AND SON[1]

ALMOST incredible as it may seem, there is more truth than fiction in the following story. Whatever of the latter element may have been added, it is for the purpose of throwing that disguise around the real facts of the former which is due to the feelings of a respectable family. The principal parties alluded to have left the stage of life many years since; but I am well aware there are not a few yet alive who, should they, as is very probable, read this narration, will have their memories carried back to scenes and persons of much more substantial existence than the mere creation of an author's fancy. I have given it the form of a confession in the first person, partly for the sake of convenience, partly of simplicity, but chiefly because such was the form in which the main incidents were a long time ago repeated to me by my own informant. It is a strange story—the true solution of which will probably be found in the supposition of a certain degree of unsoundness of mind, on the one part, manifesting itself in the morbid and unnatural paternal antipathy; and of its reproduction on the other, by the well known though mysterious law of hereditary transmission. W. W.

. . . . . .

My appointed number of years has now almost sped. Before I sink to that repose in the bosom of the great common mother, which I have so long and earnestly coveted, I will disclose the story of a life which one fearful event has made, through all its later stages, a continued stretch of wretchedness and remorse. There may possibly be some parents to whom it may serve a not useless lesson.

[1]From the *Democratic Review*, December, 1841, Vol. IX, pp. 560–568.

This story, no less than such fanciful ones as "The Angel of Tears" (*post*, I, pp. 83–86), and "Eris; A Spirit Record" (*post*, I, pp. 86–89), would seem to show that Whitman had come under the influence of Poe, for whose *Broadway Journal* he later contributed a brief sketch on American music, *post*, I, pp. 104–106. However, instead of being the creation of a morbid imagination, the present story may have been told to the author in the manner stated, for he seldom claims complete originality for his plots (*cf.* "Complete Prose," p. 196). If so, it argues his ability in early youth to inspire a high degree of confidence. Whatever the origin of the plot, Whitman's interest in it must have been stimulated by the fact that two of his own brothers were subnormal mentally. One, Edward, was at this time a six-year-old imbecile, while his brother Jesse, a year or two older than Walt, was to die in the King's County Lunatic Asylum in 1870. It is not clear, however, that the insanity of the elder brother was congenital. There is a letter in the Bucke collection written by Jefferson Whitman to Walt attributing Jesse's mental disorder to his own follies.

I was born, and have always lived, in one of the largest of our American cities. The circumstances of my family were easy; I received a good education, was intended by my father for mercantile business, and upon attaining the proper age, obtained from him a small but sufficient capital; and in the course of a few years from thus starting, found myself sailing smoothly on the tide of fortune. I married; and, possessed of independence and domestic comfort, my life was a happy one indeed. Time passed on; we had several children; when about twenty years after our marriage my wife died. It was a grievous blow to me, for I loved her well; and the more so of late, because that a little while before, at short intervals, I had lost both my parents.

Finding myself now at that period of life when ease and retirement are peculiarly soothing, I purchased an elegant house in a fashionable part of the city; where, surrounding myself and my family with every resource that abundance and luxury can afford for happiness, I settled myself for life—a life which seemed to promise every prospect of a long enjoyment. I had my sons and daughters around me; and, objecting to the boarding-school system, I had their education conducted under my own roof, by a private tutor who resided with us. He was a mild, gentlemanly man, with nothing remarkable about his personal appearance, unless his eyes might be called so. They were gray —large, deep, and having a softly beautiful expression that I have never seen in any others; and which, while they at times produced an extraordinary influence upon me, and yet dwell so vividly in my memory, no words that I can use could exactly describe. The name of the tutor was Alban.

Of my children, only two were old enough to be considered anything more than boys and girls. The eldest was my favorite. In countenance he was like the mother, whose first-born he was; and when she died, the mantle of my affections seemed transferred to him, with a sadly undue and unjust degree of preference over the rest. My second son, Luke, was bold, eccentric, and high-tempered. Strange as it may seem, notwithstanding a decided personal resemblance to myself, he never had his father's love. Indeed, it was only by a strong effort that I restrained and concealed a positive aversion. Occasions seemed continually to arise wherein the youth felt disposed to thwart me, and make himself disagreeable to me. Every time I saw him, I was conscious of something evil in his conduct or disposition. I have since thought that a great deal of all this existed only in my own imagination, warped and darkened as it was, and disposed to look upon him with an "evil eye." Be that as it may, I was several times made very angry by what I felt sure were intended to be wilful violations of my rule, and contemptuous taunts toward me for that partiality to his brother which I could not deny. In the course of time, I grew to regard the heedless boy with a feeling almost amounting— I shudder to make the confession—to hatred. Perhaps, for he was very cunning, he saw it, and, conscious that he was wronged, took the only method of revenge that was in his power.

I have said that he was eccentric. The term is hardly strong enough to mark what actually was the case with him. He occasionally had spells which approached very nearly to complete derangement. My family physician spoke learnedly of regimen, and drugs, and courses of treatment which, if carefully persevered in, might remove the peculiarity. He said, too, that cases of that kind were dangerous, frequently terminating in confirmed insanity. But I laughed at him, and told him his fears were idle. Had it been my favorite son instead of Luke, I do not think I would have passed by the matter so contentedly.

Matters stood as I have described them for several years. Alban, the tutor, continued with us; as fast as one [child] grew up, so as to be beyond the need of his instructions, another appeared in the vacant place. The whole family loved him dearly, and I have no doubt he repaid their affection, for he was a gentle-hearted creature, and easily won. Luke and he seemed great friends. I blush now as I acknowledge that this was the only thing by which Alban excited my displeasure.

I shall pass over many circumstances that occurred in my family, having no special relation to the event which, in the present narrative, I have chiefly in view. One of my favorite amusements was afforded by the theatre. I kept a box of my own, and frequently attended, often giving my family permission also to be present. Luke I seldom allowed to go. The excuse that I assigned to myself and to others was, that he was of excitable temperament, and the acting would be injurious to his brain. I fear the privilege was withheld quite as much from vindictiveness toward him, and dislike of his presence on my own part. So Luke himself evidently thought and felt. On a certain evening—(were it last night, my recollection of it all could not be more distinct)—a favorite performer was to appear in a new piece; and it so happened that every one of us had arranged to attend—every one but Luke. He besought me earnestly that he might go with the rest—reminded me how rarely such favors were granted him—and even persuaded Alban to speak to me on the subject.

"Your son," said the tutor, "seems so anxious to partake of this pleasure, and has set his mind so fully upon it, that I really fear, sir, your refusal would excite him more than the sight of the play."

"I have adopted a rule," said I, "and once swerving from it makes no rule at all."

"Mr. Bervance will excuse me," he still continued, "if I yet persevere in asking that you will allow Luke this indulgence, at least for this one evening. I am anxious and disturbed about the boy—and should even consider it as a great personal favor to myself."

"No, sir," I answered, abruptly, "it is useless to continue this conversation. The young man cannot go, either from considerations of his pleasure or yours."

Alban made no reply; he colored, bowed slightly, and I *felt* his eye fixed upon me with an expression I did not at all like, though I could not analyze it. I was conscious, however, that I had said too much; and if the tutor had not at that moment left the room, I am sure I should have apologized for my rudeness.

We all went to the theatre. The curtain had hardly risen, when my attention was attracted by some one in the tier above, and right off against my box, coming noisily in, talking loudly, and stumbling along, apparently on purpose to draw the eyes of the spectators. As he threw himself into the front seat, and the glare of the lamps fell upon his face, I could hardly believe my eyes when I saw it was Luke. A second and a third observation were necessary to convince me. There he sat, indeed. He looked over to where I was seated, and while my sight was riveted upon him in unbounded astonishment, he deliberately rose—raised his hand to his head—lifted his hat, and bowed low and long—a cool, sarcastic smile playing on his features all the time—and finally breaking into an actual laugh, which even reached my ears. Nay—will it be believed!—the foolish youth had even the effrontery to bring down one of the wretched outcasts who are met with there, and seat himself full in our view—he laughing and talking with his companion so much to the annoyance of the house that a police officer was actually obliged to interfere! I felt as [if] I should burst with mortification and anger.

At the conclusion of the tragedy we went home. Reader, I cannot dwell minutely on what followed. At a late hour my rebellious boy returned. Seemingly bent upon irritating me to the utmost, he came with perfect nonchalance into the room where I was seated. The remainder of that night is like a hateful dream in my memory, distinct and terrible, though shadowy. I recollect the sharp, cutting, but perfectly calm rejoinders he made to all my passionate invectives against his conduct. They worked me up to a phrensy, and he smiled all the more calmly the while. Half maddened by my rage, I seized him by the collar, and shook him. My pen almost refuses to add—but justice to myself demands it—the Son felled the Father to the earth with a blow! Some blood even flowed from a slight wound caused by striking my head, as I fell against a projecting corner of furniture—and the hair that it matted together was gray!

What busy devil was it that stepped noiselessly round the bed, to which I immediately retired, and kept whispering in my ears all that endless night? Sleep forsook me. Thoughts of a deep revenge—a fearful redress—but it seemed to me hardly more fearful than the crime—worked within my brain. Then I turned, and tried to rest, but vainly. Some spirit from the abodes of ruin held up the provocation and the punishment continually before my mind's eye. The wretched youth had his strange fits: those fits were so thinly divided from insanity that who should undertake to define the difference? And for insanity was there not a prison provided, with means and appliances, confinement, and, if need be, chains and scourges? For a few months it would be nothing more than wholesome that an unnatural child, a brutal assaulter of his parent, should taste the discipline of such a place. Before my eyes closed, my mind had resolved on the scheme—a scheme so cruel that, as I think of it now, my senses are lost in wonder that any one less than a fiend could have resolved to undertake it.

The destinies of evil favored me. The very next morning Luke had one of his strange turns, brought on, undoubtedly, by the whirl and agitation of the previous day and night. With the smooth look and quiet tread with which I doubt not Judas looked and trod, I went into his room and enjoined the attendants to be very careful of him. I found him more violently affected than at any former period. He did not know me; I felt glad that it was so, for my soul shrank at its own intentions, and I could not have met his conscious eye. At the close of the day, I sent for a physician; not him who generally attended my family, but one of those obsequious gentlemen who bend and are pliant like the divining rod, that is said to be attracted by money. I sent, too, for some of the officers of the lunatic asylum. Two long hours we were in conversation. I was sorry, I told them, very sorry; it was a dreadful grief to me; the gentlemen could not but sympathize in my distress; but I felt myself called upon to yield my private feelings. I felt it best for my unhappy son to be, for a time at least, removed to the customary place for those laboring under his miserable disease. I will not say what other measures I took—what *tears* I shed. Oh, to what a depth may that man be sunk who once gives bad passions their swing! The next day, Luke was taken from my dwelling to the asylum, and confined in what was more like a dungeon than a room for one used to all the luxurious comforts of life.

Days rolled on. I do not think any one suspected aught of what really was the case. Evident as it had been that Luke was not a favorite of mine, no person ever thought it possible that a father could place his son in a mad-house from motives of any other description than a desire to have him cured. The children were very much hurt at their brother's unfortunate situation. Alban said nothing; but I knew that he sorrowed in secret. He frequently sought, sometimes with success, to obtain entrance to Luke; and after a while began to bring me favorable reports of the young man's recovery. One day, about three weeks after the event at the theatre, the tutor came to me with great satisfaction on his countenance. He had just returned from Luke, who was now as sane as ever. Alban said he could hardly get away from the young man, who conjured him to remain, for solitude there was a world of terror and agony. Luke had besought him, with tears streaming down his cheeks, to ask me to let him be taken from that place. A few days longer residence there, he said, a conscious witness of its horrors, and he should indeed be its fit inmate for ever.

The next morning I sent private instructions to the asylum, to admit no person in Luke's apartment without an order from me. Alban was naturally very much surprised, as day after day elapsed and I took no measures to have my son brought home. Perhaps, at last, he began to suspect the truth; for in one of the interviews we had on the subject those mild and beautiful eyes of his caused mine to sink before them, and he expressed a determination, dictated as he said by an imperious duty, in case I did not see fit to liberate the youth, to take some decided steps himself. I talked as smoothly and as sorrowfully as possible—but it was useless.

"My young friend, I am sure," said he, "has received all the benefits he can possibly derive from the institution, and I do not hesitate to say, any longer continuance there may be followed by dangerous—even fatal—consequences. I cannot but think," and the steadfast look of that gray eye settled *at* me, as if it would pierce my inmost soul, "that Mr. Bervance desires to see his unlucky child away from so fearful an abode; and I have no doubt that I shall have his approval in any proper and necessary measures for that purpose."

I cursed him in my heart, but I felt that I had to submit. So I told him that if in two days more Luke did not have any relapse, I would then consider it safe to allow him to be brought home.

The swift time flew and brought the evening of the next day. I was alone in the house, all the family having gone to a concert, which I declined attending, for music was not then suited to my mood. The young people stayed later than I had expected; I walked the floor till I was tired, and then sat down on a chair. It was a parlor at the back of the house, with long, low windows opening into the garden. There and then, in the silence of the place, I thought for the first time of the full extent of the guilt I had lately been committing. It pressed upon me, and I could not hide from my eyes its dread enormity. But it became too painful, and I rose, all melted with agonized yet tender emotions, and determined to love my injured boy from that hour as Father should love Son. In the act of rising, my eyes were involuntarily cast toward a large mirror, on the chimney-piece. Was it a reflection of my own conscience, or a horrid reality? My blood curdled as I saw there an image of the form of my son—my cruelly treated Luke—but oh, how ghastly, how deathly a picture! I turned, and there was the original of the semblance. Just inside one of the windows stood the form, the pallid, unwashed, tangly-haired, rag-covered form, of Luke Bervance. And that look of his—there was no deception there—it was the vacant, glaring, wild look of a *maniac*.

"Ho, ho!"

As I listened, I could hardly support myself, for uncontrollable horror.

"My son, do you not know me? I am your father," I gasped.

"You are Flint Serpent. Do you know *me*, Flint? A little owl screeched in my ear, as I came through the garden, and said you would be glad to see me, and then laughed a hooting laugh. Speak low," he continued in a whisper: "big eyes and bony hands are out there, and they would take me back again. But you will strike at them, Flint, and scatter them, will you not? Sting them with poison; and when they try to seize me knock them down with your heart, will you not?"

"Oh, Christ! what a sight is this!" burst from me, as I sank back into the chair from which I had risen, faint with agony. The lunatic started as I spoke, and probably something like a recollection lighted up his brain for a moment. He cast a fierce glance at me.

"Do you like it?" he said, with a grim smile; "it is of your own doing. You placed me in a mad house. I was not mad; but when I woke, and breathed *that* air, and heard the sounds, and saw what is to be seen *there*—Oh, now I am mad! Curse you! it is your work. Curse you! Curse you!"

I clapped my hands to my ears, to keep out the appalling sounds that seemed to freeze my very blood. When I took them away, I heard the noise of the street door opening, and my children's voices sounding loud and happily. Their maniac brother heard them also. He sprang to the window.

"Hark!" he said; "they are after me, Flint. Keep them back. Rather than go there again, I would jump into a raging furnace of fire!" He glided swiftly into the garden, and I heard his voice in the distance. I did not move, for every nerve seemed paralyzed.

"Keep them back, Flint! It is all your work! Curse you!"

When my family came into the apartment, they found me in a deep swound, which I fully recovered from only at the end of many minutes.

My incoherent story, the night, and the strangeness of the whole affair, prevented any pursuit that evening, though Alban would have started on one if he had had any assistance or

clue. The next morning, the officers of the asylum came in
search of the runaway. He had contrived a most cunning plan
of escape, and his departure was not found out till daylight.

My story is nearly ended. We never saw or heard of the
hapless Luke more. Search was extensively made, and kept
up for a long time; but no tidings were elicited of his fate.
Alban was the most persevering of those who continued the task,
even when it became hopeless. He inserted advertisements in
the newspapers, sent emissaries all over the country, had hand-
bills widely distributed, offering a large reward; but all to no
purpose. The doom, whatever it was, of the wretched young
man is shrouded in a mantle of uncertainty as black as a veil of
the outer darkness in which his form had disappeared on that
last memorable night; and in all likelihood it will now never be
known to mortals.

A great many years have gone by since these events. To
the eyes of men, my life and feelings have seemed in no respect
different from those of thousands of others. I have mixed with
company—laughed and talked—eaten and drunk; and, now
that the allotted term is closing, must prepare to lay myself in
the grave. I say I have lived many years since then, and have
laughed and talked. Let no one suppose, however, that time
has banished the phantoms of my busy thoughts and allowed
me to be happy. Down in the inward chamber of my soul
there has been a mirror—large, and very bright. It has pic-
tured, for the last thirty years, a shape, wild and haggard, and
with tangly hair—the shape of my maniac son. Often, in the
midst of society, in the public street, at my own table, and in
the silent watches of the night, that picture stands out in
glaring brightness; and, without a tongue, tells me that it is
all my work, and repeats that terrible cursing which, the last
time the tyrant and victim stood face to face together, rang
from the lips of the Son, and fell like a knell of death on the
ear of the Father.

THE TOMB–BLOSSOMS[1]

A PLEASANT, fair-sized country village—a village embosomed
in trees, with old churches, *one* tavern, kept by a respectable

[1]From the *Democratic Review*, January, 1842, Vol. X, pp. 62–68. Reprinted in
James J. Brenton's "Voices from the Press," 1850, and, with illustrations, in a Phila-
delphia paper, probably in 1892.

widow, long, single-storied farm-houses, their roofs mossy, and their chimneys smoke-blacked—a village with much grass, and shrubbery, and no mortar nor bricks, nor pavements, nor gas—no *newness:* that is the place for him who wishes life in its flavor and its bloom. Until of late, my residence has been in such a place.

Men of cities! what is there in all your boast of pleasure—your fashions, parties, balls, and theatres—compared to the simplest of the delights we country folk enjoy?[1] Our pure air, making the blood swell and leap with buoyant health; our labor and our exercise; our freedom from the sickly vices that taint the town; our not being racked with notes due, or the fluctuations of prices, or the breaking of banks; our manners of sociality, expanding the heart and reacting with a wholesome effect on the body;—can anything which citizens possess balance these?

One Saturday, after paying a few days' visit at New York, I returned to my quarters in the country inn. The day was hot, and my journey a disagreeable one. I had been forced to stir myself beyond comfort, and dispatch my affairs quickly, for fear of being left by the cars. As it was, I arrived panting and covered with sweat, just as they were about to start. Then for many miles I had to bear the annoyance of the steam-engine smoke; and it seemed to me that the vehicles kept swaying to and fro on the track, with a more than usual motion, on purpose to distress my jaded limbs. Out of humor with myself and everything around me when I came to my travel's end, I refused to partake of the comfortable supper which my landlady had prepared for me; and rejoining to the good woman's look of wonder at such an unwonted event, and her kind inquiries about my health, with a sullen silence, I took my lamp, and went my way to my room. Tired and head-throbbing, in less than half a score of minutes after I threw myself on my bed I was steeped in the soundest slumber.

When I awoke, every vein and nerve felt fresh and free. Soreness and irritation had been swept away, as it were, with the curtains of night; and the accustomed tone had returned again. I arose and threw open my window. Delicious! It was a calm, bright Sabbath morning in May. The dew-drops

---

[1] This phrasing, taken with the sentiment expressed in "Young Grimes," *infra,* pp. 3–4, may indicate that the sketch was originally written while Whitman was living on the Island.

glittered on the grass; the fragrance of the apple-blossoms which covered the trees floated up to me; and the notes of a hundred birds discoursed music to my ear. By the rays just shooting up in the eastern verge, I knew that the sun would be risen in a moment. I hastily dressed myself, performed my ablutions, and sallied forth to take a morning walk.

Sweet, yet sleepy scene! No one seemed stirring. The placid influence of the day was even now spread around, quieting everything, and hallowing everything. I sauntered slowly onward, with my hands folded behind me. I passed round the edge of the hill, on the rising elevation and top of which was a burial-ground. On my left, through an opening in the trees, I could see at some distance the ripples of our beautiful bay; on my right, was the large and ancient field for the dead. I stopped and leaned my back against the fence, with my face turned toward the white marble stones a few rods before me. All I saw was far from new to me; and yet I pondered upon it. The entrance to that place of tombs was a kind of arch—a rough-hewn but no doubt hardy piece of architecture that had stood, winter and summer, over the gate there, for many, many years. O fearful arch! if there were for thee a voice to utter what has passed beneath and near thee; if the secrets of the earthy dwelling that to thee are known could be by thee disclosed—whose ear might listen to the appalling story and its possessor not go mad with terror!

Thus thought I; and, strangely enough, such imagining marred not in the least the sunny brightness which spread alike over my mind and over the landscape. Involuntarily, as I mused, my look was cast to the top of the hill. I saw a figure moving. Could someone beside myself be out so early, and among the tombs? What creature odd enough in fancy to find pleasure there, and at such a time? Continuing my gaze, I saw that the figure was a woman. She seemed to move with a slow and feeble step, passing and repassing constantly between two and the same graves, which were within half a rod of each other. She would bend down and appear to busy herself a few moments with the one; then she would rise and go to the second, and bend there and employ herself as at the first. Then to the former one, and then to the second again. Occasionally the figure would pause a moment, and stand back a little, and look steadfastly down upon the graves, as if to see whether her work were done well. Thrice I saw her walk with a tottering gait, and stand midway between the two, and look alternately at each. Then she would go to one and arrange something, and come back to the midway place, and gaze first on the right and then on the left, as before. The figure evidently had some trouble in suiting things to her mind. Where I stood, I could hear no noise of her footfalls; nor could I see accurately enough to tell what she was doing. Had a superstitious man beheld the spectacle, he would possibly have thought that some spirit of the dead, allowed the night before to burst its cerements and wander forth in the darkness, had been belated in returning, and was now perplexed to find its coffin-house again.

Curious to know what was the woman's employment, I undid the simple fastenings of the gate, and walked over the rank wet grass toward her. As I came near, I recognized her for an old, a very old inmate of the poor-house, named Delaree. Stopping a moment, while I was yet several yards from her and before she saw me, I tried to call to recollection certain particulars of her history which I had heard a great while past. She was a native of one of the West India islands, and, before I who gazed at her was born, had with her husband come hither, to settle and gain a livelihood. They were poor; most miserably poor. Country people, I have noticed, seldom like foreigners. So this man and his wife, in all probability, met much to discourage them. They kept up their spirits, however, until at last their fortunes became desperate. Famine and want laid iron fingers upon them. They had no acquaintance; and to beg they were ashamed.[1] Both were taken ill; then the charity that had been so slack came to their destitute abode, but came too late. Delaree died, the victim of poverty. The woman recovered after a while; for but many months was quite an invalid, and was sent to the alms-house, where she had ever since remained.

This was the story of the aged creature before me, aged with the weight of seventy winters. I walked up to her. By her feet stood a large rude basket, in which I beheld leaves and buds. The two graves which I had seen her passing between so often were covered with flowers—the earliest but sweetest flowers of the season. They were fresh, and wet, and very fragrant—those delicate soul-offerings. And this, then, was her employment. Strange! Flowers, frail and passing, grasped

---

[1] *Cf.* "Luke," xvi: 3.

by the hand of age, and scattered upon a tomb! White hairs, and pale blossoms, and stone tablets of Death!

"Good morning, mistress," said I, quietly.

The withered female turned her eyes to mine, and acknowledged my greeting in the same spirit wherewith it was given.

"May I ask whose graves they are that you remember so kindly?"

She looked up again, probably catching from my manner that I spoke in no spirit of rude inquisitiveness, and answered,

"My husband's."

A manifestation of a fanciful taste, thought I, this tomb-ornamenting, which she probably brought with her from abroad. Of course, but one of the graves could be her husband's; and one, likely, was that of a child, who had died and been laid away by its father.

"Who else?" I asked.

"My husband's," replied the aged widow.

Poor creature! her faculties were becoming dim. No doubt her sorrows and her length of life had worn both mind and body nearly to the parting.

"Yes, I know," continued I, mildly; "but there are two graves. One is your husband's, and the other is——"

I paused for her to fill the blank.

She looked at me a minute, as if in wonder at my perverseness, and then answered as before,

"My husband's. None but my Gilbert's."

"And is Gilbert buried in both?" said I.

She appeared as if going to answer, but stopped again and did not. Though my curiosity was now somewhat excited, I forebore to question her further, feeling that it might be to her a painful subject. I was wrong, however. She had been rather agitated at my intrusion, and her powers flickered for a moment. They were soon steady again; and, perhaps gratified with my interest in her affairs, she gave in a few brief sentences the solution of the mystery. When her husband's death occurred, she was herself confined to a sick bed, which she did not leave for a long while after he was buried. Still longer days passed before she had permission, or even strength, to go into the open air. When she did, her first efforts were essayed to reach Gilbert's grave. What a pang sunk to her heart when she found it could not be pointed out to her! With the careless indifference which is shown to the corpses of outcasts, poor

Delaree had been thrown into a hastily dug hole, without any one noting it, or remembering which it was. Subsequently, several other paupers were buried in the same spot, and the sexton could only show two graves to the disconsolate woman, and tell her that her husband's was positively one of the twain. During the latter stages of her recovery, she had looked forward to the consolation of coming to his tomb as to a shrine, and wiping her tears there; and it was bitter that such could not be. The miserable widow even attempted to obtain the consent of the proper functionaries that the graves might be opened, and her anxieties put at rest! When told that this could not be done, she determined in her soul that at least the remnant of her hopes and intentions should not be given up. Every Sunday morning, in the mild seasons, she went forth early, and gathered fresh flowers, and dressed *both* the graves. So she knew that the right one was cared for, even if another shared that care. And lest she should possibly bestow the most of this testimony of love on him whom she knew not, but whose spirit might be looking down invisibly in the air, and smiling upon her, she was ever careful to have each tomb adorned in exactly similar manner. In a strange land, and among a strange race, she said, it was like communion with her own people to visit that burial-mound.

"If I could only know which to bend over when my heart feels heavy," thus finished the sorrowing being as she rose to depart, "then it would be a happiness. But perhaps I am blind to my dearest mercies. God in his great wisdom may have sent that I should not know which grave was his, lest grief over it should become too common a luxury with me, and melt me away."

I offered to accompany her, and support her feeble steps; but she preferred that it should not be so. With languid feet she moved on. I watched her pass through the gate and under the arch; I saw her turn, and in a little while she was hidden from my view. Then I carefully parted the flowers upon one of the graves, and sat down there, and leaned my face in my hands and thought.

What a wondrous thing is woman's love! Oh Thou whose most mighty attribute is the Incarnation of Love, I bless Thee that Thou didst make this fair disposition in the human heart, and didst root it there so deeply that it is stronger than all else, and can never be torn out! Here is this aged wayfarer, a woman of trials and griefs, decrepid, sore, and steeped in poverty; the most forlorn of her kind; and yet, through all the storm of misfortune, and the dark cloud of years settling upon her, the Memory of her Love hovers like a beautiful spirit amid the gloom, and never deserts her, but abides with her while life abides.   Yes; *this* creature loved; this wrinkled, skinny, gray-haired crone had her heart to swell with passion, and her pulses to throb, and her eyes to sparkle.   Now, nothing remains but a Loving Remembrance, coming as of old, and stepping in its accustomed path, not to perform its former object, or former duty—but from long habit.   *Nothing* but that!—Ah! is not that a great deal?

And the buried man—he was happy to have passed away as he did.   The woman—she was the one to be pitied.   Without doubt she wished many times that she were laid beside him. And not only she, thought I, as I cast my eyes on the solemn memorials around me; but at the same time there were thousands else on earth who panted for the Long Repose, as a tired child for the night.[1]   The grave—the grave—what foolish man calls it a dreadful place?   It is a kind friend, whose arms shall compass us round about, and while we lay our heads upon his bosom, no care, temptation, nor corroding passion shall have power to disturb us.   Then the weary spirit shall no more be weary; the aching head and aching heart will be strangers to pain; and the soul that has fretted and sorrowed away its little life on earth will sorrow not any more.   When the mind has been roaming abroad in the crowd, and returns sick and tired of hollow hearts, and of human deceit—let us think of the grave and of death, and they will seem like soft and pleasant music. Such thoughts then soothe and calm our pulses; they open a peaceful prospect before us.   I do not dread the grave.   There is many a time when I could lay down and pass my immortal part through the valley of the shadow as composedly as I quaff water after a tiresome walk.   For what is there of terror in taking our rest?   What is there here below to draw us with such fondness?   Life is the running of a race—a most weary race, sometimes.   Shall we fear the goal, merely because it is shrouded in a cloud?

I rose, and carefully replaced the parted flowers, and bent my steps homeward.

If there be any sufficiently interested in the fate of the aged

[1] *Cf. infra*, p. 11, and other juvenile verse of the "graveyard" type.

woman, that they wish to know further about her, for those I will add that ere long her affection was transferred to a Region where it might receive the reward of its constancy and purity. Her last desire—and it was complied with—was that she should be placed midway between the two graves.

BOZ AND DEMOCRACY[1]

Is IT not your fortune, reader, occasionally, in your path through life, to meet with one whose custom it is to look alway upon the dark points of a picture—to seek out faults, and where they do not really exist, to fancy them—whose disposition is sour and whose soul seems anxious to condemn all that other people praise? A man of this description is to cheerfulness and soul-confidence what a cloud is to the sun. Malignant and envious, he would rob a patriot of his countrymen's love—a saint of his reverence—a glorious writer of his well-deserved fame.

The Washington *Globe* discourseth after the following manner:

If to delineate the human character in its lowest stage of ignorance, vice and degradation, and give it the most unbounded scope in every species of wickedness and crime, is to be a Democratic writer, then most assuredly Mr. Dickens is emphatically one. He has exhibited human nature in its naked, ragged deformity, reeking with vice and pollution; as ignorant as wicked, and absolutely below the standard of the very beasts of the field. He has made his exhibitions of human character more disgusting and abhorrent, by a degree of brutal ignor-ance and stupendous depravity, which constitute, in their combination, a spectacle so absolutely and exclusively hateful, as to absorb all con-sideration of the means by which this miserable desecration of human-ity was produced, and all sympathy for the brutes who to us, as it were, misrepresent their fellow creatures. Incidentally, these spectacles may connect themselves in our minds, with the means by which this extrem-ity of vice and ignorance was produced, but the overwhelming feeling is that of disgust and abhorrence. There are physical diseases so re-volting to the senses as to convert pity into sickening disgust, and there is a degree of moral corruption and wickedness which annihilates all sympathy.

[1] From *Brother Jonathan*, February 26, 1842. Dickens was at the time being fêted in New York.

The editor of the *Brother Jonathan*, in referring to this communication, declares that it "bears the initials of as true and honest a democrat as the editor of the *Globe*, or any of the correspondents of that paper."

To call this the literature of Democracy is to make Democracy as brutal as this gentleman has been pleased to represent it in his native country. It may suit there, where it has perhaps its prototypes, so numerous as to constitute a class, but it does not actually belong to the United States, nor is it applicable to the state of society in this country. Such a school of literature can only aid the course and progress of vice among us, by placing before the already degraded, examples of new modes of wickedness, with which they were hitherto unacquainted, and degrees of degradation of which they never had any perception, until they became so conspicuous in the polite and fashionable literature of the day. The extraordinary cheapness with which these works have been got up among us, and the allurements they present in a series of embellishments with the grossness of the scenes they are intended to illustrate, have given them a general circulation among those classes most likely to overlook the latent imperceptible moral, if any such exists, and to concentrate their attention on those broad caricatures of wickedness, which are too often represented by the author in combination with ludicrous circumstances, admirably calculated to make those who have no very distinct notions of right and wrong, consider the whole an excellent joke, worthy of all imitation.

I cannot, for my part, comprehend how a writer can be fairly entitled to the credit of being the champion of that class of mankind which he pictures in colors so revolting to our feelings and sympathies; nor by what process of induction this intimate association with this perpetual contemplation with all the varieties of extreme degradation coupled with a boundless latitude of crime, can be converted into a school of morals. If this is indeed the tendency of such contemplations and associations, let us send our children to bridewells and penitentiaries for their education, and to the quarter sessions for lessons of morality. Indeed it seems to me that Mr. Dickens' moral writings are very much on a par with Le Boeuf's great moral picture of Adam and Eve, in the moment of being tempted by the serpent. They were represented as large as life, perfectly naked, the female in the attitude of a lascivious courtesan, tempting a bashful youth; and if the artist had not fortunately bethought himself of calling it a great moral picture, no decent female would have dared to visit its exhibition. At this rate, I should not be at all surprised at seeing some strenuous amateur writing a criticism to prove the displays of Fanny Elssler[1] a great moral spectacle.

The above is evidently the offering of no unpracticed hand. I wish I could speak as favorably of the author's appreciation of merit, and of his candor and judgment.

A "democratic writer," I take it, is one the tendency of whose pages is to destroy those old land-marks which pride and fashion

·A German *danseuse* (1810–1884).

have set up, making impassable distinctions between the brethren of the Great Family[1]—to render in their deformity before us the tyranny of partial laws—to show us the practical workings of the thousand distortions engrafted by custom upon our notions of what justice is—to make us love our fellow-creatures, and own that although social distinctions place others far higher or far lower than we, yet are human beings alike, as links of the same chain; one whose lines are imbued, from preface to finis, with that philosophy which teaches to pull down the high and bring up the low.   I consider Mr. Dickens to be a democratic writer.

The mere fact of a man's delineating human character in its lowest stages of degradation, and giving it unbounded scope in every species of wickedness, proves neither his "democracy" nor its opposite.   If it be done in such a way as that a kind of charm is thrown all the time around the guilty personage described—in such a way that excuses and palliations for his vice are covertly conveyed, every now and then—such writings, most assuredly, would have no fair claim to rank among "the literature of democracy."   But when these specimens of naked, ragged deformity, as ignorant as wicked, are drawn out before us, and surrounded with their fit accompaniments, filth and darkness, and the deepest discomfort—when crime is portrayed, never so that by any possibility the reader can find the slightest temptation to go and do likewise—when we see how evil doing is followed by its sure and long and weary punishment—when our minds are led to the irresistible conclusion that iniquity is loathsome, and by the magic of the pen-painter have its pictures so stamped upon them that we ever after associate depraved actions with lowness and the very vulgarity of pollution—in such case, I say, the delineations of life in its lowest aspect, and even characterized by grossest ignorance and brutality, do not militate against their author's claim for admiration from all true democrats.   And, then, the effect of the contrast which Mr. Dickens seems fond of forcing us to make between these wicked ones and the beings of purity and truth whom he also draws with a master hand!   How he brings these characters together, and places them side by side, and makes them play into each other's hands, as it were, for the purpose of bringing out their distinctive traits!   He not only teaches his readers to abhor vice, but he exhibits before them, for imitation, examples

[1] *Cf. infra*, pp. 46-48.

of the beauty of honesty—not as in the abstract style of the essayist, or the lofty dreams of the poet—but by examples that everyone can copy, examples in familiar life, that come home to us all. Who is not in love with truth when he follows, through trouble, poverty, and temptation, a little child that never swerves, but in its simplicity conducts itself as though there were no such thing as falsehood? What impropriety is there in the process of induction which calls that a school of morals where the pupil sees mapped out before him the parish boy's progress through sin and ignorance—resisting the tempter when yielding would have procured ease—steadily holding to the truth at all risks—living like an angel of light amid spirits of darkness—never giving up, though often his prospects seemed desperate—and being rewarded, at last, with prosperity?

The writer in the *Globe* thinks that the spectacles of misery pictured in the Boz novels constitute a combination so exclusively hateful as to absorb all consideration of the means which produce them, and all sympathy for the performers themselves. Did not the writer in the *Globe*, when he read the graphically drawn and deeply colored picture of the life led by Oliver Twist and his mates in the poor house, and of all the transactions there, and of the conduct of those who had to do with the institution—did he not have some reflections upon the evils of such a state of society as led to the existence of these things? When he read of Squeers and Do-the-boys hall, did he not entertain the most distant idea of how such a boarding-school system, if prevalent, might be rooted out, by thus showing it up?

The critic in the *Globe* compares Mr. Dickens' portraitures to the exhibition of those physical diseases so revolting to the senses as to create nothing but horror and sickening disgust. I suppose that in order to please our critic, a writer must speak mincingly, and with much delicacy lest he should introduce a vigorous turn or idea, which would offend him for its grossness. I fear me he is too dainty. Such exquisite sensitiveness—such affectation of being overcome by the strength of description in the novelist—such refined horror at some fancied overstepping of the limits wherein an author should confine himself, if he aspires to please the polite taste—bespeak the literary fop much more than they mark a man really fit to measure the length and breadth of that genius he so maligns. Besides, Mr. Dickens makes a sparing use of these strong features. The criticism in the *Globe* seems imbued throughout with the notion that the

Boz works tell of nothing but the horrible and the awful—of desperate crime, and sensual vice. Surely it is not so. Boz is not altogether a feeder upon Newgate Calendars, and Police Reports, and whatever else reflects from the mind of him who looks thereon a sombre and a sorrowful hue. Pickwick,[1] and the Wellers,[1] and the Fat Boy,[1] forbid! Dick Swiveller[2] and the Marchioness[2]—Kit,[2] and pony—Miggs[3] and Joe Willett,[3] condemn the imputation. And thy sweet face, Kate Nickleby,[4] and thy Christian nature, Cheeryble brothers[4]—and thou, poor Nell[2]—and thou, G. Varden[3]—repel the slander!

The familiarity with low life wherein Mr. Dickens places his readers is a wholesome familiarity. For those moving in a kindred sphere it is wholesome, because it holds out to them continually the spectacle of beings of their own grade, engaged either in worthy actions which are held up to emulation, and shown to be rewarded both in themselves and in their results—or engaged in avocations of guilt which in themselves and their results are fearful, and only to be thought of with shuddering. For the richer classes this familiarity is wholesome because they are taught to feel, in fancy, what poverty is, and what thousands of fellow-creatures, as good as they, toil on year after year, amid discouragements and evils, whose bare relation is enough to make the hearer heart-sick. The rich cannot taste the distresses of want from their own experience; it is something if they are made to do so through the power of the pen.

He cannot comprehend, this critic tells us, how a writer can be called the champion of that class of mankind which he pictures in colors so revolting. A good parent or teacher sometimes has to lay before those whom he would reform the strong, naked, hideous truth. But Mr. Dickens never maligns the poor. He puts the searing iron to wickedness, whether among poor or rich; and yet when he describes the guily, poor and oppressed man, we are always in some way reminded how much need there is that certain systems of law and habit which lead to this poverty and consequent crime should be remedied.

I would say more, but my limits prevent me. I cannot,

---

[1] Characters in the "Pickwick Papers," 1836.

[2] Characters in "The Old Curiosity Shop," 1840–41.

[3] Characters in "Barnaby Rudge," 1841.

[4] Characters in "Nicholas Nickleby," 1839.

It would appear from the above list that Whitman had devoured Dickens's novels as fast as they came from the press, for he alludes to all that had been published in 1842, the date of "Boz and Democracy."

however, close this paper without alluding once more, as in the beginning of the article, to those men who are always prone to carping and detraction. Mr. Dickens' charming manners, his modesty, his freedom from haughtiness, his *lovable* nature, his pleasant tenor of mind, as displayed in his personal conduct —might, it would seem, have saved him from those snappish and sour flings which some of the third-rate editorial fry are indulging in toward him. There are men among us with that unfortunate disposition—unfortunate as well for themselves as for those who have any intercourse with them—which picks out by preference every chance to snarl, and bite, and find fault. Honor paid to a fellow-creature is hateful to them: they turn pale with envy and malignance.

As I think that my humble lance, wielded in defense of Mr. Dickens, may meet the sight of that gentleman himself, I cannot lose the opportunity of saying how much I love and esteem him for what he has taught me through his writings—and for the genial influence that these writings spread around them wherever they go. Never having seen Boz in the body, we have yet had many a tête-à-tête. And I cannot tamely hear one whom I have long considered as a personal friend, and as a friend to his species, thus falsely and uncharitably and groundlessly attacked.

THE LAST OF THE SACRED ARMY[1]

THE memory of the WARRIORS OF OUR FREEDOM!— let us guard it with holy care. Let the mighty pulse which throbs responsive in a nation's heart at utterance of that nation's names of glory never lie languid when their deeds are told or their example cited. To him of the Calm Gray Eye,[2] selected by the Leader of the Ranks of Heaven as the instrument for a people's redemption;—to him, the bright and brave, who fell in the attack at Breed's;[3]—to him, the nimble-footed soldier of the swamps of Santee;[4]—to the young stranger from the luxuries of his native France;[5]—to all who fought in that long weary fight for

[1] From the *Democratic Review*, March, 1842, Vol. X, pp. 259–264.
[2] General George Washington.
[3] Major General Joseph Warren.
[4] Francis Marion.
[5] The Marquis de Lafayette.

disenthralment from arbitrary rule—may our star fade, and our good angel smile upon us no more, if we fail to chamber them in our hearts, or forget the method of their dear-won honor!

For the fame of these is not as the fame of common heroes. The mere gaining of battles—the chasing away of an opposing force—wielding the great energies of bodies of military—rising proudly amid the smoke and din of the fight—and marching the haughty march of a conqueror—all this, spirit-stirring as it may be to the world, would fail to command the applause of the just and discriminating. But such is not the base whereon American warriors found their title to renown. *Our* storied names are those of the Soldiers of Liberty; hardy souls, encased in hardy bodies—untainted with the effeminacy of voluptuous cities, patient, enduring much for principle's sake, and wending on through *blood, disease,* destitution, and prospects of gloom to attain the Great Treasure.

Years have passed; the sword-clash and the thundering of the guns have died away; and all personal knowledge of those events—of the fierce incentives to hate, and the wounds, and scorn, and the curses from the injured, and wailings from the prisoners—lives now but in the memory of a few score of gray-haired men; whose number is, season after season, made thinner and thinner by death. Haply, long, long will be the period ere our beloved country shall witness the presence of such or similar scenes again. Haply, too, the time is arriving when War, with all its train of sanguinary horrors, will be a discarded custom among the nations of earth. A newer and better philosophy—teaching how evil it is to hew down and slay ranks of fellow-men, because of some disagreement between their respective rulers—is melting away old prejudices upon this subject, as warmth in spring melts the frigid ground.

The lover of his race—did he not, looking abroad in the world, see millions whose swelling hearts are all crushed into the dust beneath the iron heel of oppression; did he not behold how kingcraft and priestcraft stalk abroad over fair portions of the globe, and forge the chain, and rivet the yoke; and did he not feel that it were better to live in one flaming atmosphere of carnage than slavishly thus—would offer up nightly prayers that this new philosophy might prevail to the utmost, and the reign of peace never more be disturbed among mankind.

On one of the anniversaries of our national independence, I was staying at the house of an old farmer, about a mile from a thriving country town, whose inhabitants were keeping up the spirit of the occasion with great fervor. The old man himself was a thumping patriot. Early in the morning, my slumbers had been broken by the sharp crack of his ancient musket, (I looked upon that musket with reverence, for it had seen service in *the* war), firing salutes in honor of the day. I am free to confess, my military propensities were far from strong enough (appropriate as they might have been considered at such a time) to suppress certain peevish exclamations toward the disturber of my sweet repose. In the course of the forenoon, I attended the ceremonials observed in the village; sat, during the usual patriotic address, on the same bench with a time-worn veteran that had fought in the contest now commemorated; witnessed the evolutions of the uniform company; and returned home with a most excellent appetite for my dinner.

The afternoon was warm and drowsy. I ensconced myself in my easy-chair, near an open window; feeling in that most blissful state of semi-somnolency, which it is now and then, though rarely, given to mortals to enjoy. I was alone, the family of my host having gone on some visit to a neighbor. The bees hummed in the garden, and among the flowers that clustered over the window frame; a sleepy influence seemed to imbue everything around; occasionally the faint sound of some random gunfire from the village would float along, or the just perceptible music from the band, or the tra-a-a-ra- of a locust. But these were far from being jars to the quiet spirit I have mentioned.

Insensibly, my consciousness became less and less distinct; my head leaned back; my eyes closed; and my senses relaxed from their waking vigilance. I slept.

. . . How strange a chaos is sometimes the outset to a dream![1]—There was the pulpit of the rude church, the scene of the oration—and in it a grotesque form whom I had noticed as the drummer in the band, beating away as though calling scattered forces to the rescue. Then the speaker of the day pitched coppers with some unshorn hostler boys; and the grave personage who had opened the services with prayer was half stripped and running a foot-race with a tavern loafer. The places and the persons familiar to my morning excursion about the country town appeared as in life, but in situations all fantastic and out of the way.

[1] *Cf. post*, II, pp. 200-204.

After a while, what I beheld began to reduce itself to more method. With the singular characteristic of dreams, I knew— I could not tell how—that thirty years elapsed from the then time, and I was among a new generation. Beings by me never seen before, and some with shrivelled forms, bearing an odd resemblance to men whom I had known in the bloom of manhood, met my eyes.

Methought I stood in a splendid city. It seemed a gala day. Crowds of people were swiftly wending along the streets and walks, as if to behold some great spectacle or famous leader.

"Whither do the people go?" said I to a Shape who passed me, hurrying on with the rest.

"Know you not," answered he, "that the Last of the Sacred Army may be seen to-day?"

And he hastened forward, apparently fearful lest he might be late.

Among the dense ranks I noticed many women, some of them with infants in their arms. Then there were boys, beautiful creatures, struggling on, with a more intense desire even than the men. And as I looked up, I saw at some distance, coming toward the place where I stood, a troop of young females, the foremost one bearing a wreath of fresh flowers. The crowd pulled and pushed so violently that this party of girls were sundered one from another, and she who carried the wreath being jostled, her flowers were trampled to the ground.

"O, hapless me!" cried the child; and she began to weep.

At that moment her companions came up; and they looked frowningly when they saw the wreath torn.

"Do not grieve, gentle one," said I to the weeping child. "And you," turning to the others, "blame her not. There bloom more flowers, as fair and fragrant as those which lie rent beneath your feet."

"No," said one of the little troop, "it is now too late."

"What mean you?" I asked.

The children looked at me in wonder.

"For whom did you intend the wreath?" continued I.

"Heard you not," rejoined one of them, "that to-day may be seen the Last of His Witnesses? We were on our way to present this lovely wreath—and she who would give it was to say, that fresh and sweet, like it, would ever be His memory in the souls of us, and of our countrymen."

And the children walked on.

Yielding myself to the sway of the current, which yet continued to flow in one huge human stream, I was carried through street after street, and along many a stately passage, the sides of which were lined by palace-like houses. After a time, we came to a large open square, which seemed to be the destination—for there the people stopped. At the further end of this square stood a magnificent building, evidently intended for public purposes; and in front of it a wide marble elevation, half platform and half porch. Upon this elevation were a great many persons, all of them in standing postures, except one, an aged, very aged man, seated in a throne-like chair. His figure and face showed him to be of a length of life seldom vouchsafed to his kind; and his head was thinly covered with hair of a silvery whiteness.

Now near me stood one whom I knew to be a learned philosopher; and to him I addressed myself for an explanation of these wonderful things.

"Tell me," said I, "who is the ancient being seated on yonder platform."

The person to whom I spoke stared in my face surprisedly.

"Are you of this land," said he, "and have not heard of him—the Last of the Sacred Army?"

"I am ignorant," answered I, "of whom you speak, or of what Army."

The philosopher stared a second time; but soon, when I assured him I was not jesting, he began telling me of former times, and how it came to be that this white-haired remnant of a past age was the object of so much honor. Nor was the story new to me—as may it never be to any son of America.

We edged our way close to the platform. Immediately around the seat of the ancient soldier stood many noble-looking gentlemen, evidently of dignified character and exalted station. As I came near, I heard them mention *a name*—that name which is dearest to our memories as patriots.

"And you saw the Chief with your own eyes?" said one of the gentlemen.

"I did," answered the old warrior.

And the crowd were hushed, and bent reverently, as if in a holy presence.

"I would," said another gentleman, "I would you had some relic which might be as a chain leading from our hearts to his."

"I have such a relic," replied the aged creature; and with

trembling fingers he took from his bosom a rude medal, sus-
pended round his neck by a string. "This the Chief gave me,"
continued he, "to mark his good-will for some slight service I
did the Cause."

"And has it been in *his* hands?"[1] asked the crowd, eagerly.

"Himself hung it around my neck," said the veteran.

Then the mighty mass was hushed again, and there was no
noise—but a straining of fixed eyes, and a throbbing of hearts,
and cheeks pale with excitement—such excitement as might be
caused in a man's soul by some sacred memorial of one he
honored and loved deeply.

Upon the medal were the letters "G. W."

"Speak to us of him, and of his time," said the crowd.

A few words the old man uttered; but few and rambling as
they were, the people listened as to the accents of an orator.

Then it was time for him to stay there no longer. So he
rose, assisted by such of the by-standers whose rank and repu-
tation gave them the right, and slowly descended. The mass
divided, to form a passage for him and his escort, and they
passed forward. And as he passed, the young boys struggled to
him, that they might take his hand, or touch his garments.
The women, too, brought their infants, to be placed for a mo-
ment in his arms; and every head was uncovered.

I noticed that there was little shouting, or clapping of hands—
but a deep-felt sentiment of veneration seemed to pervade them,
far more honorable to its object than the loudest acclamations.

In a short time, as the white-haired ancient was out of sight,
the square was cleared, and I stood in it with no companion but
the philosopher.

"Is it well," said I, "that such reverence be bestowed by a
great people on a creature like themselves? The self-respect
each one has for his own nature might run the risk of effacement
were such things often seen. Besides, it is not allowed that man
pay worship to his fellow."

"Fear not," answered the philosopher; "the occurrences you
have just witnessed spring from the fairest and manliest traits
in the soul. Nothing more becomes a nation than paying its
choicest honors to the memory of those who have fought for
it or labored for its good. By thus often bringing up their ex-
amples before the eyes of the living, others are incited to follow
in the same glorious path. Do not suppose, young man, that it

[1] *Cf. post*, II, pp. 3, 285, 286.

is by sermons and oft-repeated precepts we form a disposition great or good.[1] The model of one pure, upright character, living as a beacon in history, does more benefit than the lumbering tomes of a thousand theorists.

"No: it is well that the benefactors of a state be so kept alive in memory and in song, when their bodies are mouldering. Then will it be impossible for a people to become enslaved; for though the strong arm of their old defender come not as formerly to the battle, his spirit is there, through the power of remembrance, and wields a better sway even than if it were of fleshy substance."

. . . The words of the philosopher sounded indistinctly to my ears—and his features faded, as in a mist. I awoke and looking through the window, saw that the sun had just sunk in the west—two hours having passed away since the commencement of my afternoon slumber.

A LEGEND OF LIFE AND LOVE[2]

A VERY cheerless and fallacious doctrine is that which teaches to deny the yielding to natural feelings, righteously directed, because the consequences may be trouble and grief as well as satisfaction and pleasure. The man who lives on from year to year, jealous of ever placing himself in a situation where the chances can possibly turn against him—ice, as it were, surrounding his heart, and his mind too scrupulously weighing in a balance the results of giving way to any of those propensities his Creator has planted in his heart—may be a philosopher, but can never be a happy man.

Upon the banks of a pleasant river stood a cottage, the residence of an ancient man whose limbs were feeble with the weight of years and of former sorrow. In his appetites easily gratified, like the simple race of people among whom he lived, every want of existence was supplied by a few fertile acres. Those acres were tilled and tended by two brothers, grandsons of the

---

[1] *Cf.* "Logic and sermons never convince."   ("Leaves of Grass," 1917, I, p. 70.)

[2] From the *Democratic Review*, July, 1842, Vol. XI, pp. 83–86.
This unsuccessful attempt to write the Hawthornesque allegorical tale has, perhaps, a secondary significance because of the fact that Whitman's recent return to the city forced upon him just such a decision as he describes in the tale.

old man, and dwellers also in the cottage. The parents of the boys lay buried in a grave near by.

Nathan, the elder, had hardly seen his twentieth summer. He was a beautiful youth. Glossy hair clustered upon his head, and his cheeks were brown from sunshine and open air. Though the eyes of Nathan were soft and limpid, like a girl's, and his cheeks curled with a voluptious swell, exercise and labor had developed his limbs into noble and manly proportions. The bands of hunters, as they met sometimes to start off together after game upon the neighboring hills, could hardly show one among their number who in comeliness, strength, or activity, might compete with the youthful Nathan.

Mark was but a year younger than his brother. He, too, had great beauty.

In course of time the ancient sickened, and knew that he was to die. Before the approach of the fatal hour, he called before him the two youths, and addressed them thus:

"The world, my children, is full of deceit. Evil men swarm in every place; and sorrow and disappointment are the fruits of intercourse with them. So wisdom is wary.

"And as the things of life are only shadows, passing like the darkness of the cloud, twine no bands of love about your hearts. For love is the ficklest of the things of life. The object of our affection dies, and we thenceforth languish in agony; or perhaps the love we covet dies, and that is more painful yet.

"It is well never to confide in any man. It is well to keep aloof from the follies and impurities of earth. Let there be no links between you and others. Let not any being control you through your dependence upon him for a portion of your happiness. This, my sons, I have learned by bitter experience, is the teaching of truth."

Within a few days afterward, the old man was placed away in the marble tomb of his kindred, which was built on a hill by the shore.

Now the injunctions given to Nathan and his brother—injunctions frequently impressed upon them before by the same monitorial voice—were pondered over by each youth in his inmost heart. They had always habitually respected their grandsire: whatever came from his mouth, therefore, seemed as the words of an oracle not to be gainsaid.

Soon the path of Nathan chanced to be sundered from that of Mark.

And the trees leaved out, and then in autumn cast their foliage; and in due course leaved out again, and again, and many times again—and the brothers met not yet.

Two score years and ten! what change works over earth in such a space as two score years and ten!

As the sun, an hour ere his setting, cast long slanting shadows to the eastward, two men, withered, and with hair thin and snowy, came wearily up from opposite directions, and stood together at a tomb built on a hill by the borders of a fair river. Why do they start, as each casts his dim eyes toward the face of the other? Why do tears drop down their cheeks, and their frames tremble even more than with the feebleness of age? They are the long separated brothers, and they enfold themselves in one another's arms.

"And yet," said Mark, after a few moments, stepping back and gazing earnestly upon his companion's form and features, "and yet it wonders me that *thou* art my brother. There should be a brave and beautiful youth, with black curls upon his head, and not those pale emblems of decay. And my brother should be straight and nimble—not bent and tottering as thou."

The speaker cast a second searching glance—a glance of discontent.

"And I," rejoined Nathan, "I might require from *my* brother, not such shrivelled limbs as I see—and instead of that cracked voice the full swelling music of a morning heart—but that half a century is a fearful melter of comeliness and of strength; for half a century it is, dear brother, since my hand touched thine, or my gaze rested upon thy face."

Mark sighed, and answered not.

Then, in a little while, they made inquiries about what had befallen either during the time past. Seated upon the marble by which they had met, Mark briefly told his story.

"I bethink me, brother, many, many years have indeed passed over since the sorrowful days when our grandsire, dying, left us to seek our fortunes amid a wicked and a seductive world.

"His last words, as thou, doubtless, dost remember, advised us against the snares that should beset our subsequent journeyings. He portrayed the dangers which lie in the path of love; he impressed upon our minds the folly of placing confidence in human honor; and warned us to keep aloof from too close communion with our kind. He then died but his instructions lived, and have ever been present in my memory.

"Dear Nathan, why should I conceal from you that at that
time I loved. My simple soul, ungifted with the wisdom of our
aged relative, had yielded to the delicious folly, and the brown-
eyed Eva was my young heart's choice. O brother, even now—
the feeble and withered thing I am—dim recollections, pleasant
passages, come forth around me, like the joy of old dreams. A
boy again, and in the confiding heart of a boy, I walk with Eva
by the river's bank. And the gentle creature blushes at my
protestations of love, and leans her cheek upon my neck. The
regal sun goes down in the west, and we gaze upon the glory of
the clouds that attend his setting, and while we look at their
fantastic changes, a laugh sounds out, clear like a flute, and
merry as the jingling of silver bells. It is the laugh of Eva."

The eye of the old man glistened with unwonted brightness.
He paused, sighed, the brightness faded away, and he went on
with his narration.

"As I said, the dying lessons of him whom we reverenced were
treasured in my soul. I could not but feel their truth. I feared
that if I again stood beside the maiden of my love, and looked
upon her face, and listened to her words, the wholesome axioms
might be blotted from my thoughts, so I determined to act as
became a man: from that hour I never have beheld the brown-
eyed Eva.

"I went amid the world. Acting upon the wise principle
which our aged friend taught us, I looked upon everything
with suspicious eyes. Alas! I found it but too true that iniquity
and deceit are the ruling spirits of men.

"Some called me cold, calculating, and unamiable; but it
was their own unworthiness that made me appear so to their
eyes. I am not—you know, my brother—I am not, naturally,
of proud and repulsive manner; but I was determined never to
give my friendship merely to be blown off again, it might chance
as a feather by the wind; nor interweave my course of life with
those that very likely would draw all the advantage of the con-
nection, and leave me no better than before.

"I engaged in traffic. Success attended me. Enemies said
that my good fortune was the result of chance—but I knew it
the fruit of the judicious system of caution which governed me
in matters of business, as well as of social intercourse.

"My brother, thus have I lived my life. Your look asks me
if I have been happy. Dear brother, truth impells me to say
no. Yet, assuredly, if few glittering pleasures ministered to me

on my journey, equally few were the disappointments, the hopes blighted, the trusts betrayed, the faintings of the soul, caused by the defection of those in whom I have laid up treasures.

"Ah, my brother, the world is full of misery!"

The disciple of a wretched faith ceased his story, and there was silence a while.

Then Nathan spoke:

"In the early years," he said, "I too loved a beautiful woman. Whether my heart was more frail than thine, or affection had gained a mightier power over me, I could not part from her I loved, without the satisfaction of a farewell kiss. We met,— I had resolved to stay but a moment,—for I had chalked out my future life after the fashion [in which] thou hast described thine.

"How it was I know not, but the moments rolled on to hours; and still we stood with our arms around each other.

"My brother, a maiden's tears washed my stern resolves away. The lure of a voice rolling quietly from two soft lips, enticed me from remembrance of my grandsire's wisdom. I forgot his teachings and married the woman I loved.

"Ah! how sweetly sped the seasons! We were blessed. True, there came crossings and evils; but we withstood them all, and holding each other by the hand, forgot that such a thing as sorrow remained in the world.

"Children were born to us—brave boys and fair girls. Oh, Mark, that, *that* is a pleasure—that swelling of tenderness for our offspring—which the rigorous doctrines of your course of life have withheld from you!

"Like you, I engaged in trade. Various fortunes followed my path. I will not deny but that some in whom I thought virtue was strong proved cunning hypocrites and worthy no man's trust. Yet are there many I have known [to be] spotless, as far as humanity may be spotless.

"Thus, to me, life has been alternately dark and fair. Have I lived happy?—No, not completely; it is never for mortals so to be. But I can lay my hand upon my heart and thank the Great Master that the sunshine has been far oftener than the darkness of the clouds.

"Dear brother, the world had misery—but it is a pleasant world still, and affords much joy to the dwellers!"

As Nathan ceased, his brother looked up in his face, like

a man unto whom a simple truth had been for the first time revealed.

THE ANGEL OF TEARS[1]

HIGH, high in space floated the angel Alza. Of the spirits who minister in heaven, Alza is not the chief; neither is he employed in deeds of great import, or in the destinies of worlds and generations. Yet if it were possible for envy to enter among the Creatures Beautiful, many would have pined for the station of Alza. There are a million million invisible eyes which keep constant watch over the earth—each Child of Light having his separate duty. Alza is one of the angels of tears.

Why waited he, as for commands from above?

There was a man upon whose brow rested the stamp of the guilt of Cain. The man had slain his brother. Now he lay in chains awaiting the terrible day when the doom he himself had inflicted should be meted to his own person.

People of the Black Souls!—beings whom the world shrinks from, and whose abode, through the needed severity of the law, is in the dark cell and massy prison—it may not be but that ye have, at times, thoughts of the beauty of virtue, and the blessing of a spotless mind. For if we look abroad in the world, and examine what is to be seen there, we will know, that in every human heart resides a mysterious prompting which leads it to love goodness for its own sake. All that is rational has this prompting. It never dies. It can never be entirely stifled. It may be darkened by the tempests and storms of guilt, but ever and anon the clouds roll away, and it shines out again. Murderers and thieves, and the most abandoned criminals, have been unable to deaden this faculty.

It came to be, that an hour arrived when the heart of the imprisoned fratricide held strange imagining. Old lessons and long forgotten hints, about heaven, and purity, and love, and gentle kindness, floated into his memory—vacillating, as it

---

[1] From the *Democratic Review*, XI, pp. 282-284, September, 1842.

Professor Bliss Perry finds this sketch "chiefly interesting as proving how very neatly the young journalist could play, if need be, upon the flute of Edgar Allan Poe." (*Loc. cit.* p. 24.) As this shows the influence, perhaps, of Poe's prose-poetry, so "Bervance; or Father and Son" shows a Poesque decadence. Tales like "A Legend of Life and Love" may have been written under the influence of another contributor to the *Democratic Review*, Nathaniel Hawthorne; but if so, the imitation was far less successful in the latter case.

were, like delicate sea-flowers on the bosom of the turgid ocean.
He remembered him of his brother as a boy—how they played
together of the summer afternoons—and how, wearied out at
evening, they slept pleasantly in each other's arms.   O, Master
of the Great Laws!   Couldst thou but roll back the years and
place that guilty creature a child again by the side of that
brother!   Such were the futile wishes of the criminal.   And as
repentance and prayer worked forth from his soul, he sank
on the floor drowsily, and a tear stood beneath his eyelids.

Repentance and prayer from *him!*   What hope could there
be for aspirations having birth in a source so polluted?   Yet the
Sense which is never sleepless heard that tainted soul's desire,
and willed that an answering mission should be sent straight-
way.

When Alza felt the mind of the Almighty in his heart—for it
was rendered conscious to him in the moment—he cleaved the
air with his swift pinions, and made haste to perform the cheer-
ful duty.   Along and earthward he flew—seeing far, far below
him mountains, and towns, and seas, and stretching forests.
At distance, in the immeasurable fields wherein he travelled,
was the eternal glitter of countless worlds—wheeling and whirl-
ing, and motionless never.   After a brief while, the Spirit be-
held the city of his destination; and, drawing nigh, he hovered
over it—that great city shrouded in the depths of night, and its
many thousands slumbering.

Just as his presence, obedient to his desire, was transferring
itself to the place where the murderer lay, he met one of his
own kindred spreading his wings to rise from the ground.

"O Spirit," said Alza, "what a sad scene is here!"

"I grow faint," the other answered, "at looking abroad
through these guilty places.   Behold that street to the right."

He pointed, and Alza, turning, saw rooms of people, some
with their minds maddened by intoxication, some uttering horrid
blasphemies—sensual creatures, and wicked, and mockers of all
holiness.

"O, brother," said the Tear-Angel, "let us not darken our
eyes with the sight.   Let us on to our appointed missions.   What
is yours, my brother?"

"Behold!" answered the Spirit.

And then Alza knew for the first time that there was a third
living thing near by.   With meek and abashed gesture, the
soul of a girl just dead stood forth before them.   Alza, without

I took the liberty, two or three weeks since, of forwarding you a M.S. tale "The Angel of Tears," intended for the "Boston Miscellany."—

Be so kind, if you accept it, to forward a note, informing me thereof, to this place (your agency in New York), and if you decline, please return the M.S.—

My stories, I believe, have been pretty popular, and extracted liberally. Several of them in the Democratic Review have received public favor, instance "Death in the School-Room," &c &c.

Walter Whitman

Tuesday June 14th.

Wishes Manuscript

Messrs Bradbury Soden & Co
Mr. Hale Jr. Boston Mass

WHITMAN'S EARLIEST MANUSCRIPT

A letter of 1842, offering for publication the tale which begins on the opposite page. Reproduced through the courtesy of the owner, Mr. Thomas B. Harned.

asking his companion, saw that the Spirit had been sent to guide and accompany the stranger through the Dark Windings.

So he kissed the brow of the re-born, and said,

"Be of good heart! Farewell, both!"

And the soul and its monitor departed upward, and Alza went into the dungeon.

Then, like a swinging vapor, the form of the Tear-Angel was by and over the body of the sleeping man. To his vision night was as day, and day as night.

At first, something like a shudder went through him, for when one from the Pure Country approaches the wickedness of evil, the presence thereof is made known to him by an instinctive pain. Yet a moment, and the gentle Spirit cast glances of pity on the unconscious fratricide. In the great Mystery of Life, Alza remembered, though even he understood it not, it had been settled by the Unfathomable that Sin and Wrong *should* be. And the angel knew too, that Man, with all the darkness and the clouds about him, might not be contemned, even by the Princes of the Nighest Circle to the White Throne.

He slept. His hair, coarse and tangly through neglect, lay in masses about his head, and clustered over his neck. One arm was doubled under his cheek, and the other stretched straight forward. Long steady breaths, with a kind of hissing sound, came from his lips.

So he slumbered calmly. So the fires of a furnace, at night, though not extinguished, slumber calmly, when its swarthy ministers impel it not. Haply, he dreamed some innocent dream. Sleep on, sleep on, outcast! There will soon be for you a reality harsh enough to make you wish those visions had continued alway, and you [had] never awakened.

Oh, it is not well to look coldly and mercilessly on the bad done by our fellows. That convict—that being of the bloody hand—who could know what palliations there were for his guilt? Who might say there was no premature seducing aside from the walks of honesty—and no seed of evil planted by others in his soul during his early years? Who should tell he was not so bred that had he at manhood possessed aught but propensities for evil it would have been miraculous indeed? Who might dare cast the first stone?[1]

The heart of a man is a glorious temple; yet its Builder has seen fit to let it become, to a degree, like the Jewish structure

[1] *Cf. post,* I, pp. 97–103, 108–110.

of old, a mart for gross traffic, and the presence of unchaste things. In the Shrouded Volumes doubtless it might be perceived how this is a part of the mighty and beautiful Harmony; but our eyes are mortal, and the film is over them.

The Angel of Tears bent him by the side of the prisoner's head. An instant more, and he rose, and seemed about to depart; as one whose desire had been attained. Wherefore does that pleasant look spread like a smile over the features of the slumberer?

In the darkness overhead yet linger the soft wings of Alza. Swaying above the prostrate mortal, the Spirit bends his white neck, and his face is shaded by the curls of his hair, which hang about him like a golden cloud. Shaking the beautiful tresses back, he stretches forth his hands, and raises his large eyes upward, and speaks murmuringly in the language used among the Creatures Beautiful:

"I come. Spirits of Pity and Love, favored children of the Loftiest[1]—whose pleasant task it is with your pens of adamant to make record upon the Silver Leaves of those things which, when computed together at the Day of the End, are to outcancel the weight of the sum of evil—your chambers I seek!"

And the Angel of Tears glided away.

While a thousand air-forms, far and near, responded in the same tongue wherewith Alza had spoken:

"Beautiful, to the Eye of the Centre, is the sight which ushers repentance!"

ERIS; A SPIRIT RECORD[2]

WHO says that there are not angels or invisible spirits watching around us? The teeming regions of the air swarm with bodiless ghosts—bodiless to human sight, because of their exceeding and too dazzling beauty!

And there is one, childlike, with helpless and unsteady movements, but a countenance of immortal bloom, whose long-lashed eyes droop downward. The name of the Shape is Dai.

[1] Cf. infra, p. 47; and post, II, p. 71.

[2] From the Columbian Magazine, I, 3, pp. 138–139, March, 1844. The fanciful sketch was announced in the February number of the Columbian.

In Greek mythology Eris was the goddess of discord, daughter of Nyx (Night), sister of Mars (War), and mother of Strife. It was she who, being uninvited to the nuptials of Pelius and Thetis, provoked the strife among the goddesses which resulted in the Trojan War.

When he comes near, the angels are silent, and gaze upon him
with pity and affection. And the fair eyes of the Shape roll,
but fix upon no object; while his lips move, but a plaintive tone
only is heard, the speaking of a single name. Wandering in the
confines of earth, or restlessly amid the streets of the beautiful
land, goes Dai, earnestly calling on one he loves.

Wherefore is there no response?

Soft as the feathery leaf of the frailest flower—pure as the
heart of flame—of a beauty so lustrous that the sons of Heaven
themselves might well be drunken to gaze thereon—with fleecy
robes that but half apparel a maddening whiteness and grace—
dwells Eris among the creatures beautiful, a chosen and cher-
ished one. And Eris is the name called by the wandering angel
—while no answer comes, and the loved flies swiftly away, with
a look of sadness and displeasure.

It had been years before that a maid and her betrothed lived
in one of the pleasant places of earth. Their hearts clung to
one another with the fondness of young life, and all its dreamy
passion. Each was simple and innocent. Mortality might
not know a thing better than their love, or more sunny than
their happiness.

In the method of the rule of fate, it was ordered that the maid
should sicken, and be drawn nigh to the gates of death—nigh,
but not through them. Now to the young who love purely
High Power commissions to each a gentle guardian, who
hovers around unseen day and night. The office of this spirit
is to keep a sleepless watch, and fill the heart of its charge with
strange and mysterious and lovely thoughts. Over the maid
was placed Dai, and through her illness the unknown presence
of the youth hung near continually.

To the immortal, days, years and centuries are the same.

Erewhile, a cloud was seen in Heaven. The delicate ones
bent their necks, and shook as if a chill blast had swept by—
and white robes were drawn around shivering and terrified forms.

An archangel with veiled cheeks cleared the air. Silence
spread through the hosts of the passed away, who gazed in
wonder and fear. And as they gazed they saw a new companion
of wondrous loveliness among them—a strange and timid crea-
ture, who, were it not that pain must never enter those borders
of innocence, would have been called unhappy. The angels
gathered around the late comer with caresses and kisses, and
they smiled pleasantly with joy in each other's eyes.

Then the archangel's voice was heard—and they who heard it knew that One mightier spake his will therein:

"The child Dai!" said he.

A far reply sounded out in tones of trembling and apprehension.

"I am here!"

And the youth came forth from the distant confines, whither he had been in solitude. The placid look of peace no more illumined his brow with silver light, and his unearthly beauty was as a choice statue enveloped in mist and smoke.

"Oh, weak and wicked spirit!" said the archangel, "thou hast been false to thy mission and thy Master!"

The quivering limbs of Dai felt weak and cold. He would have made an answer in agony—but at that moment he lifted his eyes and beheld the countenance of Eris, the late comer.

Love is potent, even in Heaven! and subtle passion creeps into the hearts of the sons of beauty, who feel the delicious impulse, and know that there is a soft sadness sweeter than aught in the round of their pleasure eternal.

When the youth saw Eris, he sprang forward with lightning swiftness to her side. But the late comer turned away with aversion. The band of good-will might not be between them, because of wrongs done, and the planting of despair in two happy human hearts.

At the same moment, the myriads of interlinked spirits that range step by step from the throne of the Uppermost (as the power of that light and presence which is unbearable even to the deathless, must be tempered for the sight of any created thing, however lofty) were conscious of a motion in the mind of God. Quicker than electric thought the command was accomplished! The disobedient angel felt himself enveloped in a sudden cloud, impenetrably dark. The face of Eris gladdened and maddened him no more. He turned himself to and fro, and stretched out his arms—but though he knew the nearness of his companions, the light of Heaven, and of the eyes of Eris, was strangely sealed to him. The youth was blind forever.

So a wandering angel sweeps through space with restless and unsteady movements—and the sound heard from his lips is the calling of a single name. But the loved flies swiftly away in sadness, and heeds him not. Onward and onward speeds the angel, amid scenes of ineffable splendor, though to his sight the splendor is darkness. But there is one scene that rests before him alway. It is of a low brown dwelling among the children of men; and in an inner room a couch, whereon lies a young maid, whose cheeks rival the frailness and paleness of foam. Near by is a youth, and the filmy eyes of the girl are bent upon him in fondness. What dim shape hovers overhead? He is invisible to mortals; but oh! well may the blind spirit, by the token of throbs of guilty and fiery love beating through him, know that hovering form! Thrust forward by such fiery love, the shape dared transcend his duty. Again the youth looked upon the couch, and beheld a lifeless corpse.

This is the picture upon the vision of Dai. His brethren of the bands of light, as they meet him in his journeyings, pause awhile for pity; yet never do the pangs of their sympathy, the only pangs known to those sinless creatures, or arms thrown softly around him, or kisses on his brow, efface the pure lineaments of the sick girl—the dead.

In the portals of Heaven stands Eris, oft peering into the outer distance. Nor of the millions of winged passengers that hourly come and go, does one enter whose features are not earnestly scanned by the watcher. And the fond joy resides in her soul, that the time is nigh at hand; for a thread yet binds the angel down to the old abode, and until the breaking of that bond, Eris keeps vigil in the portals of Heaven.

The limit of the watch comes soon. On earth, a toil-worn man has returned from distant travel, and lays him down, weary and faint at heart, on a floor amid the ruins of that low brown dwelling. The slight echo is heard of moans coming from the breast of one who yearns to die. Life, and rosy light, and the pleasant things of nature, and the voices and sight of his fellows, and the glory of thought—the sun, the flowers, the glittering stars, the soft breeze—have no joy for him. And the coffin and the cold earth have no horror; they are a path to the unforgotten.

Thus the tale is told in Heaven, how the pure love of two human beings is a sacred thing, which the immortals themselves must not dare to cross. In pity to the disobedient angel he is blind, that he may not gaze ceaselessly on one who returns his love with displeasure. And haply Dai is the spirit of the destiny of those whose selfishness would seek to mar the peace of gentle hearts, by their own unreturned and unhallowed passion.

THE LITTLE SLEIGHERS[1]

A Sketch of a Winter Morning on the Battery

Just before noon, one day last winter, when the pavements were crusted plentifully with ice-patches, and the sun, though shining out very brightly by fits and starts, seemed incapable of conveying any warmth, I took my thick overcoat, and prepared to sally forth for a walk. The wind whistled as I shut the door behind me, and when I turned the corner it made the most ferocious demonstrations toward my hat, which I was able to keep on my head not without considerable effort. My flesh quivered with the bitter coldness of the air. My breath appeared steam. Qu—foo-o! how the gust swept along!

Coming out into Broadway, I wended along by the Park, St. Paul's Church, and the icicle-tipped trees in Trinity graveyard. Having by this time warmed myself into a nice glow, I grew more comfortable, and felt ready to do any deed of daring that might present itself—even to the defiance of the elements which were growling so snappishly around me.

When I arrived at Battery-place—at the crossing which leads from that antique, two-story corner house, to the massive iron gates on the opposite side—I must confess that I was for a moment in doubt whether I had not better, after all, turn and retrace my steps. The wind absolutely roared. I could hear the piteous creaking of the trees on the Battery as the branches grated against one another, and could see how they were bent down by the power of the blast. Out in the bay the waves were rolling and rising, and over the thick rails which line the shore-walk dashed showers of spray, which fell upon the flagstones and froze there.

But it was a glorious and inspiriting scene, with all its wildness. I gave an extra pull of my hat over my brows—a closer adjustment of my collar around my shoulders, and boldly ventured onward. I stepped over the crossing, and passed through the gate.

Ha! ha! Let the elements run riot! There is an exhilarating sensation—a most excellent and enviable fun—in steadily pushing forward against the stout winds!

---

[1] From the *Columbian Magazine*, Vol. II, pp. 113–114, September, 1844.
This sketch was written before July 1, 1844, since in the issue of the *Columbian* for September of that year the editor, in accepting the present sketch, informed correspondents that contributions had all been read up to July 1.

The whole surface of the Battery was spread with snow. It seemed one mighty bride's couch, and was very brilliant, as though varnished with a clear and glossy wash. This huge, white sheet, glancing back a kind of impudent defiance to the sun, which shone sharply the while, was not, it seemed, to be left in its repose, or without an application to use and jollity. Many dozens of boys were there, with skates and small sleds— very busy. Oh, what a noisy and merry band!

The principal and choicest of the play tracts was in that avenue, the third from the water, known to summer idlers as "Lovers' Walk." For nearly its whole length it was a continued expanse of polished ice, made so partly by the evenness of the surface and partly by the labor of the boys. This fact I found out to my cost; for, turning in it before being aware that it was so fully preoccupied and so slippery, I found it necessary to use the utmost caution or run the certainty of a fall.

"Pawny-guttah!" Gentle lady, (I must here remark,) or worthy gentleman, as the case may be, whose countenance bends over this page, and whose opportunities have never led you to know the use, meaning and import, conveyed in the term just quoted—call to your side some bright-eyed boy—a brother or a son, or a neighbor's son, and ask *him*.

"Pawny-guttah!" I stepped aside instinctively, and, with the speed of an arrow there came gliding along, lying prone upon a sled, one of the boyish troop. The polished steel runners of this little vehicle sped over the ice with a slightly grating noise, and he directed his course by touching the toe of either boot, behind him, upon the ice, as he wished to swerve to the right or left.

Who can help loving a wild, thoughtless, heedless, joyous boy? Oh, let us do what we can—we who are past the time— let us do what we may to aid their pleasures and their little delights, and heal up their petty griefs. Wise is he who is himself a child at times. A man may keep his heart fresh and his nature youthful, by mixing much with that which is fresh and youthful. Why should we, in our riper years, despise these little people, and allow ourselves to think them of no higher consequence than trifles and unimportant toys?

I know not a prettier custom than that said to be prevalent in some parts of the world, of covering the coffins of children with flowers.[1] They pass away, frail and blooming, and the blossom

[1] *Cf. infra*, p. 35.

of a day is their fittest emblem. Their greatest and worst crimes were but children's follies, and the sorrow which we indulge for their death has a delicate refinement about it, flowing from ideas of their innocence, their simple prattle, and their affectionate conduct while living. Try to love children. It is purer, and more like that of angels, than any other love.

Reflections somewhat after this cast were passing in my mind as I paused a moment and gazed upon those little players. What a miniature, too, were they of the chase of life. Every one seemed intent upon his own puny objects—every one in pursuit of "fun."

The days will come and go, and the seasons roll on, and these young creatures will grow up and launch out in the world. Who can fortell their destinies? Some will die early and be laid away in their brown beds of earth, and thus escape the thousand throes, and frivolities, and temptations, and miserable fictions and mockeries which are interwoven with our journey here on earth. Some will plod onward in the path of gain—that great idol of the world's worship[1]—and have no higher aspirations than for profit upon merchandize. Some will love, and have those they love look coldly upon them; and then, in the sickness of their heart, curse their own birth hour. But all, all will repose at last.[2]

Why, what a sombre moralist I have become! Better were it to listen to the bell-like music of those children's voices; and, as I turned to wend my way homeward, imbue my fancy with a kindred glee and joyishness! Let me close these mottled reveries.

TEAR DOWN AND BUILD OVER AGAIN[3]

HE WHO at some future time shall take upon himself the office of writing the early history of what is done in America, and of how the American character was started, formed, and finished—with some analysis of its materials, and the parts that entered from time to time into its make—will surely have much cause to mention what may be called "the pull-down-and-build-over-again spirit." This name is so descriptive,

[1] Cf. infra, pp. 37–39, 45; also post, I, pp. 123–125, II, p. 63, 67–68.
[2] Cf. the poem "We All Shall Rest At Last," infra, p. 10–11.
[3] From the American Review, Vol. II, pp. 536–538, November, 1845.

that it hardly needs any very elaborate explanation to tell what is meant by it.

Simultaneously with the departure of winter last April, (he feigned to go away, it will be remembered, in February, but it was only a trick of the old rascal, who came back again more grim than ever, as people's frosty noses soon bore witness,) and as the warmth of spring penetrated the frozen ground, some of those subtle agencies that hold sway over the human will, penetrated five hundred New York hearts with a greater but very different warmth. Then these five hundred hearts prompted their owners to put their hats on their heads and walk forth, and view their tenements and lands, for they were men of substance. Then they communed with themselves, and said in their own hearts, "Let us level to the earth all the houses that were not built within the last ten years; let us raise the devil and break things!" In pursuance of this resolve, they procured workmen, purchased hooks, ladders and battering rams, and went to work. Then fled tenants from under roofs that had sheltered them when in their cradles, and had witnessed their parents' marriages—roofs aneath which they had grown up from childhood, and that were filled with memories of many years. Then wept old men and old women, that they were not to die within the walls that they had loved so long—rather a foolish weeping, too, when we consider that by staying there a few hours longer their desire could have been accomplished. Then fell beams and rafters—then were unearthed the dust and decay of the past—then mortar and old lime, originally plastered by hands the worms had eaten long ago, filled Manhattan island with showers almost as pestiferous as the sand-clouds of Sahara. Then exulted each jolly Irishman who owned, or could hire, a dirt-cart and a patient horse— exulted, and was to be talked to by tax-paying citizens, not as a favor, but as one who could grant a favor. Then spoke hammer to axe, which spoke again to pick, while their triumphant din was answered by the melancholy fall of post, cornice and clapboard, and the piteous creaking of divorced floors and riven ceilings. Then was razed to the ground many a beam, rough-coated on the outside, but stout and sound at heart, like the men of the former age!

Good-bye, old houses! There was that about ye which I hold it no shame to say I loved passing well. It is true, ye had not the smart jaunty air, the brazen varnished look, of our modern buildings; but I liked ye all the better for it. Ah! how many happy gatherings some of ye have held in your capacious embrace, years ago! Births , too, and funerals as well, might ye tell of. Who that now walks the pavement, or droops away on some distant shore, a gray-headed and care-worn man, yet was in your knowledge a fair-lipped baby, and a playful boy! What vows of love were breathed in your hearing, and passed into the air to disolve—but passed also into human hearts, waking sweet echoes where now are the ashes of decay and death! Answer, ye crumbling walls! have ye heard, in the night's silence, no bitter groans from young men, sickened of life, even before they knew its darkest trials, and wearied with themselves and their own follies? Have ye never witnessed solitary tears, shed by eyes the world got only glances of pride and coldness from? Has the moaning of sick children vibrated through your chambers, and the merry shout of the gay, and the smooth tongue of wedded affection, and the manly voice of true friendship? In awe and stillness have ye beheld death? And how sped the departing then? Looked he back with a soul fainting at its former vanities, or cheerfully like a soldier over the conquered battle-field? Ah! deep were the lessons ye might teach, could these questionings be answered.

Some of our citizens—those of them who have the say on the subject—want old St. Paul's Church pulled down and built over again. When we come to consider how indecorous it is to worship our Maker in a place whose foundations were laid near a hundred years ago, and which has so many larger and handsomer temples around it; when we reflect on the probable gratification of the Lord at having a new house, of such greater convenience and splendor than the old one; when we behold how much more likely Christians are to entertain humble, meek and heavenly thoughts in a church of marble, guilding [gilding] and showy carved work, than in one of a plainer make; when we remember how there are no starving poor in the world, no children growing up totally devoid of all moral or scientific instruction for want of means; when we see that in the present happy and perfect state of mankind there is little room for the exercise of that virtue whereof Christ said, "Inasmuch as ye refused it to the least of these your brethren, ye refused it to me;" when we are so clearly convinced that it is consistent for doctrines teaching love, simplicity and contempt for worldly show, to be expounded in a place whose corner-stones rest upon pride, and whose walls are built in vain-glory; when we bethink us how good it is to leave no land-marks of the past standing, no pile honored by its association with our storied names, with the undying memory of our Washington, and with the frequent presence of his compatriots; when we consider, also, what a sad botch the present St. Paul's Church is, and how it mars the elegant beauty of Clirehugh's barber's shop on the opposite corner; then we shall feel glad and delighted at the sagacity which has discovered the pressing need there is for a better church, and eager to see the old one destroyed forthwith. Moreover, let there be no half-way work about it. Let those miserable old trees be cut away at the same time. What good do they there? Why cumber they the ground? There is one large elm in particular, whose shade falls darkly at mid-day on the graves of two men, soldiers who fought stoutly for that freedom we now enjoy. Let that old elm most especially be cut down. Its wild arms would split with horror from its blistered, weather-beaten trunk, to see the sacred tombs it has so long stood sentry over, desecrated by piles of brick and lime, for a spruce new church, for a generation that should "forget the burial-places of their fathers."

Not many months since, amid a small, slow-moving procession of white-haired ancients, we entered that building, in attendance on the funeral ceremonies of General Morgan Lewis the chief officer of the Society of the Cincinnati. It was a chilling, solemn business. As we sat in one of the side pews, we looked around at the few withered men, the remnants of the Revolution, the testimony of old times, that were near us. Erect and stern, unbent with age, there was one whose eyes had been undismayed with the smoke of Bunker Hill, and who had faltered not after the hapless battle of Long Island. Those dim gray orbs, moreover, had gazed upon that paragon of men, whose glory is almost more than mortal. "I was with him here," I heard him say, an hour afterwards, "to give thanks after the British had left the city." *With Washington there!* Oh, hallowed be the spot where his footsteps fell! Thrice hallowed be the temple where the purest prayers ever breathed from a patriot's heart, went forth toward Heaven![1]

There may be, and no doubt are, those in this utilitarian age who will smile with contempt at sympathies like these, if offered as reasons why St. Paul's Church here, or any other

[1] *Cf. infra*, pp. 72-78; *post*, II, pp. 117-118.

such noble old building, shall not give place to modern "improvements." Thank Heaven! there are also those who can enter into such feelings, and act upon them. There are those whose ideas of beauty, worth and grandeur are not altogether fixed, as far as such things are concerned, on buildings of imposing height, great breadth, and showy exterior. There are those who would, in examining some crowded city, hold more attention for that spot in an obscure street where the early days of an undying genius were passed than for the proudest palace owned by the richest capitalist. There are those who would go farther to view even Charlotte Temple's grave, than Mr. Astor's stupid-looking house in Broadway[1]—would bear more bother for a sight of the "Field of the Grounded Arms," than to scan—when it is completed—the famous Girard College. To such, greatness and goodness are things intrinsic—mental and moral qualities. To the rest of the world, and that is nine-tenths of it, *appearance* is everything. And yet, perhaps I am wrong. It *is* the world, which in spite of itself, pays homage to every sacred spot where a great deed has been performed, or which a truly great man has sanctified by birth or death. Can Irishmen forget where Emmet lies buried, that it should be marked by no grave-stone, and the proudest columns loom up everywhere around? And how many centuries will bring the day when Mount Vernon is an indifferent spot to America?

Let us not be mistaken. We are by no means desirous of retaining what is old, merely because it is old. We would have all dilapidated buildings, as well as all ruinous laws and customs, carefully levelled to the ground, forthwith, and better ones put in their places. Wherever the untiring fingers of time have done their work of decay, there we would neutralize the danger with the hand of reformation—imitating thus the great copy of Nature, the mother of the only wise philosophy. No friend are we to the rotten structures of the past, either of architecture or government. It is only where upstarts would pull down something noble, stout and true, that we cry, "Stay your hand, leveler!" It is only when honorable and holy memorials of the good which the past has sent us, with its many evils, is jeopardized, that we would raise our voice in warning and indignation. To all destruction which is a necessary precedent to man's glory, comfort, or freedom, we say, "God speed!" and

[1] *Cf. post*, I, p. 219.

are willing to lend our humble strength withal! This, but no more. What we have that is good, that is fully equal to our present capacities and wants, that, if destroyed, would doubtless be replaced by something not half as excellent: let it stand!

And I must add—and I hope it is [in] no spirit of harshness—that whoever is opposed to *such* conservatism, whoever moves under the impulse of a rabid, feverish itching for change, a dissatisfaction with proper things as they are, through the blindness which would peril all in the vague chance of a remotely possible improvement, has something of the same mischief of the soul that "brought death into the world, and all our wo,"[1] a prompting which, even though it comes to put up a new church, comes from that father of restlessness, the Devil.

———

A DIALOGUE[2]

WHAT would be thought of a man who, having an ill humor in his blood, should strive to cure himself by only cutting off the festers, the outward signs of it, as they appeared upon the surface? Put criminals for festers and society for the diseased man, and you may get the spirit of that part of our laws which expects to abolish wrong-doing by sheer terror—by cutting off the wicked, and taking no heed of the causes of wickedness. I have lived long enough to know that national folly never deserves contempt; else I should laugh to scorn such an instance of exquisite nonsense!

Our statutes are supposed to speak the settled will and voice of the community. We may imagine, then, a conversation of the following sort to take place—the imposing majesty of the people speaking on the one side, a pallid, shivering convict on the other.

"I have done wrong," says the convict; "in an evil hour a kind of frenzy came over me, and I struck my neighbor a heavy blow, which killed him. Dreading punishment, and the disgrace of my family, I strove to conceal the deed, but it was discovered."

"Then," says society, "you must be killed in return."

[1] "Paradise Lost," I, l. 3.

[2] From the *Democratic Review*, Vol. XVII, pp. 360–364, November, 1845. *Cf. post*, I, pp. 108–110, II, pp.15–16. There were many editorials on the subject in the *Eagle* during Whitman's editorship.

"But," rejoins the criminal, "I feel that I am not fit to die. I have not enjoyed life—I have not been happy or good. It is so horrid to look back upon one's evil deeds only. Is there no plan by which I can benefit my fellow-creatures, even at the risk of my own life?"

"None," answers society; "you must be strangled—choked to death. If your passions are so ungovernable that people are in danger from them, we shall hang you."

"Why that?" asks the criminal, his wits sharpened perhaps by his situation. "Can you not put me in some strong prison, where no one will be harmed by me? And if the expense is anything against this, let me work there, and support myself."

"No," responds society, "we shall strangle you; your crimes deserve it."

"Have you, then, committed no crimes?" asks the murderer.

"None which the law can touch," answers society.

"True, one of us had a mother, a weak-souled creature, that pined away month after month, and at last died, because her dear son was intemperate, and treated her ill. Another, who is the owner of many houses thrusts a sick family into the street because they did not pay their rent, whereof came the deaths of two little children. And another—that particularly well-dressed man—effected the ruin of a young girl, a silly thing who afterward became demented, and drowned herself in the river. One has gained much wealth by cheating his neighbors—but cheating so as not to come within the clutches of any statute. And hundreds are now from day to day practising deliberately the most unmanly and wicked meannesses. We are all frail!"

"And *these* are they who so sternly clamor for my blood!" exclaims the convict in amazement. "Why is it that I alone am to be condemned?"

"That they are bad," rejoins society, "is no defense for you."

"That the multitude have so many faults—that none are perfect," says the criminal, "might at least make them more lenient to me. If my physical temperament subjects me to great passions, which lead me into crime, when wronged too—as I was when I struck that fatal blow—is there not charity enough among you to sympathize with me—to let me not be hung, but safely separated from all that I might harm?"

"There is some reason in what you say," answers society; "but the clergy, who hate the wicked, say that God's own voice has spoken against you. We might, perhaps, be willing to let you off with imprisonment; but Heaven imperatively forbids it, and demands your blood. Besides, that you were wronged gave you no right to revenge yourself by taking life."

"Do you mean me to understand, then," asks the convict, "that Heaven is more blood-thirsty than you? And if wrong gives no right to revenge, why am I arraigned thus?"

"The case is different," rejoins society. "We are a community—you are but a single individual. You should forgive your enemies."

"And are you not ashamed," asks the culprit, "to forget that as a community which you expect me to remember as a man? While the town clock goes wrong, shall each little private watch be abused for failing to keep the true time? What are communities but congregated individuals? And if you, in the potential force of your high position, deliberately set examples of retribution, how dare you look to me for self-denial, forgiveness, and the meekest and most difficult virtues?"

"I cannot answer such questions," responds society; "but if you propose no punishment for the bad, what safety is there for citizens' rights and peace, which would then be in continual jeopardy?"

"You cannot," says the other, "call a perpetual jail no punishment. It is a terrible one. And as to your safety, it will be outraged less by mild and benevolent criminal laws than by sanguinary and revengeful ones. They govern the insane better with gentleness than severity. Are not men possessing reason more easily acted on through moral force than men without?"

"But, I repeat it, crimes will then multiply," says society (not having much else to say); "the punishment must be severe, to avoid that. Release the bad from the fear of hanging, and they will murder every day. We must preserve that penalty to prevent this taking of life."

"I was never ignorant of the penalty," answers the criminal; "and yet I murdered, for my blood was up. Of all the homicides committed, not one in a hundred is done by persons unaware of the law. So that you see the terror of death does not deter. The hardened and worst criminals, too, frequently have no such terror, while the more repentant and humanized suffer in it the most vivid agony. At least you could try the experiment of no hanging."

"It might cost too much. Murder would increase," reiterates society.

"Formerly," replies the criminal, "many crimes were punished by death that now are not; and yet those crimes have not increased. Not long since the whipping-post and branding-iron stood by the bar of courts of justice, and were often used, too. Yet their abolition has not multiplied the evils for which they were meted out. This, and much more, fully proves that it is by no means the dread of terrible punishment which prevents terrible crime. And now allow me to ask you a few questions. Why are most modern executions private, so called, instead of public?"

"Because," answers society, "the influence of the spectacle is degrading and anti-humanizing. As far as it goes, it begets a morbid and unhealthy feeling in the masses."

"Suppose all the convicts," goes on the prisoner, "adjudged to die in one of your largest States, were kept together for two whole years, and then in the most public part of the land were hung up in a row—say twenty of them together—how would this do?"

"God forbid!" answers society with a start. "The public mind would revolt at so bloody and monstrous a demonstration. It could not be allowed."

"Is it anything less horrible," resumes the questioner, "in the deaths being singly and at intervals?"

"I cannot say it is," answers society.

"Allow me to suppose a little more," continues the criminal, "that all the convicts to be hung in the whole republic for two years—say two hundred, and that is a small estimate—were strangled at the same time, in full sight of every man, woman and child—all the remaining population. And suppose this were done periodically every two years. What say you to that?"

"The very thought sickens me," answers society, "and the effect would be more terrible and blighting upon the national morals and the health of the popular heart than it is any way possible to describe. No unnatural rites of the most barbarous and brutal nations of antiquity ever equalled this; and our name would always deserve to be written literally in characters of blood. The feeling of the sacredness of life would be utterly destroyed among us. Every fine and Christian faculty of our souls would be rooted away. In a few years, this hellish oblation becoming common, the idea of violent death would be the theme of laughter and ribald jesting. In all the conduct and opinions of men, in their every-day business, and in their private meditations, so terrible an institution would some way, in some method of its influence, be seen operating. What! two hundred miserable wretches at once! The tottering old, and the youth not yet arrived at manhood; women, too, and perhaps girls who are hardly more than children! The spot where such a deed should be periodically consummated would surely be cursed forever by God and all goodness Some awful and poisonous desert it ought to be; though, however awful, it could but faintly image the desert such horrors must make of the heart of man, and the poison it would diffuse on his better nature."

"And if all this appalling influence," says the murderer, "were really operating over you—not concentrated, but cut up in fractions and frittered here and there—just as strong in its general effect, but not brought to a point, as in the case I have imagined—what would you then say?"

"Nay," replies society, with feverish haste, "but the executions are now required to be private."

"Many are not," rejoins the other; "and as to those that are nominally so, where everybody reads newspapers, and every newspaper seeks for graphic accounts of these executions, such things can never be private. What a small proportion of your citizens are eye-witnesses of things done in Congress; yet they are surely not private, for not a word officially spoken in the Halls of the Capitol, but is through the press made as public as if every American's ear were within hearing distance of the speaker's mouth. The whole spectacle of those two hundred executions is more faithfully seen, and much more deliberately dwelt upon, through the printed narratives, than if people beheld it with their bodily eyes, and then no more. Print preserves it. It passes it from hand to hand, and even boys and girls are imbued with its spirit and horrid essence. Your legislators have forbidden public executions; they must go farther. They must forbid the relation of them by tongue, letter, or picture; for your physical sight is not the only avenue through which the subtle virus will reach you. Nor is the effect lessened because it is more covert and more widely diffused. Rather, indeed, the reverse. As things are, the masses take it for granted that the system and its results are right. As I have supposed them to be, though the nature would remain the same, the difference of the form would present the monstrous evil in a vivid and utterly new light before men's eyes."

"To all this," says society, "I answer—*what*"? What shall it be, thou particular reader, whose eyes now dwell on my fanciful dialogue? Give it for thyself—and if it be indeed *an answer*, thou hast a logic of most surpassing art.

O, how specious is the shield thrown over wicked actions, by invoking the Great Shape of Society in their defense! How that which is barbarous, false, or selfish for an individual becomes singularly proper when sanctioned by the legislature, or a supposed national policy! How deeds wicked in a man are thus applauded in a number of men!

What makes a murder the awful crime all ages have considered it? The friend and foe of hanging will unite in the reply —Because it destroys that cunning principle of vitality which no human agency can replace—invades the prerogative of God, for God's is the only power that can give life—and offers a horrid copy for the rest of mankind. Lo! thou lover of strangling! with what a keen razor's sharpness does every word of this reply cut asunder the threads of that argument which defends thy cause! The very facts which render murder a frightful crime, render hanging a frightful punishment. To carry out the spirit of such a system, when a man maims another, the law should maim him in return. In the unsettled districts of our western states, it is said that in brutal fights the eyes of the defeated are sometimes torn bleeding from their sockets. The rule which justifies the taking of life, demands gouging out of eyes as a legal penalty too.

I have one point else to touch upon, and then no more. There has, about this point, on the part of those who favor hanging, been such a bold, impudent effrontery—such a cool sneering defiance of all those greater lights which make the glory of this age over the shame of the dark ages—a prostitution so foul of names and influences so awfully sacred—that I tremble this moment with passion, while I treat upon it. I speak of founding the whole breadth and strength of the hanging system, as many do, on the Scriptures. The matter is too extensive to be argued fully, in the skirts of an essay; and I have therefore but one suggestion to offer upon it, though words and ideas rush and swell upon my utterance. When I read in the records of the past how Calvin burned Servetus at Geneva, and found his defense in the Bible—when I peruse the reign of the English Henry 8th, that great champion of Protestantism, who, after the Reformation, tortured people to death, for refusing to acknowledge his spiritual supremacy, and pointed to the Scripture as his authority—when, through the short reign of Edward 6th, another Protestant sovereign, and of the Bloody Mary, a Catholic one, I find the most barbarous cruelties and martyrdoms inflicted in the name of God and his Sacred Word—I shudder and grow sick with pity. Still I remember the gloomy ignorance of the law of love that prevailed then, and the greater palliations for bigotry and religious folly. I bethink me how good it is that the spirit of such horrors, the blasphemy which prostituted God's law to their excuse, and the darkness of superstition which applauded them, have all passed away. But in these days of greater clearness, when clergymen call for sanguinary punishments in the name of the Gospel![1]— when, chased from point to point of human policy, they throw themselves on the supposed necessity of hanging in order to gratify and satisfy Heaven—when, instead of Christian mildness and love, they demand that our laws shall be pervaded by vindictiveness and violence—when the sacrifice of human life is inculcated as in many cases acceptable to Him who they say has even revoked his consent to brute sacrifices—my soul is filled with amazement, indignation and horror, utterly uncontrollable. When I go by a church, I cannot help thinking whether its walls do not sometimes echo, "Strangle and kill in the name of God!" The grasp of a minister's hand produces a kind of choking sensation; and by some kind of optical fascination, the pulpit is often intercepted from my view by a ghastly gallows frame. "O, Liberty!" said Madame Roland, "what crimes have been committed in thy name!"[2] "O, Bible!" say I, "what follies and monstrous barbarities are defended in *thy* name!"

---

[1] In 1842 the Rev. W. Patton, D.D., published a pamphlet in New York entitled "Capital Punishment Sustained by the Word," and a similar volume had been published by the Rev. George B. Cheever in 1843. The *Brother Jonathan* and the *Democratic Review* had espoused the opposite side of the controversy, the latter publishing, in March, 1842, a reply to Wordsworth's "Sonnets on the Punishment of Death" and in October of the same year Whittier's "Lines on the Abolition of the Gallows," while Lowell had five sonnets in reply to Wordsworth in the issue for May.

In old age Whitman said: "I was in early life very bigoted in my anti-slavery, anti-capital-punishment and so on, but I have always had a latent toleration for the people who choose a reactionary course." (See "With Walt Whitman in Camden," I, p. 193.)

[2] "O Liberty! Liberty! how many crimes are committed in thy name!" (Quoted in Macaulay's "Essay on Mirabeau.")

ART–SINGING AND HEART–SINGING[1]

GREAT is the power of Music over a people! As for us of America, we have long enough followed obedient and child-like in the track of the Old World. We have received her tenors and her buffos [buffas]; her operatic troupes and her vocalists, of all grades and complexions; listened to and applauded the songs made for a different state of society—made, perhaps, by royal genius, but made to please royal ears likewise; and it is time that such listening and receiving should cease. The subtlest spirit of a nation is expressed through its music—and the music acts reciprocally on the nation's very soul. Its effects may not be seen in a day, or a year, and yet these effects are potent invisibly. They enter into religious feelings—they tinge the manners and morals—they are active even in the choice of legislators and high magistrates. Tariff can be varied to fit circumstances—bad laws can be obliterated and good ones formed —those enactments which relate to commerce or national policy, built up or taken away, stretched or contracted, to suit the will of the government for the time being. But no human power can thoroughly suppress the spirit which lives in national lyrics, and sounds in the favorite melodies sung by high and low.

There are two kinds of singing—heart-singing and art-singing.[2] That which touches the souls and sympathies of other communities may have no effect here—unless it appeals to the throbbings of the great heart of humanity itself—pictures love, hope, or mirth in their comprehensive aspect. But nearly every nation has its peculiarities and its idioms, which make its best intellectual efforts dearest to itself alone, so that hardly any thing which comes to us in the music and songs of the Old World, is strictly good and fitting to our own nation.

[1] From the *Broadway Journal*, Vol. II, pp. 318–319, November 29, 1845. This essay is interesting in revealing an early form taken by Whitman's enthusiasm for American democracy, and also in preserving the only record, other than Whitman's own reminiscences, of what Edgar Allan Poe thought of the work of the young writer. This brief record appears in the following footnote to the original article:

"The author desires us to say, for him, that he pretends to no scientific knowledge of music. He merely claims to appreciate so much of it (a sadly disdained department, just now) as affects, in the language of the deacons, 'the natural heart of man.' It is scarcely necessary to add that we agree with our correspondent throughout. ED. B. J. [Edgar Allan Poe]."

Whitman reprinted this essay, somewhat altered, under the caption "Music that *is* Music," as an editorial in the Brooklyn *Daily Eagle*, December 4, 1846. (See "The Gathering of the Forces," II, pp. 346–349.)

[2] *Cf. post*, I, p. 257.

With all honor and glory to the land of the olive and the vine, fair-skied Italy—with no turning up of noses at Germany, France or England—we humbly demand whether we have not run after their beauties long enough.

"At last we have found it!" exclaimed we, some nights since, at the conclusion of the performances by the Cheney Family,[1] in Niblo's saloon.[2] At last we have found, and heard, and seen something original and beautiful in the way of American musical execution. Never having been present at any of the Hutchinsons' Concerts[3] (the Cheneys, we are told, are after the same token,) the elegant simplicity of this style took us completely by surprise, and our gratification was inexpressible. This, said we in our heart, is the true method which must become popular in the United States—which must supplant the stale, second-hand, foreign method, with its flourishes, its ridiculous sentimentality, its anti-republican spirit, and its sycophantic influence, tainting the young taste of the republic.

The Cheney young men are such brown-faced, stout-shouldered fellows as you will see in almost any American church, in a country village, of a Sunday. The girl is strangely simple, even awkward, in her ways. Or it may possibly be that she disdains the usual clap-trap of smiles, hand-kissing, and dancing-school bends. To our taste, there is something refreshing about all this. We are absolutely sick to nausea of the patent-leather, curled-hair, "japonicadom" style. The Cheneys are as much ahead of it as real teeth are ahead of artificial ones—even those which Dodge, (nature-rival, as he is,) sent to the late Fair. We beg these young Yankees to keep their manners plain alway. The sight of them, as they are, puts one in mind of health and fresh air in the country, at sunrise—the dewy,

---

[1] The Cheneys composed a quartette, three brothers and a sister, children of a distinguished New Hampshire preacher. They first appeared in New York City in October, 1845. Though tempted by flattering offers, Simeon Pease Cheney refused to give up his teaching of country singing classes (a work shared by his two brothers). Later he compiled "The American Singing-Book," and collected materials for "Wood-Notes Wild," posthumously published, in which he records bird notes.

[2] *Cf.* "Franklin Evans," *post*, II, pp. 130, 145, 211.

[3] Later Whitman heard the Hutchinsons, both in New York and in Brooklyn, and admired their singing very much. *Cf.* "Complete Prose," p. 517.

Though there were thirteen brothers and sisters in this once famous musical family, Whitman probably refers to the quartette who first took New York City by storm in 1843. They spent their summers on a New England farm, their falls and winters singing in New England and in New York. Later (1845) they went to England, Scotland and Ireland. (See "National Encyclopedia of American Biography.")

earthy fragrance that comes up then in the moisture, and touches the nostrils more gratefully than all the perfumes of the most ingenious chemist.

These hints we throw out rather as suggestive of a train of thought to other and more deliberate thinkers than we—and not as the criticisms of a musical connoisseur. If they have pith in them, we have not much doubt others will carry them out. If not, we at least know they are written in that true wish for benefitting the subject spoken of, which should characterize all essays.

————

SLAVERS AND THE SLAVE TRADE[1]

PUBLIC attention within the last few days has been naturally turned to the slave trade—that most abominable of all man's schemes for making money, without regard to the character of the means used for the purpose. Four vessels have, in about as many days, been brought to the American territory, for being engaged in this monstrous business! It is a disgrace and a blot on the character of our republic, and on our boasted humanity!

Though we hear less now-a-days of this trade—of the atrocious slave hunt—of the crowding of a mass of compact human flesh into little more than its equal of space—we are not to suppose that such horrors have ceased to exist. The great nations of the earth—our own first of all—have passed stringent laws against the slave traffic. But Brazil openly encourages it still. And many citizens of Europe and America pursue it not withstanding its illegality. Still the negro is torn from his simple hut—from his children, his brethren, his parents, and friends—to be carried far away and made the bondsman of a stranger. Still the black-hearted traitors who ply this work, go forth with their armed bands and swoop down on the defenseless villages, and bring their loads of human trophy, chained and gagged, and sell them as so much merchandise!

[1] From the Brooklyn *Daily Eagle*, March 18, 1846.
Cf. post, I, pp. 160–162, 171–174, II, pp. 8–10.
Whitman's editorship of the *Eagle* began shortly after the death of his predecessor, William B. Marsh, which occurred on February 26, 1846; his connection with the *Eagle* was terminated by a "row with the boss and the party" in the latter part of January, 1848 (on or just before January 18, as shown by references in the contemporary press of the city and in the style of the *Eagle's* pages themselves). See *post*, II, p. 88. Except for a few special contributions, Whitman did all the editorial writing for the *Eagle*. (See *post*, I, p. 116.) The authorship of the selections here reprinted is therefore easily determined.

The slave-ship! How few of our readers know the beginning of the horrors involved in that term! Imagine a vessel of the fourth or fifth class, built more for speed than space, and therefore with narrow accommodations even for a few passengers; a space between decks divided into two compartments, three feet three inches from floor to ceiling—one of these compartments, sixteen feet by eighteen, the other forty by twenty-one—the first holding two hundred and twenty-six children and youths of both sexes—the second, *three hundred and thirty-six men and women*—and all this in a latitude where the thermometer is at eighty degrees in the shade! Are you sick of the description? O, this is not all, by a good sight. Imagine neither food nor water given these hapless prisoners—except a little of the latter, at long intervals, which they spill in their mad eagerness to get it; many of the women advanced in pregnancy—the motion of the seas sickening those who have never before felt it—dozens of the poor wretches dying, and others already dead (and they are most to be envied!)—the very air so thick that the lungs cannot perform their office—and all this for filthy lucre! Pah! we are almost a misanthrope to our kind when we think they will do such things!

Of the 900 negroes, (there were doubtless more,) originally on board the *Pons* not six hundred and fifty remained when she arrived back, and landed her inmates at Monrovia! It is enough to make the heart pause its pulsations to read the scene presented at the liberation of these sons of misery.—Most of them were boys, of from twelve to twenty years. What woe must have spread through many a negro mother's heart, from this wicked business!

It is not ours to find an excuse for slaving, in the benighted condition of the African. Has not God seen fit to make him, and leave him so? Nor is it any less our fault because the chiefs of that barbarous land fight with each other, and take slave-prisoners. The whites encourage them, and afford them a market. Were that market destroyed, there would soon be no supply.

We would hardly so insult our countrymen as to suppose that any among them yet countenance a system only a little portion of whose horrors we have been describing—did not facts prove the contrary. The "middle passage" is yet going on with all its deadly crime and cruelty. The slave-trade yet exists. *Why?* The laws are sharp enough—too sharp. But

who ever hears of their being put in force, further than to con-
fiscate the vessel, and perhaps imprison the crews a few days?
But the laws should pry out every man who helps the slave-
trade—not merely the sailor on the sea, but *the cowardly rich
villain and speculator on the land*—and punish *him*. It cannot
be effectually stopped until that is done—and Brazil forced by
the black muzzles of American and European men-of-war's can-
non, to stop her part of the business too!

HURRAH FOR HANGING![1]

WE ARE going to say some bold truths! We are going to
dash at once into the impassioned errors of probably four out
of every five who will read this article.

—If ever the present system of criminal law, and of the treat-
ment of criminals, offered an instance of one of its fruits, that
instance is the precocious monster *Freeman*—the butcher of five
human beings last week in Cayuga co., in this state—as we have
already published the dark and dreadful narrative. Reader!
you may meet such a remark as the foregoing with a scowl, or
an impatient jibe—but if we are not, in our own mind, clear in
its truth, may we never get sight of Heaven hereafter!

The present excited state of public feeling will, of course,
lead the representatives of society in due time to paddle in *his*
blood, as he in that of his victim's. The murder will surely be
revenged. We can therefore do no harm by seizing the occasion
to draw as profitable a lesson as we may from the whole case.
It is no inviting task; but few tasks are inviting.

—Let us examine somewhat of the murderer's life:

So far as anything can be gathered from the facts brought to
light, Freeman seems to be an uneducated, friendless outcast.
He has never had the benefit of any kind of teaching or counsel;
and never lived within any fixed moral or religious influences.
His whole character is of the most blindly brutal cast—a mere
human animal. At the early age of nineteen, he is accused of
a crime of which he says he is not guilty, and, through the in-
fluence of Mr. Van Ness, is sent to the State Prison for five years.
Now consider how few of better fortune, even of virtuous and
religious character, would not deeply feel the wrong and injus-

[1] From the Brooklyn *Daily Eagle*, March 23, 1846.
Cf. infra, pp. 97–103; *post*, II, pp. 15–16.

tice of such proceedings, and be roused to the fiercest hate against those who had been instrumental in bringing them to it. How much more terrible the effect then on this neglected, ignorant and depraved negro, in whom the brute had been allowed to rule the man.

For five long and weary years he is shut up in prison, and left to brood over his wrongs. He can make no distinction between the inevitable mistakes of the law and human testimony, and what he imagines is a determination to crush him. He thinks only of his laborious imprisonment day after day, month after month, till it has taken possession of all his thoughts; and the purpose of revenge, which to him is justice, has become to him the very breath of life. If society had dealt tenderly with him during this awful period; if some ministering angel[1] had come and heard his sorrowful story, and sought to bring him under kindly influences, and taught him the beautiful Christian law, "Love your enemies; bless those who curse you;" if this had been done, he might have been saved, and his victims been still in the midst of the living.

But this was not done. The neglected wretch was left to his fate, left to be haunted by his foul passions, and at last to be turned out to do their own bidding without a word of warning, or one friend to guide or bless. Is it a matter of wonder, then, that the result is what we have seen? Is it strange that the wild beast prevailed?

That the wretch had worked himself into a terribly calm and blind ferocity appears from the whole account of the murder. The idea of revenge seems to have swallowed up all things else. He seems to have become perfectly bewildered and blinded by his purpose of blood. He not only strikes the object of his spite, the man who did him the supposed wrong, but indiscriminately, as though running the bloody muck. With a frightful coolness, he plunges his knife into all whom he meets, sacrificing guilty and innocent alike. He destroys those who never did him harm, whom he never saw, and against whom he could have had no possible hatred or ill-feeling! This very horror of the butchery shows how thoroughly diseased and confused the whole moral being of the murderer had become.

—What remains then? *Hang him.* In the work of death, let the law keep up with the murderer, and see who will get the victory at last. Homicides are increasing in every part of the

[1] *Cf. infra*, pp. 83-86.

land. We are amazed that the gallows don't stop 'em. Let its advocates not be backward, however. Let them stick it out staunchly and kill and slay the faster—and, even if the more they hang the more they prepare to hang, let them keep it up still—*for is not such the command of God?*[1]

"MOTLEY'S YOUR ONLY WEAR!"[2]

A CHAPTER FOR THE FIRST OF APRIL.

AHA! *this* is all Fool's day, is it? What right or reason has any body to select one day from the whole year, and give it such a name? Just as if our world was weak and wicked a three hundred and sixty-fifth fraction of its existence only. Why, sirs, the rule should run the other way altogether. If there were a day of universal common sense all over the earth, *that* would indeed be something wonderful. The great axis would cease in its revolutions in dismay and confusion, at any-thing of *that* kind!

But we must not run off in this manner.

We salute you, Fools! The time is yours; politeness demands that you should have the compliments of the season; and we are going to give up to your services a part of one of our columns. And as your name is legion, it were well to pick out the few among you who, standing prominently forward, are entitled to the first benefit of our courtesy.

The sour tempered grumbler at humanity, and at this beau-tiful earth which the good God has made so well—the man whose actions sing "love not," forever, though his mouth sings not at all—*he* is one to whom this day is most particularly dedicated. He will not smile, not he; but he will snarl and snap—the tart vinegar fellow! He will not bless the bright sunshine, and the fragrant flowers, and the innocence of young children, and the soothing wind that brings health and vigor. No, no. He plods discontentedly along. He sees but the bad that is in his fellow creatures; he has sharp eyes for every stum-bling block, and quick ears for every discord, (a harmony to the hearing largely tuned,)[3] in the great anthem of life. Weak;

[1] *Cf. infra*, p. 103.

[2] From the Brooklyn *Daily Eagle*, April 1, 1846.

[3] This would seem to argue that Whitman's theory of evil had already been formulated. *Cf. post*, I, p. 231.

miserable one! Wilt thou walk through the garden, and perversely prick thy hand with the thorns, and put thy nose only to the scentless blossom, while all around thee is so much goodly roses, and ever fresh verdure, and sweets budding out perpetually? Wilt thou cast thy glance morosely on the ground, and never toward that most excellent canopy, the cloud-draped and star-studded sky above thee?

Ah, open thyself to a better and more genial philosophy, Fool. There are griefs and clouds and disappointments, in the lot of man; but there are comforts and enjoyments too.[1] And we must glide aside by the former smoothly, and hold fast to the latter, and foster them, that like guests treated hospitably, they may come again, and haply take up their abode with us. It is habit, after all, that makes the largest part of the discontents of life. Fight against that wicked habit, Fool, that thou may'st be a happier man, and not be thought of simultaneously with the First of April.

—And you, sir, with the muck-rake—you feverish toiler and burrower for superfluous wealth[2]—you must not be forgotten, either. Cease your weary application, an hour or two—for your class should hold high revel, to-day. No? you have houses to build, and accounts to compute, and profits to reap? But, man, you already own houses enough; and the profits of your past labor warrant the ample competence of the future. Still, argue you, *business* engages all your time—*must* occupy it? Oh, Fool! The little birds, and the sheep in the field, possess more reason than thou; for when once their natural wants are satisfied, they repose themselves and toil no more.[3] The lambs gambol. The birds sing, in joy and gratitude, as it were, to the good God; and *you* will do nothing but plod, and plod. Go to, Fool! It is not well to labor in servile offices, while the great banquet is spread in many princely halls, and all who would partake are welcome.

—Gently turn we to another band of the erring mortal. Gently: For *guilt*, though often tough, to an iron hardness, cannot be bettered by other hardness—by stern vindictive punishment,[4] and angry reproof. Apart and by themselves—in silence and

---

[1] *Cf. infra*, pp. 78–83.   [2] *Cf. infra*, pp. 37–39; *post*, I, pp. 123–125, 245; II, pp. 63, 67.

[3] Such a paraphrase of the Bible as this suggests a probable source of Whitman's inspiration in the moral didacticism with which the *Eagle* editorials are replete; and it also helps to account for his prophetic rôle's assuming so decidedly religious a form. See *post*, II, pp. 91–92.

[4] *Cf. infra*, pp. 97–103, 108–110.

tears—with repentance, and vows of reformation, should the *doers of crime* keep this day. No taunt or insult of their more fortunate brethren should come to deepen their oppressive sadness. But the words of encouragement and sympathy should come—the friendly glance such as the Pardoner himself disdained not to throw on sin and sinners—the thought of the frailness of mortality, and its self-retrieving strength, also, these, like good spirits, should surround the sons and daughters of vice and cheer them to the working out of a better heart.

—Nor must we forget the political fool—the unbeliever in human goodness and progress, and worth: nor the little manœuvrer and plotter who is mighty in bar-rooms, and blusters loudly with the sacred names of towering ideas—which are to him but the base counters to pass away in exchange for food for his own silly and selfish ambition. He is truly a foolish Fool, and ofttimes inoculates others with the contagion.

—And as we must stop in the category somewhere—long as the list could be made—we wind up with that multitude, (if it be not a bull to say so,) of single fools, the bachelors and maids who are old enough to be married—but who, from appearances, will probably "die and give no sign."[1] If seizing the means of the truest happiness—a home, domestic comfort, children, and the best blessings—be wisdom, then is the unmarried state a great folly. There be some, doubtless, who may not be blamed—whom peculiar circumstances keep in the bands of the solitary; but the most of both sexes can find partners meet for them, if they will.[2] Turn Fools, and get discretion. Buy candles and

---

[1] *Cf.* "He dies, and makes no sign" ("King Henry VI," Pt. 2, III, 3, 29).

[2] Such a passage is perplexing rather than illuminating; for, though it clearly shows that, previous to Whitman's first Southern journey, he strongly approved of marriage as an institution and the married state as an avenue to happiness, we cannot be sure that the writer is Whitman the man instead of Whitman the philosophizing editor, nor can we be sure that, if this be a personal revelation, it was not qualified by the prophetic inspiration which descended upon the poet about 1847. Moreover, does he excuse himself along with the individuals whom "peculiar circumstances keep in the bands of the solitary"? If so, what were the peculiar circumstances alluded to—the mere inability to find a mate or something in his emotional nature which made it unlikely that he would ever find a mate? (See *infra*, pp. lxix-l, 92.) That the latter may have been the case seems a little more probable when the final appeal to the bachelors is made, for this appeal is based, not on romantic or hedonistic grounds, but on the duty to "do the state some service," an appeal which is made very prominent in "Children of Adam." An undated scrap of Whitman manuscript, owned by Mr. Alfred Goldsmith, records the following melancholy query: "Why is it that a sense comes always crushing on me, as of one happiness I have missed in life? and one friend and companion I have never made?" However, the passage in the text above is too ambiguous to be very valuable as evidence either way, when taken by itself. (See *infra*, p. 48, note 1.)

double beds; make yourself a reality in life—and do the state some service.

We cease; even though yet but on the first leaf of the ponderous catalogue.   And if in the wild spirit of the day, we have expressed our fancies in defiance of the sober methods of editors, let us find our license amid the wide privileges of the First of April—or, if it please you better, sweet madam, or good sir, jot us down as one who himself, by good right, deserves a patch o' the motley.

SOMETHING ABOUT THE CHILDREN OF EARLY SPRING [1]

THE flowers! the sweet and beautiful flowers, are beginning now to bud forth and bloom!   With the first mildening of the air came the proud camelia, in all its simple splendor of pure red, or unmottled white.   We saw it weeks ago on the stands, and in the parlor windows, as we passed along, with its glossy clean leaves, and its peculiar aristocratic bend, as if conscious that it should be the queen of all the tribe of grace.   The waxe like [wax-like] precision of its delicate blossom-leaves, and the early greeting it gives us, of all flowers of the year, make it one of our chosen favorites.

And the oriental-looking cactus is out too, with its innumerable points, like the turrets of some old gothic architecture. And the azalia, likewise, one of the sisters of the April circle. But the perennial blooming rose, the beautiful one! ah, *it* comes like a loved child's smiling face, that greets us daily and grows into our hearts deeper and deeper through the passing time.   In summer and winter blooms the good rose—in the severity of the latter season, requiring, of course, to be sheltered with a kindly hand from the cold kiss of the snows and frosts. Blessings on the fragrant Daughter of the Morning Clouds! It is the choice and cherished blossom of our variable clime. In its plenty and luxuriance, it spreads by the sides of the fields in the country, and repays the slightest care of the gardener. Without the good rose, we were to lose much of the loveliness that covers the surface of our northern earth.

And should we forget the humble, and modest,—the sweet downward-hidden violet?   Timid as a soft-eyed babe, it nestles

[1] From the Brooklyn *Daily Eagle*, April 9, 1846.

its face in the breast of Earth, its mother! Flower of the faint sweet perfume, and the purple blush! we pluck thee never—but love to bend down and part carefully away the grass leaves, and inhale thy fragrance—but ever place back around thee thy bolder friend, and leave thee then unharmed. Ah, there is to us a deep sacred charm in humility! And is it not so to all?—How wicked the heart that can, in the black corruption of its selfishness, outrage that charm, and bruise the innocent weakness of a modest fragile one!

The heath-blossom and the blue-bell, too, exhibit their colored tints to the sun, and draw back again life and vigor from his smiles. And the geranium, that sweet among the sweetest, opens its little red buds, and fills the air with the refreshing scent of its lemon-smelling leaves. Nor are there wanting other manifestations of the bounty of the good Father above; but on these we forbear now to expatiate.

——If you have none of these silent orators of devotion about you, gentle reader, go forthwith and procure them, and place them where you will see them every day. Their mute mouths are a perpetual hymn to the holy God—and it were well for you to listen to them. Miss Bremer[1] tells us a beautiful and sublime thought which she learned from flowers.—In the resemblance, as they are widely and incessantly drawing life, beauty, and virtue from the sun, *while yet that luminary lessens not in those qualities which it is constantly bestowing on other things*—so the Almighty, the fountain of goodness, truth and all vitality, though throwing off that vitality and truth forever, yet stays eternally the same, and loses nought.

——Ah, we may learn many a fine moral from the flowers!

OURSELVES AND THE *EAGLE*[2]

We have arrayed ourselves in new apparel, and present us to the public with a "clean face," to-day—as per the current paragraph, and all after it! We might say a great deal, herewith, about what we are going to do, etc.; but we think it about as well to "let our acts speak for us." We shall do as well as we can; and our journal will be "devoted" to—what is put into it.

[1] *Cf. post*, I, p. 128.
[2] From the Brooklyn *Daily Eagle*, June 1, 1846.

The democratic party of Brooklyn should (*and do*) hand-somely support a handsome daily paper.—For our part, too, we mean no mere lip-thanks when we say that we are truly con-scious of the warm kindness with which they have always treated this establishment. To those in Brooklyn who, not taking a daily local print, feel inclined to subscribe to one, we respect-fully suggest that they "try us," now. If at the end of a fort-night, or month, they don't think they get the worth of their money, we will cheerfully mark them off again. We really feel a desire to talk on many subjects, to *all* the people of Brooklyn; and it *ain't* their ninepences we want so much either. There is a curious kind of sympathy (haven't you ever thought of it before?) that arises in the mind of a newspaper conductor with the public he serves. He gets to *love* them. Daily communion creates a sort of brotherhood and sisterhood between the two parties. As for us, we like this. We like it better than the more "dignified" part of editorial labors—the grave political disquisition, the contests of faction, and so on. And we want as many readers of the *Brooklyn Eagle*—even unto the half of Long Island—as possible, that we may increase the number of such friends. For are not those who daily listen to us, friends? —Perhaps no office requires a greater union of rare qualities than that of a *true editor*. No wonder, then, that so few come under that flattering title! No wonder that we are all derelict, in some particular! In general information, an editor should be com-plete, particularly with that relating to his own country. He should have a fluent style: elaborate finish we do not think requisite in daily writing. His articles had far better be earnest and terse than polished; they should ever smack of being uttered on the spur of the moment, like political oratory.—[1] In temper,

[1] This statement of Whitman's editorial creed, made shortly before he did the first known writing on "Leaves of Grass," was in part, perhaps unconsciously, transferred to his poetic work. But in the matter of polish, he seems to have come to see the weak-ness of his position, in regard to both editorial writing and poetic composition. In an editorial in the Brooklyn *Daily Times* (January 25, 1858) under the heading "Wanted, A Critic," he writes:

"We never glance over our own columns or those of our contemporaries without wishing that some monarch of journalism would arise, and hold all the small fry of the profession to a rigid accountability in regard to the style and grammar of their manifold effusions. . . . How much of the turbid bombast and buncombe of political speak-ers might be choked in the utterance, if the newspapers would only conform themselves, and compel others to conform, to a stern and rigid rectitude of expression. . . .

"We firmly believe that a loose and ungrammatical style leads to heterodoxy of senti-ment—that the writer who would deliberately infringe the rules of composition would not long hesitate attempting to make the worse appear the better reason.

". . . . The *Evening Post* is perhaps the model journal as regards its rhetoric

Job himself is the lowest example he should take. And even that famed ancient, we trow, cannot be said to have achieved the climax of human endurance—since types and printing presses were not in vogue at his era. An editor needs, withal, a sharp eye, to discriminate the good from the immense mass of unreal stuff floating on all sides of him—and always bearing the counterfeit presentment of the real. This talent is so rare that many newspapers have built up quite a reputation on the merit of their selections[1] alone. Here, in this country, most editors have far far *too much to do*,[2] to make good work of what they do. Abroad, it is different. In London or Paris, the payment for a single "leader" is frequently more than the month's salary of the best remunerated American editor. Crowding upon one individual the duties of five or six, is, indeed, the greatest reason of all why we have in America so very few daily prints that are artistically equal to the European ones. Is it not astonishing, then—not that the press of the United States don't do better, but that it don't do worse?

With all and any drawbacks, however, much good can always be done, with such [a] potent influence as a well circulated newspaper. To wield that influence, is a great responsibility. There are numerous noble reforms that have yet to be pressed

---

but it circulates only among the classes who stand least in need of an instructor. . . . The slovenliness of journalistic composition reacts with tenfold effect upon public speakers. We have sat in the Board of Education and listened to the grossest errors of utterance, such as 'It don't matter'—'I was a-going to propose'—'I motion that,' etc., until our fingers have tingled with the desire to box the speakers' ears, and set them at the bottom of the lowest classes, instead of placing them at the head of school affairs."

[1] This refers to the miscellany of copied poetry and prose, occasionally including a serial story such as Whitman's own "Fortunes of a Country Boy" (see *post*, II, p. 103, note), which the better papers of the day usually printed on the first of their four pages.

[2] There is no doubt that the duties of an editor were, in the forties, both so complex and so bothersome as to excuse occasional carelessness in composition. But tradition is positive on the point that Whitman, for his part, was so alive to the danger of having the creative part of him destroyed by the more commonplace duties of his profession that he usually left the office for a stroll of two or three hours, or a swim at Carey's Baths, in the middle of every fine day, sometimes taking a member of the office force with him for company. Nor are we dependent on tradition alone. The following brief editorial dealing with a line of city omnibuses shows where Whitman was likely to be found in the afternoons: ". . . After our editorial morning toils are over—weary and fagged out with them—we have no greater pleasure than to get into one of these handsome easy carriages (imagining it is our private establishment, and the other passengers our guests)—and drive out to some of the beautiful avenues beyond Fort Greene (*are* we to have that Park?) and there alight, and walk about—stretching over the hills, and down the distant lanes—till after sunset; and then walk home again with a tremendous appetite for supper, and limbs that invite sleep. We always find the carriages of the East Brooklyn line 'comfortable,' and the drivers civil and obliging." (Brooklyn *Daily Eagle*, August 25, 1846.)

upon the world. People are to be schooled, in opposition per-
haps to their long established ways of thought.—In politics, too,
the field of improvement is wide enough yet; the harvest is
large, and waiting to be reaped—and each paper, however
humble, may do good in the ranks. Nor is it a mere monoto-
nous writer after old fashions that can achieve the good we speak
of. . . . We shall have more to say on this theme, at a very
early period.

A PLEASANT MORNING[1]

LIKE what we have had to-day, deserves special notice, after
the late abominable "spell" of damp and darkness. How fair
and glorious was to-day's rising of the sun! All nature seemed
glad, like a gleesome youth. The cool, clear air, with the fresh-
ness that always hangs in it, at sun-rise, were especially grateful.
We noticed invalids drawn out; and doubtless the Battery has
heard the mirth of children loudly to-day.

And the *ladies!* it has seemed to us in our peregrinations,
that they look more beautiful to-day than ever before! We
had occasion to go through a part of Broadway, in the great
Babel over the river, about 11 o'clock. Ah, the handsome
faces and poetical forms we were mildened by there! And
how hot it was withal. The water-carts should be on the alert,
such weather as this.

On the side opposite our office, we see at this moment bevies
of our Brooklyn belles on their way to the ferry. They have
those lithe graceful shapes such as the American women only
have—the delicately cut features, and the intellectual cast of
head. Ah, woman! the very sight of you is a mute prayer of
peace. Without your refining presence the late sulky fit of
weather, "wouldn't be a beginning," to the darkness that would
spread over the earth.

ANDREW JACKSON[2]

ONE year ago passed a noble spirit to heaven!—One year ago,
to-day, Andrew Jackson, yielded up his life—and yielded it up

[1] From the Brooklyn *Daily Eagle*, June 3, 1846.

[2] From the Brooklyn *Daily Eagle*, June 8, 1846. Whitman's worship of the hero of
democracy was doubtless imbibed from his father, a staunch Democrat, who named one
of his sons for Jackson and another for Jefferson.

calmly and gracefully, and (for who shall say otherwise?) with
the consciousness of duties well performed. "Heaven gave
him length of days, and he filled them with deeds of glory."
Noble! yet simple-souled old man! We never saw him but
once. That was when we were but a little boy, in this very
city of Brooklyn.[1] He came to the north, on a tour, while he
was President. One sweet fragrant summer morning, when the
sun shone brightly, he rode up from the ferry in an open ba-
rouche. His weather-beaten face is before us at this moment,
as though the scene happened but yesterday—with his snow-
white hair brushed stiffly up from his forehead, and his piercing
eyes quite glancing through his spectators—as those rapid eyes
swept the crowds on each side of the street.

The whole city—the ladies first of all—poured itself forth
to welcome the Hero and Sage. Every house, every window,
was filled with women, and children, and men—though most of
the latter were in the open streets. The President had a big-
brimmed white beaver hat, and his arm must have ached some,
from the constant and courteous responses he made to the inces-
sant salutations which greeted him every where—the waving of
handkerchiefs from the females, and shouts from the men.

Massive, yet most sweet and plain character! in the wrangle
of party and the ambitious strife after political distinctions,
which mark so many even of our most eminent men, how grate-
ful it is to turn to *your* unalloyed patriotism! Your great soul
never knew a thought of self, in questions which involved your
country! Ah, there has lived among us but *one* purer!

EAST LONG ISLAND[2]

A FLYING PIC-NIC—GREENPORT, &c.—God bless us all!
what an idea! To take breakfast as usual in Brooklyn—ride a
hundred miles—"spend the day"—and then return over the
same hundred miles to sup at nine o'clock, where we started
from—and all just as quietly as a man ties his neckcloth in
the morning! Such a feat, (we flatter ourself,) is not unworthy
of special record, even in this era of heaven-telegraphs, and
democratic "annexation."—Yes, gentle madam—or sir, with

[1] In the summer of 1833; Whitman was fourteen years old.
[2] From the Brooklyn *Daily Eagle*, June 27, 1846.

upturned nose—it *is* true. In far less than the mean time when the sun shone (or ought to have shone,) yesterday, *we* achieved the aforesaid feat. We started at half-past seven, A. M.,—went to Greenport—analyzed that pretty town, talked with the ladies, roamed hither and yon, dined, and did many other things needless to mention here. At five o'clock, P. M. (after spending twice as long a "day" as the Constitutional Convention has at any time worked, yet,) westward came we, and at nine, our boot-soles were duly whopping the pavement of Henry street, in this most pious city of churches.

Certes, a pleasanter country town (and a stiff place, withal, that knows the fashions, and can tell the taste of modern French cookery!) than Greenport, it were a cruel task to give even "tricksy Ariel."[1] Going down with the L. I. R. R., you are dumped (the said R. R. going no farther,) on a long wharf, cluttered with rubbish of the most nondescript kind. After you have picked yourself up from the bewilderment of a jaunt whose rapidity has left you somewhat in doubt whether you are really awake, you sweep your eyes around, and lo! a few rods to the south, a goodly habitation, of potent dimensions, and flags flying—a most christian looking house, and a satisfactory assurance, after fifty miles of "plains" and scrub oak, that you are *not* among heathen, but will surely get you a good civilized dinner. As a further enlightenment, in the premises, let us transcribe the following card:

PECONIC HOUSE,
Greenport, L. I.
At the termination of the Rail Road.
(Good Sea Bathing and Fishing).
D. R. FLEEMAN, ⎫ Proprietors.
GEO. FLEEMAN, ⎬

To this house (if you know what's what,) you will forthwith transport yourself. It is a jewel of a hotel—and the dinner yesterday is "not to be beat," we vouch for it. Mr. Fleeman was formerly of the Pearl street House, in New York; he has, at the Peconic, the fullest and finest accommodations that may be desired. "Some" gentlemen or families can either or both be "at home" there—and we recommend 'em to try it.

The village of Greenport contains about sixteen hundred inhabitants. It lies handsomely, in respect to situation; and we

[1] "My tricksy spirit [Ariel]," "The Tempest," V, 1, 226.

should judge would be unsurpassable for health. Streets are opened in every direction. Neat new houses line them, and gardens, with many pretty flowers, adorn them. There are three churches, all in a bunch together,—Presbyterian, Baptist, and Methodist, under the Rev. Messrs. Woodbridge, Leech, and Collins. Some eleven or twelve whaleships go out of Greenport, which makes something of an item of business there. The persons largest engaged in whaling are Ireland, Wells, & Carpenter. There are two ship yards—Post's and Bishop's. A spirited competition is kept up in county trading, &c., we should judge from the shops. The *Watchman*, a weekly print, is published at Greenport. And besides the Peconic House (which is first, by all odds,) there are the Greenport House, by Mr. Terry, and the Temperance Hotel by old Capt. Clark.

The beauty and the wealth of Long Island lie mostly along its shores, or near to them. Thus it is, that an unfavorable impression often results from travelling over the railroad—which, just beyond Jamaica, pursues the most dreary tract afforded by Suffolk and Queen's co's. It cuts the immense tract called Hempstead Plains, and afterwards keeps a picket of "brush" on its sides, with little intermission, till it gets to Greenport. If the traveller were to go a short distance either north or south, almost anywhere along this tract, he would be quite sure to find a rich and thrifty settlement—rich in fertile acres, agricultural productions, and the comforts of farm life. He would also find himself contiguous either to the Sound or South Bay—both full of good fish, of the scaly or shelly order. Much of the simplicity of patriarchial times, too, yet prevails among the farmers of Suffolk—much of the *honesty*, besides. Even the Railroad had not yet been able to eradicate it.[1]

The farmers of Suffolk county! A sturdier faction of that "country's pride," which, "once lost, can never be supplied,"[2] does not exist. Our whig neighbours of the New York *Tribune* and the Brooklyn *Star* affect to look with sovereign contempt on them, we know; they point annual jokes (about election times,) with their "benighted" state, and so on. And yet a more generally intelligent race of men and women exists nowhere,—certainly not in any of our Atlantic cities—than the farmers of Suffolk county. They have little parlor polish,

[1] *Cf. post*, I, p. 179; II, p. 14.
[2] From Goldsmith's "The Deserted Village."

perhaps—that miserable paint with which a poor heart so often daubs itself; but they are well-informed on general topics, clear in their political views, and hospitable to a fault. Every body knows how *democratic* they are: and here's the rub to the whig prints aforementioned. We consider the wit which aims itself at the honest simplicity of that part of our state to be an evidence unquestionable of either a very silly brain or a very bad heart.

We shall remember yesterday's excursion for some time, with pleasure. The company was excellent—no small portion being ladies. A car was attached, filled with first-rate refreshments; and the obliging waiters served the passengers just as the latter might have been served in an ordinary public dining or ice-cream room. On the return, nearly every body had a prodigious bouquet. Take it altogether, it was creditable to each one engaged in getting it up—and to the L. I. Railroad Co. as much as any.

"HOME" LITERATURE[1]

He who desires to see this noble Republic independent, not only in name but in fact, of all unwholesome foreign sway must ever bear in mind the influence of European literature over us—its tolerable amount of good, and its, we hope, "not to be endured" much longer, immense amount of evil. That there is often some clap-trap in denunciations of English books, we have no disposition to deny,—but the evil generally leans on the other side: we receive with a blind homage whatever comes to us stamped with the approbation of foreign critics— merely because it *is* so stamped. We have not enough confidence in our own judgment; we forget that God has given the American mind powers of analysis and acuteness superior to those possessed by any other nation on earth.

For the beautiful creations of the great intellects of Europe— for the sweetness of majesty of Shakespeare,[2] Goethe,[3] and some of the Italian poets—the fiery breath of Byron,[4] the fascinating melancholy of Rousseau,[5] the elegance and candor of Hume

[1] From the Brooklyn *Daily Eagle*, July 11, 1846.

[2] For Shakespeare's influence on Whitman, see the Subject Index.

[3] *Cf. post*, I, pp. 132, 139–141.   [4] *Cf. infra*, p. 48, note 1.

[5] *Cf. post*, I, p. 243. Professor Perry has pointed out (*loc. cit.*, pp. 52, 69, 266, 277-280) numerous points of similarity between Whitman and Rousseau.

and Gibbon—and much more beside—we of the western world bring our tribute of admiration and respect. Presumptious and vain would it be for us to decry their glorious merits. But it must not be forgotten, that many of the most literary men of England are the advocates of doctrines that in such a land as ours are the rankest and foulest poison.—Cowper teaches blind loyalty to the "divine right of kings,"—Johnson[1] was a burly aristocrat—and many more of that age were the scorners of the common people, and pour adulation on the shrine of "toryism." Walter Scott, Croly,[2] Alison,[3] Southey, and many others well known in America, exercise an evil influence through their books, in more than one respect; for they laugh to scorn the idea of republican freedom and virtue.

And what perfect cataracts of trash come to us at the present day from abroad! The tinsel sentimentality of Bulwer is but a relief from the inflated, unnatural, high-life-below-stairs, "historical" romances of Harrison Ainsworth. As to the vulgar coarseness of Marryatt,[4] the dish-water senility of Lady Blessington,[5] and the stuff (there is no better word,) of a long string of literary quacks, tapering down to the nastiness of the French Paul de Kock (who in reality has perhaps more talent than all the others put together—malgre his awfully murderous translations into English,)—who can say they have any qualities which recommend them to that wide circulation they enjoy on this side of the Atlantic? Let us be more just to ourselves and our own good taste. Why, "Professor" Ingraham,[6] and those— their name is legion—Misters and Madams who write tales (does any body ever really read them through?) for the monthly magazines, have quite as much genuine ability as these coiners of unwholesome reading from abroad!

[1] *Cf. post*, I, pp. 127–128.

[2] George Croly (1780–1860), an Irish poet, clergyman, and writer of such romances as "Salathiel."

[3] Probably Sir Archibald Alison (1792–1867), the Scotch historian, author of "History of Europe during the French Revolution."

[4] Frederick Marryat (1792–1848), captain in the British navy and author of "Mr. Midshipman Easy" and other novels.

[5] Marguerite Power, Countess of Blessington (1789–1849), a literary patroness, author of "Conversations with Lord Byron."

[6] Joseph Holt Ingraham (1809-1860), a sailor, a graduate of Bowdoin College, professor of languages in Jefferson College (Natchez, Miss.) in 1832, and a Protestant Episcopal rector of St. Thomas' Hall, a boy's school (Holly Springs, Miss.), after 1855. He wrote stories of adventure, notably "Lafitte; or the Pirate of the Gulf," and religious romances, such as "The Prince of the House of David," which did much to remove the odium from fiction reading in America.

But where is the remedy? says the inquisitive reader. *In ourselves* we must look for it. Let those who read (and in this country who does not read?) no more condescend to patronize an inferior foreign author, when they have so many respectable writers at home. Shall Hawthorne get a paltry *seventy-five dollars* for a two-volume work—shall real American genius shiver with neglect—while the public run after this foreign trash? We hope, and we confidently expect, that the people of this land will come to their "sober second thought" upon the subject, and that soon.

MORBID APPETITE FOR MONEY[1]

IN THE course of an article on the subject of the influence of wealth, &c., in one of our exchange papers, we find this sentiment:

Poverty—poverty, in the common acceptation of the term—is a thing dreaded by mankind, and is often placed among the catalogue of *crimes*. Such is the poverty that fellowships with rags and beggary. But there is another species of poverty, the most despicable that can be imagined, and more to be dreaded than all other earthly ills and maladies combined. We mean the *poverty of soul*, with which rich men are often afflicted, and the only poverty to be abhorred and despised. Men who oppress and cheat the poor—men who make wealth the standard of worth and respectability—men who make gold their god, and whose devotions consist of *Dollar-Worship*, are the self-made victims of this *poverty of soul*, compared to which destitution is a Heaven sent blessing.

On no particular matter is the public mind more unhealthy than the appetite for money. The wild schemes of visionary men—the religious excitements of misled enthusiasts—the humbugs of ignorant pretenders to knowledge—the quackery of the thousand imposters of all descriptions who swarm through the land—have their followers and believers for a time; though the weakness which always attends error soon carries them to oblivion.—They glitter for a moment—swim for a day on the tide of public favor—and then sink to a deserved and endless repose. But the mad passion for getting rich does not die away in this manner. It engrosses all the thoughts and the time of men. It is the theme of all their wishes. It enters into their

hearts and reigns paramount there. It pushes aside the holy
precepts of religion, and violates the purity of justice. The
unbridled desire for wealth breaks down the barriers of morality,
and leads to a thousand deviations from those rules, the observ-
ance of which is necessary to the well-being of our people. It
is that, and nothing else, which has led to the commission of
those robberies of the public treasury that have in years past
excited the astonishment and alarm of the American nation.
It is the feverish anxiety after riches that leads year after year
to the establishment of those immense moneyed institutions,
which have so impudently practised in the face of day, frauds
and violations of their engagements, that ought to make the
cheek of every truly upright man burn with indignation.[1]
Reckless and unprincipled—controlled by persons who make
them complete engines of selfishness—at war with everything
that favors our true interests—unrepublican, unfair, untrue,
and unworthy—these bubbles are kept afloat solely and wholly
by the fever for gaining wealth. . . . The same unholy
wish for great riches enters into every transaction of society,
and more or less taints its moral soundness. And from this it is
that the great body of the working-men should seek to guard
themselves. Let them not think that the best thing on earth, and
the most to be desired, is money. For of all the means neces-
sary to happiness, wealth is at least a secondary one; and yet all
of us tacitly unite in making it the main object of our desire.—
For it we work and toil, and sweat away our youth and man-
hood, giving up the improvement of our minds and the cultiva-
tion of our physical nature; weakly thinking that a heap of
money, when we are old, can make up to us for these sacrifices.
And yet when we see the universal homage paid to the rich man,
it appears not very wonderful that people are so greedy for
wealth. But let us think again, of what avail or of what true
gratification is that respect which is paid merely to money? Is
it to win this at the last—to hear men admire—and listen to
the deferential accents of the low—for which hundreds plod on,
and on, and on—making that which was intended as the pleas-
antest part of our journey here a burden or a useless waste? Is
it to gain these ends that men fritter away the sweet spring and
summer of their lives, sinking premature wrinkles into their
brows, closing their hearts to the sweet promptings of nature to
enjoy; and finding themselves, at an advanced stage of their

[1] *Cf. post*, II, pp. 136–142.

existence, with abundance of worldly means for happiness, but past the legitimate season for it? Foolish and miserable error! All the time of such men is devoted to their one great aim; and all their fear is that they may be poor. Want of wealth is, in their idea, the greatest of miseries. They look abroad into the world, and their souls seem to grasp at but one object—filthy lucre. . . . Now let us be more just to our own nature. Let us cast our eyes over this beautiful earth, where so much of fair joy, of pure happiness, of grandeur, of love, of sunshine, exist; looking on the human race with the gentle orbs of benevolence and philosophy; sending our glance through the cool and verdant lanes—by the sides of the blue rivers—over the busy and crowded city—among those who dwell far on the prairies—or along the green savannahs—or where the monarch of rivers pours his dark tide into the sea; and we shall see poor men everywhere; and we shall see that those men are not wretched because they are poor; and we shall see that if they were to prove luckier than they have been, and were to become rich, they would not be better men—or happier men. And many of the most truly great men that ever lived have been poor—have passed their days in the vale—and never had their names sounded abroad by applauding mouths. Silent and unknown—enjoying the treasures of soul inherent within them—superior to the common desire for notoriety—they have lived and died in obscure stations. The world heard not of them—statues were not built to them—nor domes consecrated to them—nor cities honored with being named after them. But they were nevertheless of characters really sublime and grand: not the grandeur of common heroes, but the grandeur of some mighty river, existing in a part of the world as yet undiscovered, holding its broad course through untrodden banks, and its capacious riches not open to the world.

CRITICISM—NEW BOOKS[1]

By AN old and excellent custom—a custom good for the public, for the publishers of books, and for editors of newspapers—new books are presented to editors, that they may mention the same, and thus bring them before their readers. A newspaper that does not give such notices is "behind the age;"

[1] From the Brooklyn *Daily Eagle*, November 9, 1846.

for brief as those notices generally are, they enable a man to keep up with what is doing in the literary world, and to see the gradual steps made in the advancement of every thing. *This is true*—as any one will acknowledge after a moment's reflection; for he who gets no inkling of any of the new developments constantly made, through books (and he *will* get that inkling through honestly written book-notices,) lives quite in the Past. . . . The custom alluded to has another good effect also—it enables *editors* to keep up, in some sort, with the foremost ones of the age. For though it cannot be expected that they will study from top to bottom every book they have—that skimming tact which an editor gets after some experience, enables him to take out at a dash the meaning of a book—and his paper and his readers are invariably the gainers by it. An editor thus surrounded by the current literature of the age—by thoughts and facts evolved from master-minds, as well as imitators—*cannot lag behind.* In a thousand invisible but potent ways the result is good for his professional labors.

As to the book-notices in this journal, we hope to say nothing amiss, when we say that our readers lose something when they lose the reading of them. They are our candid opinions; leaning, as we prefer to lean, to a kindly vein—as it is not our province to "cut up" authors. . . . (A new book was sent to us the other day with a highly eulogistic written notice, to be inserted as editorial. We can't do *such things*.)[1] . . . It certainly were no compliment to the taste of Brooklynites, to assume that they feel no interest in literary matters.

———

[EXTRACTS FROM WHITMAN'S CRITICISMS OF BOOKS AND AUTHORS, CULLED FROM THE BROOKLYN *DAILY EAGLE* OF 1846–1848][2]

"Arabian Nights' Entertainment"
    They bring up the loving and greedy eagerness with which boyhood read these tales—a love surpassing the love for puddings and confectionery. . . . The minds of boys

[1] *Cf. post*, pp. 153, 157.

[2] I believe it safe to say that Whitman reviewed more books, and knew more about books, than any contemporary editor in Brooklyn, if not in New York, exclusive of the editors of the literary periodicals. It was he who introduced the literary miscellany into the *Eagle* and who first gave prominence to book reviewing through its columns.

and girls warm and expand—become rich and generous—
under the aspect of such florid pages as those of Robinson
Crusoe, the Arabian Nights, Marco Polo, and the like.
[October 11, 1847.]

"Bible, The Holy," Harper's Illuminated Edition.
It is almost useless to say that no intelligent man can
touch the Book of Books with an irreverent hand. [October 21, 1846.]

Boswell James: "The Life of Samuel Johnson, LL.D., Including a Journal of a Tour of the Herbrides", Croaker,
John Wilson, ed., in two volumes.
We are no admirer of such characters as Dr. Johnson.
He was a sour, malicious, egotistical man. He was a
sycophant of power and rank, withal; his biographer narrates that he "always spoke with rough contempt of popular liberty." His head was educated to the point *plus*,
but for his heart, might still more unquestionably stand

In the course of two years he quoted from nearly a hundred more or less well-known
authors and reviewed more than a hundred other books. In some cases, he merely
glanced at preface and table of contents; in other cases he skipped through the volume;
but good books sometimes received more than one reading at his hands and more than
one notice. In all cases, his library was being steadily increased. That the student
may have a better idea of what Whitman was reading just before, and at the time of,
his first work on the "Leaves of Grass," I append a list of the more important books
noticed or reviewed in the *Eagle*:

William Harrison Ainsworth's "The Miser's Daughter"; Anthon's 'Dictionary of Greek
and Roman Antiquities"; Baxter's (Richard) "Life and Writings"; Robert Bell's
"Life of the Rt. Hon. George Canning"; Berrian's "An Historical Sketch of Trinity
Church, N. Y."; J. D. Blake's "History of the American Revolution"; William Bolles's
"Phonographic Pronouncing Dictionary of the English Language"; J. R. Boyd's "Eclectic
Moral Philosophy"; E. L. Bulwer's "Lucretia; or The Children of the Night"; Chambers' "Encyclopædia of English Literature"; Chambers' "Miscellany of Useful and
Entertaining Knowledge"; A. B. Chapin's "Puritanism Not Genuine Protestantism";
Lydia Maria Child's "Fact and Fiction" and "Memoirs of Madame de Stael and of
Madame Roland"; Coleridge's "Aids to Reflection"; Colman's "Juvenile Publications";
D'Aubigne's "History of the Reformation of the Sixteenth Century"; J. H. Merle
D'Aubigne's "The Protector; A Vindication"; Father P. J. DeSmet's "Oregon
Missions"; Charles D. Desher's "Chaucer and Selections from His Poetical Works";
Dickens's "The Cricket on the Hearth," "The Chimes," "A Goblin Story," "A Christmas Carol," etc., in one volume; Dumas's "The Duke of Burgundy"; Duncan's "Sacred
Philosophy of the Seasons"; Theodore Dwight's "Summer Tours"; Mrs. E. F. Ellet's
"Rambles About the Country"; Thomas F. Farnham's "Mexico: Its Geography, Its
People, and Its Institutions" and "Life, Travels, and Adventures in California and
Scenes in the Pacific Ocean"; "Father Darcy"; Mrs. S. Ferrier's "The Inheritance";
Richard Ford's "Spaniards and Their Country"; John Foster's "The Statesmen of
the Commonwealth of England"; L. N. Fowler's "Marriage, Its History and Ceremonies"; O. S. Fowler's "Physiology, Animal and Mental" and "Memory and Intellectual

the sign *minus*. * * * Nor were the freaks of this man the mere "eccentricities of genius": they were provably the faults of a vile low nature. His soul was a bad one. [But Whitman gives Doctor Johnson a certain amount of credit for his "Dictionary".] [December 7, 1846.]

BREMER, FREDERIKA:[1] Harper's Edition of her works, containing "The Neighbours," "The Home," "The President's Daughter," "Nina," "Strife and Peace," "Life in Delacardia," etc. [Translated by Mary Howitt.]
If we ever have children, the first book after the New Testament, (with reverence we say it) that shall be made their household companion—a book whose spirit shall be infused in them as sun-warmth is infused in the earth in spring—shall be Miss Bremer's novels. We know nothing more likely to melt and refine the human character—particularly the young character. In the study of the soul portraits therein delineated—in their motives, actions, and the results of those actions—every youth, of either sex, will be irresistibly impelled to draw some moral, and make some profitable application to his or her own case. [August 18, 1846.]

BRYANT, WILLIAM CULLEN[2]
We have called Bryant one of the best poets in the world. This smacks so much of the exaggerated that we are half a mind to alter it, true as we sincerely believe it to be. But

---

Improvement"; John G. Galt's "Treatment of Insanity"; Goodwin's "Lives of the Necromancers"; Mrs. Gore's "The Courtier of the Days of Charles II"; William Augustus Guy's "Doctor Hopper's Physicians' Vade Mecum"; Henry Hallam's "The Constitutional History of England"; Headley's "Washington and His Generals"; Henry William Herbert's "Roman Traitor, A True Tale of the Republic"; "Jack Long, or Shot in the Eye"; Douglas Jerrould's "St. Giles and St. James"; "Julia Ormond, or The New Settlement"; Mrs. C. M. Kirkland's "Spenser and the Fairy Queen"; James Sheridan Knowles's "Fortesque"; "Laneton Parsonage"; Mrs. R. Lee's "Memoirs of Baron Cuvier"; "Life of Christ in the Words of the Evangelists"; "Lives of Eminent Individuals Celebrated in American History," three volumes; Abiel Abbott Livermore's "Lectures to Young Men"; "Locke Amsden, or The Schoolmaster"; B. C. Edwards Lester's "Houston and His Republic"; Benson J. Lossing's "Seventeen Hundred and Seventy-Six"; "Martyrs and Covenanters of Scotand"; A. Slidell Mackenzie's "Spain Revisited"; Mary J. McIntosh's "Two Lives, or To Seem and To Be"; A. D. Mayo's "Balance" (on universalism); "Memoirs of the Most Eminent American Mechanics"; Thomas Miller's "The Poetical Language of Flowers"; Dr. George Moore's "The Use of the Body in Relation to the Mind"; Morse's "School Geography and Atlas"; Baron John von Muller's "History of the World" (trans. by Alexander H. Everett); Olmstead's "Letters on Astronomy"; Francis Sargent Osgood's "A Birth-Day Bijou"; Miss Par-

[1] Cf. infra, p. 114.   [2] Cf. infra, p. 115, note; post, I, p. 242, note.

we will let it stand.   *   *   *   Moreover, there will come a time when the writings of this beautiful poet shall attain their proper rank—a rank far higher than has been accorded to them by many accomplished men, who think of them by no means disparagingly. [September 1, 1846.]

CARLYLE, THOMAS: "Heroes and Hero Worship."

Under his rapt, wierd (grotesque?) style the writer of this work has placed—we may almost say *hidden*—many noble thoughts.   That his eyes are clear to the numerous ills which afflict humanity, and that he is a Democrat in that enlarged sense [in] which we would fain see more men Democrats;—that he is quick to champion the down-trodden, and earnest in his wrath at tyranny—is evident enough in almost any one page of Mr. Carlyle's writings. . . . We must confess, however, that we would have preferred to get the thoughts of this truly good thinker, in a plainer and more customary garb.   No great writer achieves anything worthy of him, by merely inventing a new *style*. Style in writing, is much as dress in society; sensible people will conform to the prevalent mode,[1] and it is not of infinite importance anyhow, and can always be so varied as to fit one's peculiar way, convenience, or circumstance. [October 17, 1846.]

---

doe's "Louis the Fourteenth"; Samuel Parker's "Journal of an Exploring Tour Beyond the Rocky Mountains"; Mrs. Phelps's "The Fireside Friend, or Female Student"; Prescott's "Conquest of Peru"; Joseph Salkeld's "Classical Antiquities"; M. B. Sampson's "Rationale of Crime"; Epes Sargent's "Songs of the Sea and Other Poems"; Dr. Leonard Schmitz's "History of Rome"; Mrs. Sigourney's "Water-Drops"; William Gilmore Simms's "Guy Rivers: A Tale of Georgia"; Frederick Soulie's "Pastourel" and "Countess of Morion"; Alden Spooner's "The Grape Vine"; J. G. Spurzheim's "Phrenology"; Story's "Commentaries on the Constitution of the United States"; Eugene Sue's "Martin the Foundling" and "The Wandering Jew"; W. C. Taylor's "Modern British Plutarch"; "Thornberry Abbey"; Henry Thornton's "Family Prayers"; Thomas Timpson's "Memoirs of Mrs. Elizabeth Fry"; "Michael Angelo Titmarsh's" "Notes on a Journey From Cornhill to Cairo"; Turnbull's "Genius of Scotland"; Thomas C. Upham's "Life of Madame de la Mothe Guyon, With Some Account of Fenelon, Archbishop of Cambray"; J. Van Lennep's "The Adopted Son" (trans. by W. E. Hoskins); Dr. von Tschudi's "Travels in Peru"; John Ware's "Memoir of the Life of Henry Ware, jr."; James F. Warner's "Rudimental Lessons in Music"; Dr. Francis Wayland's "The Pursuit of Knowledge Under Difficulties"; J. K. Wellman's "Illustrated Botany"; Francis C. Wemyss' "Twenty-Six Years of the Life of an Actor and Manager"; N. P. Willis's "Sacred Poems"; Marcius Willson's "American History"; Whittier's "Supernaturalism in New England." Total—100 volumes.

As further showing the scope of Whitman's literary information and his taste at the time, I have compiled the following list of authors, American and foreign, from whom he

[1] *Cf. post*, I, p. 162.

"The French Revolution. A History." [Revised edition.]
Mr. Carlyle's genius, as evolved in the work whose title we
have given above, is too broad a subject, and provokes too
many inferences, to be properly treated in one of these short
notices. [November 23, 1846.]

"Past and Present, and Chartism," in two parts.
One likes Mr. Carlyle, the more he communes with him;
there is a sort of fascination about the man. His wierd
wild way—his phrases, welded together as it were, with
strange twistings of the terminatives of words—his startling
suggestions—his taking up, fish-hook like, certain matters
of abuse—make an *original* kind of composition, that gets,
after a little usage, to be strangely agreeable! This "Past
and Present, and Chartism," now—who would ever puzzle
out the drift of the book from the chapter-heads? from
such phrases as "Plugson on undershot," or "the One in-
stitution," or "Gospel of Dilletantism"? And yet there
lies rich ore under that vague surface. [April 14, 1847.]

CHANNING, WILLIAM ELLERY: "Self-Culture."
We have always considered it an unsurpassed piece, either
as to its matter or manner. [June 28, 1847.]

---

has quoted either in his Miscellany or in his Sunday Reading columns. These are in
addition to the reviews given above. In some cases the quotations are in verse, in others
they are in prose. Many of the quotations fill a column or less, while some are novel-
ettes and run for several issues. The numbers in parenthesis indicate the frequency of
quotation, except where only one extract is made.

James Aldrich, T. S. Arthur, Honoré Balzac, Miss Barrett, Park Benjamin (2),
Blackwood's Magazine, Frederika Bremer, William Cullen Bryant (7), J. H. Bright (2),
Lord Byron, Thomas Carlyle, William M. Campbell, J. Maria Child, M. Constant,
Eliza Cook (6), *The Dial*, Charles Dickens, E. J. Eames, Thomas Dunn English, Goethe,
John D. Godman, Theodore A. Gould (11), Mrs. Gove, Washington Irving (3), Mrs.
Sarah J. Hale, Nathaniel Hawthorne (2), William Hazlitt, Johann Gottfried von Herder
(4), Mrs. Hemans, George Herbert (2), Mrs. Mary H. Hewitt, Mary Howitt (5), William
Howitt, Thomas Hood (2), Oliver Wendell Holmes (2), William Henry Cuyler Hosmer,
R. Hoyt, Leigh Hunt (3), Victor Hugo (2), Mrs. C. M. Kirkland, Karl Theodor Korner,
Friedrich Wilhelm (?) Krummacher, Henry Wadsworth Longfellow (22), Samuel Lover
(4), James Russell Lowell (2), Charles Mackay, Thomas Mackellar, Jean François Mar-
montel (2), R. M. Milnes, Miss Mitford, William Motherwell, Mrs. Norton, Joseph A.
Nunes, Susan Pindar, Edgar Allan Poe, "Jean Paul" Richter, William Rogers, Epes
Sargent (2), Schiller, Mrs. Sedgewick, Mrs. Sigourney (6),——Simpson (a traveller), Mrs.
Seba Smith, Mrs. Southey, Alfred B. Street, Charles Swain (2) J. B. Taylor, T. B. Thayer
——Thompson, Albert Tracy, Johann Ludwig Uhland (2), Heinrich Voss, John Green-
leaf Whittier (6), N. P. Willis (2), Johann Heinrich Daniel Zschokke (2). Total—75
authors.

Some of the book reviews given here in brief excerpts may be found in full in "The
Gathering of the Forces," II, pp. 260 ff., *passim*.

COLERIDGE, SAMUEL TAYLOR: "Letters, Conversations, and Recollections."
Indeed anything relating to Coleridge—that legitimate child of imagery, and true poet—will for many years yet be interesting. [February 20, 1847.]

"Biographia Literaria," in two volumes.
To a person of literary taste, the first pleasure of reading any thing written by Coleridge will be, that it is written in such choice and unaffected style—next that the author evidently lays open his whole heart with the artlessness of a child—and next that there is no commonplace or cant. These are exceedingly rare merits, at the present day. . . . "Biographia Literaria" will reach the deepest thoughts of the "choice few" among readers who can appreciate the fascinating subtleties of Coleridge; and both volumes will be entertaining to the general reader, from their fund of anecdote, and the good humor that will rise to the surface even of such a poetical nature as that child of song's. In some respects we think this man stands above all poets: he was passionate without being morbid—he was like Adam in Paradise, and almost as free from artificiality. [December 4, 1847.] ·

DIXON, DR. EDWARD H.: "Woman and Her Diseases, From the Cradle to the Grave."
"To the pure all things are pure" is the not inappropriate motto of this work: and the mock delicacy that condemns the widest possible diffusion among females of such knowledge as is contained in this book, will receive from us no quarter. Let any one bethink him a moment how rare is the sight of a well-developed, healthy, *naturally* beautiful woman: let him reflect how widely the customs of our artificial life, joined with ignorance of physiological facts, are increasing the rarity (if we may be allowed such an approach to a bull,)—and he will hardly dispute the necessity of such publications as this. [March 4, 1847.]

DUMAS, ALEXANDER: "The Count of Monte-Christo."
[Whitman mentions this but has not read it; in Dumas's earlier works he finds "a pleasant gracefulness and vivacity."] [September 30, 1846.]

"Sylvandire."
We like this better as a story, than the foregoing, by the
same author ["Diana of Meridor"]. Indeed, we think there
are not many books, of its scope, with superior interest.
[April 14, 1847.]

"Memoirs of a Physician"
* * * a wild, hurrying, exciting affair; full of its author's
characteristics. [May 31, 1847.]

EMERSON, RALPH WALDO[1]
* * * one of Ralph Waldo Emerson's inimitable lectures
[that on "Spiritual Laws," which he quotes]. [December
15, 1847.]

FULLER, MARGARET: "Papers on Literature and Art."
[Though some treat with supercilious contempt such works
when essayed by women] we are not thus disposed. We
think the female mind has peculiarly the capacity, and
ought to have the privilege, to enter into the discussion of
high questions of morals, taste, &c. We therefore welcome
Miss Fuller's papers, right heartily. [November 9, 1846.]

GOETHE, JOHANN WOLFGANG VON: "The Autobiography of
Goethe." [Third and Fourth Parts; translated by Parke
Godwin.][2]
The *truthful* truthfulness which characterizes its revelations
is especially refreshing, for in these days there is an im-
mense contagion of *affected* truthfulness, beyond all bearing,
and nauseous to an extreme, general as it is! We like
Goethe's autobiography because it throws off quite all of
this affectation, and writes as an intelligent man would
write to a refined and sincere friend. [June 28, 1847.]

GUIZOT, FRANÇOIS: "History of the English Revolution of
1640," in two volumes.
Here is one of the really valuable books of the age. [But
Whitman has not read it thoroughly "as yet."] [March
5, 1846.]

---

[1] *Cf. post*, II, pp.53–54.
[2] *Cf. post*, I, pp. 139–141.

HAZLITT, WILLIAM: "Napoleon Bonaparte."
This masterpiece of style, earnestness, clearness, and spirit—this best (to our notion) of all the histories of the great "soldier of fortune". . . . We have on a former occasion[1] expressed, more fully, our opinions of the *democracy* of this work. [April 2, 1847.]

HOWITT, MARY: "Ballads."
Among the Brooklyn *Eagle's* most favored favorites stands the sweet authoress of these poems! [February 2, 1847.]

IRVING, WASHINGTON:[2] "Life and Voyages of Christopher Columbus." [Abridged edition.]
Our poor commendation is not needed for any writings of such a man as Irving. [March 12, 1847.]

KEATS, JOHN: "Poetical Works," in two volumes.
Keats—peace to his ashes—was one of the pleasantest of modern poets, and, had not the grim monster Death so early claimed him, would doubtless have become one of the most distinguished. [March 5, 1846.]

LAMB, CHARLES[3]
* * * the pleasant Elia, the delicate-humored. [February 13, 1847.]

LAMARTINE, ALPHONSE: "History of the Girondists."
* * * it is, we think we can say, the most dramatic work we ever read—too dramatic, perhaps, for the higher purposes of history—though its intensity of interest is increased bv the same cause. [August 10, 1847.]

LONGFELLOW, HENRY WADSWORTH: "Poems," Harper's Edition.
* * * We consider Mr. Longfellow to be gifted by God with a special faculty of dressing beautiful thoughts in beautiful words. The country is not half just to this eloquent writer; an honor and a glory as he is to the American name—and deserving to stand on the same platform with

---

[1] March 15, 1847; this interesting comment on the French Revolution may be found in "The Gathering of the Forces," II, pp. 284–287.

[2] *Cf. post*, II, p. 5.

[3] *Cf. post*, II, p. 156.

Bryant and Wordsworth. [Whitman then quotes from "The Rain"] as a suggestion of how the commonest occurrences offer themes of great thoughts to the true poet. [October 12, 1846.]

"Evangeline—A Tale of Acadie."

And so ends the poem like a solemn psalm, the essence of whose deep religious music still lives on in your soul, and becomes a part of you. You have soon turned over its few pages, scanned every line, and reached the issue of the story, and perhaps idly regret that there is no more of it,

"But a thing of beauty is a joy forever;"

and we may thank Mr. Longfellow for some hours of pure religious, living tranquility of soul. [November 20, 1847.]

MELVILLE, HERMAN: "Omoo," in two volumes.
    * * * most readable sort of reading. [May 5, 1847.]

MICHELET, JULES: "History of France." [Translated by G. H. Smith.]
Of the many standard works from his pen, the history of France is on some accounts the best: he appears to have taken pride and pains in making it the fullest and clearest. [April 22, 1847.]

MILTON, JOHN: "Poems," Harper's Edition, in two volumes.
As a writer Milton is stern, lofty, and grand; his themes are heavenly high, and profoundly deep. A man must have something of the poet's own vast abruptness (if we [may] use such a term), in order to appreciate this writer, who, apparently conscious of his own gigantic proportions, disdains the usual graces and tricks of poets who are read more widely, and understood more easily, because they have *not* his qualities. The towering pile of cliffs, with yawning caverns in the side, the mysterious summits piercing the clouds, while the lightning plays on their naked breasts, is not, to the usual world, half so favorite an object as the landscape of cultivated meadows fringed with a little wood, and watered by a placid stream. [January 10, 1848.]

RAUMER, FREDERICH LUDWIG GEORG VON: "America."
[Whitman is reading it for the second time since its publication "last summer," and rates it highly as a defense of

American institutions.] As a turner aside of the sneers and falsehoods of our distant libellers, it is perhaps well that the work is so strong in our favor. But here at home it will do no harm to remember that we have not by any means reached perfection. The abuse has prevailed so thoroughly in foreigners' accounts of us, however, that probably the baron has allowed himself deliberately to lean to the other side as far as possible. Heaven bless him for it! and heaven bless him, too, for his imperturbable good temper, which spreads through all he writes! [October 8, 1846.]

RUSKIN, JOHN: "Modern Painters," first American edition.
It is indeed worthy of the reading of every lover of what we must call intellectual chivalry, enthusiasm, and a high-toned sincerity, disdainful of the flippant tricks and petty arts of small writers. [July 22, 1847.]

"SAND, GEORGE":[1] "The Journeyman Joiner." [Translated by George Shaw.]
That Madame Sand's works are looked upon by a portion of the public, and of critics, with a feeling of great repugnance, there is no denying. But the talented French woman is nevertheless one of a class much needed in the world— needed lest the world stagnate in wrongs merely from precedent. We are fully of the belief that "free discussion," upon any subject of general and profound interest, is not only allowable, but in most cases desirable. And this is all we have to say to those who put Madame Sand's books down by a mere flourish of prejudice. . . . The "Journeyman Joiner" is a work of very great interest as a story. Indeed we know of few that are more so. [September 27, 1847.]

SCHLEGEL, FREDERICK VON: "The Philosophy of Life and Philosophy of Language." [Translated by A. J. W. Morrison.]
Disquisitions on the most solemn subjects that can engage human thought form the first sections of this book. [December 7, 1847.]

[1] Cf. post, II, p. 53.

SEDGWICK, THEODORE: "The American Citizen; his True Position, Character and Duties."
It is a noble discourse! [November 8, 1847.]

SIMMS, WILLIAM GILMORE: "The Wigwam and the Cabin," Second Series.
Simms is unquestionably one of the most attractive writers of the age; and yet some of his characters—to our mind at least—are in exceedingly bad taste. It *may* be all well enough to introduce a "foul rabble of lewd spirits," in order to show that "Virtue can triumph even in the worst estates," but it is our impression that ladies and gentlemen of refinement—to say nothing of heads of families— would rather take the maxim upon trust than have it exemplified to them or their children through the medium of a picture so very coarse and indelicate in its details, as that drawn by Mr. Simms in his "Caloya." [But praise is accorded to other tales in the volume.] [March 9, 1846.]

TAYLOR, BAYARD: "Views Afoot."
We have scanned them with much enjoyment. [December 4, 1846.]

THOMSON, JAMES: "The Seasons."
His "Seasons" is not surpassed by any book with which we are acquainted, in its happy limning of the scenes it professes to represent; in its faculty of bringing before the reader the clear sight of everything in its scope. [November 24, 1847.]

TUPPER, MARTIN [FARQUHAR]: "Probabilities, An Aid to Faith."
[It] has a lofty, an august scope of intention! It treats of the great mysteries of the future, of God and his attributes, of the fall of man, of heaven and hell! The author, Mr. Tupper, is one of the rare men of the time. He turns up thoughts as with a plow, on the sward of monotonous usage. We should like well to go into this book, in a fuller article; but justice to it would require many pages. [February 20, 1847.]

WALTON, IZAAC: "The Lives of Dr. John Donne, Sir Henry
Wotten, Mr. Richard Hooker, Mr. George Herbert, and
Dr. Robert Sanderson."
It is refreshing to peruse a style of charming simplicity,
ingrained with a manly natural elegance. The life of gen-
tle Izaac himself is the most interesting part of the book.
[But Whitman finds the volume refreshing as a whole.]
[December 21, 1846.]

WORKING-WOMEN[1]

THE evils and horrors connected with the payment, in this
quarter of the country, for women's labor—sewing, book-
folding, umbrella-work, etc., etc.—are a monotonous subject of
complaint enough; and people are quite ready to say, It's of no
use to write about *that*. But when we see how the continued,
persevering, incessant, honest efforts at reforming any old
abuse, by means of newspaper-writing, at last succeed, (though
the world, which seldom looks very deeply, is apt to give the
credit to a later agent, and heeds not where the motion was given
and what kept it up,) we are inclined to think that in this sub-
ject of poor pay for females' work, good results would sooner
or later follow from the faithful adherence of the press to an
advocacy of "the rights of women" in the matter.[2] Why,
there are hundreds and hundreds of poor girls and women here-
about—and not a few in Brooklyn—who suffer the most shame-
ful impositions from those who employ them to work. These
girls and women make from *fifty cents* (!) to two dollars per
week—very few in the neighbourhood of the latter sum, how-
ever. The price paid for making one of those heavy stout over-
coats, such as our firemen wear, is but fifty cents, at the highest
—and pantaloons and vests, ("slop-work") from six to fifteen
cents! . . . What remedy for this miserable system, we
are not prepared to suggest; but the first thing is to make the
public aware that it is an evil—and that it sows a public crop of
other evils.

[1] From the Brooklyn *Daily Eagle*, November 9, 1846.
Cf. post, I, p. 233.
[2] *Cf. infra*, pp. 116-117. In advocating women's rights, industrial as well as political,
Whitman was an early champion of the sex though Emerson and Greeley had both
shown the way, to say nothing of the Transcendentalists in general.

THE OLD BLACK WIDOW[1]

(A NARRATIVE THE TRUTH OF WHOSE ESSENTIALS IS VOUCHED
FOR BY THE EDITOR OF THIS PRINT.)

SOME years ago, (and not many, either) an aged black woman, a widow, occupied a basement in one of the streets leading down to the North river, in New York city. She had employment from a number of families who hired her at intervals to cook, nurse, and wash for them; and in this way she gained a very decent living. If we remember right, the old creature had no child, or any near relation, but was quite alone in the world, and lived, when at home, in the most solitary manner. She always had her room and humble furniture as clean as a new glove, and was remarkable every where for her neatness, agreeable ways, and good humor—and all this at an age closely bordering on seventy. Opposite to where this ancient female lived, was a row of stables for horses, cabs, private vehicles on livery, and such like. At any hour of the day and evening, groups of hostlers and stout stable boys were working or lounging about there—and the ears of the passer-by could hardly fail to hear joking and laughter, and often coarse oaths and indecent ribaldry. The old black woman, smoking her pipe of an evening, at her door on the opposite side of the way, suffered considerable annoyance from their swearing and obscenity. She was a pious woman, not merely in profession but practice, and faithfully tried to worship God, and walk in the paths of duty. For several weeks at intervals she had noticed a barefooted young girl of twelve or thirteen years, strolling about, and frequently stopping at the stables. This girl was a deaf mute,[2] the daughter of a wretched intemperate couple in the neighbourhood, who were letting her grow up as the weeds grow. With no care and guidance for her young steps, she had before her the darkest and dreariest of prospects. What under such circumstances could be expected of her future years, but degradation, misery, and crime? The old black widow had many anxious thoughts about this little girl, and shuddered at the fate which seemed prepared for her. She at last determined to make an effort in behalf of the hapless one. She had heard of the institutions

---

[1] From the Brooklyn *Daily Eagle*, November 12, 1846.

[2] Whitman wrote another tale about a deaf mute, "Dumb Kate," "Complete Prose," pp. 370-371.

provided for the deaf and dumb, and how the sealed avenues of the senses are almost opened to them again there. Upon making inquiry, she found that in the case of her young neighbor, the payment of a certain sum of money, (two hundred dollars, we think it was,) would be necessary, preparatory to her admission into the New York Institution. Whether any payment was required after this, we have forgotten, but the sum in advance was indispensable. The old woman had got quite well acquainted with the child, and discovered in her that quickness and acuteness for which her unfortunate kind are remarkable. She *determined* to save her—to turn her path aside from darkness to light.—Day after day then, and night after night, whenever her work would permit, went forth the old woman, with papers and letters, to beg subscriptions from the charitable, for that most holy object. Among the families where she was known, she always succeeded in getting something—sometimes half a dollar, sometimes two—and in a few instances five, and even ten dollars. But where she was a stranger, she rarely received any answer to her request except a rude denial, or a contemptuous sneer.—Most of them suspected her story to be a fabrication—although she had provided herself with incontestible proofs of its truth, which she always carried with her. It seemed a hopeless effort, and yet she persevered—contributing from her own scanty means every cent that she could spare. Need we say that Heaven blessed this poor creature's sacred work—that she succeeded in getting the requisite sum, and that the girl was soon afterward placed an inmate of the asylum? Whether the aged widow yet lives in her basement, and what has happened since in the life of the girl, we know not. . . .—In all that we have ever heard or read, we do not know a better refutation of those scowling dogmatists who resolve all the actions of mankind into a gross motive of pleasing the abstract self.

INCIDENTS IN THE LIFE OF A WORLD–FAMED MAN[1]

"THE AUTO-BIOGRAPHY OF GOETHE." Truth and Poetry: from My Life. From the German of Goethe, by Parke Godwin. Two vols. Wiley & Putnam, 161 Broadway, N. Y.

[1] From the Brooklyn *Daily Eagle*, November 19, 1846.

WHAT a prodigious gain would accrue to the world, if men who write well would as much think of writing LIFE, as they (most of them) think it necessary to write one of the million things evolved from life—Learning! What a gain it would be, if we could forego some of the heavy tomes, the fruit of an age of toil and scientific study, for the simple easy truthful narrative of the existence and experience of a man of genius,—how his mind unfolded in his earliest years—the impressions things made upon him—how and where and when the religious senti- ment dawned in him—what he thought of God before he was inoculated with books' ideas—the developement of his soul— when he first loved—the way circumstance imbued his nature, and did him good, or worked him ill—with all the long train of occurrences, adventures, mental processes, exercises within, and trials without, which go to make up the man—for *character* is the man, after all. Such a work, fully and faithfully per- formed, would be a rare treasure! . . . . This Life of Goethe—this famous *Wahrheit und Dichtung*—seems shaped with the intention of rendering a history of soul and body's growth, such as alluded to. It is not full enough, perhaps; but it is a real history, and no man but will learn much in the reading of it. It (like Shakspere's writing) does not bear every now and then the inscription, "See the moral of this!" or "Behold how vice is punished!" It goes right on, stating what it has to say, exuberant in its seeds of reflection and infer- ence—though it doesn't reflect or draw the inference.

Cf. infra, p. 132.
This book review is selected for presentation at length not only because it is a fair sample of Whiman's reviewing (see *infra*, pp. 125–126) but also because it throws light upon the germination of the literary ideals which, during the next year, began to shape some parts of the "Leaves of Grass" (see *post*, II, p. 63, note). A kinship between Whit- man and Goethe has more than once been noted, but apparently it has not been known that Whitman was acquainted with the German writer before beginning his own book. In Doctor Bucke's "Notes and Fragments" (privately printed, 1899, pp. 105–106) is given Whitman's critical opinion of Goethe, together with copious notes concerning the life of the latter, dated January, 1856. In this, however, he confesses his inadequate reading of Goethe. It may have been that Goethe's "Autobiography," in the American translation (Whitman did not know German), introduced him to the great German ro- manticist. In any case, the present book review shows that Whitman was longing for a biographical work—whether in prose or verse seemed to matter little—which should express the entire man very much as his own "Leaves of Grass" set out to do. *Cf.* the following bit of off-hand criticism reported in "With Walt Whitman in Camden" (III, p. 159): "Goethe impresses me as above all to stand for essential literature, art, life —to argue the importance of centering life in self—in perfect persons—perfect you, me: to force the real into the abstract ideal: to make himself, Goethe, the supremest example of personal identity: everything making for it: in us, in Goethe: every man repeating the same experience."

Mr. Parke Godwin, the translator, (assisted), deserves more than ordinary thanks for this labor—one long needed, for we are told that there has been hitherto but a miserable imperfect elliptical translation, published in London some time since, and now out of print. John Henry Hopkins, jr., of Vermont owns also a hand in the new translation—he having rendered the second volume. . . The print, paper, &c. are good. We notice one or two errors, however, in the text; one, for instance, on the 18th page of volume 1st, which makes the great earthquake in Lisbon happen in 1775. It should be 1755.

Our readers will need no apology from us for our transferring one or two extracts from this Auto-Biography to our columns.

[Then are introduced four lengthy extracts.—EDITOR.]

MATTERS WHICH WERE SEEN AND DONE IN AN AFTERNOON RAMBLE[1]

THE luscious air (mellow as a full-ripe peach) and the cloudless skies, forbade any return that day (17th) to indoor avocations.—Merely to live, (out of doors) amid such fresh and welcome beauty, was enough;—but to "go to work" immediately after tasting it, was too much! . . . Who says Brooklyn is not a growing place? He surely cannot have walked lately, as we then walked, through East Brooklyn and South Brooklyn. At this present writing we think we could go and count full three hundred houses in process of erection in those two parts of our city! In Atlantic street there are several rows of noble buildings, and in quite every cross street can be heard the sound of carpenters' hammers and masons' trowels. . . . And by the bye, speaking of East Brooklyn, we wonder that some public-spirited personage or personages do not set on foot measures for the construction of *Churches* thereabout, or even in the wide scope between it and Fulton street—for they are much needed there. There is, it is true, the New Methodist now being built in Bridge street, and a small but neat wooden Church (on speculation) in Prince street; but the exuberant population there requires many and large houses of worship. No person who walks often through that part of our city, and beholds the immense proportion of *young people* resident in it, but will surely

[1] From the Brooklyn *Daily Eagle*, November 19, 1846.

agree with us.   West of Fulton street is well supplied with the most magnificent Churches, and this makes the paucity on the other side more apparent.

. Crossing to N. Y. at the South Ferry, (what mortal could wish a better-managed mode of passage than appertains to our Brooklyn ferries?) we lingered awhile on the Battery—that be- loved spot[1]—and reflected whether the new *Washington Park*, on the heights of Fort Greene,[2] would not be quite as noble a promenade, even without the water-front: it would have a far more magnificent *water-view*, you know.   .   .   .   Stores, and very handsome ones, we observed, are encroaching on the south side of Broadway, from the Bowling Green up to the site of the old Waverley House—the stretch made vacant by the fire of last summer.   The last gaps in the line are now being filled up, and the New Year's callers on that route will behold not a single evidence of the ruin made by the   "devouring element" so short a while since.   .   .   .   What a fascinating chaos is Broadway, of a pleasant sunny time!   We know it is all, (or most of it,) "fol-de-rol," but still there is a pleasure in walking up and down there awhile, and looking at the beautiful ladies, the bustle, the show, the glitter, and even the gaudiness.   But alas! what a prodigious amount of means and time might be much better and more profitably employed than as they are there!

After giving a passing glance in the rooms of the Art Union, (a perpetual free exhibition of Paintings, Broadway, near Pearl st., which we advise our Brooklyn folk to visit often: it will cost them nothing, and there are always good things there,) we ascended the wide winding stair-case of the Society Library, to the room where *Brown's Statuary* is exhibiting.   Mr. B. is a young American, and deserves well; for he shows genius and industry.   We particularly liked two marble Bas Reliefs—one of the Pleiades, and another of the Hyades.   (These latter "weep- ing sisters," by the by, seem lately to have been in the ascendant.) An Adonis, quite the size of life, would perhaps be considered the most attractive "feature" of the exhibition.   Though a noble statue, it did not, however, come up to our (perhaps too lifted)

---

[1] *Cf. infra*, pp. 90–92.

[2] Whitman never lost an opportunity to urge the preservation of the site of old Fort Greene as a public park.   Though other newspapers in Brooklyn were interested in the same enterprise, none were more zealous in the cause than the *Eagle*, so that Whitman's pride in the successful results of the journalistic campaign was justified (see the letter from Whitman in Stephen M. Ostrander's "History of Brooklyn," 1894, II, p. 89).

ideas of "Myrrha's immortal son". . . . Just crossing Broadway, (to 341) our taste for the Ideal—for the exquisite in form, the gracefully quaint, and the chastely gorgeous—experienced a sort of "new development" in looking over *Banks's* new stock and saloon; for surely no mortal man, (except the proprietor himself, who seems to devote his life enthusiastically to it,) could ferret out, or "get up" so many superb things, in a super-superb style! Vases that would add wonder to the palaces of the Persian Shas—glitteringly grotesque mantel-ornaments—tiara brilliants that princesses might wear—bracelets, rings, and a maze of etc.!—such are but a portion of the star-like things that are collected here! True Democrat as we are, we did like to look on shapes and things of beauty, ever.

—The deafening flourish of trumpets and roll of drums ushered up the curtain of the Park theatre, just as we entered and took a seat amid a well-filled house, to see a counterfeit presentment of "The Troublesome Raigne of John, King of England," (which is probably more Marlowe's play than Shakspere's after all.) And there sat the monarch so "infirm of purpose," on his throne —surrounded by bold barons, and all the things of the Feudal age! Whatever may be said of Mr. Kean's acting, the public owe him something for the perfection of costume, scenery, properties, &c. in the plays produced under his control. It is not to be denied that a New York audience never before had anything in the neighborhood of the truthfulness and appropriateness which mark the present representation of King John. *That* shows something like a court, and the movements of royalty, and of armies. There are scores of knights and men-at-arms, that bring to one's mind the stamps on old English coins, the pictures and effigies in old Abbeys, and such like. And instead of the ludicrous stiffness that usually prevails on the stage, in such scenes, there are colloquial groupings, and all the adjuncts, as near as possible, of reality. . . . But what shall we say of Mrs. Kean's Queen Constance? a piece of artistic work which we shall not soon forget. We are not given to superlatives in these things—but if there be any *perfection* in acting, Mrs. K. evinces it in her portrayal of that widowed and crownless Queen! From first to last it was a continuous stretch of unsurpassed by-play and fine elocution. The harrowing close of the third act was marked by the tears of half the audience, men as well as women. The character of Constance is such as Mrs. Kean can (and almost she only) truly represent—the following bit of delivery, as she gave it, was perhaps never better done, on the stage. It is the rejoinder she gives to the remonstrances of Cardinal Pandulph and King Philip, against her overwhelming grief for the loss of her little son, Prince Arthur, who was taken prisoner by his usurping uncle:

> Grief fills the room up of my absent child,
> Lies in his bed, walks up and down with me;
> Puts on his pretty looks, repeats his words,
> Remembers me of all his gracious parts,
> Stuffs out his vacant garments with his form;
> Then have I reason to be fond of grief.
> Fare you well: had you such a loss as I,
> I could give better comfort than you do—
> I will not keep this form upon my head,
> When there is such disorder in my wit.
> Oh, lord! my boy, my Arthur, my fair son!
> My life, my joy, my food, my all in the world,
> My widow-comfort, and my sorrow's cure!

We must confess, though we are no admirer of Mr. Kean, that he, in King John, left little to be asked for more, by the reasonable spectator. His elocution was good, and his air and bearing such as became royalty. The two last acts, which depend quite altogether upon him, were deeply interesting; and we think the common cant hitherto about the play, that it "lacks dramatic effect," must pretty effectually get its quietus, now. The play really is full of dramatic interest—and not the least of it flows from its historical associations. Only the morbid appetite for unnatural strained effect can complain of want of interest in such a play as King John. . . . Mr. Vanderhoof's Faulconbridge was acting of the liveliest, heartiest, most refreshing sort, and gave a light grace to the massiveness of the rest. The young creature who played Arthur took the sympathies of the whole house; she played with quiet, grace, and modesty.

EDUCATION—SCHOOLS, Etc.[1]

In our prevalent system of Common School Instruction, there is far too much of mere forms and words. Boys and girls learn "lessons" in books, pat enough to the tongue, but vacant

[1] From the Brooklyn *Daily Eagle*, November 23, 1846.

to the brain.   Many wearisome hours are passed in getting this rote, which is almost useless, while the proper parts of education have been left unattended to.   Of what use is it, for instance, that a boy knows the technical definition of a promontory or a gulf—and can bound states, as they are bounded in the book, north, and east, and south, and west, when he has no practical idea of the situation and direction of countries, and of the earth's different parts?   Of what use is it that he can recite the rules of grammar, and speak off all its book terms, when he does not apply it in his conversation, knows not a tittle of the meaning of what he says, and is hourly committing the grossest violations of it?   Of what use is it to a child that he has "ciphered through the book," to use the common phrase, when he cannot apply the various rules to the transactions of business, and is puzzled by a little simple sum perhaps in the very elementary parts of arithmetic?

Unless what is taught in a school be understood, and has some greater value than merely a knowledge of the words which convey it, it is all a sham.   In schools (as too much in religion) many people have been too long accustomed to look at the *mere* form—the outward circumstance—without attending to the reality.   It matters little that a teacher preserves the most admirable discipline—performs all the time-honored floggings and thumpings and cuffings[1]—and goes through with all the old-established ceremonies of school-teaching—unless the pupils are aided in forming sharp, intelligent minds—and are properly advanced in the branches they may be pursuing.   Without these follow, his education is a mockery—a make believe.   The forms of a school are of small account, except as they contribute to the main object—improvement.

The proper education of a child comprehends a great deal more than is generally thought of.   Sending him to school, and learning him to read and write, is not educating him.   That brings into play but a small part of his powers.   A proper education unfolds and develops every faculty in its just proportions.   It commences at the beginning, and leads him along the path step by step.   Its aim is not to give so much book-learning, but to polish and invigorate the mind—to make it used to thinking and

---

[1] Whitman had much to say in the *Eagle* against flogging school children, a practice which he appears to have avoided as a school-teacher himself.   He wrote one of his earliest tales on the theme, "Death in a School-Room" ("Complete Prose," pp. 336–340).

acting for itself, and to imbue it with a love for knowledge. It seeks to move the youthful intellect to reason, reflect and judge, and exercise its curiosity and powers of thought. True, these powers, this reason and judgment have to be exercised at first on childish subjects—but every step carries him further and further. What was even at first not difficult, becomes invaluable as an easy habit. And it is astonishing how much may be done in this way; how soon a child acquires, by proper training, a quickness of perception and a ready facility of drawing on stores of its own, that put to the blush the faculties of many, even of mature age. We consider it a great thing in education that the learner be taught to rely upon himself. The best teachers do not profess to *form* the mind, but to *direct* it in such a manner—and put such tools in its power—that it builds up itself.[1] This part of education is far more worthy of attention, than the acquiring of a certain quantity of school knowledge. We would far rather have a child possessed of a bright, intelligent, moderately disciplined mind, joined to an inquisitive disposition, with very little of what is called learning, than to have him versed in all the accomplishments of the most forward of his age, arithmetic, grammar, Greek, Latin, and French, without that brightness and intelligence.

A FACT-ROMANCE OF LONG ISLAND[2]

On the Huntington south shore of Long Island is a creek near the road called "Gunnetaug"—and the mouth of this creek, emptying into the bay, is reported to be so deep that no lines have ever yet sounded its bottom. It sometimes goes by the name of "Drowning Creek," which was given to it by a circumstance that we will relate. It is a universal summer custom on Long Island to have what are called "Beach parties:" that is, collections of people, young and old, each bringing a lot of provisions and drink, and who sail over early in the morning to the beach which breaks off the Atlantic waves from our island's "green girt shore," and spend the day there. Many years ago such a party went over from Gunnetaug. They formed a cheerful and healthy set, full of animal spirits. They

[1] *Cf. post*, I, pp. 148–149, 220–221; II, pp. 13–15.
[2] From the Brooklyn *Daily Eagle*, December 16, 1846.

bathed in the surf—danced—told stories—ate and drank—
amused themselves with music, plays, games, and so on—and
ranged upon the beach in search of the eggs of the sea-gull, who
lays them in no nest except the warm sand, exposed to the sun,
which makes a first rate natural Eccallobeon.[1] (I have some-
times gathered a hundred of these eggs on similar excursions,
in an hour: they are palatable and about half the size of hen's
eggs.) The owner of the boat which carried the party over the
bay was a young farmer who had his sister and his sweetheart
on board. Towards the latter part of the afternoon, they set
out on their return—and made the greater haste, as a thunder
shower seemed to be gathering overhead. They had crossed
the bay, and were just entering the mouth of the creek we have
mentioned when the storm burst, and a sudden flaw of wind
capsized the boat. Most Long-Islanders are good swimmers;
and as the stream was but a few yards wide, the men supported
the women and children to the banks. The young man, the
owner of the boat, grasped his sister in one arm and struck out
for the shore with the other. When he was within a rod of it,
he heard a slight exclamation from the upturned boat, and
turning his head saw the girl he loved slip into the water!
Yielding to a sudden impulse, he shook off his sister, swam back,
dived, and clutching the sinking one by her hair and dress,
brought her safely to the shore. Then he again swam back for
his sister—and for many long and dreadful minutes, beat the
dark waters, and dived—*but beat and dived in vain.* The girl
drowned, and her body was never more seen. . . . . . .
From that time forth, the young man's character was changed.
He laughed no more, and never again engaged in any of the
country jollities. He married his sweetheart: but it was a cold
and unfriendly union—and about a year from the time of his
sister's drowning, he began to pine and droop. He had no dis-
ease—at least none that is treated of in medical works; but his
heart withered away, as it were. In dreams, the chill of his
sister's dripping hair was against his cheek—and he would
awake with a cry of pain. Moping and sinking thus, he gradu-
ally grew weaker and weaker, and at last died. . . . The
story is yet told among the country people, thereabouts, and
often when sailing out of the creek, I have looked on the spot
where the poor girl sank, and the shore where the rescued one
escaped.

[1] A kind of incubator.

A FEW WORDS TO THE YOUNG MEN OF BROOKLYN[1]

It DESERVES to be remembered that education is not a thing for schools, or children merely. The acquirement of knowledge concerns those who are grown, or nearly grown, men more than children. Let no one suppose that when a person becomes eighteen or twenty or thirty years old, he is past the season for learning. Some of the wisest and most celebrated men, whose names adorn the page of history, educated themselves after they had lost the season of youth. They began, many of them, without even a knowledge of reading and writing, and raised themselves by their industry and study to high eminences. The biographies of men of science present accounts of people born and nurtured amid the deepest poverty and toil, with hardly money enough to buy a sheet of paper or the commonest book—who yet, by a resolute application and improving of odd hours, acquired learning far beyond others who were living in comfort and enjoying all the advantages of schools. . . . No period is too late to attend to the improvement of the mind. No station has cares so numerous, or disadvantages so great, but that the one who fills it may cultivate his intellect. There have been young men—young men whose lot it was to labor hard, and to possess but few aids in acquiring what they sought —and these same persons, thirsting for knowledge, and feeling how noble a thing it is to raise oneself above the level of ignorance, and equality with the low and debased, resolutely set themselves to work in studying—and attained distinction and fame in that sphere. And more than this: not only have poverty and suffering and weakness been overcome by those bent on advancing, but even blindness and deafness which seem to present unsurmountable obstacles, have not been able to stop the exertions of the knowledge-seeking spirit. Some of the greatest scholars have labored under these afflictions, and have surmounted them. . . . To those who are just entering upon manhood, the paths of science present pleasures of the most alluring kind. If the young men of Brooklyn, instead of spending so many hours idling in bar-rooms,[2] and places of vapid, irrational un-amusement, were to occupy that time in improving

---

[1] From the Brooklyn *Daily Eagle*, December 17, 1846.
Cf. infra, pp. 144-146; *post*, I, pp. 220-221, II, pp. 13-15.

[2] *Cf.* "Franklin Evans," *passim.*, and the sub-title of "Sketches of the Sidewalks and Levees," *post*, I, p. 199; also p. 193.

themselves in knowledge, happy would it be for them, and the city too! If, instead of engaging in scenes, associating with companions, and haunting places, that lead them to become fond of gambling, that meanest and most debasing of vices— or of intemperance, that dreadful canker that cuts off the fairest flowers and the finest fruits in the human garden, they would but covet the far higher and the far purer pleasures of literature, half the misery and guilt that generally afflict men would be precluded them.

_____

"IMPORTANT ANNOUNCEMENT"[1]

THE Brooklyn *Eagle* wishes everybody in general, and some persons in particular, to understand that it considers its presence at any public place—at *any* place, where it goes in its capacity as the B. E.—to be a *special favor*, a thing for the place and persons visited to show themselves thankful for, and to bless their stars for. As to the "courtesy" of gratuitous tickets, little gifts, (to be noticed in the paper, which notice brings more good to them than ten times the value of said gifts,) and all that sort of thing, long custom has quite staled us to the delicious privilege. The *Eagle* will always like to go among its friends—will always like to be generous in the bestowal of its favors—but it must be with the clear understanding that no obligation is conferred upon it. . . . These words are said in complete good nature—and without any special application— but for "all future time." Moreover, when the *Eagle's* presence at a given place is wished for, it must be solicited by the polite means of special invitation, accompanied by ample "cards of admission," &c.; it not being in the range of human possibilities or condescensions for the *E.* to explain at the doors of places that it *is* the *E.*

_____

AN INCIDENT ON LONG ISLAND FORTY YEARS AGO[2]

WHEN my mother was a girl, the house where her parents and their family lived was in a gloomy wood, out of the way from

[1] From the Brooklyn *Daily Eagle*, December 22, 1846.
    Whitman attempted to live up to the high conception of the function of the newspaper editor outlined in "Ourselves and the *Eagle*," (*infra*, pp. 114–117); and in this characteristic bit of straight talk to offending readers he seeks (without complete success) to maintain a proportionate dignity.

[2] From the Brooklyn *Daily Eagle*, December 24, 1846.

any village or thick settlement.[1] One August morning my grandfather had some business a number of miles from home, and he put a saddle on the back of his favorite horse, "Dandy," (a creature he loved next to his wife and children,) and rode away to attend to it. When nightfall came and my grandfather did not return, my grandmother began to feel a little uneasy. As the night advanced, she and her daughter sitting up impatient for the return of the absent husband and father, a terrible storm came, in the middle of which their ears joyed to hear the well-known clatter of Dandy's hoofs. My grandmother sprang to the door, but upon opening it, she almost fainted into my mother's arms; for there stood Dandy, bridled and saddled, but no signs of my grandfather. My mother stepped out and found that the bridle was broken, and the saddle soaked with rain and covered with mud. They returned sick at heart into the house. . . . It was just after midnight, and the storm was passing off, when in the dreary stillness of their sleepless watch, they heard something in the room adjoining (the "spare room,") which redoubled their terror. They heard the slow heavy footfalls of a man walking. Tramp! tramp! tramp! it went—three steps solemnly and deliberately, and then all was hushed again. By any who in the middle of the night have had the chill of a vague unknown horror creep into their very souls, it can well be imagined how they passed the time now. My mother sprang to the door, and turned the key, and spoke what words of cheer she could force through her lips, to the ears of her terrified parent. The dark hours crept slowly on, and at last a little tinge of day-light was seen through the eastern windows. Almost simultaneously with it, a bluff voice was heard some distance off, and the quick dull beat of a horse galloping along a soft wet road. That bluff merry halloo came to the pallid and exhausted females like a cheer from a passsing ship to starving mariners on a wreck at sea. My grandmother opened the door this time to behold the red laughing face of her husband, and to hear him tell how, when, after the storm was over and he went to look for Dandy, whom he had fastened under a shed, he discovered that the skittish creature had broken his fastening and run away home—and how he could not get another horse for love or money, at that hour—and how he was fain forced to stop until nearly daylight. . . .

[1] This homestead was near Cold Spring, Long Island. Whitman has described it in "Complete Prose," pp. 5–6.

Then told my grandmother her story—how she had heard
heavy footfalls in the parlor—whereat my grandfather laughed,
and walked to the door between the rooms, and unlocked it,
and saw nothing but darkness; for the shutters were closed, and
it was yet quite a while to sunrise. My mother and grand-
mother followed timidly, though they now began to feel a little
ashamed. My grandfather threw open the shutters of one win-
dow, and his wife those of the other. Then with one sweep of
their eyes round the room, they paused a moment—after which
such a guffaw of laughter came from the husband's capacious
mouth, that Dandy away up in the barnyard sent back an
answering neigh in recognition!

Three or four days previously, my mother had broken off
from a peach tree in the garden a branch uncommonly full of
fruit of a remarkable beauty and ripeness. She brought it in,
and stuck it amid the flowers and other simple ornaments on
the high shelf over the parlor fire-place. The night before,
while the mother and daughter were watching, three of the
peaches, over-full in their ripeness, had dropped, one after the
other, on the floor, and my mother's and grandmother's terri-
fied imaginations had converted the harmless fruit into cowhide
heels! Here was the mystery—and there lay the beautiful
peaches, which my grandfather laughed at so convulsively
that my provoked grandmother, after laughing a while too,
picked them up, and half-jokingly and half-seriously thrust
them so far into the open jaws of her husband that he was nigh
to have been choked indeed.

THE WEST[1]

RADICAL, true, far-scoped, and thorough-going Democracy
may expect, (and such expecting will be realized,) great things
from the West! The hardy denizens of those regions, where
common wants and the cheapness of the land level convention-
ism, (that poison to the Democratic vitality,) begin at the roots
of things—at first principles—and scorn the doctrines founded
on mere precedent and imitation. . . . There is something
refreshing even in the extremes, the faults, of Western character.
Neither need the political or social fabric expect half as much
harm from those untutored impulses, as from the staled and

[1] From the Brooklyn *Daily Eagle*, December 26, 1846.

artificialized influence which enters too much into politics amid richer (not really richer, either) and older-settled sections.[1]

WHY DO THE THEATRES LANGUISH? AND HOW SHALL THE AMERICAN STAGE BE RESUSCITATED?[2]

To HIM who has anything like a proper appreciation of the noble scope of good of which an American drama might be made capable, the inquiry now-a-days must often suggest itself. Is it not amazing that we have not before this thrown off our slavish dependence even in what some would call a comparatively small matter of theatricals? *It is full time.*—English managers, English actors, and English plays, (we say it in no spirit of national antipathy, a feeling we hate) must be allowed to die among us, as usurpers of our stage. The drama of this country *can* be the mouth-piece of freedom, refinement, liberal philosophy, beautiful love for all our brethren, polished manners and an elevated good taste. It can wield potent sway to destroy any attempts at despotism—it can attack and hold up to scorn bigotry, fashionable affectation, avarice, and all unmanly follies. Youth may be warned by its fictitious portraits of the evil of unbridled passions. Wives and husbands may see perhaps for the first time in their lives, a long needed lesson of the absurdity of contentious tempers, and of those small but painful disputes that embitter domestic life—contrasted with the pleasant excellence of a forbearing, forgiving and affectionate spirit. The son or daughter just entering the door of dissipation may get timely view of that inward rottenness which is concealed in such an outside of splendor. All— every age and every condition in life—may with profit visit a well regulated dramatic establishment, and go away better than when they came.—In order to reap such by no means difficult results, the whole method of theatricals, as at present pursued in New York, needs first to be overthrown.—The great and good reformer who should with fearless hand attempt the task of a new organization, would meet with many difficulties and much ridicule; but that he would succeed is in every respect probable, if he possessed ordinary perseverance and discretion. New York City is the only spot in America where such a revolu-

[1] *Cf. post,* I, p. 185.
[2] From the Brooklyn *Daily Eagle,* February 12, 1847.

tion could be attempted, too. With all our servility, to foreign fashion, there is at the heart of the intelligent masses there, a lurking propensity toward what is original, and has a stamped American character of its own. In N. York, also, are gathered together a number of men—literary persons and others—who have a strong desire to favor anything which shall extricate us from the entangled and by no means creditable position we already hold of playing second fiddle to Europe. These persons —most of them young men, enthusiastic, democratic, and liberal in their feelings—are daily acquiring a greater and greater power. And after all, anything appealing to the national heart of the people, as to the peculiar and favored children of freedom,—as to a new race and with a character separate from the kingdoms of other countries—would meet with a ready response, and strike at once the sympathies of all the true men who love America, their native or chosen land.

As to the particular details of the system which should supplant theatricals as they now exist, the one who in greatness of purpose conceives the effort only can say. That effort must be made by a man or woman of no ordinary talent—with a clear comprehensiveness [comprehension?] of what is wanted—not too great a desire for pecuniary profit—little respect for old modes and the accustomed usage of the stage—an *American* in heart and hand—and liberal in disposition to provide whatever taste and propriety may demand.[1] The assistance of writers of genius will of course be required. The whole custom of paid newspaper puffs should be discarded, entirely and utterly.[2] There is hardly anything more contemptible, and indeed unprofitable in the long run, than this same plan of some paid personage writing laudatory notices of the establishment which pays him, and then sending them to the newspapers, to be printed as spontaneous opinions of the editors. A person of genius, we say again, must effect this reform—and about genius there is something capable of seeing its course instinctively for itself, which makes trifling hints, details, and minor particulars, altogether impertinent. Until such a person comes forward, and works out such a reform, theatricals in this country will continue to languish, and theatres be generally more and more deserted by

---

[1] This description of the needed reformer fits well the character of Whitman himself, who was, it must be remembered, at this very period making earnest efforts to find a new instrument of song.

[2] *Cf. infra*, p. 126, and *post*, I, p. 157.

men and women of taste, (rightfully too) as has been the case
for eight or ten years past.

A CITY FIRE[1]

AMONG the "sights" of New York city—(and more frightful
duplicates are to be feared in Brooklyn, unless we have larger
and plentier corporation cisterns)—few possess a vivider interest
for the time, than the public fires. Alarming as they are, too,
there is a kind of hideous pleasure about them.[2] To ask a deni-
zen hereabouts, if he have ever visited a fire, would of course be a
superfluous question. But for those elsewhere, (and even for
our own citizens,) it may not be uninteresting to have a de-
scription of one of these sudden and sad accidents peculiar to
large towns, that sometimes plunge happy families in the depth
of sorrow. A season since, there was a fire in the upper part
of N. Y., which entirely consumed twelve or fourteen houses
inhabited by the middling class of people—and partially dam-
aged several others; besides frightening every family for many
squares around. I visited the place just after dark, when the
flames, (thanks to the Croton!) had begun to be got under.
For several blocks before arriving there, all passage was im-
peded by squads of people hurrying to and fro with rapid and
eager pace. Women carrying bundles—men with sweaty and
heated faces—little children, many of them weeping and sob-
bing,—met me every rod or two. Then there were stacks of
furniture upon the sidewalk, and even in the street. Puddles of
water, and frequent lengths of hose-pipe, endangered the pedes-
trian's safety; and the hubbub, the trumpets of the engine fore-
men, the crackling of the flames, and the lamentations of those
who were made homeless—all sounded louder and louder as we
approached, and at last grew to one continued and deafening
din! It was a horrible yet imposing sight! When my eyes
caught a full view of it, I beheld a space of several lots, all
covered with smouldering ruins, mortar, red hot embers, piles
of smoking, half-burnt walls—a sight to turn a man's heart
sick, and make him tremble when he should awake sleepless in

[1]From the Brooklyn *Daily Eagle*, February 24, 1847.
Cf. "Song of Myself," Sec. 33, "Leaves of Grass," 1917, I, p. 81; 1855, p. 39; also *post*,
II, pp. 278–283.
[2]*Cf.* DeQuincey's essay, "Murder Considered as one of the Fine Arts."

the silence of the midnight. I stood off against the fire. In
every direction around, except the opposite front, there was one
compact mass of human flesh, upon the stoops, and along the
sidewalks, and blocking up the street, even to the edge of where
the flames were raging. The houses at the right hand were as
yet unharmed, with the exception of blistered paint, and win-
dows cracked by the strong heat over the way. I looked
through those windows to the rooms within. The walls were
bare and naked; no furniture, no inhabitant, no sign of life—
but everything bearing the stamp of desolation and flight. . . .
Every now and then would come a suffocating whirlwind of
smoke and burning sparks. Yet I stood my ground—I and
the mass—gazing at the wreck and the brightness before us.
The red flames rolled up the sides of a house newly caught, like
the forked tongues of serpents licking their prey.—It was terri-
bly grand. And then all the noise would cease, and for a min-
ute or two nothing would break in upon silence except the hoarse
voices of the engineers and their subordinates, and the hissing
and dull roaring of the fire. A few moments more, and the clat-
ter and the clang sounded out again with redoubled loudness.
The most pitiful thing in the whole affair was the sight of shiv-
ering women, their eyes red with tears, and many of them dash-
ing wildly through the crowd, in search, no doubt, of some
member of their family, who, for what they knew, might be
burned in the smoking ruins near by. Of all the sorrowful
spectacles of the world, perhaps no one could be more sorrowful
than such as this! . . . And those crumbled ashes! what
comforts were entombed there—what memories of affection
and brotherhood—what preparation, never to be consum-
mated—what hopes, never to see their own fruition—fell down
as the walls fell down, and were crushed as they were crushed!
But twelve hours before, the sun rose pleasantly; and all prom-
ised fair. The most distant idea of this misery, it entered into
the brain of no man to conceive. *Now*, what a change! People
who commenced the day with comfort before them, closed it
penniless. Those who had a house to shelter them at sunrise,
at sunset owned no pillow whereon to lay their heads. Wives
and husbands who parted in the morning with jocund words,
met at night to mingle their tears together, and to grieve over
blighted prospects. On the minds of many there, doubtless,
these and similar reflections forced themselves. I saw it in the
sombre countenances of the spectators, and heard it in their

conversation one to another. . . . And so, elbowing and pushing for rods through the crowd, one at last made out to get where the air was less hot and stifling, and the press of people less intense.

———

WHAT AN IDEA![1]

THE N. Y. *Sun* (24th,) says, in an article against the *unity* of the United States as one government: "The liberty of the country is centered in the independence of the states, and with a good understanding with each other a general government might be dispensed with.   Our government is a union of free states, and not a consolidation of states." . . . Our government, for certain purposes, *is* a "consolidation."   The wisdom of that principle is proved in the past and present; but in the local matters of the states, this consolidation does not give congress the right to interfere.—Perhaps no human institution—from which so much clashing was expected—has ever turned out better, than the "separate independence" of the federal and state governments.   With one exception, (and even that, in its result, only proves the sanatory powers of the consolidation,) they have never jarred.   Each has its sphere apart from the other—and each keeps in its sphere.

But the worst of such insidious articles as the *Sun's* is that they depress the idea of the sacredness of the *bond of union of these states*.   That bond is the foundation of incomparably the highest political blessings enjoyed in the world!   And the position of things at present demands that its sacredness should be recognized by *every and all* American citizens—however they may differ on points of doctrine or abstract rights.

———

DRAMATIC AFFAIRS, AND ACTORS[2]

IN THE heaviness that of late years seems spread, like a Lethean fog, over the prospects of a high-developed drama in this country, there is yet but little sign of the "curtain's rising."

[1] From the Brooklyn *Daily Eagle*, February 24, 1847.
Cf. post, II, p. 277.
[2] From the Brooklyn *Daily Eagle*, April 19, 1847.

At the Park theatre, a new piece, "Wissmuth & Co.,"[1] has been produced, but it is doubtless one of those amphibious things that balk the good appetite of the times for a better drama—for an improvement on the antiquated non-pleasant method of the past. . . . To-night, at the Park, Mrs. Mason[2] commences an engagement, playing Bianca in "Fazio"—Mr. Wheatley[3] as the latter character. (A morbid affair, this Fazio play, much like the worst of Bulwer's novels.) Mrs. M. is spoken of in high terms by the critics of the N. Y. press; but then there is really no dependence to be placed on those notices of public performers —they are half of the time paid for by parties concerned, and much of the other half is the result of favoritism.[4] . . . At the Olympic theatre, they are giving a run, after the old sort, of the popular operas, very neatly got up on a small scale; Miss Taylor[5] appears to-night as Zorlina in "Fra Diavolo"; (the best played parts at this theatre are Diavolo's two fellow robbers). . . . At the Bowery, Mrs. Shaw,[6] "takes" the countess in Knowles's[7] "Love"—a good play. At the Chatham, Yankee Hill[8] enacts his miserably exaggerated burlesques upon New England manners. . . . At the opera house in Chambers street, they are continuing the representation of a narrow few—

[1] "Wismuth and Co., or the Noble and the Merchant," a four-act drama founded on an old German play. With Chanfrau and Mrs. Hunt in the cast, it was nevertheless unsuccessful when produced, for the first time, on April 13, 1847.

[2] Mrs. James Mason, formerly Miss Emma Wheatley, a sister of William Wheatley, with whom she often acted. Whitman would probably have expressed his own opinion of her acting when he wrote the present essay but for the fact that Mrs. Mason was just then breaking a nine-year retirement from the stage.

[3] William Wheatley (1816-1876) first appeared on the stage at the age of ten, acting in "William Tell" with Macready. He was a "brilliant, finished, and versatile" Shakespearean actor, and a successful manager, first of the Arch Street Theatre in Philadelphia, and later of Niblo's Garden in New York (1862-1868).

[4] *Cf. infra*, p. 153.

[5] Miss Mary Celia Taylor, whose "delicious voice" and ease of acting made her a favourite at the Olympic from 1840 to 1849, as well as at the Bowery and elsewhere.

[6] Mrs. Shaw—later Mrs. Shaw-Hamblin—an actress in comedies and Shakespearean tragedy, first appeared in America on July 25, 1836, as Mariana in Knowles's "The Wife." She was from the first a favourite at the Park Theatre. She also acted, after 1839, at the Bowery.

[7] James Sheridan Knowles (1784-1862), born in Ireland; a preacher, physician, educator, poet, dramatist, and actor. He was the author of "Virginius," "The Hunchback," "William Tell," "Love," and "The Wife."

[8] George Handel Hill, whose burlesque interpretation of the Yankee character was very popular with theatregoers, particularly his acting of Solon Shingle in J. S. Jones's "The People's Lawyer." He also played Jonathan Plowboy in Samuel Woodworth's "The Forest Rose." See Mr. Montrose J. Moses's "The American Dramatist," Boston, 1917, p. 50.

those not even the second best—of the Italian operas; tonight, "Lucrezia Borgia."[1] On Wednesday night, it will be pleasanter to go, for then they give "Lombardi."[2] Nor must we overlook the new musical corps, late from Havana, now giving operas at the Park, two evenings a week: after the next representation by this corps, our readers will get a plain man's opinions of them.[3]

We reiterate an idea often advanced by us before—a suggestion that some great revolution must take place here, modernizing and Americanizing the drama, before it can reach that position among the first rank of intellectual entertainments, and as one of those agents of refining public manners and doing good, where it properly belongs. The same style and system of theatricals now exists that existed a hundred years ago,—while nearly every thing else is changed. What would be thought of writing novels and publishing newspapers on the plans that prevailed then? How long too shall we continue a mere inheritor of what is discarded in the old world? For the noble specimens in all the departments of literature which England has given—for the varied beauties of Shakspeare, the treasures of her honest sturdy old comedies, with their satire upon folly and vice of all kinds,—we are thankful, and would spread their influence for ever. Let them hold possession of the stage as long as may be—but not at the expense of our independence, and by making us a set of provincial imitators. It is no disrespect to those glorious old pieces and their authors to say that God's heavenly gift of genius has not been confined to them and their method of development alone. We have here in this land a new and swarming race, with an irrepressible vigour for working forward to superiority in *every thing*. As yet, it is true, all seems crude, chaotic, and unformed; but over the surface of the troubled waters, we think we see far ahead the Ararat, and the olive tree growing near. The drama *must* rise: the reign of English managers and English local plays must have its end.

---

[1] An Italian opera in four acts, the text by Felice Romain, the music by Donizetti. Champlain says this was first sung in New York in 1854; but it will be noted that Whitman, writing at the time, places its first production at least as early as 1847.

[2] "*Lombardi Alla Prima Crociata*" ("The Lombards in the First Crusade").

[3] A promise which was not kept.

[THE DEMOCRATIC SPIRIT][1]

To ATTACK the turbulence and destructiveness of the democratic spirit, is an old story—a tale told by many an idiot, and often signifying indeed "nothing"[2] save that the teller is too shallow to be more than a mechanical walker in the paths of the ignorant black past, and [to] look on those who turn aside therefrom as heretics and dangerous ones. Why, all that is good and grand in any political organization in the world, is the result of this turbulence and destructiveness; and controlled by the intelligence and common sense of such a people as the Americans, it never has brought harm, and never can. A quiet contented race sooner or later becomes a race of slaves— and when so become, there are always among them *still worse* slaves, bound mentally, who argue that it is better so, than to rise and destroy the tyranny that galls them. But with the noble democratic spirit—even accompanied by its freaks and its excesses—no people can ever become enslaved; and to us all the noisy tempestuous scenes of politics witnessed in this country— all the excitement and strife, even—are *good* to behold. They evince that *the people act;* they are the discipline of the young giant, getting his maturer strength. Is not this better than the despairing apathy wherewith the populace of Russia and Austria and the miserable German states—those *well-ordered* governments—endure the black-hearted rapacity of their rulers? We trow it is. And it is from such materials—from the democracy with its manly heart and its lion strength, spurning the ligatures wherewith drivellers would bind it—that we are to expect the great FUTURE of this western world! a scope involving such unparalleled human happiness and rational freedom, to such unnumbered myriads, that the heart of a true *man* leaps with a mighty joy only to think of it![3] God works out his greatest results by such means; and while each popinjay priest of the mummery of the past is babbling his alarm, the youthful Genius of the people passes swiftly over era after era of change and improvement, and races of human beings erewhile down in gloom or bondage rise gradually toward that majestic developement which the good God doubtless loves to witness. . . .

---

[1] From the Brooklyn *Daily Eagle*, April 20, 1847. In this volume captions enclosed in parentheses have been supplied by the editor when none appeared in the original text. *Cf. post*, I, pp. 259–264.

[2] *Cf.* "Macbeth," V, 5, 26–28. [3] *Cf. infra*, pp. 15–16.

It is the fashion of a certain set to assume to despise "politics" and the "corruption of parties," and the unmanageableness of the masses: they look at the fierce struggle, and at the battle of principles and candidates, and their weak nerves retreat dismayed from the neighborhood of the scenes of such convulsion. But to our view, the spectacle is always a grand one—full of the most august and sublime attributes. When we think how many ages rolled away while political action—which rightly belongs to every man whom God sends on earth with a soul and a rational mind—was confined to a few great and petty tyrants, the ten thousandth of the whole; when we see what cankerous evils gradually accumulated, and how their effect still poisons society—is it too much to feel this joy that among *us* the whole *surface* of the body politic is expanded to the sun and air, and each man feels his rights and *acts* them? Nor ought any member of our republic to complain, as long as the aggregate result of such action is what the world sees it is. Do we not behold evolving into birth, from it, the most wondrous nation, the most free from those evils which bad government causes, the really widest extending, possessing the truest riches of people and moral worth and freedom from want, ever yet seen aneath the broad heavens? . . . We know, well enough, that the workings of the democracy are not always justifiable, in every trivial point. But the great winds that purify the air, and without which nature would flag into ruin—are they to be condemned because a tree is prostrated here and there, in their course?[1]

NEW STATES: SHALL THEY BE SLAVE OR FREE?[2]

IT IS of not so much importance, the difference in the idea of a proper time to discuss, if we are only united in the *principle* that whatever new territory may be annexed to the United States, shall be free territory, and not for slaves. With the present slave

[1] *Cf. post*, I, pp. 197–198.

[2] From the Brooklyn *Daily Eagle*, April 22, 1847.

It was this editorial, "American Workingmen *versus* Slavery," and others of the sort, no doubt, which threw the weight of the *Eagle's* influence toward the "Barnburner" wing of the Democratic Party and resulted in the "rows with the boss and the party" (see "Complete Prose," p. 188) which ultimately set the young editor adrift. William Cullen Bryant, who was probably then, as later, a friend of Whitman, had this comment to make in the columns of the New York *Evening Post* on the occasion of Whitman's dismissal (January 21, 1848):

"Democracy in Kings County, L. I.—To a person familiar with the fact as to who

states, of course, no human being any where out from them-
selves has the least shadow of a right to interfere;[1] but in new
land, added to our surface by the national arms, and by the
action of our government, and where slavery does not exist, it
is certainly of momentous importance one way or the other,
whether that land shall be slave land or not. All ordinarily
"weighty issues" are insignificant before this: it swallows them
up as Aaron's rod swallowed the other rods. It involves the
question whether the mighty power of this republic, put forth
in its greatest strength, shall be used to root deeper and spread
wider an institution which Washington, Jefferson, Madison,
and all the old fathers of our freedom, anxiously, and avowedly
from the bottom of their hearts, sought the extinction of, and
considered inconsistent with the other institutions of the land.
And if those true and brave old men were now among us, can
any candid person doubt which "side" they would espouse in
this argument? Would the great apostle of democracy—in his
clear views of right and wrong, and their linked profit and loss—
would he *now*, seeing the stalwart giants of the free young west,
contrasted with the meagre leanness of the south—meagre with
all her noble traits—would *he* hesitate in bending his divine en-
ergies to the side of freedom?

The man who accustoms himself to *think*, when such matters
are put before him, and does not whiff his opinion rapidly out,

---

among the democrats of the western end of Long Island have been for years past in
command of the movements there, the following news will not be very astonishing:

"Old Hunkers vs. Barnburners.—Probably our readers know that the democrats
of this state are divided at the present time under the above heads; and of all ferocity,
there seldom has been seen any to equal that which seems to actuate these two sections.
The democratic party in Brooklyn—the *Eagle*—has for two years past been edited by
Mr. Walter Whitman, who, it seems, is a 'Barnburner.' In consequence of this fact
a disagreement has arisen, because the 'Old Hunkers' wanted one of their own men
there; and Mr. W. has had to give way to one of the other side.'—Brooklyn *Star*.

"It is intimated in another Brooklyn paper that the radicals are now anxious to have a
press of their own—and the late editor of the *Eagle*, mentioned above, is to engage in
such an enterprise."

In the fall of 1848 that is precisely what Whitman did (see *infra*, p. lii). It is pos-
sible, but unlikely, that Whitman went south with the intention of remaining only until
the "radicals" had the new sheet (the Brooklyn *Freeman*) ready for him. Still, it seems
a little strange that a radical "Barnburner" should have gone south at all at the time,
and more strange that he should have willingly worked on a paper which carried slave
auction announcements, though it did not, during his connection with it, defend slav-
ery. However, Whitman was not a man of one reform; least of all was he an Abolition-
ist crank (see *post*, II, p. 9, note 3). He had felt the call to become the poet of the whole
nation and must needs see it, north and south. If that meant self-contradiction then
he would reply, "I am large, I contain multitudes."

[1] *Cf. post*, II, p. 57.

from mere heedlessness, or from a more degrading motive, will see the wide and radical difference between the unquestionable folly, and wicked wrong, of "abolitionist" interference with slavery in the southern states—and this point of establishing slavery in fresh land. With the former we have nothing to do; but with the latter, we should all be derelict to our highest duties as christians, as men, and as democrats, if we did not throw ourselves into the field of discussion, using the utmost display of every energy wherewith God has endowed us, in behalf of the side which reason and religion proclaim as the right one. Is *this* the country, and *this* the age, where and when we are to be told that slavery must be propped up and extended? And shall any respectable portion of our citizens be deluded either by the sophisms of Mr. Calhoun, or those far, very far, lower influences of the darkest and meanest phases of demagougism [demagoguism], which are rife more at the north than at the south, to act in a matter which asks consideration purely on points of high justice, human rights, national advantage, and the safety of the union in the future?

THE AMBITION TO "MAKE A SHOW" IN DRESS.— HINTS TO BROOKLYN YOUNG WOMEN AND MEN

ALL people should endeavor to dress neatly, and with scrupulous cleanliness and tidiness. But the ambition—particularly in young people—to have shining new clothes is of the paltriest and most vulgar kind. You rarely see a young man or woman of real good sense, and possessing any true accomplishments, who makes a marked display in the way of apparel. Generally speaking, in nature, the gaudiest objects have the least real worth. The peacock is not really as valuable as the despised goose; the mackaw "can't begin" with the plain-looking nightingale. . . . We all like to see a *well*-dressed young woman or man; that is one whose clothes are gracefully made, are plain, clean, full, and not awkward. But the mere displayer of shining cloth, with an *attractive* look from top to toe, is not likely to please the sober judgment. . . . Hear

¹From the Brooklyn *Daily Eagle*, April 23, 1847.
    This editorial would seem to indicate that Whitman's bohemianism in dress has not yet been assumed, but, on the other hand, that he is no longer the dandy he was a few years previous. *Cf. post*, I, pp. 208–210.

what somebody says of that class whose life is nothing but a
devotion to the appearance of their persons:

LIFE OF A DANDY.—He gets up leisurely, breakfasts comfortably,
reads the paper regularly, dresses fashionably, eats a tart gravely,
talks superfluously, kills time indifferently, sups elegantly, goes to bed
stupidly, and lives uselessly.

ANTI-DEMOCRATIC BEARING OF SCOTT'S NOVELS[1]

THE novels of Walter Scott are in some respects unsurpassed
—but cannot be altogether praised. This great writer delin-
eates kings and queens and celebrated historic personages'
more private life, perhaps even better where he excites every
reader's profoundest sympathy by their losses, their defeats
in war, or their severe calamities. Nor does he fail in a lower
sphere. Who will not follow Jeanie Deans with every warm
feeling on her venturous journey to London? And upon the
whole, we think the "Heart of Mid Lothian," the best of the
great North Man's productions. Considered artistically it is
certainly faultless; and judging by our own heart while reading
it, (as we have done four or five times) there are no others more
capable of deeply interesting the brain that peruses it.

But Scott was a tory and a high church and state man. The
impression after reading any of his fictions where monarchs or
nobles compare with patriots and peasants, is dangerous to the
latter and favorable to the former. In the long line of those
warriors for liberty, and those large-hearted lovers of *men* before
classes of men, which English history has recorded upon its
annals, and which form for the fast-anchored isle a far greater
glory than her first Richard, or her tyrannical Stuarts, Scott
has not thought one fit to be illustrated by his pen. In him as in
Shakspere, (though in a totally different method,) "there's
such divinity does hedge a king,"[2] as makes them something
more than mortal—and though this way of description may be
good for poets or loyalists, it is poisonous for freemen. The
historical characters of Scott's books, too, are not the characters
of truth. He frequently gets the shadow on the wrong face.
Cromwell, for instance, was in the main, and even with severe

[1]From the Brooklyn *Daily Eagle*, April 26, 1847.
Cf. infra, pp. 67–72; *post*, II, pp. 57–58, 105.
[2]"Hamlet," IV, 5, 106.

faults, a heroic champion of his countrymen's rights—and the young Stuart was from top to toe a licentious, selfish, deceitful, and unprincipled man, giving his fastest friends to the axe and his subjects to plunder, when a spark of true manly nerve would have saved both. But the inference to be drawn from Scott's representation of these two men makes the villain a good-natured pleasant gentleman, and the honest ruler a blood-seeking hypocrite! Shame on such truckling! It is a stain black enough, added to his atrocious maligning of Napoleon, to render his brightest excellence murky!

————

RIDE TO CONEY ISLAND, AND CLAM–BAKE THERE[1]

NEVER was there a time better fitted than yesterday for an excursion from city to country, or from pavement to the sea-shore! The rain of the previous evening had cooled the air, and moistened the earth; there was no dust, and no unpleasant heat. It may well be imagined, then, that a jolly party of about sixty people, who, at 1 o'clock, P. M., met at the house of Mr. King, on the corner of Fulton and Orange streets, (where they laid a good *foundation* for after pleasures,) had every reason to bless their stars at the treat surely before them. Yes: there was to be a clam-bake—and, of all places in the world, a clam-bake at Coney-Island! Could mortal ambition go higher, or mortal wishes delve deeper? . . . At a little before 2, the most superb stages, four of them from Husted & Kendall's establishment, were just nicely filled, (no crowding, and no vacant places, either,) and the teams of four and six horses dashed off with us all at a merry rate. The ride was a most in-spiriting one. After crossing the railroad track, the signs of country life, the green fields, the thrifty corn, the orchards, the wheat lying in swathes, and the hay-cocks here and there, with the farming-men at work all along, made such a spectacle as we dearly like to look upon. And then the clatter of human tongues, inside the carriages—the peals upon peals of laughter! the jovial witticisms, the anecdotes, stories, and so forth!—Why, there were enough to fill ten octavo volumes! The members of the party were numerous and various—embracing all the professions, and nearly all the trades, besides sundry aldermen, and other officials.

[1]From the Brooklyn *Daily Eagle*, July 15, 1847.

Arrived at Coney Island, the first thing was to "take a dance," at which sundry distinguished personages shook care out of their heads and dust from their heels, at a great rate. Then a bathe in the salt water; ah, that was good indeed! Divers marvellous feats were performed in the water, in the way of splashing, ducking, and sousing, and one gentleman had serious thoughts of a sortie out upon some porpoises who were lazily rolling a short distance off. The beautiful, pure, sparkling, sea-water! one yearns to you (at least we do,) with an affection as grasping as your own waves![1]

Half-past five o'clock had now arrived, and the booming of the dinner bell produced a sensible effect upon "the party," who ranged themselves at table without the necessity of a second invitation. As the expectation had been only for a "clambake" there was some surprise evinced at seeing a regularly laid out dinner, in handsome style, too, with all the et-ceteras. But as an adjunct—by some, made the principal thing—in due time, on came the roasted clams, well-roasted indeed! in the old Indian style, in beds, covered with brush and chips, and thus cooked in their own broth. When hunger was appeased with these savory and wholesome viands, the champaigne (good stuff it was!) began to circulate—and divers gentlemen made speeches, introductory to, and responsive at, toasts. A great many happy hits were made, and, in especial, one of the aldermen, at the head of one of the tables, conceived a remarkable toast, at which the people seemed tickled hugely. The healths of Messrs. Masterton, Smith, and King, of Mr. Murphy,[2] and of the corporation of Brooklyn, etc., were drank. Nor were the artisans and workmen forgotten; nor were the ladies, nor the Brooklyn press, which the member of congress from this district spoke in the most handsome manner of, and turned off a very neat toast upon.

The return to Brooklyn, in the evening, was a fit conclusion to a day of enjoyment. The cool air, the smell of the new mown

[1] *Cf.* "Leaves of Grass," 1917, I, p. 59:

You see! I resign myself to you also—I guess what you mean
I behold from the beach your crooked inviting fingers,
I believe you refuse to go back without feeling of me, etc.

This and similar passages in Whitman's verse evidently describe a temperament characteristic of his young manhood. On them certain writers (especially Doctor W. C. Rivers in his "Walt Whitman's Anomaly," pp. 40 ff.) have based their assertion of Whitman's "sexual hyperesthesia."

[2] Henry C. Murphy; see *post*, II, pp. 1, 2, 5, 225, 295.

hay, the general quiet around, (there was anything but quiet, however, inside our vehicles,) made it pleasant indeed. We ascended to the tower-like seat, by Mr. Camfield,[1] the driver of the six-horse stage, and had one of the pleasantest sort of eight-mile rides back to Brooklyn, at which place our party arrived a little after 9 o'clock. All thanks, and long and happy lives, to the contractors on the new city hall! to whose generous spirit we were indebted for yesterday's pleasure.

NEW LIGHT AND OLD[2]

THERE are many people among us—and generally intelligent ones, too—who are in the habit of talking, writing, and reasoning on the principle that *government* is the power whose influence, properly wielded, ought to make men virtuous, happy, and possessed of a competence. We find the following extract in the last number of that valuable weekly, the *American Statesman:*

WHICH IS THE MOST PERFECT POPULAR GOVERNMENT?—"That," said Bias, "where the laws have no superior."

"That," said Thales, "where the inhabitants are neither too rich nor too poor."

"That," said Anacharsis, the Scythian, "where virtue is honored and vice detested."

"That," said Pattacus, "whose dignities are always conferred upon the virtuous, and never upon the base."

"That," said Cleopolus, "where the citizens fear blame more than punishment."

"That," said Chilo, "where the laws are regarded more than the orators."

"That," said Solon, "where any injury done to the meanest subject is an insult to the whole community."

"But," said the wisest of them all, "that is the most perfect government, where the earth is not monopolized by the few to the injury of the many, and where labor, receiving a just remuneration for its toil, is guaranteed to all. In that government you will find neither misery, nor crime, nor poverty."

It may seem a tall piece of coolness and presumption for a humble personage like ourself to put *his* opinions of government

[1] This is probably a misprint for *Canfield,* for no *Camfields* appear in the city directories of the period.

[2] From the Brooklyn *Daily Eagle,* July 26, 1847.
Cf. "Song of the Broad-Axe," 1856, in "Leaves of Grass," 1917, I, pp. 228–230.

on the same page with those of the wise men of the ancient days; but, as a common engineer, now, could tell Archimedes things to make the latter stare, so the march of improvement has brought to light truths in politics which the wisest sages of Greece and Rome never discovered. And it is, at the same time, painful to yet see the servile regard paid by the more enlightened present to the darker past. The recognized doctrine that the people are *to be governed* by some abstract power, apart from themselves, has not, even at this day and in this country, lost its hold—nor that to any thing more than the government must the said people look for their well-doing and the prosperity of the state. In such a form of rule as ours this dogma is particularly inconvenient; because it makes a perpetual and fierce strife between those of opposing views, to get their notions and doctrines realized in the laws.

In plain truth, "the people expect too much of the government." Under a proper organization, (and even to a great extent as things are,) the wealth and happiness of the citizens could be hardly touched by the government—could neither be retarded nor advanced. *Men* must be "masters into [unto?] themselves," and not look to presidents and legislative bodies for aid. In this wide and naturally rich country, the best government indeed is "that which governs least."[1]

One point, however, must not be forgotten—ought to be put before the eyes of the people every day; and that is, that although government can do little positive *good* to the people, it may do an *immense deal of harm.* And here is where the beauty of the democratic principle comes in. Democracy would prevent all this harm. It would have no man's benefit achieved at the expense of his neighbors. It would have no one's rights infringed upon and that, after all, is pretty much the sum and substance of the prerogatives of government. How beautiful and harmonious a system! How it transcends all other codes, as the golden rule, in its brevity, transcends the ponderous tones [tomes?] of philosophic lore! While mere politicians, in their narrow minds, are sweating and fuming with their complicated statutes, this one single rule, rationally construed and applied, is enough to form the starting point of all that is necessary in government: *to make no more laws than those useful for preventing a man or a body of men from infringing on the rights of other men.*

[1] *Cf. post,* I, pp. 259–264; also "To the States," "Leaves of Grass," 1917, I, p.10.

We conclude our article by the following extract from a dis-
course by the great Channing,[1] which we mean more particularly
for those who think that *poor* citizens are the great difficulty in
the way of national happiness:

Mere wealth adds nothing to a people's glory.   It is the nation's soul,
which constitutes its greatness.   Nor is it enough for a country to pos-
sess a select class of educated, cultivated men; for the nation consists
of the many not the few; and where masses are sunk in ignorance and
sensuality, there you see a degraded community, even though an aris-
tocracy of science be lodged in its bosom.   It is the moral and intellec-
tual progress of the people to which the patriot should devote himself
as the only dignity and safeguard of the state.

PHILOSOPHY OF FERRIES[2]

OUR Brooklyn ferries teach some sage lessons in philosophy,
gentle reader, (we like that time-honoured phrase![3]) whether you
ever knew it or not.   There is the Fulton, now, which takes pre-
cedence by age, and by a sort of aristocratic seniority of wealth
and business, too.   It moves on like iron-willed destiny.   Pas-
sionless and fixed, at the six-stroke the boats come in; and at the
three-stroke, succeeded by a single tap, they depart again, with
the steadiness of nature herself.   Perhaps a man, prompted by
the hell-like delirium tremens, has jumped over-board and been
drowned: still the trips go on as before.   Perhaps some one has
been crushed between the landing and the prow—(ah! that most
horrible thing of all!) still, no matter, for the great business of
the mass must be helped forward as before.   A moment's pause
—the quick gathering of a curious crowd, (how strange that they
can look so unshudderingly on the scene!)—the paleness of the
more chicken hearted—and all subsides, and the current sweeps
as it did the moment previously.   How it deadens one's sym-
pathies, this living in a city!
    But the most "moral" part of the ferry sights, is to see the
conduct of the people, old and young, fat and lean, gentle and

[1] I presume this is William Ellery Channing, Unitarian minister, pulpit orator, and
writer, but I have been unable to locate the passage in his works.

[2] From the Brooklyn *Daily Eagle*, August 13, 1847.
    This early editorial has interest, not only in itself, but also because Whitman was such
a frequenter of the ferries and because one of his truest poems was written about, if not
on, them ("Crossing Brooklyn Ferry").   *Cf.* also "Complete Prose," p. 11, and *post*,
II, pp. 292–293.

[3] *Cf. post*, II, p. 262.

simple, when the bell sounds three taps. Then follows a spec-
tacle, indeed—particularly on the Brooklyn side, at from seven
o'clock to nine in the morning. At the very first moment of
the sound, perhaps some sixty or eighty gentlemen are plodding
along the side walks, adjacent to the ferry boat—likewise some
score or so of lads—with that brisk pace which bespeaks the
"business individual." Now see them as the said three-tap is
heard! Apparently moved by an electric impulse, two thirds
of the whole number start off on the wings of the wind! Coat
tails fly high and wide! You get a swift view of the phantom-
like semblance of humanity, as it is sometimes seen in dreams—
but nothing more—unless it may be you are on the walk your-
self, when the chances are in favor of a breath-destroying punch
in the stomach. In their insane fury, the rushing crowd spare
neither age nor sex. Then the single stroke of the bell is heard;
and straightway what was rage before comes to be a sort of
extatic fury! Aware of his danger, the man that takes the toll
has ensconced himself behind a stout oaken partition, which
seems only to be entered through a little window-looking place:
but we think he must have more than ordinary courage, to
stand even there. We seriously recommend the ferry superin-
tendent to have this place as strong as iron bars can make it.

   This rushing and raging is not inconsistent, however, with
other items of the American character. Perhaps it is a devel-
opment of the "indomitable energy" and "chainless enter-
prise" which we get so much praise for. But it is a very ludi-
crous thing, nevertheless. If the trait is remembered down to
posterity, and put in the annals, it will be bad for us. Posterity
surely cannot attach anything of the dignified or august to a
people who run after steam-boats, with hats flying off, and skirts
streaming behind! Think of any of the Roman senators, or
the worthies of Greece, in such a predicament.—(The esteem
which we had for a certain acquaintance went up at least
a hundred per cent, one day, when we found that, though a daily
passenger over the ferry, he never accelerated his pace in the
slightest manner, even when by so doing, he could "save a
boat.")

   A similar indecorum and folly are exhibited when the boat
approaches the wharf. As if some avenging fate were behind
them, and the devil indeed was going to "take the hindermost,"
the passengers crowd to the very verge of the forward parts, and
wait with frightful eagerness till they are brought within three

or four yards of the landing—when the front row prepare them-
selves for desperate springs. Among many there is a rivalry
as to who shall leap on shore over the widest stretch of water!
The boat gets some four or five feet from the wharf, and then
the springing begins—hop! hop! hop!—those who are in the
greatest hurry generally stopping for several minutes when
they get on the dock to look at their companions behind on the
boat, and how *they* come ashore! Well: there is a great deal of
inconsistency in this world.

The Catherine ferry at the foot of Main street has plenty
of business, too, though not near as much as the one whose
peculiarities we have just been narrating. It has lately had
some new boats—or new fixings and paint, we don't know which
—and presents, (we noticed the other day, in crossing,) quite a
spruce appearance. The Catherine ferry is used by many work-
ing people: in the morning they cross there in prodigious num-
bers. Also, milk wagons, and country vehicles generally. Dur-
ing the day a great many of the Brooklyn dames go over this
ferry on shopping excursions to the region of Grand street and
Catherine street on the other side. The desperation to get to
the boat, which we have mentioned above, does not prevail
so deeply here. Long may the contagion "stay away"! for
we must confess that we don't like to see it. This ferry, (like
all the others,) is a very profitable investment; and from those
profits we are warranted in saying—as we have said once or
twice before—that the price for foot passengers should be put
down to one cent, and horses and wagons in proportion.

The South ferry has a more dainty and "genteel" character
than either of the other places. The broad avenue which
leads to it, and the neighborhood of the aristocratic heights,
from whom it receives many of its passengers, keep it so. Busi-
ness is not so large there as at either of the other ferries we have
mentioned; but the accommodations are of the first quality.
The boats are large and clean; and the more moderate bustle
and clatter make it preferable, during the summer afternoons,
for ladies and children—the latter often taken by their nurses
and remaining on board the boats for an hour, for the pleasant
sail.

Besides these, we have the ferry from the foot of Jackson
street on the Brooklyn side, to Walnut st. New York side.
This consists of only one boat, and a rather shabby one at that.
Many workmen at the navy yard use this means of conveyance;

and it is also of course patronized by citizens in that vicinity. We should think much better and more rapid accommodations would be desirable there.—The boat is half the time prevented by her own unwieldness from getting into her slip under half an hour's detention. She seems to be some old affair that has been cast off for years.

We have also two other ferries, in the limits of Brooklyn, which in time will be as much avenues of business as either of the rest. One of these goes from Whitehall to the foot of Hamilton avenue, and accommodates the region of the Atlantic dock, and of farther South Brooklyn, which is daily assuming more and more importance. The other goes also from Whitehall to the long wharf near Greenwood cemetery. This also is necessary for the accommodation of a rapidly increasing mass of citizens who are attracted by the salubrity of that section of Brooklyn joined with the cheapness of the land and the nearness of the beautiful grounds of the cemetery.

The ferry at the foot of Montagu[e] street is in progress; and will probably be in operation next spring. The Bridge street ferry is also determined upon, and may be completed by the same time.

———

AMERICAN WORKINGMEN, *VERSUS* SLAVERY[1]

THE question whether or no there shall be slavery in the new territories which it seems conceded on all hands we are largely to get through this Mexican war, is a question between *the grand body of white workingmen, the millions of mechanics, farmers, and operatives of our country*, with their interests, on the one side—and the interests of the few thousand rich, "polished," and aristocratic owners of slaves at the south, on the other side. Experience has proved, (and the evidence is to be seen now by any one who will look at it) that a stalwart mass of respectable workingmen cannot exist, much less flourish, in a thorough slave state. Let any one think for a moment what a different appearance New York, Pennsylvania, or Ohio would present—how much less sturdy independence and family happiness there would be—were slaves the workmen there, instead of each man as a general thing being his own workman. We wish

[1]From the Brooklyn *Daily Eagle*, September 1, 1847.
Cf. infra, pp. 160–162; *post*, II, pp. 8–10.

not at all to sneer at the south; but leaving out of view the educated and refined gentry, and coming to the "common people" of the whites, everybody knows what a miserable, ignorant, and shiftless set of beings they are. Slavery is a good thing enough, (viewed partially,) to the rich—the one out of thousands; but it is destructive to the dignity and independence of all who work, and to labor itself. An honest poor mechanic, in a slave state, is put on a par with the negro slave mechanic—there being many of the latter, who are hired out by their owners. It is of no use to reason abstractly on this fact—farther than to say that the price of a northern American freeman, poor though he be, will not comfortably stand such degredation.

The influence of the slave institution is to bring the dignity of labor down to the level of slavery, which, God knows! is low enough. And this it is which must induce *the workingmen of the north, east, and west, to come up, to a man, in defense of their rights, their honor, and that heritage of getting bread by the sweat of the brow, which we must leave to our children.* Let them utter forth, then, in tones as massive as becomes their stupendous cause, that their calling shall *not* be sunk to the miserable level of what is little above brutishness—sunk to be like owned goods, and driven cattle!—We call upon every mechanic of the north, east, and west—upon the carpenter, in his rolled up sleeves, the mason with his trowel, the stone-cutter with his brawny chest, the blacksmith with his sooty face, the brown-fisted ship-builder, whose clinking strokes rattle so merrily in our dock yards—upon shoemakers, and cartmen, and drivers, and paviers, and porters, and millwrights, and furriers, and ropemakers, and butchers, and machinists, and tinmen, and tailors, and hatters, and coach and cabinet makers —upon the honest sawyer and mortar-mixer, too, whose sinews are their own—and every hard-working man—to speak in a voice whose great reverberations shall tell to all quarters that the *workingmen* of the free United States, and their business, are not willing to be put on the level of negro slaves, in territory which, if got at all, must be got by taxes sifted eventually through upon them, and by their hard work and blood. But most of all we call upon *the farmers*, the workers of the land— that prolific brood of brown faced fathers and sons who swarm over the free states, and form the true bulwark of our republic, mightier than walls or armies—upon them we call to say whether *they* too will exist "free and independent" not only in name but also by those social customs and laws which are greater than constitutions—or only so by statute, while in reality they are put down to an equality with slaves!

There can be no half way work in the matter of slavery in the new territory: we must either have it there, or have it not. Now if either the slaves themselves, or their owners, had fought or paid for or gained this territory, there would be some reason in the pro-slavery claims. But every body knows that the work and the cost come, forty-nine fiftieths of it, upon the free men, the middling classes and workingmen, who do their own work and own no slaves. Shall *these* give up all to the aristocratic owners of the south? Will even the poor white freemen of the south be willing to do this? It is monstrous to ask such a thing!

Not the least curious part of the present position of this subject is, the fact *who* advances the claims of slavery, and the singular manner in which those claims are half-allowed by men at the north who ought to know better. The truth is that all practice and theory—the real interest of the planters themselves—and the potential weight of the opinions of all our great statesmen, southern as well as northern, from Washington to Silas Wright—are strongly arrayed in favor of limiting slavery to where it already exists. For this the clear eye of Washington looked longingly; for this the great voice of Jefferson plead, and his sacred fingers wrote; for this were uttered the prayers of Franklin and Madison and Monroe. But now, in the south, stands a little band, strong in chivalry, refinement, and genius—headed by a sort of intellectual Saladin—assuming to speak in behalf of sovereign states, while in reality they utter their own idle theories; and disdainfully crying out against the rest of the republic, for whom their contempt is but illy concealed. The courage and high-tone of these men are points in their favor, it must be confessed. With dextrous but brazen logic they profess to stand on the constitution against a principle whose very existence dates from some of the most revered formers of that constitution! And these—this band, really little in numbers, and which could be annihilated by one pulsation of the stout free heart of the north—these are the men who are making such insolent demands, in the face of the working farmers and mechanics of the free states—the nine-tenths of the population of the republic. We admire the chivalric bearing (sometimes a sort of impudence) of these men. So we admire, as it is told in history, the dauntless conduct of kings and nobles when arraigned for punishment before an outraged and a too long-suffering people. . . . But the course of moral light and human freedom, (and their consequent happiness), is not to be stayed by such men as they. Thousands of noble hearts at the north—the entire east—the uprousing giant of the free west —will surely, when the time comes, sweep over them and their doctrines as the advancing ocean tide obliterates the channel of some little brook that erewhile ran down the sands of its shore. Already the roar of the waters is heard; and if a few short-sighted ones seek to withstand it, the surge, terrible in its fury, will sweep them too in the ruin.

EAST LONG ISLAND CORRESPONDENCE[1]

LETTER I

Starting on the Railroad—Bedford—East New York—Jamaica—
"characters" there—Hempstead—Hicksville—Farmingdale,
(formerly "Hardscrabble,") finis.

RIVERHEAD, SUFFOLK COUNTY, SEPTEMBER 10TH.—At half-past one o'clock yesterday afternoon, I started on the L. I. railroad from the South ferry on my way to the eastern section of "old Nassau." The usual splutter which precedes a start attended us, of course. Little boys with newspapers, friends taking leave, women uttering "last words," Emerald ladies with peaches, (oranges now are among the things that *were,*) and small fry with various wares, surrounded the cars; and these, with the assistance of the furious steam pipe, and certain obstreperous iron work that certes seemed to have some rickety disorder, made up a scene that would make the fortune of a melo-drama, if brought in at the close of an act—but which I was glad enough to escape from, I assure you.

The first stopping place was at Bedford. So near to Brooklyn, our readers are most of them familiar enough with the aspect of this pretty little hamlet; it has a great amount of

---

[1] From the Brooklyn *Daily Eagle*, September 16, 1847.

It was not very uncommon in Whitman's editorial days for an editor to travel occasionally, keeping in touch with his newspaper or magazine by means of "correspondence." During his editorship of the *Eagle* Whitman appears to have made two trips to the eastern end of the Island (see *infra,* pp. 118–121), and another while writing for the *Standard* (see *post,* II, pp. 306-321). *Cf. post,* II, pp. 275-278. The present journey lasted, apparently, about two weeks.

shrubbery and trees, and that same richness of vegetation gives it, with all its rurality, something of a fever-and-aguish aspect, which I should hardly like to live in the midst of, more than long enough to visit my hospitable friend W., at his cottage there.

East New York comes next on the line.   This settlement is quite a flat.   To the north rises a spur of that range of hills which runs nearly through the island, and gives the settlement a relief from the character of monotony which most flat places possess.   East New York *was* going to be, once, a very great city, and arrangements were made on a corresponding scale to have it so.   A post office was established, also a school and church, ditto a "land agency"; after which there was some talk of a bank—(all this was years ago, in the "speculation times"[1]) —and your humble servant himself was spoken to about going there and establishing a newspaper.—Numerous lots were sold, and buildings erected.—The place did really offer a pretty natural situation, and the land presenting no obstacle to convenience of every kind in forming a village, golden dreams were paramount in the heads of more than its principal proprietor, Mr. Pitkin.   But alas! like all the false business that was superinduced by the poisonous influence of the United States bank, and the paper speculators of those days, the bubble burst at last—and East New York almost burst with it.   I observe that some clusters of buildings are still there, and most of them seem to be occupied.   But the whole village is devoid of that aspect of vitality which notes [denotes?] a thriving and growing place, where the inhabitants are "making money."

After passing the Union race course—the scene of so many feverish contests, and of the changing ownership of cash, and which presents, in its every-day look so wondrous a difference from the days when great races are to come off—we arrived at Jamaica.   This is truly a charming place, and is occupied by many intellectual and wealthy people.   It consisted a few years ago mostly of one main street, the turnpike; but of late years this has been intersected by a great many thoroughfares, and now Jamaica can almost present its claims to a cityfied character.   It has as many churches, in proportion, as Brooklyn— including that of "the old dominie," Mr. Schoonmaker, who used to preach alternately in Dutch and English.—Also the old Methodist church, with its little panes of window glass, about as

[1] *Cf. post*, II, p. 297.

big as boarding house pancakes. At this last, is stationed one of the old fathers, the venerable presiding elder of the Long Island district, Mr. Matthias, whose age and estimable character make him much endeared to everybody. Jamaica has two newspapers, the *Democrat*,[1] whose politics are signified by its name, and the *Farmer*,[2] a whig print.—Some good schools, for both sexes, and any quantity of stores and public houses, are also in Jamaica.

We then stopped a moment at Brushville, two or three miles to the east, where the Hempstead turnpike turns off from the one which leads down unto Jericho; and the next "station," as called out by the conductor, is Hempstead "and Branch,"—something like "Boston and New England." The railroad, as you probably know, does not run through the village of Hempstead, which is somewhat to be regretted. Said village lies some two miles to the south; and the stopping place is a settlement built up right in the middle of the plains, on the strength of that *being* the stopping place. It does not look so bare, though, as one would expect, from the character of the surrounding country. A track has been laid to connect with the village of Hempstead so that passengers can go from Brooklyn there, without getting out of the car: it goes down from the main track by horse-engine instead of steam.—Hempstead is an old village, mostly celebrated for its clams, (indeed it is by some called Clamtown.) It is pretty in its situation, very wholesome, has a worthy population, and is considerable of a trading town. There is one newspaper there, the *Inquirer*,[3] neutral in politics, an excellent academy, and divers churches. To the southeast from it stretches the great turnpike that leads down along our island's "sea-girt shore," even through the gates of Jerusalem and into the recess of Babylon the great.

Hicksville comes next, (not stopping to make particular mention of Carl place and Westbury). Ah, how are the mighty fallen! Hicksville was going to be "one of the cities," when the railroad was first finished to it.[4] We remember the time. Why, people bought lots there, (only think of it,) and speculated in them, just the same as the corn and flour dealers, last winter, went into *their* speculations.—And full as bitterly bitten were the dreamers of this "city on the plain," as were our floury neighbours at the western end of South street. Hicksville now

[1] *Cf. infra*, xxxii and notes. [3] *Cf. infra*, p. 32, note 2.
[2] *Cf. infra*, p. 48, note 2. [4] In 1837.

consists of one very large tavern, with a remarkably meagre aspect, and standing much in want of a coat of paint—one huge car house—sundry pig-pens unoccupied—and a few houses, also unoccupied.—The only thing in which Hicksville has ample room and verge enough, and which a man might take without any one saying him nay, would be yard room—for potato patches, drying clothes, or any other purpose he saw fit.   In every direction you look on nothing but the flat plains—of which I shall have more to say in one of these rambling epistles.

Farmingdale lies some seven or eight miles farther east. In the vernacular hereabout it was called Hardscrabble (this is the veritable place!) but the rage for improvement, not agreeing with Juliet, (wasn't it Shakespere's Juliet, who asked about *that* "rose"?[1]) wisely thought that *any* other name would be more inviting than Hardscrabble.[2]   I think it was right.

——But I have made my letter already long enough for this day of short newspaper articles.   Though I have headed my letter "East Long Island correspondence,"—and though it has, as yet, got no farther than Farmingdale, I shall let the heading stand in view of what I shall write in future.   I have dated it at Riverhead, too, though I must describe several localities yet before I catch up, (or rather get the reader to catch up,) to Riverhead.   We are "enjoying" a pretty dull, continued, chilly rain, this morning—after having had said rain, in a still heavier development, during the night—and a prospect of "the same subject continued," during the day, and perhaps longer.

EAST LONG ISLAND CORRESPONDENCE[3]

LETTER II

Scenery after leaving Farmingdale (otherwise Hardscrabble,) Huntington and Babylon; Deer Park; scenery at the "stations"; West Hills; Medford, Yaphank, and St. George's manor; practicability of cultivating the wild land here; stopping at Riverhead; &c.

AFTER leaving Farmingdale, we trudged east with our steam steed through brush, plains, pine, scrub oak, and all the other peculiarities of those singular diggins, at a speed considerably

[1] "Romeo and Juliet," II, 2, 43.

[2] See the Index for other evidence of Whitman's interest in place names.

[3] From the Brooklyn *Daily Eagle*, September 18, 1847.

faster than ordinary wind.   The next station to Farmingdale is
Deer Park, somewhat half way between the village of Hunting-
ton on the north and Babylon the great on the south.   You
must not suppose, from the name of this station, that it really
is a park, or that deer are very plentiful here.   On the contrary,
few spots can peresent a more dreary and barren appearance.
The blackened stumps of pine trees, the uninviting glimpses of
a bit of soil here and there, the monotonous pine tree, and one
single house, used as a tavern, are all that *relieve* the eye.   But
it is very different both to the north and south.   There lie the
ample and rich farms of the good old democratic town of Hunt-
ington.   Thousands and thousands of the best soil on Long
Island are comprised in them.   To the north are apple orchards
and grass lands, so thrifty that the eye of an agriculturist might
gloat for hours in the mere seeing of them.   The land is diver-
sified into hills and valleys; and on the tops of the highest eleva-
tions are little lakes of the purest water, which form brooks
down the valleys, and irrigate many of the neighboring fields.
What is called the highest point of land on the island is at
West Hills, in the town of Huntington; it was made much use
of by Mr. Hassler, the U. S. chief of engineers, in the great plan
of coast survey which has been going on for some years past.
The other part of Huntington, lying along the south bay, is of a
different character; it partakes of *fish*, both on the land as well
as water.   Fish is one of the most powerful manures known,
and under its influence the corn grows to an astonishing height
and size.   I have thought, indeed, that the fault among the
farmers here was in putting too much of it, at a time, on their
land.   Like Macbeth's ambition, it o'erleaps itself and falls
on the other side of fertility.[1]

Beyond Deer Park are numerous petty "stations," which al-
ways make me think of new single habitations in the far west[2]—
with their cheerless looking houses, barefooted children, and
general slovenliness.   These "stations" are appointed gener-
ally with respect to some village or town off against them on the
north or south turnpikes, and consist mostly of but one or two
structures, and those of the shabbiest kind.   Sometimes a little
spot for gardening is cleared around them; but the energy of
their owners seems to give out before any great good has been
done.   You see the dwarfed and sickly yellow corn, and the

[1] "Macbeth," I, 9, 27–28.
[2] There is no evidence that Whitman had himself visited the West previous to this time.

poor beans and potatoes; but no care is taken of them when they promise so wretchedly, which redoubles their dwarfedness and sickliness.—I am firmly convinced, however, that a little intelligent knowledge of agriculture, aided by its great hand-maiden chemistry, would do wonders here, and soon make even these sterile spots to bud and blossom like the rose. It is a pity that there is, among the farmers of Long Island, an unusual share of the contempt of their craft for "book-farming."

Medford, Yaphank, St. George's manor, and so forth, are the names of some of the stopping places here—to the south and north of which lie many rich and fertile neighborhoods. The railroad seems to have been built with the design of running thro' the most unproductive and the most uninviting parts of the island.   For while on both sides, adjacent to the shore, one could hardly go amiss of pleasant places, athwart the line of the rails the eye rests, soon after leaving Jamaica, upon one continued spread of apparently useless land, uncultivated and almost valueless—and this quite down to Greenport.   The question as to the practicability of cultivating this land has lately been started.   A very large portion of it doubtless *is* susceptible of cultivation.

Never having been to Riverhead, the county town of old Suffolk, I suddenly resolved, when the conductor sung out its name, and the cars stopped there, to stop there too.   Accordingly, I clutched my carpet bag, and, in obedience to the prevailing spirit of haste, was soon out upon the platform.—The village itself lies a little south from the stopping place of the railroad, and is one of the oldest on Long Island.   Of its character, peculiarities, and what I have delved out here in the way of incident—as well as how I am "getting along" myself—I shall advise you more fully in another epistle.

Since my setting down here, we have been blessed with a refreshing time in the way of a cold, dull, dark, blue-devilish, north-east rain—not a bit of sunshine or clear sky being even momentarily visible.   I was in hopes, last evening, that a change was coming over the spirit of the dream,[1] but at the moment of the present writing, (Saturday morning, 11th,) the clouds are as heavy as ever.   But never mind: is a man made to grumble merely because the skies look dark?   Are not the skies *there* still?

---

[1] *Cf.* "A change came o'er the spirit of my dream," Byron's "The Dream," Stanza 3, line 1.   *Cf.* I, *post*, p. 218.

I heard last night that authentic news of Scott's victories at the city of Mexico had been received in town. Consider me as on the top of the tallest pine tree in the present neighborhood, wafting my gratified patriotism to you in the loudest sort of a "holler."

———

EAST LONG ISLAND CORRESPONDENCE[1]

LETTER III

SOUTHOLD, SEPTEMBER 14TH.—Seeing, to-day, as I passed one of the country stores, a real *Indian*, (at least as far as there are any of that race now-a-days; that is, perhaps, an Indian whose blood is only thinned by only two or three degrees of mixture,) my thoughts were turned toward the aboriginal inhabitants of this island. A populous and powerful race! for such they once were. Some authorities assert that, at the earliest approach of the whites to this part of the continent, and for a time after, the Indian inhabitants of Long Island numbered a million and a half. This may be an over-estimate; but the red race here was certainly very numerous, as is evidenced by many tokens. "An ancient Indian," says one tradition, "more than a hundred years ago, declared to one of the earliest inhabitants of Easthampton, that within his recollection the natives were *as many as the spears of grass*. And if, said he, stretching his hands over the ground, you can count these, then, when I was a boy, you could have reckoned their number." . . . Another token is the immense shell-banks, at intervals, all along the shores of the island—some of them literally "mountain high." Another is the immense tract devoted to the fields of Indian corn.

Unlike the present arrangement, the seat of the greatest aboriginal population and power was on the eastern extremity of Long Island. On the peninsula of Montauk dwelt the royal tribe;—and there lived and ruled the noble Wyandanch; (*will* not the Union ferry company be persuaded to take off that miserably wrong terminative of "dank" from the boat they pretend to christen after the old chief).[2] This chief held a position not

[1] From the Brooklyn *Daily Eagle*, September 20, 1847.

[2] William Wallace Tooker, in his "Indian Place Names on Long Island" (Putnam's, New York, 1911), pp. 294–295, gives ten different spellings, apparently preferring *Wyandance*, in which form the name supplanted that of Deer Park (*infra*, p. 178) on January 1, 1889. Wyandance was Sachem of Paumanack (Whitman's spelling, *Paumanok*, is not given by Tooker at all), after the death of his elder brother in 1652. His name means "the wise speaker." *Cf. post*, II, pp. 274–275, 315–316.

unlike our American president. On the Island were thirteen
separate tribes, (our King's county was occupied by the "Can-
arsees,") who were united in one general confederacy, at the
head of which was Wyandanch. From Montauk, whose white
sides resounded forever with the mighty voice of the sea, went
forth the supreme commands and decisions. Here, too, was the
holiest of the burial places, the sacred spots to all savage na-
tions, and peculiarly so to our North American Indians. On
Montauk, even now, may also be seen remains of aboriginal
fortifications, one of which at what is now called "Fort Hill"
must have been a work of art indeed. It had ramparts and
parapets, ditches around, and huge towers at each of four cor-
ners—and is estimated to have afforded conveniences for three
or four hundred men, and to evince singular knowledge of war-
fare, even as understood by what we call civilized nations.
Wars, indeed, added to pestilence, and most of all the use of the
"fire-water,"[1] thinned off the Indian population from the earlier
settlement of the whites, until there are hardly any remaining.
I believe there are but two clusters of Indian families that can
be called settlements, now on the island. One is at Shinnecock,
and consists of some hundred and forty or fifty persons: the
other is down on Montauk, and does not comprise a baker's
dozen. Sad remnants, these, of the sovereign sway and the old
majesty there!

EXCERPTS FROM A TRAVELLER'S NOTE BOOK— [No. 1][2]

CROSSING THE ALLEGHANIES

WE LEFT Baltimore on Saturday morning at seven o' clock,
on the railroad for Cumberland, which is about a hundred and
seventy miles distant, at the eastern edge of the Alleghanies.
Of course, at this season of the year the country is not remark-

---

[1] *Cf.* post, II, p. 111. For other evidences of Whitman's interest in the Indians, see
post, II, pp. 233–235, 260–261, 274–275, 314–317.

[2] From the *Daily Crescent* (New Orleans), March 5, 1848.

Whitman's connection with the *Crescent* extended from its first issue, Sunday, March
5, 1848 (thereafter it was issued only on week days), until he resigned, May 24, 1848
(see *post*, II, p. 78). Since he was not in sole editorial charge of the paper, as he had been
in the *Eagle* office, it is necessary to identify his contributions. Some of these are signed
"W" or "W. W." The latter form of initial was affixed to the only poem known to
have been published by him in the *Crescent*, "The Mississippi at Midnight." The ori-

ably fascinating anywhere; and here a very large portion of the road is bounded on one side or the other by cliffs and steeps of an Alp-like loftiness.   We seemed, for at least a hundred miles, to follow the course of an interminable brook, winding with its windings, and twisting with its twists, in a, to me, singular fashion.   But even with so many circuits, the road had to be cut through very many bad places; and was probably one of the most expensive railroads ever built.   It pays enormous profits, however; and they seriously "talk" about having it continued to some place on the Ohio, perhaps Wheeling.   After "talking about it" awhile, it will very likely be done; it only wants money enough—and an enormous lot of that it *will* want, too!

At Harper's Ferry, where they gave us twenty minutes to dine, the scenery is strikingly abrupt and varied.   Houses were perched up over our heads—backs in the ground—and others perched up over *their* heads, and so on.   The finest scenery, though, even here, (if it be not a bull to say so,) is about half a mile off.   As soon as the cars stopped, a frightful sound of bells

---

ginal version, which differs in many respects from that in the "Complete Prose" (pp. 373–374), is to be found in Doctor Bucke's "Notes and Fragments" (pp. 41–42), in the *Yale Review*, October, 1915, and in the "Publications of the Louisiana Historical Society," Vol. VII, pp. 102–103.   Other contributions given here are identified (1) by their being in Whitman's particular province as described by himself (this applies only to "Fourierism," *post*,I, p. 229; see *post*, II, p. 78); (2) by their unambiguous similarity to Whitman's preserved writings (as "General Taylor at the Theatre," *post*, I, p. 225); (3) by the detailed statements of one of Whitman's fellow journalists of the New Orleans press of 1848 (James Edmunds, author of "Kant's Ethics," Louisville, 1884) to Mr. William Kernan Dart, whose article on "Walt Whitman in New Orleans" ("Publications of the Louisiana Historical Society," Vol. VII) mentions most of the important articles which can with assurance be ascribed to Whitman; or (4) by two or more of these methods of identification.   It may be said also that there is nothing in any of these articles to contradict the statements of Mr. Dart, but, on the other hand, that the internal evidence of Whitman's authorship is very strong.

As to the "Excerpts from a Traveller's Note Book," they follow the known route of the Whitmans (see "Complete Prose," pp. 14–15) in their journey to New Orleans and was published immediately after their arrival.   As they were not published as "communicated" matter, it is extremely unlikely that they were written by any other pen, even were there no authority for ascribing them to Whitman.   In addition, the internal evidence is so strong as to be practically conclusive in itself.   Curiously enough, the first and longest of these sketches was not mentioned by Mr. Dart in his article, since (as appeared upon investigation) he had examined only the file of the *Crescent* in the Hunter Memorial Library, which happened to lack the first number.   A complete file is to be seen in the Library of the Louisiana Historical Society.   This oversight on the part of Mr. Dart, whose work is otherwise careful, became the basis for the erroneous assertion, made both by Professor George Rice Carpenter and by Professor Perry (whose information was obtained from Professor Carpenter), to the effect that the *Crescent* was first issued on March 6—a curious though trifling error.

These three sketches are here numbered and dated as in the *Crescent*, but, as the third obviously should precede the second, the *Crescent's* accidental or careless twisting of the travel-story is here corrected so as not to confuse the reader.

and discordant screams surrounded us, and we were all but torn in pieces by the assault, as it were! Recovering from the first shock of such an unexpected salute, we found that there were several "hotels," each moved by a bitter rivalry for getting the passengers to eat their dinner. One "opposition house," in particular, seemed bent upon proceeding to extremities—and most of the passengers were fain to go quietly in. For a good dinner here, the price was only twenty-five cents.

Cumberland, at which we arrived about sunset, is a thriving town, with several public edifices, a newspaper or two, and those [institutions] invariably to be found in every western and southern community, some big "hotels." The town has a peculiar character, from its being the great rendezvous and landing place of the immense Pennsylvania wagons, and the drovers from hundreds of miles west. You may see Tartar-looking groups of these wagons, and their drivers, in the open grounds about,— the horses being loosed—and the whole having not a little the appearance of a caravan of the Steppes. Hundreds and hundreds of these enormous vehicles, with their arched roofs of white canvas, wend their way into Cumberland from allq uarters, during a busy season, with goods to send on eastward, and to take goods brought by the railroad. They are in shape not a little like the "Chinese junk," whilom exhibited at New York— being built high at each end, and scooping down in the waist. With their teams of four and six horses, they carry an almost incalculable quantity of "freight"; and if one should accidentally get in the road-ruts before their formidable wheels, they would perform the work of a Juggernaut upon him in most effectual order. The drivers of these vehicles and the drovers of cattle, hogs, horses, &c., in this section of the land, form a large slice of "society."

Night now falling down around us like a very large cloak of black broadcloth, (I fancy *that* figure, at least, hasn't been used up by the poets[1]) and the Alleghanies rearing themselves up "some pumpkins"[2] (as they say here,) right before our nasal members, we got into one of the several four-horse stage coaches

---

[1] Du Bartas came very near it in "Night's black mantle covers all alike" ("Divine Weeks and Works," Sylvester translation, First Week, First Day). The important fact, however, is that Whitman has begun his war on the conventionality of existing poetry. The early notebook specimens belong to this period.

[2] "A term in use at the South and West, in opposition to the equally elegant phrase 'small potatoes.' The former is applied to anything large or noble; the latter to any thing small or mean." (Bartlett, "Dictionary of Americanisms," p. 626.)

of the "National Road and Good Intent Stage Company," whereby we were to be transported over those big hills. They did the thing systematically, whatever may be said elsewise. All the passengers' names were inscribed on a roll, (we purchased tickets in Philadelphia, at $13 a head, to go to Wheeling,) and a clerk stands by and two or three negroes with a patent weighing machine. The clerk calls your name—your baggage is whipped on the machine, and if it weighs over fifty pounds, you have to pay extra. You are then put in the stage, (literally put in, like a package, unless you move quickly,) your baggage packed on behind—and the next name called off—baggage weighed—and so on to the end of the chapter. If six passengers desire it, or any smaller number who will pay for six, they can wait and have a coach sent with them the next morning, or at any hour they choose. One cunning trick of the company is, that they give you no check or receipt for your baggage, for which they pretend not to be responsible. It is best, therefore, if possible, for each passenger to have some witness to his baggage and its amount, in which case, if it be lost, the company will have to pay up—whatever they publish to the contrary.

So they boxed us up in our coach, nine precious souls, and we dashed through the town and up the mountains, with an apparent prospect of as comfortable a night as could be expected, considering all things. One or two of the passengers tried to get up a conversational entertainment; one old gentleman, in particular, *did* talk. He resided on a farm in the interior of Ohio. He had been on to Washington, (I heard the fact at least twenty-five times in the course of that night and the next day,) to claim a certain $5,000 from the Government for capturing a British merchant brig off the coast of Maine, in the last war. She got becalmed, or something of that sort, and he being thereabout, in command of a fishing smack, sailed or rowed up, captured her and brought her into port, where the Government functionaries took possession of her and sold her cargo for some $30,000. Our old gentleman, however, (not *then* old, of course,) had no privateering papers, and [was] consequently not a dollar the gainer. He had now been on to Washington to see about it, and was in hopes of getting at least his share of the sale. (Poor old man! if he lives till he gets Congress to pay him, he will be immortal.) This famous old gentleman moreover informed us that his wife had had thirteen

children, one in every month of the year, and one over besides—
all being alive and kicking! He did not know exactly what to
think about the Mexican war; but he thought that Congress
might at least grant decent pensions to those who were severely
maimed in it, and to the widows of both officers and privates
who were killed. Sage and sound conclusions, thought the
rest of us too.[1] And here I may say, once for all, that, though
expecting to find a shrewd population as I journeyed to the
interior, and down through the great rivers,[2] I was by no means
prepared for the sterling vein of common sense that seemed to
pervade them—even the roughest shod and roughest clad of
all. A satirical person[3] could no doubt find an ample field for
his powers in many of the manners and the ways of the West;
and so can he, indeed, in the highest circles of fashion. But I
fully believe that in a comparison of actual manliness and what
the Yankees call "gumption," the well-to-do *citizens* (for I am
not speaking so much of the country,) particularly the young
men, of New York, Philadelphia, Boston, Brooklyn and so on,
with all the advantages of compact neighborhood, schools, etc.,
are not up to the men of the West. Among the latter, probably,
attention is more turned to the *realities* of life, and a habit
formed of thinking for one's self; in the cities, frippery and arti-
ficial fashion are too much the ruling powers.[4]

Up we toiled, and down we clattered, (for the first fifty miles
it was nearly *all* up,) over these mighty warts on the great breast
of nature. It was excessively cold; the moon shone at intervals;
and whenever we stopped, I found the ground thickly covered
with snow. The places at which we changed horses, (which
was done every ten miles,) were generally long, old, one-story
houses, with stupendous fires of soft coal that is so plentiful
and cheap here. In the night, with the mountains on all sides,
the precipitous and turning road, the large, bare-armed trees
looming up around us, the room half filled with men curiously
enwrapped in garments of a fashion till then never seen—and the
flickering light from the mighty fire putting a red glow upon
most objects, and casting others into a strong shadow—I can
tell you these stoppages were not without interest. They might,

---

[1]Whitman had advocated the granting of homesteads in the West to the veterans
of this war. (See "The Gathering of the Forces," II, pp. 229–230.)

[2]*Cf. infra*, pp. 151–152.

[3]Possibly a reference to Dickens's "American Notes," which, though distasteful to
Whitman, the latter forgave his English favourite.

[4]*Cf. post*, II, p. 30.

it seems to me, afford first rate scenes for an *American* painter—one who, not continually straining to be merely second or third best, in *imitation*, seizes original and really picturesque occasions of this sort for his pieces.[1] There was one of the Alleghany inns, in particular, that we stopped at about an hour after midnight. (All the staging across these mountains, both to and fro, is done in the night, which engrafts a somewhat weird character upon the public houses—their busy time being from sunset to sunrise.) There were some ten or twelve great strapping drovers, reclining about the room on benches, and as many more before the huge fire. The beams overhead were low and smoke-dried. I stepped to the farther end of the long porch; the view from the door was grand, though vague, even in the moonlight. We had just descended a large and very steep hill, and just off on one side of us was a precipice of apparently hundreds of feet. The silence of the grave spread over this solemn scene; the mountains were covered in their white shrouds of snow—and the towering trees looked black and threatening; only the largest stars were visible, and they glittered with a tenfold brightness. One's heart, at such times, is irresistibly lifted to Him of whom these august appearances are but the least emanation. Faith! if I had an infidel to convert, I would take him on the mountains, of a clear and beautiful night, when the stars are shining.

Journeying in this manner, the time and the distance slipped away, until we welcomed the gray dawn of the morning. Half an hour more brought us to Uniontown, at the western side of the Alleghanies—and glad enough were "all hands" to arrive there.

EXCERPTS FROM A TRAVELLER'S NOTE BOOK— [No. 3][2]

WESTERN STEAMBOATS—THE OHIO

HAVING crossed the Alleghanies during Saturday night, and spent the ensuing day in weary stages, from Uniontown onward, we arrived at Wheeling a little after 10 o'clock on Sunday night, and went aboard the steamer *St. Cloud*, a freight and packet boat, lying at the wharf there, with the steam all up, and ulti-

[1] This call for a native American school of painting was a logical sequel to his demand for a native music and drama. *Cf. infra*, pp. 104–106, 152–154; *post*, I, p. 158.

[2] From the *Daily Crescent*, March 10, 1848.

mately bound for New Orleans. This was my "first appearance" on a Western steamboat. The long cabin, neatly carpeted, and lit with clusters of handsome lamps, had no uncomfortable look; but the best comfort of the matter lay in (what I myself soon laid in) a good state room, of which I took possession, and forthwith was oblivious to all matters of a waking character. Roused next morning by the clang of the breakfast bell, I found that we had during the night made a good portion of our way toward Cincinnati.

Like as in many other matters, people who travel on the Ohio, (that most beautiful of words!) for the first time, will stand a chance of being somewhat disappointed. In poetry and romance, these rivers are talked of as though they were cleanly streams; but it is astonishing what a difference is made by the simple fact that they are always and altogether excessively muddy—mud, indeed, being the prevailing character both afloat and ashore. This, when one thinks of it, is not only reasonable enough, but unavoidable in the very circumstances of the case. Yet, it destroys at once the principal beauty of the rivers. There is no romance in a mass of yellowish brown liquid. It is marvellous, though, how easily a traveller gets to drinking it and washing in it. What an india-rubber principle, there is, after all, in humanity!

To one who beholds steamboat-life on the Ohio for the first time, there will of course be many fresh features and notable transpirings. One of the first and most unpleasant, is the want of punctuality in departing from places, and consequently the same want in arriving at them. All the steamers carry freight, that being, indeed, their principal business and source of profit, to which the accommodation of passengers, (as far as time is concerned) has to stand secondary. We on the *St. Cloud*, for instance, picked up all sorts of goods from all sorts of places, wherever our clever little captain made a bargain for the same. What he brought down from Pittsburg, the Lord only knows; for we took in afterward what would have been considered a very fair cargo to a New York liner. At one place, for instance, we shipped several hundred barrels of pork; ditto of lard; at another place, an uncounted (by me) lot of flour—enough, though, it seemed, to have fed half the office-holders of the land—and that *is* saying something. Besides these, we had bags of coffee, rolls of leather, groceries, dry goods, hardware, all sorts of agricultural products, innumerable coops filled with live geese, turkeys, and fowls, that kept up a perpetual farm-yard concert. Then there were divers living hogs, to say noth-ing of a horse, and a resident dog. The country through which the Ohio runs is one of the most productive countries—and one of the most buying and selling—in the world; and nearly all the transportation is done on these steamboats. Putting those two facts together, one can get an idea of the infinite variety, as well as amount of our cargo. To my eyes it was enormous; though people much used to such things didn't seem to consider it any wonder at all.

About half past 6 o'clock, on board these boats—I begin at the beginning, you see—the breakfast bell is rung, giving the passengers half an hour to prepare for the table. Of edibles, for breakfast, (as at the other meals, too,) the quantity is enor-mous, and the quality first rate. The difference is very wide between the table here and any public table at the northeast; the latter, as many a starved wight can bear testimony, being, in most cases, arranged on a far more economical plan. The worst of it is, on the Western steamboats, that everybody gulps down the victuals with railroad speed. With that dis-tressing want of a pleasant means to pass away time, which all travellers must have experienced, is it not rather astonishing that the steamboat breakfast or dinner has to be dispatched in five minutes?

During the day, passengers amuse themselves in various ways. Cheap novels are in great demand, and a late newspaper is a gem almost beyond price. From time to time, the boat stops, either for wood or freight; sometimes to pick up a passenger who hails from the shore. At the stopping places on the Kentucky side, appear an immense number of idlers, boys, old farmers, and tall, strapping, comely young men. At the stopping places on the northern shore, there seems to be more thrift and ac-tivity. The shore, each way, is much of it barren of interest; though the period must arrive when cultivation will bend it nearly all to man's use. Here and there, already, is a comfort-able house; and, at intervals, there are tracts of well-tilled land, particularly on the Ohio line.

In the evening, (the reader must remember that it is not for *one* evening only, but sometimes for ten or twelve,) the passenger spends his time according to fancy. In our boat, the *St. Cloud*, the two large cabin tables were sometimes surrounded by readers; and the stove by smokers and talkers. The ladies appeared to have rather a dull time of it in their place. Most of them would sit listlessly for hours doing nothing—and, so far as I could learn, saying nothing!

Among the principal incidents of the voyage was crossing the falls of the Ohio, just below Louisville. Our boat was very deeply laden; and there is a canal around the ticklish pass; our captain, with Western hardihood, determined to go over the "boiling place." For my own part, I didn't know till afterwards, but that it was an every hour occurence. The bottom of the boat grated harshly more than once on the stones beneath, and the pilots showed plainly that they did not feel altogether as calm as a summer morning. We passed over, however, in perfect safety. The Ohio here has a fall of many feet in the course of a mile. Does not the perfection to which engineering has been brought afford some means of remedying this ugly part of the river? Besides the canal around on the Kentucky side, the Indiana Legislature has lately granted a charter for one on its shore, too.

From Louisville down, one passes through a long stretch of monotonous country—not varied at all, sometimes for dozens of miles. The Ohio retains its distinctive character of mud, till you get to the very end of it.

Cairo, at the junction of the Mississippi, pointed our passage into the great Father of Waters. Immense sums of money have been spent to make Cairo something like what a place with such a name ought to be. But with the exception of its position, which is unrivalled for business purposes, everything about it seems unfortunate. The point on which it is situated is low, and liable to be overflowed at every high flood. Besides, it is unwholesomely wet, at the best. It is doubtful whether Cairo will ever be any "great shakes," except in the way of ague.

EXCERPTS FROM A TRAVELLER'S NOTE BOOK— [No. 2][1]

CINCINNATI AND LOUISVILLE

IT MAY well be doubted whether any large city in Christendom can show a more plentiful, or cheaper, supply of what are

[1] From the *Daily Crescent*, March 6, 1848.

In lapping back over the narrative of the last paper, this article indicates how careless Whitman often was as a journalist. He seldom planned ahead, or if he did, he seldom carried out his plans. *Cf. infra*, p.158; *post*, I, pp. 255, 293.

termed "provisions" than Cincinnati. All the richest and wholesomest products of the earth pour in there, as into a sort of cornucopia—all that grows on these farms or is rendered from the dairy, or the care of the poulterer. You can buy a pair of the fattest sort of chickens, in the markets there, for a quarter of a dollar, and many other things that are in proportion. If it were possible, though, to make the side bank which rises up from the Ohio anything else except the ungainly *mud* which it is nearly all the time, the city in question would be hugely the gainer among that large class "people in general." That miry bank gives anything but an agreeable character to those who see Cincinnati from the river: it could certainly be remedied, and to the profit, too, of passengers, drays, and horses. A favorite name for the shops, as a prefix, is that of the "Queen City." One may notice many a "Queen City Segar Store," and "Queen City Clothing Emporium," etc. The princely invitation of "Walk In" is also inscribed on about one-third of the shop window lights. With New York and New Orleans, Cincinnati undoubtedly makes the trio of business places in this republic—though Philadelphia must not be forgotten either. There are very large and flourishing manufactories at Cincinnati, and the retail stores vie with those of the sea-board. If the advice be not considered impertinent, however, we should advise the city papers to have the streets cleaned, and kept so, "regardless of expense."

Louisville, one hundred and fifty miles further down on the Ohio, is a smaller and considerably quieter city than the one above named. It has a substantial look to him who walks through it for the first time; and, withal, does not a little business in provisions, too. Most of the boats passing on the Ohio rendezvous here—and if it were not for the ugly "falls" just below the city, (avoided by a canal on the Kentucky side,) doubtless there would be still more from below. Louisville has many noble and hospitable citizens, whose family circles make a "happy time" for him who gets on visiting terms with them.[1]

[1]Whether this observation is based on hear say or on experience I do not know. But *Cf. infra*, p. 24, note.

MODEL ARTISTS[1]

HALF the newspapers we get from the North[2] have something tc say about the "Model Artists," often in a tone of very severe condemnation. They say the sight of such things is *indecent;* if that be so, the sight of nearly all the great works of painting and sculpture—pronounced by the united voice of critics of all nations to be master-pieces of genius—is, likewise, indecent. It is a sickly prudishness that bars all appreciation of the divine beauty evidenced in Nature's cunningest work—the human frame, form and face.

There may be some petty attempts, in the low by-places, which all cities have, to counterfeit these groupings, after a vile method. Such, however, are only to be seen by those who go especially to see them. Of the graceful and beautiful group-ings—most of them—after models in sculpture—exhibited by persons of taste and tact, it is hard to see what harm can be said.

A QUESTION OF PROPRIETY[3]

OUR contemporary of the Mobile *Herald* disagrees altogether from some humble remarks of ours, last week, on the subject of "Model Artists"—and, (as near as we remember, for the paper containing the remarks alluded to has been mislaid,) disagrees also from our opinion of the perfect propriety of sculptures and paintings after a similar sort with these "Artists." In what we said, and in what we have to say, it is not so much about the Model Artists, but the general principle, in this country; for among the nations on the continent of Europe it has been settled long ago. A portion of England holds out still; but they do it more from the proverbial obstinacy of John Bull than from any other reason.

The only objection that we conceive of to the undraped figure arises from an assumption of coarseness and grossness intended.

[1] From the *Daily Crescent*, March 6, 1848.
Cf. post, I, p. 194; also II, pp. 5–8. The courageous defense of the nude in art here given provoked sharp passage of arms with a writer in the Mobile *Herald;* see "A Question of Propriety" above.

[2] *Cf.* Whitman's description of his duties in the *Crescent* office, *post,* II, p. 78.

[3] From the *Daily Crescent,* March 14, 1848.

Take away this, and there is no need (in the cases under discussion) of any objection at all. Eve in Paradise—or Adam either[1]—would not be supposed to shock the mind. Neither would the sight of those inhabitants of the Pacific Islands, whose nakedness is, or was, the innocent and usual custom. Neither does the sight of youth, among us or anywhere else. And, so stern and commanding is the potency of genius, even over the vulgar, neither do copies of the Venus de Medicis; for the prude dare not open his mouth against what the world, for many a year, has pronounced divine. It is only when people *will* try hard to think exclusively of what they assume to be a grossness intended, that they are "shocked" at such spectacles. But would not a woman of sense, (to say nothing of a man of sense, whose delicacies are not supposed to be so super-refined,) even if her education has been rigid in this respect, do better to take it for granted that *no* grossness is intended? Is there any absolute need of directing the mind in the worser way?

Amid all the works of that Power which, in the most stupenous systems and the smallest objects in them, shows such unspeakable harmony and perfection, nothing can compare with the *human* master-piece, his closing and crowning work! It is a master-piece in *itself*, not as it is furbelowed off by the milliner and tailor.[2] Nor would it be altogether uninteresting to pursue the inquiry how far artificial ideas on the subject of swaddling this work, so much in vogue among civilized nations—and barring off the contemplation of its noble and beautiful proportions—how far, we say, these practices may have aided in the effect of diminishing the average amplitude and majesty of the form, which effect must be confessed to when comparing present times with the age of the old Grecians and Latins.

As for the Model Artists, we know excellent women, and men, too, who have attended their performances with rational gratification. We have witnessed them[3] with the like result. It is somewhat a matter of taste, however; and we do not wish to quarrel with anybody because his taste differs from ours. In conclusion, it may be well to state that there are perhaps, in bye-places, exaggerated exhibitions of these groupings—as

---

[1] It was obviously reasoning such as this which suggested to Whitman the collective title for his poems of sex and nakedness, "Children of Adam." *Cf.* "Complete Prose," pp. 296–300.

[2] *Cf. post*, I, pp. 245–246.

[3] *Cf.* "Complete Prose," p. 440.

gluttony or drunkenness is the depravity of a wholesome appetite. Such, from what we hear, are so abominable as to be beneath even the merit of condemnation.[1]

THE HABITANTS OF HOTELS[2]

THERE is no actual need of a man's travelling around the globe in order to find out a few of the principles of human nature. The observer needn't even go to a college or a primary school, but if he is determined to supply himself with knowledge, let him visit the precincts of some of our "first-rate, tip [-top]" bar-rooms on Saturday or Sunday night.[3]

The young gentleman with the shiny black coat and the unexceptionable pantaloons is the very pink of propriety. He is very particular about the quality of the crepe that he wears upon his hat, and is excessively fond of mild Havana segars. He invariably uses a toothbrush with an ivory handle, and is partial to watering-places in the summer-time, and gambling houses when the "Norwegian season" takes place. A large diamond brest-pin and a massive gold chain attached to a galvanized watch are generally his ornaments. The cockpit for him is a favorite place of resort, and he occasionally "splurges" himself at a game of cards. When the yellow fever season commences, the gentleman in question darts like an arrow northward, and spends his summer at Saratoga or Niagara Falls.

Now yonder is an elderly gentleman, who seems to desire to bite the head off a gold-mounted cane. By way of varying his mode of enjoyment, he occasionally twirls his watch-seal and about twice in every half hour motions the bar-keeper to mix him a brandy toddy. Gentlemen of this class generally live in the West, in South America, or Mexico. This description of gentlemen are generally adepts in all matters pertaining to horse-flesh, and in the selection of Bowie knives and shooting-galleries, are philosophers "beyond compare." Their con-

---

[1] The *Herald* writer returns to the attack, insisting on discussing the matter as it relates to the voluptuous passions. To Whitman this seems to beg the point and he refuses, ending his part in the discussion with this curt dismissal: "He or she is the best conservator of purity who starts from the point of the innate purity of nature; it is only the vulgar who draft coarse ideas thereon. Shall the Arts be brought to the test of such ideas? Shall the high come down to the low?"

[2] From the *Daily Crescent*, March 10, 1848.

[3] *Cf. infra*, p. 148;, *post*, II, pp. 103, 221, *passim*.

versational powers are generally devoted to descriptions of duels, awful conflicts by sea and land, and stories of how bluff old Major So-and-So gave a terrible flogging to Col. This-and-That more than twenty years ago.

How gracefully he leans back in his chair, and what a "Count D'Orsay"[1] fling there is to his blue broadcloth cloak! How beautifully the gold spectacles set upon his pallid proboscis!—and his teeth—why, bless us! they glisten like pearls. See, he inserts a silver tooth-pick between the interstices of his ivories, and smiles as though he felt extremely happy. What can he be thinking of? A theory on the principle of gravitation—some beautiful idea collated from the philosophy of Emanuel Swedenborg,[2] or the price of putty? Of neither—he is thinking of nothing but the extraction of corns, of Mesmerism, and the consequences of chloroform. The gentleman alluded to will make money, buy a big seal ring, cultivate an imperial, go to Europe, get dubbed a Professor of almost anything in the way of Science or Art, bring a troupe of "Model Artists"[3] across the Atlantic, and become the "lion of the day."

That young man with the bandy legs who is standing with his back to the stove has just arrived from New York. He prides himself upon the neatness of the tie of his crimson neck-cloth, and professes to be a connoisseur in everything relating to peanuts. Whilst he puffs the smoke of a remarkably bad segar directly underneath your nostrils, he will discourse most learnedly about the classical performances in the Chatham Theatre,[4] and swear by some heathen god or goddess that "Kirby[5] was one of 'em, and no mistake." This is one of the "b'hoys of the Bowery." He strenuously contends that Mr. N. P. Willis is a humbug—that Mike Walsh[6] is a "hoss,"[7] and that the

[1] Alfred D'Orsay (1801–1852), a French leader of fashion.

[2] Probably Whitman knew something already of the Swedish mystic. *Cf. post*, II, pp. 16–18.

[3] *Cf. infra*, pp. 191–193.

[4] In New York.

[5] James Hudson Kirby (1819–1848), an actor in Shakespearean and melodramatic rôles, who made his American début in 1840, went to London in 1845 and became a popular idol at the Surrey Theatre, and died about the time of his intended return to America.

[6] Michael Walsh, popularly known as "Mike" Walsh, was an ordinary carter who by means of his gifts as an orator and his fearless championship of the rights of the masses in Tammany Hall and elsewhere, became a "Locofoco" leader and a member of Congress. (See "Sketches of the Speeches and Writings of Michael Walsh including his Poems and Correspondence," New York, 1843.)

[7] "A man remarkable for his strength, courage, etc. A vulgarism peculiar to the West." (Bartlett, "Dictionary of Americanisms," p. 298.)

DRAWINGS FROM A WHITMAN NOTEBOOK

Of the Pfaffian days, probably from Whitman's own pencil. The sketch and the caricature at the left, at least, are studies of the poet himself.

Brigadier[1] "ain't no where." The great probability is that the "b'hoy"[2] in question never saw either of the gentlemen that he attempts to lampoon. The vista of his imagination certainly does not extend beyond Baton Rouge.

A hickory stick and a hickory soul—both are stern and stalwart—both are firm and honest. Commend us to the old grey-haired farmer, whose withered fingers grasp with an iron clutch his trusty cane! Who would believe it? That old man is the father of a Senator! He subscribes for the *Union* and *National Intelligencer*, and many a times his eyes are brightened with the "silver tears of joy," when he hears the name of his first-born mentioned. The cultivation of potatoes and turnips, the threshing of the little stock of wheat, and the sale of the little field of corn, brought money to send the son to college. Intense energy, application to study, determination and industry made the farmer's son a shining light amongst his fellows. The good old farmer! his son discusses questions of the greatest importance at Washington—tells Robert Peel and John Russell that they are entirely wrong—cautions Louis Philippe against some European policy, and requests Prince Metternich to be upon his guard lest he should fail in his diplomatic conclusions. Turnips and talent—potatoes and politics—"pumpkins" (some) and professions!

The parlor of the hotel we will not enter, but when we have a pen, virgin—so far as ink is concerned—any quantity of satin paper with gilded edges, and a few gallons of cologne, we shall endeavor to describe the peculiarities of those chosen mortals who will live above board—or, at least above the bar-room.

HERO PRESIDENTS[3]

IN ALL ages of the world glory and power have been rewards of the successful warrior. Among the wandering tribes of the steppes of Tartary and sands of Arabia, as well as among the polished people of western Europe, and the naked savages of North America, the best soldier has always been recognized as the first man of his time. At this late epoch of the world it

[1] I have been unable to discover whom Whitman had in mind.

[2] A slang term of the period meaning, apparently, a second-rate "fast" young man. It was also used as a designation for the younger men in the Tammany organization, though there it was spelled in the ordinary way.

[3] From the *Daily Crescent*, March 11, 1848.

would be idle to try to change public opinion as to the uncommon merits of a man who has skilfully led the armies of his country against her enemies—who has never fought but against fearful odds, and yet has always been victorious. Nor do we wish to lessen the admiration for superior generalship and skill in the conduct of war. A long experience teaches us that it is man's nature to praise and exalt the virtues and qualities which make up the character of the triumphant hero; and as we indulge in no visionary hopes of remodelling human nature, we desire rather to direct its propensities into proper channels than to dam them up or destroy them altogether. To turn the spreading branches of human passions into new and proper directions is the aim of the philosopher and philanthropist; to cut down the tree or tear it up by the roots is the attempt of the dreamer and the fool.

He is but a poor lawgiver who legislates only for the reason and understanding, without remembering that men are also endowed with the faculties of imagination. "Let me make the ballads of a nation and I will make its laws,"[1] was a declaration suggested by the fact that the reasons of men are inferior to and under the control of their imaginations. It is a common observation that in early ages and among savage tribes, the poet, the priest and the warrior exercise more influence over men's minds than the statesman and legislator; but this remark is generally qualified by saying that as knowledge and civilization advance, the power of the latter increases while that of the former diminishes. But is man's nature changed, either by a progress from the savage to the civilized state, or by a relapse from civilization to savagism? Believing that the man is always stronger than the circumstances which surround him—that his nature is bounded by a circle beyond which the forces of matter cannot thrust him—we cannot suppose that the relative strength of reason and imagination is at all modified by the chances and changes of what we choose to denominate civilization and refinement. No! Man is the same in all his essential qualities—in the power of his reason and the vigor of his imagination—whether he struts in pantaloons or stalks in all the dignity and grace of primeval nakedness.

[1] "I knew a very wise man that believed that if a man were permitted to make all the ballads, he need not care who should make the laws of a nation." Andrew Fletcher of Saltoun, in a letter to the Marquis of Montrose. (Bartlett, "Familiar Quotations," 10th edition, p. 281.)

So long, then, as men are men, will they continue to love the pride, pomp and circumstance of glorious war—so long will they admire the leaders of armies and the gainers of victories. Quakerism can never become the creed of the race; and you might as well expect all men to adopt the straight-cut coat and plain phraseology of the followers of Fox, as to hope that the principles of peace will ever become the law of men's opinions and actions. Is it to be supposed that the framers of our constitution ever made such a chimera the basis of our civil liberties? Can we believe that the sagacity of the members of the Convention had not more correctly perceived the true nature of man than to create for him a Government incapable of enduring all the attacks of the ordinary passions of mankind? Much as the benevolent heart of Franklin might have wished for the arrival of the second golden age, when the "lion and the lamb shall lie down together," and men will dwell with each other in peace and harmony, could his practical understanding have sanctioned a system of Government whose existence would be endangered by the expression of one of the strongest and most decided tendencies of our minds? Let us rather believe that our constitution was framed by those who understood human nature as thoroughly as any set of statesmen ever did; that they were men not only deeply read in the lessons of the past, but also profoundly observant of the facts of the present. They had not only meditated the words of sages and philosophers; their souls had also been kindled to a glow by the inspiration of the bards who sang the glories and triumphs of combat. Many of them had been actors in the field as well as in the cabinet; and he who presided over them was "first in war" as well as "first in peace and first in the hearts of his countrymen."[1]

We are not, then, of those who think of the permanency of our institutions as at all threatened by our disposition to admire great generals and elevate them to the Presidency. It is the very practical nature of our government—its capability of adaptation to all states and phases of the human mind—its perfect fitness for man as he is, independent of any ideal conditions at which he may hope to arrive—that enables us to feel secure during the highest excitement of the whole people. No matter whether the nation be violently agitated by the spirit of party, or deeply moved by the feeling of gratitude which

[1] Henry Lee's "Eulogy on Washington," December 26, 1799.

prompts it to bestow the highest honors on him who has gallantly led the armies of the republic, we have full confidence in the power of the constitution to outlive any gust of passion or feeling.[1] The wisest man is often provoked to anger, and daily weeps his inability to govern his appetites and passions; but the storms of passion are transient, and when they pass away leave his wisdom high and pure like a mountain-top seen in the distance, and serving as a guide for the traveller.

But while we have none of those fears by which others are actuated when lamenting the tendency of the American people to elevate military chieftains to the Presidency, we sincerely deprecate the effort to raise any man to that high office, merely because he has shown courage and skill in manœuvring men, horses, and cannon. To be sure, it is no despicable talent which enables a man to exercise these faculties—the rather inferior qualities of even a general—with tact and success. We may assume, if you please, that the same capacity for administration is requisite in the head of an army as in the head of a people, though the assumption is falsified by many and great examples in history not a hundred years back. We will admit that all the moral and intellectual requisites of a President may be found in a good general—that the general has the quick perception, the sure yet rapid judgment, the firm will, the steady devotion to the public good so necessary in a President of the United States. Still, we cannot arrive at the conclusion that it is always best to make a President out of such a general. For to do so is, in some measure, to turn from its proper use the high office created by our fathers for certain great purposes. It is to change into an office of reward for military merit that which was intended for a place of duty and labor. The President has certain functions assigned him by the Constitution—functions arduous and difficult. His Excellency's chair is a hard and thorny seat—not a couch wreathed round with laurels, on which the soldier may recline after the toils and struggles of a successful campaign. While then we have no *fear* of a general ever using the Presidency as a means of overturning our free institutions, we have a great disinclination to turning the White House into a sort of Pension Palace, to which our triumphant generals may retire and amuse themselves and the country with four years administration of our Federal government.

[1] *Cf. infra*, pp. 159-160.

SKETCHES OF THE SIDEWALKS AND LEVEES; WITH GLIMPSES INTO THE NEW ORLEANS BAR (ROOMS) PETER FUNK, ESQ.[1]

To ILLUSTRATE the "life, fortune, and sacred honor" of the distinguished individual whose name heads off our present sketch of noted characters, is a task as tasteful as it is agreeable. The duty of the faithful chronologist and biographer is particularly a cheerful one when the subject of such notice is calculated to heighten the interest we feel in the dignity and delicate sensibilities of human nature.

Funk, like all other illustrious personages who have become so well known, as no longer to need the titulary soubriquet of *Mister*, was born and brought up—no one knows where: at least the information we have on this point is exceedingly uncertain and contradictory. Without, therefore, descending into the particulars of his early training and history, or minutely tracing up the rationale of cause and effect, by showing that a youth of moral proclivity will, in time, run into that species of moral gum-elasticity which goes to constitute the blood and bones of individuals comprising his *genus*, we shall proceed at once, *in medias res*, as the boys say at college, and make known to you, gentle reader, that Peter Funk is a young gentleman "about town" who holds the highly responsible office of by-bidder in a Mock Auction—being engaged to said work by "the man wot sells the watches."

You're a gentleman of leisure about New Orleans, may be, stranger, and lounging about ———— street. You hear the musical sound of the "human voice divine," crying out "fivenaff, five-n-aff—only going at twenty-five dollars and-n-a-ff for this elegant gold watch and chain, in prime running order, just sent in by a *gentleman leaving town*, and only five-n-aff! Did I hear you say six, sir?"

Perhaps you drop in, and if you are not careful how you look at the musical auctioneer he will accept of your look for a wink,

---

[1] From the *Daily Crescent*, March 13, 1848.

"Decoys at mock auctions are called *Peter Funk*. . . . It is an open question as to whether this name for a by-bidder was really borne by an individual." (John S. Farmer, in his "Americanisms Old and New," London, 1889, p. 53.) It is quite possible that the idea of this sketch was suggested to Whitman by Asa Greene's "The Perils of Pearl Street, By a Late Merchant," New York, 1834. Chapters VII and XIV deal with "Peter Funk."

and, according to the philosophy of the auction room, a wink passes for a bid, and you find yourself in the nominal possession of "an elegant gold watch and chain, in prime running order, just sent in to be sold by a gentleman leaving town," before you are well aware of what you are about. So take care how you look when you are in the patent auction shops. There stands the auctioneer in all the serious earnestness of a man begging for his life, and, with voice and looks and gestures, seems like one speaking sober truth, and "nothin' else." Only half a dozen individuals comprise his audience, and these half a dozen are Peter Funk and his *corps de reserve.* Peter looks somewhat stouter to-day than he was yesterday, and has exchanged his cloth cloak and cap for a blanket coat and *chapeau blanc,* and his whiskers have shared the fate of "the last rose of summer"— that is to say, they have evaporated—dropped off: they are *non est inventus*—gone!

Yes, that's Funk and his five interesting associates in business—"companions of his toil, his feelings, and his fame"— Peter the 1st, Peter the 2d, Peter the 3d, Peter the 4th and Peter the 5th—he himself being no other than Peter the Great, or the Great Peter—"Peter Funk, Esq."

Now, stranger, take care what you're about—you're the only bona fide customer—if customer you choose to call yourself— that has entered the portals of the auction shop as yet, and Peter Funk Primus and Peter Funk Secundus have done all this bidding that makes the crier keep up such a hubbaboo. Well, you don't know of this fact, and you think "a man's man for a' that,"[1] and you don't understand the secret of Peter Funk and his associates, or the service they're engaged in, and you only see a fine-*looking* watch, "just sent in to be sold by a gentleman leaving town," and going dog cheap. You nod your head, and straightway the countenance of the crier brightens up, and his voice grows even more vociferous than before. He's got a bid—a real bid—and the first and only one. He tacks on five dollars more, and now he's heard going it in fine style: "Thirty, thirty, thirty, thirty, thirty—only going at thirty dollars for a splendid elegant gold lever, with seventeen pairs of extra jewels, lately imported, and now must be sold!"

He cries on at this rate for perhaps ten minutes, occasionally casting a glance at the passers-by to see if any *greeneys* can be tolled in. Peter Funk takes the watch in his hand and examines

[1]From Burns's "A Man's a Man for a' That."

it attentively, and with a very significant look, as though his judgment was perfectly satisfied, he says deliberately, "Thirty-five!"

"Against you, sir," cries Mr. Auctioneer, and forthwith sets off with unusual volubility, crying out *ore rotundo*, "thirty-five, thirty-five—only going at thirty-five!"

"Thirty-five dollars for such an elegant gold watch is certainly cheap as dirt—they ask eighty-five or ninety at the stores"; and as these thoughts revolve in your mind, you think you might as well make five and twenty dollars as well as not, as there are plenty of boys up in your county who would jump at the bargain—and you nod again, the auctioneer having in the meantime directed the whole force of his vocable artillery at you, and launched forth in such a rigamarole of praise of said time-piece that you couldn't well resist his very passionate appeal.

"Forty dollars!" is quickly caught up. "*Only* going at forty dollars!—forty! forty! forty! forty!" and now the cryer turns to Peter, the interesting Peter, whose turn for *serious deliberation* has again come. He again examines the watch, turns it over and over again, and, as he hands it up to the cryer, says, in a very low but decided tone of voice, "forty-five!"

By this time one or two other loungers like yourself have dropped in, and monsieur cryer applies himself with exceeding earnestness in lauding the watch, as never, sure, watch was lauded before, except perhaps at a patent auction.

While you are revolving in your mind whether "to go" the *fifty*, some other greeney from one of the upper parishes, or may-be from Mississippi, with his pockets full of money, cries out "fifty, by G—d!" and you are relieved from what would have been a very dear bargain to you—the invoice price of said "elegant gold lever" having been only $17.50. Like Hodge's razors, they are "made to sell," and many are the green 'uns that are bit, by the "persuasive speech" of the auctioneer, and still more persuasive biddings of his interesting coadjutor in this pretty business, Peter Funk, Esq., the subject of our present "sketch."

I was pretty well acquainted with Funk before he went into the "auction and commission business"; we boarded a while together at the same house. Since his embarkation into the business of *buying watches*, we have grown offish with one another: he never knows me in the auction room, though we may be standing side by side; and, to tell the truth, I hardly know him half the time in the various disguises he assumes, for he scarcely ever dresses the same for two days in succession—being in cap, cloak and whiskers on one day, and the next *aliased* up in a white or green blanket. Some say he was from Old Kentuck, and others again aver he is a North Carolina Tennessean; while "other some" allege him to have been a direct importation from the nethermost corner of Down East—having resided a year or two in Texas by way of a seasoning—and that he is an "own cousin" of the "rat man," and also of kin to him "wot cleans coat collars." Of this I can say nothing—but am of opinion that if ever Peter Funk received a "fotching up" according to old-fashioned New England Puritanism, he must have become amazingly warped in his morals ere he reached the latitude of Louisiana.

To sum up the character I have to give of Peter Funk, I shall simply say that he at present thrives well, and will make a business man of himself if he keeps on. He is one of those men who reverse the saying of Hamlet, that "conscience makes cowards of us all."[1] Peter's conscience makes no coward of him—*argal*, Peter'll be rich one of these days. It's a bad thing to have

> "The native hue of resolution
> Thus sicklied o'er with the pale cast of thought."[2]

and Peter takes none of these sickly thoughts, or any other consideration, "for the morrow," except it be what coat or what colored whiskers he shall put on.

———

MISS DUSKY GRISETTE[3]

Miss Dusky Grisette is the young "lady" who takes her stand of evenings upon the pavement opposite the St. Charles Hotel, for the praiseworthy purpose of selling a few flowers by retail, showing off her own charms meanwhile, in a wholesale manner. She drives a thriving trade when the evenings are

[1] "Hamlet", III, 1, 83.

[2] *Ibidem*, III, 1, 84–85.

[3] From the *Daily Crescent*, March 16, 1848.
Cf. post, II, p. 185.
Horace Traubel reports ("With Walt Whitman in Camden," II, p. 283) Whitman as saying of this type of New Orleans society: "I have been in New Orleans—known, seen, all its peculiar phases of life. Of course my report would be forty years old or so.

pleasant. Her neat basket of choice bouquets sits by her side, and she has a smile and a wink for every one of the passers-by who have a wink and a smile for her.

Mademoiselle Grisette was "raised" in the city, and is pretty well known as a very pretty *marchande des fleurs*. She can recommend a tasteful bunch of posies with all the grace in the world, and her "buy a broom" style of addressing her acquaintance has, certainly, something very taking about it. She possesses pretty eyes, a pretty chin, and a mouth that many an heiress, grown oldish and faded, would give thousands for. The *em bon point* of her form is full of attraction, and she dresses with simple neatness and taste. She keeps her eyes open and her mouth shut, except it be to show her beautiful teeth— ah, her's are teeth that are teeth. She has sense enough to keep her tongue quiet, and discourses more by "silence that speaks and eloquence of eyes" than any other method—herein she is prudent.

Grisette is not "a blue" by any means, rather a *brune*, or, more prettily, a *brunette*—"but that's not much,"[1] the vermillion of her cheeks shows through the veil, and her long glossy hair is *nearly straight*. There are many who affect the *brune* rather than the *blonde*, at least when they wish to purchase a bouquet—and as

> "Night
> Shows stars and women in a better light,"[2]

they have a pleasant smile and a bewitching glance thrown into the bargain whilst purchasing a bunch of posies.

What becomes of the flower-girl in the day time would be hard to tell: perhaps it would be in bad taste to attempt to find

---

The Octaroon was not a whore, a prostitute, as we call a certain class of women here— and yet *was* too: a hard class to comprehend: women with splendid bodies—no bustles, no corsets, no enormities of any sort: large, luminous, rich eyes: face a rich olive: habits indolent, yet not lazy as we define laziness North: fascinating, magnetic, sexual, ignorant, illiterate: always more than pretty—'pretty' is too weak a word to apply to them." He goes on to express the opinion that race amalgamation in the South is unlikely.

In revealing his growing sensitiveness to woman's physical beauty, a sensitiveness which had cropped out in more than one *Eagle* editorial, Whitman not only reflects the influence of his new and romantic environment, but also reveals how far he has travelled from the Jamaica days in which he could declare his absolute ignorance of woman (*see infra*, p. 37). That the "caresser of life" here dominates the puritan appears from the substitution of a romantic or a satirical attitude for the youthful and unrelenting seriousness which underlay most of his previous writing.

[1] *Cf.* "yet that's not much," "Othello," III, 3.
[2] Byron's "Don Juan," Canto II, Stanza 152.

out. She is only interesting in character and association. Standing at, or reclining against, the door-cheeks of a store, with the brilliancy of the gas light falling favorably, and perhaps deceptively, upon her features and upon her person, with her basket of tasteful bouquets at her feet, and some of the choicest buds setting off her own head-dress. As such she looks in character as a *jolie grisette*, as she is, and will excite the notice of those who, beneath the light of the sun, and in the noontide gaze of men, would spurn and loathe such familiarities. Poor Grisette therefore slinks away to some retired hole or corner when the witching hours of gas light have passed by, and when the walkers upon the streets have grown tired of wandering, and with noise, [and] have thrown themselves upon their beds for repose. She sells her flowers, and barters off sweet looks for sweeter money; and with her empty basket upon her head, she takes up "the line of march" for her humble home, along with "daddy" who, being ever upon the safe lookout, has come for her.

Perhaps, in the morning, she sells coffee at one of the street corners, to the early draymen, who have an appetite for the regaling draft—becoming "all things to all men" in changing *tout à fait* her set of customers. In this last employment, she sylph-like puts on the air and manner of drudgery. Habited in a plain frock, with a check apron, and with her head "bound about" by a cotton handkerchief, she retails bad coffee at a picayune a cup, with an air of *nonchalance* entirely suited to the calling and to the customers. Hard-working men like draymen, want coffee and not glances—they need the stomach and not the appetite to be feasted. Grisette, therefore, acts well her part. Flowers and fancy for the upper ten thousand, in the glow and excitement of evening and gas-light—but neither airs nor graces attend her, nor do flowers deck her hair as, by daylight, in the cool of the morning, she repairs to her accustomed stand, with her tin coffee urn upon her head.[1]

During the day, perhaps she assists her mother, in —— street, who is a very respectable washer-woman, and highly esteemed for those exceedingly desirable qualifications, namely—the rendering of linen white and well starched. And thus, Made-

[1] Whitman himself was fond of taking his morning coffee (*cf. infra*, p. 34) at the old French market from the shining kettle of a mulatto woman; but his description of her ("Complete Prose," p. 440) does not agree with his description of "Miss Dusky Grisette." *Cf.* also *post*, I, p. 213.

moiselle Grisette fills up a very clever place of usefulness. Instead of degenerating into a mere dowd, as so many beauties become during the unenchanting hours of day-light, lounging the time away, from sofa to rocking-chair, and from rocking-chair back to sofa again, with some trifle of a novel in their hands, Grisette, who does not know a letter in the book, and is thence fortunately secure against the seductions of popular *literature*, betakes herself, with hearty good will, to the wash-tub; and they do say that her cousin Marie and herself have rare fun whilst splashing among the suds, in detailing the numerous conquests they (poor things!) supposed [themselves] to have made in the flower market the evening before.

DAGGERDRAW BOWIEKNIFE, ESQ.[1]

IT IS almost with fear and trembling, "I take my pen in hand," to attempt the portraiture of this fearful son of Mars, whose very name is almost enough to

> ——"Freeze my young blood,
> Make each particular hair to stand on end,
> Like quills upon the fretful porcupine."[2]

We do not say that our hero lives in New Orleans now, but he "used to did," and that's enough for a chap whose business it is to make "Sketches." He lived here once upon a time, and flourished extensively—went to the Legislature and to Congress, for aught we know—that is, the Congress of Texas, while that "lone star" was shining with bedimmed lustre in the political firmament.

Squire Bowieknife emigrated, some years ago, to a village in Mississippi from one of the Carolinas. He was a limb of the law, and by dint of an abundance of swagger, in a short time fought his way into notice. There are parts of Mississippi where a man may graduate into public favor, through the merits of gunpowder, with a rapidity that is astonishing. It requires a peculiar conformation and organization—a fitness of things, as it were—to constitute an individual who can thrive upon sharp steel and patent revolvers, but Bowieknife was the man, and "he went it with a rush."

[1] From the *Daily Crescent*, March 23, 1848.
[2] *Cf.* "Hamlet," I, 5, 16-20.

Thence, he found his way to Orleans, and now has gone to Texas, followed by the ghosts of no less than six hale, hearty men, at least, that were such before his "bloody-minded" shooting irons made daylight shine through them. Never did man stand more upon a point of honor than he did: he would cavil upon the hundredth part of a hair if he thought a bit of a fight was to be got out of his antagonist: and upon the most trifling misunderstanding in the world, he would attack you in a "street fight," or "call you out" and shoot you down, as though your life were of no more value than a cur dog's. Oh, he was a brave fellow, and people were afraid of him, and we cannot wonder at it.

But it so happened, that the Hon. Daggerdraw Bowieknife was not, by any manner of means, so punctual in meeting his own little liabilities as he was in being first upon the ground to take part in the murderous duel—in other words, he was one of those "d——d highminded, honorable, clever fellows," who would rather shoot a man than pay him what he owed him. There are such men in the world, and our friend was one of them: they pretend to be the very soul of honor, but an honest debt, such as an honest man would pay with entire punctuality, these sons of *honor* "pass by as the idle wind, which they regard not."[1] One day, Daggerdraw sallied out from his office to take a walk into town. He was armed and equipped, though not "according to law," but he was, in common parlance, quite "loaded down to the guards" with fashionable killing tools. In each pantaloons pocket he carried a small loaded pistol: in his bosom, and within reach, was the handle of a large bowie-knife, weighing just one pound and a half, one of those murderous weapons more efficient than the Roman short sword, and equally serviceable at cutting or thrusting. Daggerdraw had done bloody deeds with it in both ways, as more than one individual in Mississippi had experienced to his sorrow. This said big butcher-knife had run the rounds of several street fights, and was the dearly beloved of its dreaded owner. Whether the personal prowess he displayed in its use was a violation of the laws of decency and humanity, and befitted him more for the society of desperadoes and professional cut-throats, is altogether another question. No man doubted the bull-dog courage of this disciple of Blackstone, but whether any of the sym-

---

[1] *Cf.* "That they pass by me as the idle wind
  Which I respect not."   "Julius Cæsar," IV, 2, 77.

pathies of human nature, such as make man the being he is, had an abiding place in his ferocious heart, is not for us to say, though it may well be supposed there were none.

Yes, there he goes! and there is blood upon his shirt now, or at least there is revenge brooding in his thoughts, and ere long the life of some doomed one must pay the forfeit. He is not a bad-looking man either, being gentle enough in his dress and address, but

> "There was a lurking devil in his sneer,
> That raised emotions both of hate and fear."[1]

His eye was wild and restless, and there was a something in his brow that was repulsive. "And the Lord set a mark upon Cain" —can it be true that this modern Cain had his mark set upon him too? And yet there it was, the stamp and the impress of the cruel heart, legibly fixed in the very lineaments of the man's face, and no one loved to gaze upon him, for his features had that about them to freeze the heart of the beholder.

Why is it that a false sense of honor requires men to face in deadly combat such as Daggerdraw, it were hard to divine. Perhaps they suppose, as Bob Acres[2] says, that honor follows them to the grave. We are of opinion with Bob's servant, that this is the very place one might make shift to do without it, and that the honor and applause, such as it is, whips over to the adversary. Very well: Squire, take your grand rounds, and as you walk the streets, feel secure that men are afraid of you, but take good care and don't get afraid of yourself. I've heard strange stories about you—how that you never sleep o' nights—that you pace the long gallery of your boarding-house with restless and uneasy steps, and while others luxuriate in the blessings of "tired nature's sweet restorer,"[3] sleep is a stranger to your eyelids. I have heard that the lone and solemn hour of midnight is a terror to you, and that the ghosts of murdered Banquos will rise mentally to your vision, as a meet reward for your deeds of awful transgression, and your disregard fo the injunction, "Thou shalt not kill."

Some men become noted, some are celebrated, and others,

---

[1] A misquotation from Byron's "The Corsair," Canto I, Stanza ix. It should read: "a laughing Devil."

[2] A swaggering coward in Sheridan's "The Rivals." (See Act iv, Sc. I.)

[3] Young's "Night Thoughts," Night I, l. I.   *Cf. post*, I, p. 223.

again, have the stamp of notoriety fixed to their names:[1] such is the unenviable condition of him whom we have here sketched. He has made his mark through life, but it has been in the spirit of the pestilence and the destroyer.

JOHN J. JINGLEBRAIN[2]

THE subject of the present "Sketch" could never by any possible mischance be considered as one of the "B'hoys." "The lines are fallen to him in pleasant places," and if there is any peculiar blessing attached to "the ton," Jinglebrain has a chance to enjoy it.

You see him in St. Charles street, and in the haunts adjacent thereto, and you cannot fail to notice him as remarkably *distingué* in his air and appearance. His coat and his pants, his vest and his cravat, his hat and his boots are all remarkably "the thing"; and as you observe him at 10 or 12 o'clock in the morning, as he issues from some one of the fashionable *coiffeurs*, you would not be far from right in supposing that he had just made his escape from under the lid of a band box. His hair is "done to a turn," and every individual member of his side locks is in its right place, and is, indeed, as slick as grease. His whiskers and his moustache are combed and anointed with some sweet scented unguent, and he snuffs the atmosphere of St. Charles street as though the very breath of heaven was unworthy the patronage of so much clean linen and fine broadcloth, as well as a very extensive swell of personal pretensions.

Some poet or other—Shakspeare I think—makes allusion to one having small pretensions to manhood, that "the tailor made him"[3]—and if ever any individual might disclaim maternity from the common unclean mother earth, Jinglebrain is that man, for clean clothes and bear's grease have made him what he is. Nor is it in our nature, or within the bounds of our present purpose, to cavil with any man because he dresses in a seeming and becoming manner; God forbid—for we ourselves luxuriate in clean linen and goodly raiment, and are made glad

[1] A paraphrase of "some are born great, some achieve greatness, and some have greatness thrust upon 'em" (*Twelfth Night*, II, 5).

[2] From the *Daily Crescent*, March 28, 1848. *Cf. infra*, pp. 162–163; *post*, I, pp. 245–246.

[3] *Cf.* "a tailor made thee," "King Lear," II, 2, 50.

thereby: but that mortal man should be puffed up in self-importance because of his outfit from his tailor-shop, and affect a pitiful superiority over his fellows, solely on the grounds of the fit of his pants and the sleekness of his hair, is marvellously beneath what we ought to expect from the dignity of human nature.

However, it is to Jinglebrain, not so much as a dandy, nor even as a conceited numskull, that we now desire to paint him as he is, but as one of your do-nothing, nothing-to-do gentry who affect to hold all useful occupations in disgust.

Man is an eating animal, aye, a drinking one too—were it not so, the bar-keepers and the restaurants might suffer. Man, we say, is an eating animal, and as such he needs occupation to furnish him the wherewith to buy bread and butter, and those little daily necessaries, such as food and clothes to wear. The merchant toils early and toils late, and not unfrequently carries the cares of the counting room to his pillow—the professional man is full of anxiety, and very often leads a life which is the opposite extreme from pleasure and repose. If we survey the streets of our city, we see the sons of toil in their various degrees and standing, and all active in business and bustle, and wherefore? Man is an eating animal and a clothes-wearing animal, and women and children need sustenance and shelter too. There is something noble in filling up an honest and praiseworthy sphere of usefulness—in furnishing our quota toward the requirements of good citizenship—but what sphere of usefulness does Jinglebrain fill up, what niche of honest industry does he occupy?

It is said that he had a wife once—people say that he had more than one, but that he has none *now* is just the truth and "nothing else." There are some little peccadilloes which it might be unpleasant to bring to light, and which would under such development exceedingly disturb the peace and dignity of our friend Jinglebrain—all these deeds and misdoings are wrapped in the veil of oblivion, or perhaps of an "alias," and now he sports his moustache and clean linen *per se*, and is a gentleman of leisure. He has an overflowing purse too, and everybody knows how he shuffles and makes shift to keep it replenished. No man has a greater horror of the restraints which a business occupation imposes than this same dandy whom we are attempting to "Sketch." He has no ostensible occupation himself—no counting room, no business office, no fortune that he has inherited, no "old man" of a father or an uncle who is very rich and very indulgent, and yet he always has plenty of money—always flourishes in the most fashionable style and eats at the most expensive table.

Philosophers tell us of many wonders in nature—wonders of the earth, the air, and the mighty deep; but of all the wonders of a wonderful world, the way in which some people live is the greatest wonder yet. Jinglebrain boards at one of the crack hotels, and after a 10 o'clock breakfast, he patronizes the barber for an hour or two, and then *dawdles about*, as Fanny Kemble would say, until dinner. He plays a game of billiards, whiles away an hour at the green-room of one of the theatres, drinks at the most fashionable restaurants, and lunches at 12 or 1 o'clock in the most recherché manner imaginable. You see him promenading the streets, or driving dull care away with a choice regalia and a fresh newspaper, as he lolls in an arm chair on the portico of his hotel—he's a "gentleman" in a wonderfully good humor with himself and evidently feels his keeping.

Jinglebrain affects the critic too in literature—he pities the poor drudge that writes, but he condescends to notice his productions. He twirls his moustache or puffs his segar with exceeding genteel nonchalance as he passes his comment upon some work of genius—and all the while too, he, Jinglebrain, is a numskull; in learning he has hardly passed "the rudiments," and if his pretensions could only be inspected, it would be discovered that the *plus* of his self-esteem would be represented by a *minus* in the estimation of others. We have heard it said that our friend has but one standard of quality, and that is from the skin outwards. His gentlemen are made up of three parts: first, broadcloth; second, clean linen; and thirdly, of hair. No man without a moustache has ever been known to be recognized or [to] receive a street salutation at his hands. Multitudes of those who know him at other times and in other places receive no look of observation or recognition from him whatever.

What will become of Jinglebrain when he dies we cannot say. I am sure no one can tell. There are denunciations and there are blessings pronounced on the *souls* of those who do evil, and those also who do well: but what dispensation of mercy there is for those who have *no souls*, and who regard only the corporeal outside of the living man, we are by no means of sufficient wisdom to determine.

TIMOTHY GOUJON, V. O. N. O.[1]

(Vender of Oysters in New Orleans)

There is in all cities bordering nigh unto the sea, a certain species of fish ycleped oysters, very much desired by the dwellers in said cities, and very much sold by certain individuals, of rare peculiarities, called oystermen.

In this goodly city of New Orleans, (albeit, not so very good either,) there abounds a class of worthy citizens, named as above, and who exercise the office and administration of fishes of this nature, styled, as we have said, oysters. The daily duty of these individuals—free citizens of a remarkably free city— is to vend by retail the interior fleshy and somewhat savory substance of these shell-fish, as above alluded to. The outer crust, or envelope of these, being of a tough, unyielding and indigestible quality, is rejected and thrown aside as worthless, nothing being eaten by the children of men but the puffy contents thereof. To sell such, is the business and daily care of those called, in common language, oystermen—the French style them *ecaille* [*écaillers*].

It cannot have escaped the notice of the most casual observer of men and things, that the streets and well thronged thoroughfares abound in certain brick tenements, professedly devoted— not the buildings but the occupants—to the preparing and rendering fit for the mastication of all and sundry reputable citizens —at least those who possess the wherewith to pay for them— these said shell-fish, fished up by a pair of iron claws out of the briny deep. These tenements, bearing aloft the outward insignia of their rank and condition, are to be found in the crowded walks of the city—and he "who runs may read," and he who is hungry may pass in and be served, not only to his heart's content, but also to his stomach's, which is the best of the bargain. We ourselves have refreshed and regaled the "inner man," many times and oft by those luxuriating viands compounded by those disciples of the illustrious kitchener, paying our quota of current coin meanwhile, and going joyfully on our way. But of late we have ceased in our visitations to these temples—finding that a repletion of the stomach and a similar condition of the brain-pan were always in an inverse ratio the one to the other.

[1]From the *Daily Crescent*, April 4, 1848.

When the stomach was full of luxury and good eating, the brain was empty—barrenness and desolation prevailing throughout "the dome of thought, the palace of the soul."[1] In such an extremity, having ever been taught to respect mind rather than matter, we have preferred to become even as one of "Pharaoh's lean kine," in order to have use and exercise of said article of brain. Everybody remembers the story of the old Dutchman so happy and so contented, who said that "he chust eats and thrinks till he's full, and then he schmokes and schmokes, and thinks about notin at all."

'Tis not, therefore, to these Epicurean depôts we refer, or to the proprietors thereof—not by any manner of means: they are well favored men, which, as Dogberry says, "is the gift of nature":[2] they wear black coats and carry canes. These, in the strictness of speech, and the bounds of propriety, come not under the classification above alluded to. We refer to certain graceless *sans culottes*—no, not *sans culottes* either, literally, for that would be "most senseless and fit"[3]—but in the political sense of the term: men, who, in the scale of the social thermometer, do not reach boiling point by any means. It was to this enterprising portion of the body politic that Timothy Goujon belonged. Long had he lived and labored in the cause of science, for he was a practical naturalist—perhaps you may say a *conchologist*—spending his days and his nights among shellfish—he was a vendor of oysters.

Goujon made his advent in "this breathing world" in the city of Bordeaux or in some of the faubourgs thereof. His parents being grave and close-mouthed people—a national characteristic—very naturally placed Timothy, when he had come to years, at the occupation which he has followed through life—namely, a fisher and a vendor of oysters. Of the particulars of his crossing the Atlantic, and finding himself erect, like other "featherless bipeds," here upon the levee of New Orleans, we are sorry we have no well detailed account. Neither he nor his parents before him were able to exercise the art of chirography, and therefore, of the deeds of his early life—how many times with furious grasp upon the iron tongs he has dragged these unoffending fishes from their natal bed, or murderously thrust

[1] Byron's "Childe Harold's Pilgrimage," Canto II, Stanza 6.

[2] *Cf.* "To be a well-favoured man is the gift of Fortune, but to write and read comes by Nature," "Much Ado About Nothing," III, 3, 15–17.

[3] *Ibidem*, III, 3, 23.

the knife into their bosoms, and torn them from their comfortable little homes—of these things we are not informed, and must therefore, with provoking brevity, remain as mute as this same commodity in which he so perseveringly deals.

We have heard that a year or two ago he involved himself in the rent of a small box of a corner shop, where his beautiful triangular lantern, covered with red worsted, and bearing the inviting inscription of *"Always Oysters, fryd, rost & in the shel,"* hung out by night as a point of local attraction to the hungry and wayfaring, both of which varieties of worthies it is presumed every sizeable city contains. This speculation did not succeed, and Timothy sold out his stock in trade, including the beautiful red worsted emblem of gastronomy, and betook himself independently to the Levee, like a gentleman, where he might breathe a purer air, and give exercise to his lungs, at the same time vending *viva voce* the inanimate quadrupeds which lay piled up with so much *sang froid* in his boat beside him.

Often, of a Sunday morning, we have heard the melodious, guttural voice of Timothy Goujon, in that place in the city of New Orleans where men and women do, at this especial hour of the week, "most congregate," namely, in the Market-place.[1] There have we seen and heard the sentimental Goujon trill forth harmonious ditty in accents somewhat like the following, though it would require a mixture of the French horn and the bassoon to grunt out the strain with any degree of exactness, especially the chorus: "Ah-h-h-h-h-h-h-h-h a bonne marche—so cheep as navair vas—toutes frais—var fresh. Ah-h-h un veritable collection—jentlemens and plack folks. Ah-h-h come and puy de veritable poisson de la mer—de bonne hûitres—Ah-h-h-h-h-h-h-h!"

Adieu, Goujon, sell your oysters, and pocket your small gains, and live quietly and comfortably, *chaqu' un a son goût,* and *chaqu' un a son gré.*

PATRICK McDRAY[2]

STRANGER, perhaps you've seen a stout, hardy-looking Hibernian driving cotton bales along the street. He's a jolly-looking fellow, somewhat pitted by the smallpox, cracks his whip in a

[1] *Cf. infra*, p. 204.
[2] From the *Daily Crescent*, April 18, 1848.

peculiar manner, and drives a good horse—that's Patrick McDray.

He's a clever fellow, is Pat; and by dint of hard labor and plenty of it, supplies his daily wants and the animal necessities of five or six small Pats, who look for all the world like chips off the old block.

It needs no "ghost from the grave" to tell us whence came Patrick McDray; the thing *spakes* for itself, for a brogue as unerring as the pointing of the needle to the pole. True, he has some idea of becoming a native, as he says, of this country, seeing he likes it so well; but it is enough for our present purpose to acquaint you, reader, that Patrick patronized the "Green Isle of the Ocean" when he came floundering, like a great calf, into this round world of trouble, where—

> "There's nought but care on every hand,
>   In every hour that passes, O." [1]

In his own "swate" land he had endured the frowns of an ill-natured world for many years, and it was one of the blessed chances which occasionally visit the likes of Patrick McDray that brought him safe and sound upon dry land on this side of the water.

But not only in the matter of mate and dhrink and clothes was Paddy made a fortunate possessor of "virtue, liberty and independence"—and all as a natural right and consequence of breathing the blessed air that blows through the vales and over the hills of our rightful land—but Pat, by his change of soil and climate, became a sturdy patriot at the drawing nigh of the election.

Well, we may trace Patrick McDray up one side and down the other from his birth and birth place in "the swate Isle," which is to the millions, "swate" only in the "uses of adversity;" [2] we may follow him, we say, from plain Pat all the way up to his present improved condition of *Mr.* Patrick McDray, who owns his own team and drives it like a gentleman. It is a remarkable thing how a man will pick up, little by little; only give him plenty of work and sure pay, and liberty [?] united to "virtue,

[1] From Robert Burns's "Green Grow the Rashes O!" The number of quotations from Burns at this time suggests that Whitman may then have been making the acquaintance of the Scottish poet, whom he praised very highly in an essay many years later (see "Complete Prose," pp. 395-402). However, the quotations are not always accurately made and may have been culled from memory.

[2] "As You Like It," II, 1, 14.

liberty and independence" will do the balance. But Paddy was otherwise united than to the three twin sisters we speak of—Paddy had a wife, and Bridget was her name.

It would be exceedingly unbecoming to invade the sanctity of the domestic circle; and we prefer to depict Paddy as he is, either in his daily character as drayman, or in his occasional duty at the polls; but our picture would scarce be complete without one peep at Bridget, for at home she was the very "sowl of the cause."

"O Nature! all thy shows and forms
To feeling, pensive hearts have charms!
Whether the summer kindly warms,
     Wi' life and light
Or winter snows in gusty storms,
     The long dark night!" [1]

An unsophisticated child of nature was Bridget McDray, sure enough. She was a mixture of this "kindly summer" and "gusty winter," being all brightness and sunshine and good humor when things went well; but on the other hand, over-darkened with storms, "gusty" enough when ills prevailed. A strange compound was Bridget's physiognomy—the extreme of good nature and honest frankness was there, and yet as vexations are abundant in this "world of care," and abundant too in proportion to our yielding to their sway, there was to be seen in her visage a trace of a moral storm when furious passion had raged and left its lines in her brow and in the drawing down the corners of her mouth. Naturally frank to a fault, yet, notwithstanding, "they do say" when her "Irish gets up" Bridget is "rale Tipperary" over again and can flourish a broomstick or her tongue with equal rapidity and violence. O but she's a jewel of a wife, is Bridget when "she gets in one of her ways."

Patrick thrives well; he pays his day and way like an honest man, and takes good care of his horse Cashel, and this shows him to be a gentleman. He puts on his Sunday clothes when Sunday comes, and takes a walk upon the Levee by way of a variety, and when his wife Bridget "gets high" he just drops quietly out of the way and waits till the breeze has blown over and this shows him to be a man of wisdom, for in the one case a multitude of words would only have "darkened counsel,"

[1]From Robert Burns's "Epistle to William Simpson."

while giving Bridget the whole house to herself, peace was rapidly declared, there being no enemy to encounter.

We take our leave of Patrick McDray, wishing him success in life and a heap of it.

_____

SAMUEL SENSITIVE[1]

It is a fact sufficiently self-evident, neither to be gainsaid or in any manner to be disputed, that there is a deal of sweetness in the nature of a woman. Samuel Sensitive had fallen in love with one of the sex, and her name was Miss Julia Katydid.

It was a present to Julia, that Sam had, with due consideration of the consequences, resolved to abstract forty dollars and upward from his oyster and billiard account, and bestow it in a beautiful, enameled, filagree, inlaid morceau of *bijouterie*, whose value intrinsically, *per se*, was perhaps about six bits. Sam loved Katydid, and was very anxious, by all honorable means, to draw upon himself the heavenly influences of double-distilled blessedness in the shape of a sweet woman's love. For this purpose he set to work according to the manner and form in such cases "made and provided." "'Twere long to tell" the extent and the variety of Sam's amiability upon this occasion.

It was a lucky chance for the head clerk of Messrs. Pork, Produce & Co., that the star of Katydid rose on his horizon, for he was posting the turnpike of iniquity in one of the biggest omnibusses that belong to that popular line. But mesmerism, in the shape of Cupid, made his "passes" at Sam, and speedily he was a "gone hoss." Julia Katydid was a young lady with bright

[1] From the *Daily Crescent*, May 2, 1848.

It is perhaps worth noting that this extravagantly and almost vulgarly sentimental sketch was published in the *Crescent* the day following the date announced for the masked ball at Lafayette, Whitman's account of which, "A Night at the Terpsichore Ball," is reprinted in this volume (pp. 225–228). This coincidence becomes the more interesting, if not significant, when we place beside it another. The quotation on p. 217, *post*, is from Burns's "Ae Fond Kiss," addressed to his Nancy, who, it will be remembered, was also a married woman. Now, in the conversation with the fair unnamed of the Terpsichore Ball, Whitman found that she knew all the poets. Is it possible that he is here covertly sending her a message through a newspaper, alluding to a poem which his inamorata would recognize as appropriate to his feeling and their relation, but which the husband, being perhaps less literary, would miss, especially when the whole was so soaked in sentimentality as to repell the average reader? Moreover, Whitman's picture of Julia departing on a river steamer, leaving her lover to his sad meditations, reminds us of Burns's "Behold the Hour," likewise addressed to his Nancy on the occasion of her departure for Jamaica to join her husband. There is at times something sly and secretive about Whitman, and I do not believe him incapable of such an experience as I have suggested; but the evidence is so fragmentary as to have no value as proof. See in this connection Biographical Introduction, pp. xlvii ff.

eyes, very bright raven ringlets, very dark, and ruby lips, like cherries, and alabaster neck, and a very nice chin with a dimple in it. Wasn't she pretty?[1]

She was the niece of some good lady and she had had a mother —one who *was* a mother, and had brought up this feminine jewel of loveliness in a manner to develope the exceeding grace of a nature pure and exalted as those blest beings whom, in our dreams of fancy, we fondly suppose to hover about the abodes of innocence and peace. Those who only know women in the haunts and kennels of sensuality, are widely ignorant of the real nature of the sex, and while profligacy tends so purely to debase and "imbute" [imbrute] the soul, as Milton says,[2] the kindly influence of female innocense is like the quality of mercy itself, distilling like the gentle rain from heaven, and is indeed "twice blessed" whenever and wherever it is exercised.[3]

It is a curious discovery that a young fellow makes when first he becomes sensible of the existence of what is poetically termed "a heart." He is sick and he isn't sick; something is the matter, and he hardly knows what. He sits and sighs, while visions of blond lace and fancy ribbons, to say nothing of "love darting eyes and tresses like the morn,"[4] flit before his imagination, and render him very qualmish indeed. Sam never made so many blots in his day-book before, and once when he should have written "Dried Herrings," in copying an invoice, his pen insensibly traced the fair characters of the name of "Julia Katydid." He even tried to write poetry, saw beauty in the moon and stars, was frequently seen by the watchman to wander along the Levee, humming to himself, "O, meet me by moonlight alone,"[5] or apostrophizing a bale of cotton in words like these:

> Had we never loved so kindly;
> Had we never loved so blindly,
> Never met and never parted,
> I had ne'er been broken hearted![6]

Julia, it seems, had lately gone off up the river on a visit to some friends, and the self-same post to which the steamer was

[1] There are points of likeness between this description and the photograph found in Whitman's notebook; see Vol. II, facing p. 70.

[2] *Cf.* "Comus", ll. 463–469.

[3] Paraphrased from Portia's speech in "The Merchant of Venice," IV, 1.

[4] "Comus," l. 753.

[5] The title of a popular song by J. Augustus Wade (1800–1875).

[6] See *infra*, p. 216, note.

fastened when the fair Katydid stepped foot on board was like "storied urn and monumental bust,"[1] to Sam. He couldn't have thought it possible that a big post should have gained so upon his affection, and as by moonlight he stood there leaning up against the aforesaid romantic piece of timber, and gazing out upon the mighty Mississippi, which was running at that time pretty full of drift wood, Sam did feel sad, sorrowful and sober-hearted enough.

But why spin out a long story? for a long one could be told of the courtship of Sam and Katydid. Let it suffice to say, that through the benign influence of a very woman, a "change came over the spirit" of the young gentleman's dream,[2] and he who was once the prince of good fellows among a crowd of roysterers in an evening's carouse, and could laugh the loudest and longest, and emptiest, was made a different chap of as soon as

> His dream of life from morn till night,
> Was love—still love.[3]

Why lengthen the recital? Katydid was not inexorable, neither had she a heart of adamant, harder than the nether millstone. She, being wooed, was in due course of things, won, and I can show the house where they live—that is, Sam and his wife, Katydid. He visits the Levee no more by moonlight, not he: he stays at home like a decent worthy citizen, as he is. He loves Katydid, and has reason to bless the hour when she smiled and winked, and half confessed that she loved him. The merchantable firm with whom Sam was brought up, opened wide their business arms, and took him in. Altogether, Sam is looking up in the world. Who will not say that it was not that same bright-eyed Katydid that made a man of him?

———

DEATH OF MR. ASTOR OF NEW YORK[4]

AT A very advanced age this very well known personage has at length left that earth on which he had such large possessions.

---

[1] A misquotation of Gray's "Elegy Written in a Country Churchyard," l. 41.

[2] *Cf. infra*, p. 179, note. This quotation, it may be observed, is another, if a slight, evidence of the Whitman authorship of these sketches.

[3] *Cf.* Thomas Moore's "Love's Young Dream," stanza 1.

[4] From the *Daily Crescent*, April 7, 1848.
At the time of his death John Jacob Astor was the wealthiest man in the United States.

"The rich man also died." It were a trite moral to draw—to go over the oft-said maxims about the vanity of wealth, and its inability to wrestle with death; and we forbear. Wealth is good enough; but unfortunately people don't one quarter of the time enjoy it, after it comes to them.

For some years past Mr. Astor has been living in a two story brick house in Broadway, New York, opposite the old site of Niblo's Garden. The laconic door-plate, "*Mr. Astor,*" informs persons of the name of the occupant. Somehow, this dwelling always had a cold, cheerless, naked, and uninviting appearance:[1] there were no shutters to the prodigious windows, nor were pleasant faces ever seen at the panes—nor was the warm aspect of family comforts and endearments known there. Ugh! the house gave one something of a chill when passing it, even in summer.

We remember seeing Mr. A. two winters since, when going down Broadway by this house.[2] A couple of servants were assisting him across the pavement to a sleigh which was drawn up by the curb-stone. The old gentleman's head seemed completely bent down with age and sickness; he was muffled in furs and entirely unable to help himself. The very groom, a hearty young Irishman, with perhaps not two dollars in his pocket, looked with pity upon the great millionaire! Certainly no man, of the crowds that hurried along that busy promenade, would have accepted the rich capitalist's wealth tied to the condition of being "in his shoes."

Some curiosity has long been felt at the north, to know the disposition of Mr. A.'s immense wealth. It is rumored that a benevolent bequest has been made of several hundred thousand dollars; that literary institutions have been founded, and so on. We shall soon learn whether there is any truth in these stories. Fitz-Green Halleck, the poet, has for some years been the confidential clerk of Mr. Astor, and will doubtless receive a handsome legacy. One of the sons of Mr. A. is a confirmed lunatic, and is taken care of in a house built expressly for him by his father, in New York. He has servants, medical attendance, etc. The domestic affairs of Mr. Astor were never happy, or, at least, have not been so for many years.

For Whitman's attitude toward great riches, see also *infra*, pp. 37–29, iii; *post*, I, pp. 123–125, 245; II, pp. 63, 67.

[1] *Cf. infra*, p. 96.
[2] *Cf.* "Complete Prose," p. 12.

UNIVERSITY STUDIES[1]

. . . FERTILE as the age has been in plans for the improvement of the individual and social life, in no department has the human intellect been more active than in devising systems of education, fitted both for the Common School and the University. Yet, diverse as have been these schemes proposed for training the race for its duties and its pleasures, all have admitted the general principle that the object of education is rather that of developing, strengthening and directing the faculties with which nature has endowed us, than that of imparting positive knowledge, filling the mind with a heap of disjointed facts, or making it a store-house for the reception of the exploded theories of past generations. To expand and purify the soul by the contemplation of virtue, to strengthen the mind for the search after truth, and fill it with the earnest determination of resting satisfied with no other object of pursuit, should be the primary aim of all educational means. . . .

. . . We may say then that the Common School is peculiarly connected with what are generally called the material interests of society. . . . The University, while it forgets not to inculcate on the scholar the necessity of attending to the material agencies by which we are surrounded, is also occupied with teaching him that there is something more than matter in the universe, and instructs him in the art of removing the integuments which cover the ideal, and hide from all but the eye-intellectual the beauties and truths of the immaterial world. But since the University is merely a continuation of the Common School, both must be founded on a common principle; both aim, as we have said, at awakening and developing—neither at perfecting—the faculties of our nature.

If we are right in saying that the object of University education is rather to inspire the student with an ardent desire to search after truth than to infuse into his mind correct opinions on all objects within the scope of University instruction—it will be immediately perceived that it is much more important for the professors and text-writers to be thoroughly imbued with the spirit of pure and elevated philosophy than for them to come to a certain standard of orthodoxy, erected by a certain sect in politics, religion or literature. It was said by Lessing, "It

[1] From the *Daily Crescent*, April 11, 1848.
Cf. infra, pp. 144–146; *post*, II, pp. 13–15.

God held in his right hand pure and absolute truth, and in his left only the desire to search after truth, I would tell him to keep pure truth for himself, as mortal eyes are too weak to look on it, and would ask him to give me only the desire to search after truth."[1] So should the youth speak to the professor, if the latter should presume to declare his opinions as the only possible truth, and denounce all others as absolutely and unqualifiedly false. Let the professor rather tell the opinions of others and their reasonings as well as his own; then say to his hearers, "I cannot decide for you, you must inquire and decide for yourselves." Such, we are told, is the course actually pursued by the Lecturer on Constitutional Law of the Louisiana University; and how much better it is than if he merely gave his own opinions, with the reasons which led him to form them, leaving the student under the impression that there was no other rational way of considering the subject.

As with professors, so should it be with text-books. . . . Students, however, will never remain satisfied with a one-sided view of any subject; and having learned from their professors that independence of thought which is a cardinal virtue in the republic of letters, there is no danger of their receiving the words of any man as the words of a master. . . .

THE OLD CATHEDRAL[2]

THIS venerable building was, on Thursday last, resorted to by hundreds of those who wished to show their penitence and humility. The old monastic church stood, as it were, aloof from the wings on either side. The temples dedicated to the law—the higher Courts on the one side, and the Municipal Court on the other—have been renovated, and now look like modern structures by the side of some monument of old. The tall, gray Cathedral reared its ancient spire to Heaven; but the towers wherein [were] the bells that have tolled the death knell, and rung the merry marriage music of thousands, were silent. It was a day dedicated to the "King of Kings"—it was the Holy Thursday of Passion week. It commemorated the occasion of the "Last Supper" of our Saviour, who, when surrounded by his disciples, gave them his last earthly blessing. There were over two thousand communicants kneeling

[1] In his *Eine Duplik* (1778). Being ignorant of German, Whitman probably got this quotation at second hand.

[2] From the *Daily Crescent*, April 22, 1848.

at the altars, at various periods of the day, and all seemed fully sensible of the solemnity of the occasion.   Grand Mass was celebrated—after which, many persons came in to adore or communicate in spirit with the "Son of Man."   In the niche upon the right-hand side, stood a *basse relievo* of the Virgin and her Child.   Upon a table near by, was a bronze figure of the Crucifixion, and underneath a higher portion of the altar, a cross, covered with purple silk—the color emblematical of the blood that gushed from the wound inflicted by the spearman, upon the person of the Divine Nazarene.   On the other side was a niche dedicated to St. Francis; this was half covered with a particolored drapery, which entirely concealed the face of the Saint, but underneath, there was an altar composed of the most gorgeous flowers—whose radiant beauties were lighted up by innumerable candles in silver candlesticks.   The church was crowded by those devoted to the Catholic religion, and presented a scene that was solemn and interesting in the highest degree.   Our dark-eyed Creole beauties,[1] with their gilt-edged prayer-books in their hands, would walk in with an air that seemed to say that beauty was a part of religion.   Dipping their taper fingers into the holy water and crossing their foreheads, they would then walk up the aisle and kneel down to prayer. We saw many women there whose garments betokened that some dear friend had not long been laid in the grave.   They knelt before the picture of Christ carrying his cross, and prayed, no doubt, that they might have strength to carry theirs.   Persons of all classes went down before the shrine of Religion. There was the broken-hearted man of the world—the gray-haired man, whose feet were on the brink of the grave—the blooming girl whose charms were budding into womanhood— and the wrinkled, care-worn widow, to whom love was but a memory.   Then again, were the old servants of ancient families; and then ragged, pale-faced creatures, who looked as though they did not dare to approach too near the altar.   The whole scene was beautiful and solemn, and calculated to impress the heart with the purity of virtue, and endow the soul with full reliance in the power of Him who rules above.   Yesterday was Good-Friday—the anniversary of the Crucifixion.   The ceremonies on this occasion were of the most imposing nature, and showed reverence and respect for the tortures endured by the God-like Hero of Calvary, for the benefit of a sinful world.

[1] *Cf. post*, II, pp. 185 ff.

A WALK ABOUT TOWN[1]

By a Pedestrian

Got up early from my bed in my little room near Lafayette. The sun had scarcely risen, and every object seemed lazy and idle. On some German ship moored at the levee I saw about a dozen stalwart sailors with bare legs, scouring the decks. They seemed to be as happy as lords, although their wages are sometimes not more than six dollars a month. . . . Saw a negro throw a large stone at the head of his mule, because it would not pull an empty dray—wished I owned the negro—wouldn't treat him as he treated the mule, but make him a present of a cow-skin, and make him whip himself. . . . Saw a poor long-shoreman lying down on a bench; had on a real [red?] shirt and blue cottonade pantaloons; coarse brogans, but no stockings. He had spent all his money in a tippler's shop the night previous for grog, and when his last picayune was discovered to be gone, he was kicked out of the house. Thought that there were some landlords who deserved to be bastinadoed. . . . Saw a shipping master riding at full speed upon a small pony. He would have been willing to have freighted every ship in port, if he could have been "elected." Saw him go on board a vessel, and come off again, with, in all probability, a flea in his ear. He kicked the pony in his sides, and after dismounting went into the nearest grog-shop. How he kept "his spirits *up* by pouring spirits *down*." He didn't get the freight of that ship. . . . The sun had just showed his golden face above the gray clouds of the horizon, and bathes with lustre the distant scenery. Now come the bustle and business of the day. Shop-keepers are opening their stores; stevedores are hurrying aboard their respective ships. Those stevedores! they are for the most part honest men, and, physically speaking, work much harder than any other class of the community. Many of them have little tin kettles on their arms which contain their simple dinner repast. When their work is over they get their "bones," and then separate for their different homes to woo "tired nature's sweet restorer"[2]—sleep; or mayhap to spend their day's earnings in a grog-shop. . . . There's a big, red faced man walking hastily up the levee.

[1] From the *Daily Crescent*, April 26, 1848.

[2] *Cf. infra*, p. 207.

He's a Customhouse officer, and is hurrying on board his vessel for fear that if not there by sunrise, the Captain may report him to the Collector. . . . Went into St. Mary's Market, saw a man, a good old man in a blue jacket and cottonade pantaloons, with a long stick of sugar cane in his hand. Wondered who he was, and much surprised to find out that he was a lawyer of some repute. At the lower end of the market there was a woman with a basket of live crabs at her feet. Although she loved money, she had no particular affection for a press from the claws of the ungainly creatures that she handled with a pair of iron tongs. Saw the "cat fish" man, who declared that his fish were just caught, and were as tender as a piece of lamb. Went up the Market and saw rounds of beef, haunches of venison and legs of mutton, that would have made a disciple of Graham forswear his hermit-like appetite.[1] . . . Came down town—shops all open—and heard the news boys calling out the names of the different papers that they had for sale. These boys are "cute" as foxes and as industrious as ants. Some of them who now cry out "ere's yer ——, here's the ——, here's the ——," may in time be sent to Congress. . . . Went down town further—all was business and activity—the clerks placing boxes upon the pavements—the persons employed in fancy stores were bedecking their windows with their gaudiest goods, and the savory smell of fried ham, broiled beef-steaks, with onions, etc., stole forth from the half unshut doors of every restaurant. . . . Passed down Conti street and looked at the steamboat wharf. It was almost lined with steamboats; some were puffing off steam and throwing up to the sky huge columns of blackened smoke—some were lying idle, and others discharging sugar, molasses, cotton, and everything else that is produced in the great Valley of the Mississippi. Came to the conclusion that New Orleans was a great place and *no* mistake. . . . Went still further down—visited the Markets and saw that every luxury given to sinful man by sea and land, from a shrimp to a small potato, were there to be purchased. Came home again and took breakfast—tea, a radish, piece of dry toast, and an egg—read one of the morning papers, and then went about my business.

[1] Sylvester Graham (1794–1851), an American Presbyterian clergyman, vegetarian, and inventor of Graham bread.

GENERAL TAYLOR AT THE THEATRE[1]

QUITE a sensation was created in the St. Charles Theatre, last night, by the appearance of Maj. Gens. Taylor and Pillow, with some other officers of note, in the dress circle. It was just as the model artists,[2] on the stage, were in the midst of their tableaux of the "Circassian Slaves," that the hero of Buena Vista, and his companions, entered the house. In the dim light, the gas being turned off to give effect to the performances, the General's entrance was not noticed by the audience. When the lights shone out again, however, the most vociferous cheering announced that the people recognized him. The orchestra played "The Star Spangled Banner" and "Hail Columbia"—and the next tableau was one purposely complimentary to General Taylor. It was received with loud cheering and plaudits.

A NIGHT AT THE TERPSICHORE BALL[3]

BY "YOU KNOW WHO"

A STRICT adherence to the truth compels me to acknowledge that I am a bachelor, whether young or old, handsome or ugly, rich or poor, I will leave your readers to guess. I am, however, like all bachelors, one from inclination, not necessity. As all philosophers have acknowledged that every one can be suited to their minds as regards the selection of a wife, why I should be an exception to the general rule arises no doubt from the fact of my being a resident of this city of epidemics, and she *somewhere* else, with no likelihood of her ever getting here, so I have settled down [to be] as comfortable as circumstances will admit, joined the "Old Bachelor Society," intending to prove my constancy toward *her* by marrying *nobody*. If this ain't satisfactory and self-sacrificing on my part, and sufficient to immortalize me, I will *keel* over and expire.

Japhet in search of his father never had more difficulties

[1] From the *Daily Crescent*, May 9, 1848.
Cf. "Complete Prose," p. 440
[2] *Cf. infra*, p. 191.
[3] From the *Daily Crescent*, May 18, 1848.

to surmount, obstacles to contend against, and incidents to be-
fall him, than I have had in my efforts to find *her*. I did not
cease my labors night nor day, as my portfolio will prove, but
all in vain; my supplications were useless, my efforts fruitless,
my dreams and fancies of no avail. The following incident
befel me in one of my exploring expeditions after *her*.

'Twas Saturday evening, cool and pleasant, just the kind of
night for a dance, as I found myself with a few friends, com-
fortably seated in the Lafayette car. "Who knows," so ran
my mind, "but what I *may* see *her* this evening? Nature may
repay all my labors by showing me the one she intends to share
my lot." And a thousand other fanciful thoughts flitted through
my mind, when "Gentlemen will please make room for ladies"
assailed my ears from two or three stentorian voices. My
gallantry would not allow me to remain one second after this
appeal; so I got up on deck[1] as best I could, amidst the yelling
of a crowd of b'hoys trying to sing "Old Dan Tucker." I was
about taking a seat, but finding some *three inches* of the thickest
kind of dew on the bench, I *stood* it the balance of the dis-
tance.

At length we arrived at the end of our journey. The Trojan
horse could scarcely contain more persons than that car; they
were pouring out from all sides and in every direction. I
followed the crowd. Arriving at the ball-room I imagined all
trouble and inconvenience ceased, for that night. Poor deluded
being! I forgot I had a hat, and that I should provide a place
for it. I did so, but suffered some. The post-office on adver-
tizing days[2] was nothing to it. When I was clear of the crowd,
I requested one of my friends to squeeze me into *shape* again;
I felt as flat as a pancake. Did you ever put on white kid
gloves[3]—the delicate little *creatures*—without wishing they
were never known? If you did not, I did, that night. In the
hurry of the moment I bought sevens instead of nines. I
pulled; I pressed and pulled again. No go. I was determined
to have them on or burst. After a while I did both. Although
my hands looked like *cracked dumplings*, I didn't care; so I put

---

[1] The street railway cars of the New Orleans of that day were curious double-decked
affairs. The car itself was divided into four compartments—one for white women, one
for white men and women, one for those who wished to smoke, and one for negroes. A
pyramidal stairway on the outside of the car led from the first three of these compart-
ments to the upper deck, on which there was a long double seat and the driver's box.

[2] Days on which uncalled-for letters were advertized in the newspapers.

[3] It would appear that for once Whitman was in conventional evening clothes.

my *hands* behind my back and made my first *début* amidst the chivalry, beauty, loveliness, and exquisite grace congregated in that social hall.

The room was overflowing with the beauty of Lafayette,[1] with a sprinkling from New Orleans and Carrolton.   A promenade was in order when I entered and I watched each graceful form and lovely face; as they approached like sylphs of some fairy tale, in plain, fancy and mask dresses.   Each one, methought, was more lovely than the other; but no, the object of my heart,—she who has caused me so many sleepless nights and restless days,—she whom I have seen so often in my dreams and imaginings, was not among the unmasked.   I rose from my seat with a heavy heart, walked into the —— and took a drink of lemonade *without* any brandy in it.   On my return, a cotillion was in motion.   I looked upon it with stoic indifference—*she* was not there, and not being there, the place or persons had no charms for me.

While musing to myself that I would emigrate to Europe or China—get wrecked, perhaps—find her on some barren isle, etc.—I caught a glimpse of what I considered the very pink of perfection, in form, grace and movement, in fancy dress. Doctor Collyer[2] would give the world for such a figure.   My eyes were riveted on the spot.   My head began to swim.   I saw none but her.   A mist surrounded all the others, while she moved about in bold relief.   She turned.   I saw her face, radiant with smiles, ecstasy, delight.   "'Tis she!" I ejaculated, as if tossed by a pitchfork, and caught the arm of a manager, to introduce me.   He didn't know her.   It was her first appearance in the ball-room.   I imagined it was an auspicious coincidence.   It was also my first appearance.   Seeing a gentleman conversing with her, I watched my opportunity, and seeing him alone, I requested him to introduce me.   Never saw him before in my life; but what cared I—my case was getting desperate.   He willingly consented; and off we started toward her. To describe my feelings while approaching her, is impossible.   I was blind to all but her.

The agony was over; she spoke; and the deed was done.   I found that she was everything that I imagined—accomplished,

---

[1] Lafayette was then a sort of suburb, but it has long since become an integral part of New Orleans.   It appears that Whitman had a room in Lafayette for a time. (See *infra*, p. 223.)

[2] Of Doctor Collyer's Model Artists; *cf. infra*, p. 191.

pleasing in her manners, agreeable in her conversation, well versed in the authors, from Dryden down to James[1]—including all the intermediate *landings*—passionately fond of music, she said; and by her musical voice I *knew* she could sing. I was happy in every sense of the word—delighted beyond measure. She kindly consented to promenade—would carry me through a cotillion if I'd go—but, knowing nothing about the poetry of motion, I had to decline; and she,—noble, generous creature as she was!—preferred rather to talk and walk than dance. I admired her, nay, I will confess, for the first time in my life, I felt the "tender passion" creeping all over me. *I was in love!* I could not restrain myself. Candor compelled me to speak openly—I told her I had been looking for *her* since I was 18 years of age. "Looking for me!" she exclaimed with astonishment. "If not you," I answered, "some one very much like you." She guessed my object, saw and understood all, and invited me to call and see her.

I was, in my own opinion, as good as a married man—at length my toils and troubles were to cease—I was about to be repaid for my constancy, by having the one for my wife that nature intended. Just at this moment where, in any other place I would have been on my knees, the gentleman who [had] introduced me, came up to us and said—"*Wife*, ain't it time to go home?" "Yes, *my dear*," she responded. So taking his arm, casting a peculiar kind of look at me, and bidding me good night, they left me like a motionless statue on the floor. The perspiration flowed down my cheeks, like rain drops—the blood rushed to my head—my face was as red as a turkey *rooster's*— I was insensible. Some of my friends, seeing my situation, carried me into the ——, and administered another lemonade with a little brandy in it, which revived me very shortly. I jumped into a cab—in one hour afterwards I was in the arms of Morpheus.

It is very evident that she was *the* one; and yet it astonishes me how she could take her present husband for *me*. There is no similarity between us. She was still young, and no chance of being an old maid; while he appeared as careless of his wife's charms as I did of his existence.

I wish them both much happiness, altho' I am the sufferer by it.[2]

[1] George Payne Rainesford James (1801-1860), a prolific English novelist and historian.
[2] *Cf. infra*, p. 216, note.

FOURIERISM[1]

WE DON'T know much about Fourierism—that we confess; but to us it seems a great objection that nobody, as far as we learn from the system, is to do anything but *be happy*. Now who would peel potatoes and scrub the floors? The N. Y. Sunday *Dispatch* advocates Fourierism, because, under it, the *Dispatch* says, "Music, vocal and instrumental, would be everywhere cultivated, and each association would have its band, and its choir, to furnish music on all occasions. Music at sunrise would waken all from sleep. Soft music at twilight, and dancing on the green-sward in summer, or in the great saloon in winter, would be the evening recreation, and the serenade at night would make a thousand happy sleepers dream of heaven, while the solemn chorus of a thousand voices would swell the song of praise and thanksgiving for a state of happiness worthy to be called the kingdom of God on earth—for which, we pray as often as we say, '*Thy kingdom come, Thy will be done on earth as it is in heaven.*'"

THE SHADOW AND THE LIGHT OF A YOUNG MAN'S SOUL[2]

WHEN young Archibald Dean went from the city—(living out of which he had so often said was no living at all)—went down into the country to take charge of a little district school, he felt as though the last float-plank which buoyed him up on hope and happiness, was sinking, and he with it. But poverty is as stern, if not as sure, as death and taxes, which Franklin called the surest things of the modern age. And poverty compelled Archie Dean; for when the destructive New-York fire of '35 happened, ruining so many property owners and erewhile

---

[1] From the New Orleans *Daily Crescent*, May 20, 1848.
This brief notice deals with Fourierism in its economic aspects; for Whitman's views of another Fourierist idea, that of free-love, see *post*, II, p. 7, note.

[2] From the *Union Magazine of Literature and Art*, Vol. II, pp. 280–281, June, 1848.
Whitman did not return to Brooklyn from New Orleans until June 15. This sketch may have been submitted to Mrs. Kirkland's magazine before he went south or may have been submitted from among earlier manuscripts. At any rate, I find in it no reflection of the southern sojourn, though its date and theme would at first glance lead the reader to expect some indication of it.

rich merchants, it ruined the insurance offices, which of course ruined those whose little wealth had been invested in their stock. Among hundreds and thousands of other hapless people, the aged, the husbandless, the orphan, and the invalid, the widow Dean lost every dollar on which she depended for subsistence in her waning life. It was not a very great deal; still it had yielded, and was supposed likely to yield, an income large enough for her support, and the bringing up of her two boys. But, when the first shock passed over, the cheerful-souled woman dashed aside, as much as she could, all gloomy thoughts, and determined to stem the waters of roaring fortune yet. What troubled her much, perhaps most, was the way of her son Archibald. "Unstable as water," even in his youth, was not a sufficient excuse for his want of energy and resolution;[1] and she experienced many sad moments, in her maternal reflections, ending with the fear that he would "not excell." The young man had too much of that inferior sort of pride which fears to go forth in public with anything short of fashionable garments, and hat and boots fit for fashionable criticism. His cheeks would tingle with shame at being seen in any working capacity; his heart sunk within him if his young friends met him when he showed signs of the necessity of labor, or of the absence of funds. Moreover, Archie looked on the dark side of his life entirely too often; he pined over his deficiencies, as he called them, by which he meant mental as well as pecuniary wants. . . . But to do the youth justice, his good qualities must be told, too. He was unflinchingly honest; he would have laid out a fortune, had he possessed one, for his mother's comfort; he was not indisposed to work, and work faithfully, could he do so in a sphere equal to his ambition;[2] he had a benevolent, candid soul, and none of the darker vices which are so common among the young fellows of our great cities.[3]

A good friend, in whose house she could be useful, furnished the widow with a gladly accepted shelter; and thither she also took her younger boy, the sickly pale child, the light-haired little David, who looked thin enough to be blown all away by a good breeze. And happening accidentally to hear of a country district where, for poor pay and coarse fare, a school teacher was required, and finding on inquiry that Archie, who, though

[1] Cf. post, II, pp. 193–194.
[2] Cf. infra, pp. 4–5, 19–20; post, II, pp. 125, 152.
[3] Cf. post, II, pp. 5–8, 30.

little more than a boy himself, had a fine education, would fill the needs of the office, thither the young man was fain to betake himself, sick at soul, and hardly restraining unmanly tears as his mother kissed his cheek, while he hugged his brother tightly, the next hour being to find him some miles on his journey. But it *must* be. Had he not ransacked every part of the city for employment as a clerk? And was he not quite ashamed to be any longer a burthen on other people for his support?

Toward the close of the first week of his employment, the entering upon which, with the feelings and circumstances of the beginning, it is not worth while to narrate, Archie wrote a long letter to his mother, (strange as it may seem to most men, she was also his confidential friend,) of which the following is part:

"—— You may be tired of such outpourings of spleen, but my experience tells me that I shall feel better after writing them; and I am in that mood when sweet music would confer on me no pleasure. Pent up and cribbed here among a set of beings to whom grace and refinement are unknown, with no sunshine ahead, have I not reason to feel the gloom over me? Oh, poverty, what a devil thou art! How many high desires, how many aspirations after goodness and truth thou hast crushed under thy iron heel! What swelling hearts thou hast sent down to the silent house after a long season of strife and bitterness! What talent, noble as that of great poets and philosophers, thou dost doom to pine in obscurity, or die in despair![1] . . . Mother, my throat chokes, and my blood almost stops, when I see around me so many people who appear to be born into the world merely to eat and sleep, and run the same dull monotonous round—and think that I too must fall in this current, and live and die in vain!"

Poor youth, how many, like you, have looked on man and life in the same ungracious light! Has God's all-wise providence ordered things wrongly, then? Is there discord in the machinery which moves systems of worlds, and keeps them in their harmonious orbits? O, no: there is discord in your own heart; in that lies the darkness and the tangle.[2] To the young man, with health and a vigilant spirit, there is shame in despondency. Here we have a world, a thousand avenues to usefulness and to profit stretching in far distances around us. Is *this* the place for

[1] *Cf. infra*, p. 19.
[2] *Cf. infra*, p. 110.

a failing soul? Is *youth* the time to yield, when the race is just begun?

But a changed spirit, the happy result of one particular incident, and of several trains of clearer thought, began to sway the soul of Archie Dean in the course of the summer: for it was at the beginning of spring that he commenced his labors and felt his severest deprivations. There is surely, too, a refreshing influence in open-air nature, and in natural scenery, with occasional leisure to enjoy it, which begets in a man's mind truer and heartier reflections, analyzes and balances his decisions, and clarifies them if they are wrong, so that he sees his mistakes— an influence that takes the edge off many a vapory pang, and neutralizes many a loss, which is most a loss in imagination. Whether this suggestion be warranted or not, there was no doubt that the discontented young teacher's spirits were eventually raised and sweetened by his country life, by his long walks over the hills, by his rides on horseback every Saturday,[1] his morning rambles and his evening saunters; by his coarse living, even, and the untainted air and water, which seemed to make better blood in his veins. Gradually, too, he found something to admire in the character and customs of the unpolished country folk; their sterling sense on most practical subjects, their hospitality, and their industry.

One day Archie happened to be made acquainted with the history of one of the peculiar characters of the neighborhood— an ancient, bony, yellow-faced maiden, whom he had frequently met, and who seemed to be on good terms with everybody; her form and face receiving a welcome, with all their contiguity [exiguity?] and fadedness, wherever and whenever they appeared. In the girlhood of this long-born spinster, her father's large farm had been entirely lost and sold from him, to pay the debts incurred by his extravagance and dissipation. The consequent ruin to the family peace which followed, made a singularly deep impression on the girl's mind, and she resolved to get the whole

---

[1] A number of details in this sketch seem to prove it to be more autobiographical than most of the others. A school-teacher might have occasion to ride horseback every Saturday, but Whitman, as a country editor, *did* deliver his weekly papers in this manner, and more than once he has ascribed to himself Archie Dean's experience in learning to admire the common sense of the country folk. (*Cf.* "Complete Prose," p. 10; *infra*, pp. 120–121; *post*, II, p. 14, etc.) The date of Archie's being forced to leave the city for distasteful school teaching is placed in 1835; Whitman's began in 1836. Archie's unusually confiding attitude toward his mother parallels Whitman's affection for his "perfect mother." And Archie's moody pride and frustrated ambition suggest the self-revelations of Whitman's own early verse.

farm back again. This determination came to form her life—
the greater part of it—as much as her bodily limbs and veins.
She was a shrewd creature; she worked hard; she received the
small payment which is given to female labor;[1] she persisted;
night and day found her still at her tasks, which were of every
imaginable description; long—long—long years passed; youth
fled, (and it was said she had been quite handsome); many
changes of ownership occurred in the farm itself; she confided
her resolve all that time to no human being; she hoarded her
gains; all other passions—love even, gave way to her one great
resolve; she watched her opportunity, and eventually con-
quered her object! She not only cleared the farm, but was
happy in furnishing her old father with a home there for years
before his death. And when one comes to reflect on the disad-
vantages under which a woman labors, in the strife for gain,
this will appear a remarkable, almost an incredible case. And
then, again, when one thinks how surely, though ever so slowly
and step by step, perseverance has overcome apparently in-
superable difficulties, the fact—*for the foregoing incident is a fact*
—may appear so strange.

Archie felt the narrative of this old maid's doings as a rebuke
—a sharp-pointed moral to himself and his infirmity of purpose.
Moreover, the custom of his then way of life forced him into
habits of more thorough activity; he had to help himself or go
unhelped; he found a novel satisfaction in that highest kind of
independence which consists in being able to do the offices of
one's own comfort, and achieve resources and capacities "at
home," whereof to place happiness beyond the reach of variable
circumstances, or of the services of the hireling, or even of the
uses of fortune. The change was not a sudden one; few great
changes are. But his heart was awakened to his weakness;
the seed was sown; Archie Dean felt that he *could* expand his
nature by means of that very nature itself. Many times he
flagged; but at each fretful falling back, he thought of the
yellow-faced dame, and roused himself again. . . . Mean-
time changes occurred in the mother's condition. Archie was
called home to weep at the death-bed of little David. Even
that helped work out the revolution in his whole make; he felt
that on him rested the responsibility of making the widow's last
years comfortable. "I shall give up my teacher's place,"
said he to his mother, "and come to live with you; we will have

[1] *Cf. infra*, p. 137.

the same home, for it is best so." And so he did. And the weakness of the good youth's heart never got entirely the better of him afterward, but in the course of a season was put to flight utterly. This second time he *made* employment. With an iron will he substituted action and cheerfulness for despondency and a fretful tongue. He met his fortunes as they came, face to face, and shirked no conflict. Indeed, he felt it glorious to vanquish obstacles. For his mother he furnished a peaceful, plentiful home; and from the hour of David's death, never did his tongue utter words other than kindness, or his lips, whatever annoyances or disappointments came, cease to offer their cheerfullest smile in her presence.

Ah, for how many the morose habit which Archie rooted *out* from his nature, becomes by long usage and indulgence rooted *in*, and spreads its bitterness over their existence, and darkens the peace of their families, and carries them through the spring and early summer of life with no inhalement of sweets, and no plucking of flowers!

PARAGRAPH SKETCHES OF BROOKLYNITES[1]

Rev. Henry Ward Beecher

We last heard Mr. Beecher at the Anti-Slavery meeting in the Tabernacle, where the Rynders' boys made themselves so

[1] Sixteen of these brief articles were contributed by Whitman to the Brooklyn *Daily Advertizer*, a Whig paper, between May 18 and June 6, 1850. From one to four citizens were "noticed" in each article. Whitman's name is not given, but much of this material was worked over in the "Brooklyniana" and a little of it in the *Times* article on "Reminiscences of Brooklyn" (*post*, II, pp. 1–5). It is probable that Whitman also wrote the "Church Sketches" which appeared in the *Advertizer* about the same time at the rate of one a week, and which were published in the form of an illustrated booklet, "The City of Churches Illustrated," by the *Advertizer* press, in 1850. These new features of the paper were introduced shortly after the size of the sheet and its general make-up had been greatly improved. They had much to do with the sudden increase of the circulation of the paper at the time. It is also probable that certain other articles in it are from Whitman's pen, but they do not differ materially, in style or content, from those of the *Eagle* period.

The paragraph sketch of Henry Ward Beecher is given as a type of them all, because it shows that Whitman knew and admired Beecher several years before the publication of the "Leaves" (*Cf*. "With Walt Whitman in Camden," II. p. 471,) and also that he was attending not merely Free-soil but Abolition meetings. The other local personages mentioned, in paragraphs of varying lengths, are: Gen. Jeremiah Johnson, Col. Alden Spooner, Thomas Kirk, Jacob Patchen, Andre Parmentier, Samuel Willoughby, H. P. Waring, Norris L. Martin, Losee Van Nostrand, Elijah Lewis, Samuel Smith, Dr. Samuel Cox, the Rev. T. B. Thayer, the Rev. Mr. Spear, the Rev. Evan M. Johnson, Nathan B. Morse, Seymour L. Husted, Elias Pelletreau, Mr. Hartshorne, Samuel E. Clements, H. B. Pierrepont, George Hall, Judge Greenwood, Wm. M. Harris, Adrian

useful in standing up for the credit of themselves, and the city at large.[1]

Refinement and artistical beauty of style, Mr. Beecher has not. We somewhat wonder at this, for his written compositions are models of nervous beauty and classical proportion—being equal to many of the standard English authors. But refinement or not, you soon feel that a strong man is exercising his powers before you. Indeed, it has sometimes been to us, perhaps, a little more refreshing that his bold masculine discourses were *without* that prettiness and correctness of style that, say what we will, is very often accompanied by emptiness and something very akin to effeminacy.

On the occasion alluded to, Mr. Beecher, soon after the commencement of his remarks, was furiously responded to, after making a statement, by "That's a lie!" from one of the rowdies in the gallery. For a moment he turned pale—and, we have no doubt, felt the insult keenly. But abuse and prosecution [persecution?] are the spears that prick such men as Beecher on. He proceeded with his remarks, and made a very vigorous speech.[2]

Carried away by his ardor and depth of conviction, on such occasions, and repelling with the fire of an unjustly accused spirit, the taunts of those who assault him, Mr. Beecher is no doubt apt to show too palpably how the wounds smart. In one sense we honor him for it. But still we would, if we might take such a liberty, advise more coolness, even contempt or indifference, towards those who violently assault him.

The Plymouth Church, the new place of worship where Mr. B. officiates, is one of the amplest in the United States, and is always filled with a congregation when the pastor preaches. It occupies the site of the oldest Presbyterian Church of the city which, some time since, having been slightly injured by fire, was torn down to make room for the present one.

Hegeman, Cyrus P. Smith, George W. Stilwell, Rodney S. Church, the Hon. Edward Copeland, Tunis G. Bergen, John G. Cammeyer, Hiram Barney, E. J. Bartow, Jonathan Trotter, Augustus and John B. Graham, Samuel Fleet, Joseph Moser, Alfred G. Stevens, B. W. Davis, Thomas G. Gerald, John Dikeman, Joseph W. Harper, and B. W. Delamater.

The sketch of Beecher appeared in the *Advertizer* of May 25.

[1] At the annual meeting of American and Foreign Anti-Slavery Society, on May 9, 1850.

[2] A somewhat fuller account of this incident is to be found in Beecher and Scoville's "A Biography of Henry Ward Beecher," New York, 1888, pp. 252–253.

SOMETHING ABOUT ART AND BROOKLYN ARTISTS[1]

THOUGH the collection of paintings of the Brooklyn Art Union now open, includes none approaching to the highest order of merit, it is nevertheless a very agreeable collection, and contains some works of taste and talent. The association is composed mostly of young artists, who have the matter in their own hands, and, by means of judges, committees, and so forth, decide upon the pictures to be purchased, the prices to be paid, and the different other means of encouraging the painters, as well as advancing the prosperity of the "establishment." This thing of encouragement, 'specially of encouragement to the younger race of artists, commends the Brooklyn Art Union to the good will and patronage of the public. A great reason why the very large majority of our painters are distressingly feeble, is, the absence of enough of such encouragement. How would the cause of education stand now, were it not for the powerful favor which is extended to it from so many quarters, apart from those who are directly interested?

Nor is it too much to say, that nearly the same reasons which exist to compel this favor and sustenance in behalf of public education, will, if carried out, give some portion of the like wafting influences, to refined art. If we are bound, as we are by general acknowledgement, to furnish a fair education to all the children of the people, why not go a step further, and do something to add grace to that education—a polish to the raw jaggedness of the common school routine? Nearly all intelligent boys and girls have much of the artist in them, and it were beautiful to give them an opportunity of developing it in one of the fine arts.

At any rate, it seems to me that some organization of power to speak with decision, and to bring light out of the present darkness, is very much needed. For there are at the present moment ten thousand so-called artists, young and old, in this country, many of whom are working in the dark, as it were, and without aim. They want a strong hand over them. Here is a case for the imperial scepter, even in America. It is only a

[1] From the New York *Evening Post*, February 1, 1851. This is introduced with the words, "A correspondent furnishes us with the following," and appears on the editorial page. It is signed "W. W."

This criticism was reprinted, in part, in my article "Walt Whitman at Thirty-One," in the New York *Evening Post* Book Review, Saturday, June 26, 1920.

A LETTER FROM BROOKLYN[1]

Brooklyn, March 21st.

To the Editors of the Evening Post:

That part of our city called South Brooklyn, will soon present such a changed appearance, as to leave very few of the old landmarks, the hills, or natural broken places. Bergen Hill is already nearly gone; large marble houses stand where it used to slope; while swarms of sappers and miners will soon leave no sign of the noble bluff that has hitherto jutted out as a northwestern point of the graceful little cove called Gowanus Bay. It is a sad thing to lose this beautiful bluff. They fill up the shores with it, preparatory to running out piers and wharves.

In the neighborhood of the Atlantic Dock, an immense tract has been reclaimed from the water, by this filling-up process. Streets intersect it, and the prices of lots range from three hundred to fifteen hundred dollars. Hundreds of the lots are owned by the Atlantic Dock Company, who occasionally put up a batch of them at auction.

Probably this will be (the parts immediately adjacent to the dock) quite a site for manufacturing places. It has a great many advantages that way, and there is already one large manufactory there. The immense storehouses on the interior of the dock would have answered for Joseph to store the grain of Egypt, preparatory to the year of famine.

All this part of Brooklyn will have, when settled, a look of newness and modern style. For every house will have been built within the last few years. The upper streets, in the neighhorhood of Court Street, are quite of the plebeian order. Reservations are made, when the lots are sold, which cause all the houses to be of large and costly structure. Just north and east of Hamilton avenue, by the ferry, there are many very pleasant and genteel rows of houses.—Nearly all of the men who occupy them do business in New York.

Hamilton ferry is rapidly becoming one of the great channels of travel; it grows even more rapidly than the South ferry did.

---

[1] From the New York *Evening Post*, March 21, 1851.

This letter is signed "W.," and is clearly Whitman's, not only because it belongs to a period when he is known to have been writing for the *Evening Post*, but also because of the similarity between its style and content and the "Brooklyniana," to say nothing of the *Eagle* editorials. Moreover, it promises the letters from "Paumanok," easily identified as Whitman's.

It is already a much more agreeable line to cross than the Main street or Hudson avenue ferry, and will doubtless be added to, as the neighborhood which gives it sustenance shall increase.

Hamilton avenue will eventually be the principal road to Greenwood Cemetery. It is somewhat remarkable that it has not become so already. It is direct, and much shorter than any other way.

Over the Penny Bridge, and along a winding road which is nothing more than a wide dam, one reaches Third avenue, the principal thoroughfare of those *diggins,* and which generally goes by the name of Greenwood. It has lately been raised, graded, and handsomely paved, thus becoming one of the widest and finest of streets, stretching away off toward New Utrecht, along by the shore where the beautiful residences are.

Greenwood Cemetery has lately established a new general entrance, some half a mile beyond the former one, that being used merely for funerals. The old one is far the more grand and impressive. Indeed, it is doubtful whether there is a finer or more nobly picturesque scene, of its sort, any where to be found, than that old entrance to Greenwood.

The Fifth avenue, a long and wide street, which was opened and put in barely travelling order a year or two since, yet remains unpaved and unregulated. This is a pity, for it is a high, fine street, and would make an agreeable part of a drive.

The old brick house, with "1-6-9-9" on its gable end,[1] stands upon Fifth avenue. This is a famous old house, and when I can get hold of the right-sort of persons among the old Dutchmen, I intend to pump forth all that is attributed to, or connected with, that house, in the way of reminiscence, ghost-story, and such like. We have too few of those treasures, to let any of them slide away, when they can be arrested.

A good deal of the local character of the South Ferry neighborhood, comes from its being the terminus of the Long Island Railroad. This unfortunate property will, one day, without doubt, become very valuable. As the land fills up—and it is filling up, all along the road, with numerous little villages and settlements—the cars will have more and steadier passengers. Certain serious financial troubles, under which the company has labored for some time past, have been settled much less injuriously to the concern than was feared, and the road is now

[1] *Cf. post*, p. II, 226.

under fair auspices again. It is intended, the coming summer, to run two through trains between the extremities of the road, daily.

With this means of travel, running like a backbone through Long Island, and the numerous steamboat lines on the sound, who shall say that old Paumanok is not accessible? And let it be also said, by one who has learned the same from his own investigations, that many summer travellers go farther and fare worse. The eastern parts of Long Island are rich mines for those who love original and peculiar character; as I purpose to show, in notes to the *Evening Post*, some time during the summer. For thither I wend my way with the hot season, and like it far better than I could ever like Saratoga or Newport.

ART AND ARTISTS[1]

Remarks of Walt Whitman, before the Brooklyn Art Union, on the Evening of March 31, 1851

Among such a people as the Americans, viewing most things with an eye to pecuniary profit—more for acquiring than for enjoying or well developing what they acquire—ambitious of the physical rather than the intellectual; a race to whom matter of fact is everything, and the ideal nothing—a nation of whom the steam engine is no bad symbol—he does a good work who, pausing in the way, calls to the feverish crowd that in the life we live upon this beautiful earth, there may, after all, be something vaster and better than dress and the table, and business and politics.

There was an idle Persian hundreds of years ago who wrote poems; and he was accosted by one who believed more in thrift.—"Of what use are you?" inquired the supercilious son of traffic. The poet turning plucked a rose and said, "Of what use is this?" "To be beautiful, to perfume the air," answered the man of gains. "And I," responded the poet, "am of use to perceive its beauty and to smell its perfume."

It is the glorious province of Art, and of all Artists worthy the name, to disentangle from whatever obstructs it, and nourish in the heart of man, the germ of the perception of the truly great, the beautiful and the simple.

[1] From the Brooklyn *Daily Advertizer*, April 3, 1851.

When God, according to the myth, finished Heaven and Earth—when the lustre of His effulgent light pierced the cold and terrible darkness that had for cycles of ages covered the face of the deep—when the waters gathered themselves together into one place and made the sea—and the dry land appeared with its mountains and its infinite variety of valley, shore and plain—when in the sweetness of that primal time the unspeakable splendor of the sunrise first glowed on the bosom of the earth—when the stars hung at night afar off in this most excellent canopy, the air, pure, solemn, eternal—when the waters and the earth obeyed the command to bring forth abundantly, the beasts of the field, the birds of the air and the fishes of the sea—and when, at last, the superb perfection, Man, appeared, epitome of all the rest, fashioned after the Father and Creator of all—then God looked forth and saw everything that he had made, and pronounced it good. Good because ever reproductive of its first beauty, finish and freshness. For just as the Lord left it remains yet the beauty of His work. It is now spring. Already the sun has warmed the blood of this old yet ever youthful earth and the early trees are budding and the early flowers beginning to bloom:

> There is not lost, one of Earth's charms
> Upon her bosom yet
> After the flight of untold centuries,
> The freshness of her far beginning lies
> And still shall lie.[1]

With this freshness—with this that the Lord called good—the Artist has to do.—And it is a beautiful truth that all men contain something of the artist in them. And perhaps it is sometimes the case that the greatest artists live and die, the world and themselves alike ignorant what they possess. Who would not mourn that an ample palace of surpassingly graceful architecture, filled with luxuries and gorgeously embellished with fair pictures and sculpture, should stand cold and still and vacant, and never be known and enjoyed by its owner?

[1] A reprint of this speech in the Brooklyn *Daily Eagle* (July 14, 1900) failed to preserve as verse this quotation from Bryant's "Forest Hymn." The error was not corrected in Professor Perry's "Walt Whitman," he having access only to the *Eagle* reprint. But the correct version is interesting in that it shows how, by a slight alteration in the arrangement of the lines of Bryant, Whitman managed to secure an effect not unlike that of the new verse on which he was then working. It will be remembered that Whitman himself had experimented a little in blank verse. (See *infra*, pp. 19-20.)

Would such a fact as this cause your sadness? Then be sad. For there is a palace, to which the courts of the most sumptuous kings are but a frivolous patch, and, though it is always waiting for them, not one in thousands of its owners ever enters there with any genuine sense of its grandeur and glory.

To the artist, I say, has been given the command to go forth into all the world and preach the gospel of beauty. The perfect man is the perfect artist, and it cannot be other-wise.[1] For in the much that has been said of Nature and Art there is mostly the absurd error of considering the two as dis-tinct. Rousseau, himself, in reality one of the most genuine artists, starting from his false point, ran into his beautiful en-comiums upon nature and his foolish sarcasms upon art. To think of what happened when that restless and daring spirit ceased to animate one of the noblest apostles of democracy, is itself answer enough to all he ever said in condemnation of art. The shadows from the west were growing longer, as Rousseau, at the close of a beautiful summer day, felt death upon him. "Let me behold once more the glorious setting sun," was his last request. With his eyes turned toward the more than im-perial pomp and with the soft and pure harmonies of nature around him, his wild and sorrowful life came to an end, and he departed peacefully and happily. Do you think Rousseau would have passionately enjoyed the sunset, those clouds, the beauty, and the natural graces there, had such things as art and artists never existed? Was not his death made happier than his life, by what he so often ridiculed in life?

Nay, may not death itself, through the prevalence of a more artistic feeling among the people, be shorn of many of its frightful and ghastly features? In the temple of the Greeks, Death and his brother Sleep, were depicted as beautiful youths reposing in the arms of Night. At other times Death was rep-resented as a graceful form, with calm but drooping eyes, his feet crossed and his arms leaning on an inverted torch. Such were the soothing and solemnly placed influences which true

[1] This is not the place to enter in detail into a study of Whitman's indebtedness to Emerson; but inasmuch as the date and the extent of that indebtedness have been matters of dispute, it is necessary here to call attention to the close kinship between the ideas and the treatment of this address and Emerson's earlier work. This essay seems to have been written under the inspiration, first, of the lecture referred to, and second, of "The American Scholar" and "The Divinity School Address," the artist being sub-stituted for the scholar without affecting the Emersonian nature-philosophy in the least. Even the anecdote of the "idle Persian," though it may not have come through Emerson, reads like a prose "Rhodora." *Cf. infra*, p. 132.

art, identical with a perception of the beauty that there is in all the ordinations as well as all the works of Nature, cast over the last fearful thrill of those olden days. Was it not better so? Or is it better to have before us the idea of our dissolution, typified by the spectral horror upon the pale horse, by a grinning skeleton or a mouldering skull?

The beautiful artist principle sanctifies that community which is pervaded by it. A halo surrounds forever that nation. —There have been nations more warlike than the Greeks. Germany has been and is more intellectual. Inventions, physical comforts, wealth and enterprize are prodigiously greater in all civilized nations now than they were among the countrymen of Alcibiades and Plato. But never was there such an artistic race.

At a neighboring city, the other evening was given, by a lecturer,[1] a beautiful description of this character, making it a model that few in these days would think of successfully copying. The Greek form, he described as perfect, the mind well cultivated as to those things which are useful and pleasing; the man, as familiar with the history of his country, not seeking office for his emoluments or dignity, believing that no office confers dignity upon him who bears it, but that the true dignity of office arises from the character of the man who holds it, and the manner in which he administers it. He is not elated with honors or discomposed with ill success,—pursues his course with firmness, yet with moderation; and seeks not honors or profit for the services rendered his country, which he loves better than himself. He is neither penurious nor extravagant; does not court the rich nor stand aloof from the poor. He can appreciate excellence whether clothed in the apparel of the affluent or of the indigent; is no respector of persons, remembering that manly worth cannot be monopolized by any circle of society. He can mingle in festive scenes, and seek in them the feasts of *reason* as well as the flow of soul;[2] his entertainments are pre-

---

[1] This was perhaps Daniel Huntington's address before the American Artists' Association, in New York, on the evening of March 11. His subject was "Christian Art," and the lecture was repeated for the benefit of the public on March 25. Or Whitman might have had in mind Parke Godwin's lecture on "The Philosophy of Art," delivered before the Academy of Design on March 10. The press reports that I have found are too scanty to make identification easy.

[2] *Cf.* Pope's "The feast of reason and the flow of soul" ("The First Satire of the Second Book of Horace," l. 128.)

pared for the intellect as well as the physical appetite. The lyre and song, the harp and recital of heroic verse—sculpture, painting, music, poetry, as well as grave philosophical discourse—each in its turn becomes the channel of a refined and elevated pleasure. As a soldier, he acts upon the principle that "thrice is he armed who has his quarrel just,"[1] and appeals to force only when negotiations fail, but then with terrific energy. He counts no sacrifice too great for his country. Dying, his proudest boast is, that "no Athenian, through his means, ever had cause to put on mourning."

Yes, distracted by frippery, cant, and vulgar selfishness—sick even of the "intelligence of the age"—it refreshes the soul to bring up again one of that glorious and manly and beautiful nation, with his sandals, his flowing drapery, his noble and natural attitudes and the serene composure of his features. Imagination loves to dwell there, revels there, and will not turn away. There the artist appetite is gratified; and there all ages have loved to turn as to one of the most perfect ideals of man.

The orthodox specimen of the man of the present time, approved of public opinion and the tailor, stands he under the glance of art as stately? His contempt for all there is in the world, except money can be made of it;[2] his utter vacuity of anything more important to him as a man than success in "business,"—his religion what is written down in the books, or preached to him as he sits in his rich pew, by one whom he pays a round sum, and thinks it a bargain,—his only interest in affairs of state, getting offices or jobs for himself or someone who pays him—so much for some points of his character.

Then see him in all the perfection of fashionable tailordom—the tight boot with the high heel; the trousers, big at the ankle, on some rule inverting the ordinary ones of grace; the long large cuffs, and thick stiff collar of his coat—the swallow-tailed coat, on which dancing masters are inexorable; the neck swathed in many bands, giving support to the modern high and pointed shirt collar, that fearful sight to an approaching enemy—the modern shirt collar, bold as Columbus, stretching off into the unknown distance—and then to crown all, the fashionable hat, before which language has nothing to say, because sight is the only thing that can begin to do it justice—and we have indeed a model for the sculptor. Think of it; a piece of Italian marble,

---

[1] Cf. "Thrice is he arm'd that hath his quarrel just" ("King Henry VI," Pt. 2, III, 2).
[2] Cf. infra, pp. 37–39, iii, 123–125; post, II, p. 63, 67.

chiselled away till it gets to the shape of all this, hat included, and then put safely under storage as our contribution to the future ages, taste for our artistical proportion, grace, and harmony of form.[1]

I think of few heroic actions which cannot be traced to the artistical impulse. He who does great deeds, does them from his sensitiveness to moral beauty. Such men are not merely artists, they are artistic material. Washington in some great crisis, Lawrence in the bloody deck of the *Chesapeake*, Mary Stewart[2] at the block, Kossuth in captivity and Mazzini in exile, —all great rebels and innovators, especially if their intellectual majesty bears itself out with calmness amid popular odium or circumstances of cruelty and an infliction of suffering, exhibit the highest phases of the artistic spirit. A sublime moral beauty is present to them, and they realize them. It may be almost said to emanate from them. The painter, the sculptor, the poet express heroic beauty better in description; for description is their trade, and they have learned it. But the others *are* heroic beauty, the best beloved of art.

Talk not so much, then, young artist, of the great old masters, who but painted and chiselled. Study not only their productions. There is a still better, higher school for him who would kindle his fire with coal from the altar of the loftiest and purest art. It is the school of all grand actions and grand virtues, of heroism, of the death of captives and martyrs—of all the mighty deeds written in the pages of history—deeds of daring, and enthusiasm, and devotion, and fortitude. Read well the death of Socrates, and of a greater than Socrates. Read how slaves have battled against their oppressors—how the bullets of tyrants have, since the first king ruled, never been able to put down the unquenchable thirst of man for his rights.

In the sunny peninsula where Art was transplanted from Greece and, generations afterward, flourished into new life, we even now see the growth that is to be expected among a people pervaded by love and appreciation of beauty. In Naples, in Rome, in Venice, that ardor for liberty which is a constituent

---

[1] *Cf. infra*, pp. 162–163.

[2] When Whitman selected a fragment of this speech as one of the "Pieces in Early Youth" which he preserved in his "Complete Prose" (pp. 371–372), he not only corrected this error in spelling, but otherwise altered and improved this paragraph and the following one. Probably he possessed at that time only a stray page of the manuscript for certainly he could have selected few things from his writings before 1855 which better deserved to be preserved entire than this speech.

part of all well developed artists and without which a man cannot be such, has had a struggle—a hot and baffled one. The inexplicable destinies have shaped it so. The dead lie in their graves; but their august and beautiful enthusiasm is not dead:—

> Those corpses of young men,
> Those martyrs that hung from the gibbets,
> Those hearts pierced by the gray lead,
> Cold and motionless as they seem,
> Live elsewhere with undying vitality;
> They live in other young men, O kings,
> They live in brothers again ready to defy you;
> They were purified by death,
> They were taught and exalted.
> Not a grave of those slaughtered ones,
> But is growing its seed of freedom,
> In its turn to bear seed,
> Which the winds shall carry afar and re-sow,
> And the rain nourish.
> Not a disembodied spirit
> Can the weapons of tyrants let loose,
> But it shall stalk invisibly over the earth,
> Whispering, counseling, cautioning.[1]

I conclude here.—As there can be no true Artist, without a glowing thought for freedom, so freedom pays the artist back again many fold, and under her umbrage Art must sooner or later tower to its loftiest and most perfect proportions.

LETTERS FROM PAUMANOK
[No. 1][2]

Greenport, L. I., June 25.

THE PLACE AND ITS SURROUNDINGS

SWARMING and multitudinous as the population of the city still is, there are many thousands of its usual inhabitants now absent in the country. Some are sent away by the hot weather,

---

[1] Quoted from Whitman's own early free-verse poem, "Resurgemus," (*infra*, pp.27–30).

[2] From the New York *Evening Post*, June 27, 1851.
This letter is signed "N," perhaps a typographical error.

many by "the prevailing custom"; others again by desire for change.

Having neither the funds nor disposition to pass my little term of ruralizing at the fashionable baths, or watering places, I am staying awhile down here at Greenport, the eastern point of the Long Island Railroad. That is, my lodging is at Greenport; but, in truth, I "circulate" in all directions around.

Greenport is celebrated for its good harbor, its salt water, and its fish. The kind of the latter now most plentiful is the poggy (sometimes misspelt porgie[1]). It is a good fish, and easily caught. The black fish are just beginning to come in. The blue fish, however, are the most delicious, to my taste. Cooked while perfectly fresh, and not salted till fried, or broiled, they are fit for the most refined epicure.

The fish in Peconic Bay and its neighborhood are not quite so abundant as last season.[2] Still, there are enough to reward the labor of the sportsmen.

How I Amuse Myself

The best amusements in a country place, by the salt water, are the cheapest. Generally, the one who takes the most trouble to obtain pleasure, gets the least, or that which is most questionable.

Now, for instance, the fields, the waters, the trees, the interesting specimens of humanity to be scared up in all quarters of this diggins—all are, for me, ministers to entertainment.

Can there be any thing of the old gossip in my composition? For I hugely like to accost the originals I see all around me, and to set them agoing about themselves and their neighbors near by. It is more refreshing than a comedy at any of the New York theatres. The very style of their talk is a treat.

Bathing in this clear, pure, salt water, twice every day, is one of my best pleasures. Generally the water is so clear that you can see to a considerable depth. I must have the

---

[1]Whitman is, of course, in error; *porgie* is the more common spelling, though *poggy* is also correct.

[2]If this statement were based on Whitman's personal experience, it would establish definitely where he was during the summer of 1850, a matter concerning which biography is as yet largely in the dark.

bump of "aquativeness"[1] large; dear to me is a souse in the waves. Dear, oh, dear to me is Coney Island! Rockaway, too, and many other parts of sea-girt Paumanok.

Some Folks' Way of "Going in the Country"

Now all the public houses, and not a few of the private houses, in this section of Long Island, are beginning to be filled with boarders—men, women, and children—particularly the latter. It is a pity that these folks don't enjoy themselves in a more free and easy manner. They evidently preserve all the ceremoniousness of the city—dress regularly for dinner, fear to brown their faces with the sun, or wet their shoes with the dew, or let the wind derange the well sleeked precision of their hair.

Indeed, for all the good they get, they might just as well remain in a New York or Brooklyn boarding-house; except that they are a little more crowded here, perhaps. They hardly derive even the benefit of the pure air, for they remain in the house nearly all day.

I am convinced that there are really very few people who know how to enjoy the country, either for its land or water accommodations. Not many even of its permanent residents do.

Gentility in Country Boarding Houses

While I am upon such matters, let me give a word of advice to those who conduct the country boarding houses. People don't so much want any attempts at gentility in your places; to which they ought to come for relief from the glare and stiffness of the city. We folks from the region of pavements are too much used to pianos, fashionable carpets, mahogany chairs, to be seriously impressed by them when we go in the country. We would as leave, during the hot weather, when we stay among you, even be without carpets, pianos and flummery. Only let us have plenty of cleanliness, water by the wholesale, and abundance of the rich fresh fare of your country dairy, and country gardens.

[1] A humorous reference to the new science of phrenology, as it was then called, by which Whitman was really much impressed, having had his own head analyzed in detail.
    See "In Re Walt Whitman," p. 25. It was from the terminology of the phrenologists that Whitman selected a word to denote the manly friendship which inspires the "Calamus" poems—"adhesiveness."

LETTERS FROM PAUMANOK
[No. 2][1]

Greenport, L. I., June 28th.

A VILLAGE WITH A NEW NAME

THE turnpike on the peninsula of which Orient, (formerly Oysterponds,) is the eastern point, is a pleasant and thrifty looking road. It is laid quite thickly with farm cottages, none of them very grand in their appearance; but then there are hardly any that seem remarkably mean, either.

One new and costly house, on the north side of the turnpike, is the residence of Dr. Lord, formerly member of Congress, and the owner of large tracts of land here.

Strolling on through the neighborhood, I came to a thicker collection of houses, formerly known as Rocky Point, but now christened with the more romantic appellation of "Marion."

Very great confusion arises on Long Island, from the numerosity of names, belonging to one and the same place. Hardly one fourth of the neighborhoods retain the same names for twenty years in succession! Letters, packages, and even travellers are constantly getting lost, through this unfortunate propensity.

I MAKE THE ACQUAINTANCE OF AN OLD FELLOW

As I was passing the "store" at Marion, I was accosted by an old fellow, with a pipe in his mouth, and a clam-basket and hoe in his hands. He had evidently put a dram or two into his stomach, more than it could cleverly stand; but it probably made him better company than he would have been without the liquor.

I must give you a description of him, for I responded to his salute and we walked on a way together.

His trousers were originally bright blue homespun, but they had long since seen their good times, and were now variegated with patches of many colors—particularly about the "seat," which was of the style that tailors call "baggy." His vest was of a spotted dirt color, and of a cut like those you see worn

[1] From the New York *Evening Post*, June 28, 1851.

This letter and that on pp. 255–259 (*post*, I) were signed "Paumanok." *Cf.* "Complete Prose," p. 335; *infra*, p. 180, note 2; *post*, II, 277–278.

by Turkish slaves, or by "supes" in a melo-drama, at the
Bowery Theatre. Its points hung down in front. The figure
of the old man was short, squat and round-shouldered, but of
Herculean bone and muscle. His hair was not very gray, and
he showed palpable signs of strength.

But his hat! It was a hat which I am sorry now I did not
buy up and present to one of the Broadway "merchants" in
that line, or to the eating house near the Fulton ferry, whose
window has such amusing curiosities. It was a truly wonder-
ful hat! It was not a large hat; neither could it have been called
a small hat. It was unquestionably a very old hat, however.
It had probably stood the storms of many winters, and the sun
of many summers. Yet it held itself tolerably erect, with
various undulations and depressions in its surface; but an un-
fortunate paucity of brim. True, there was an apology for a
brim, but it was a very narrow apology. It was laughable
to see that hat!

While the old man was telling us that he owned a certain
windmill, which we were then and there passing, and that he
was now on his way to get a basket of soft clams, for bait to catch
fish, a waggon came along, in which he was furnished with a
ride, and so left us.

THE ROAD—THE BRIDGE—THE FISH

The various windows of Rocky Point doubtless exhibit a
flitting array of heads on all occasions of strangers passing.
It was, therefore, the case, that our walk, for a while, was quite
a public passage. Indeed, had there been a little hurrahing, we
might, (my companion and I,) have fancied ourselves some dis-
tinguished people, taking the honors.

A bend in the road brought us to an old mill, on the broad
railing of whose bridge I sat down to rest. Underneath, as I
leaned over, I saw in the stream myriads of little fish endeav-
oring to get up, but balked by an obstruction, and apparently
in council, as if at a loss what to do. The water was as clear
as glass.

Directly two or three large eels crawled lazily along, wriggling
their tails, and sucking up whatever they found on the bottom.
Then came a couple of little black fish; after which a real big
one, twenty inches long, opening his great white mouth, and
behaving in a very hoggish manner. Also, there were crabs, and
divers small fry.

Had I possessed a hook and line, there is no telling what feats might have been performed.

A couple of rods from the shore, and near at hand, was the old gentleman, with the remarkable hat; he had arrived before us, and was busily engaged with his hoe, digging a basket of soft clams, "for bait," as he said. He procured quite a mess in fifteen minutes, and then brought them up, and sat down on the bridge by me, to rest himself.

A Colloquy—"Aunt Rebby"

Lighting his pipe very deliberately, he proceeded to catechise me as to my name, birth-place, and lineage—where I was from last, where I was staying, what my occupation was, and so on. Having satisfied himself on these important points, I thought it no more than fair to return the compliment in kind, and so pitched into him.

He was born on the spot where he now lived; that very same Rocky Point. He was sixty-seven years old. For twenty years he had kept a butcher's stall in Fly Market, in New York, and left that business to move back on the "old homestead."

He volunteered the information that he was a Universalist in his religious belief, and asked my opinion upon the merits of the preachers of that faith, Mr. Chapin, Mr. Thayer, Mr. Balch, and others. He also commenced what he probably intended for a religious argument; and there was no other way than for me to stop him off, by direct inquiries into the state of his family and his real estate.

He was "well off" in both respects, possessing a farm of over a hundred acres, running from the turnpike to the Sound, and being the father of numerous sons and daughters. He expatiated on the merits of his land at great length; and was just going into those of his bodily offspring, when our confab was fated to receive a sudden interruption. For at this moment came along an old woman with a little tin kettle in her hand.

"Aunt Rebby," at once exclaimed the old gentleman, "don't you know me?"

But Aunt Rebby seemed oblivious.

"Is it possible you don't know me? Why we've bussed one another many a time in our young days!"

A new light broke upon the dim eyes of the old dame.

"Why Uncle Dan'l!" cried she, "can this be you?"

Uncle Dan'l averred that it wasn't any body else.   And then ensued a long gossip, of which I was the edified and much-amused hearer.   They had not met each other, it seems, for years, and there needed to be a long interchange of news.

"What a fine mess of clams you've got," said the old lady.

"Yes," responded Uncle Dan'l.

"But I," rejoined the old lady, in a mournful voice—"I have no body to dig clams for me now."

"No, I s'pose not," said the other composedly; "your boys are all gone now."

Supposing that the "boys" had emigrated to California, or married and moved off, I ventured an inquiry as to where they had gone.

Three young men, all the sons of the old woman, had died of consumption.   The last was buried only a short time before.

Old times were talked of.   Aunt Rebby expressed it as her positive opinion that the young folks of the present day don't enjoy half as much fun as the young folks of fifty years ago, and a little longer, did.   She was seventy years old, and remembered the days of General Washington.   Those were jovial times, but now "it was all pride, fashion and ceremony."

At the mention of pride, Uncle Dan'l interrupted her with an invitation to look at him and his apparel, and say whether he furnished any exhibition of that vice.

We Return Homeward

The afternoon being now pretty far advanced, Aunt Rebby wended on her way towards the east; and the old man, with I and my companion, turned our courses westward.   The old fellow shouldered his heavy basket, which dripped down his back.

I made him tell me the personal history of the affairs of each family, as we passed the houses on our way.   But, although I was much amused and interested with the narration, perhaps your readers wouldn't be, and so I pass it by.

About twenty-eight months ago, the old man's two eldest sons, the one of 33, the other 24 years of age, had sailed off in the new and fine sloop "Long Island," bound for some port nearly down to Florida.   He had never heard from them since. They were lost in a terrible storm that came up while they were out at sea. They owned half the sloop, which was worth $5000.

When we arrived at the old fellow's house, he invited us in and treated us to good berries. And so, at sundown, we had a nice cool walk of three miles, back to our quarters.

A PLEA FOR WATER [1]

WITH all the vaunted beauty and wholesomeness of Brooklyn, as a place of residence, our having no water better than pump-water, is enough to put us down below twenty other places, otherwise every way inferior to us. Reader, have you ever thought what this pump stuff really is?

Imagine all the accumulations of filth in a great city—not merely the slops and rottenness thrown in the streets and byways (and never thoroughly carried away)—but the numberless privies, cess-pools, sinks and gulches of abomination—the perpetual replenishing of all this mass of effete matter—the unnameable and immeasurable dirt that is ever, ever, ever filtered into the earth, through its myriad pores, and which as surely finds its way to the neighborhood of pump-water, and *into* pump-water, as that a drop of poison put in one part of the vascular system, gets into the whole system. Think of a drink, compounded of all these, and hardly one part of it clear, pure, and natural. Think of this delectable mixture being daily and hourly taken into our stomachs, our veins, our blood.

The report of the Committee of Inquiry who recommended the Croton Aqueduct (a far nobler token for New York than even her steamships, with the Trinity Churches to boot,) showed enough facts, and demonstrated realities coming home to the experience of every body who drinks water, to horrify the strongest stomach that ever existed within human ribs! I would have some Brooklyn paper get, and reprint, the essential parts of that report. [2]

Every few months there is much ados about swill-milk; (and

[1] This is a signed article in the Brooklyn *Daily Advertiser*, June 28, 1851. Whitman prided himself on the efforts he had put forth to secure for Brooklyn a good system of water works (see "Diary in Canada," pp. 64–65; Ostrander, *loc. cit*, II, p. 89). Whitman's brother Jeff was employed by "Chief Kirkwood" in the survey for and the construction of the Brooklyn water works (see "Complete Prose," p. 513).

[2] As Whitman himself had done in the *Eagle*, July 1, 1846.

the more that manufacture is shown up the better). And every body knows that rum, in all its varieties, is the declared foe of a large class of our people; and, for our part, the more they cry aloud and belabor the enemy, the better luck I wish them. But rum and bad milk are not as nasty as city pump-water; which is truly the most stinking and villainous liquid known, upon land or sea.

This hot weather, if you let a pail of pump-water stand a couple of hours, any sensitive nose must turn away, when the mouth under it drinks thereof.[1]

An abundant supply of clean, sweet, soft, wholesome water! I can conceive of no physical comfort more important. It is not only wanted for drinking, but for bathing, washing, cooking, sprinkling and cleaning streets, and so on. It is wanted to save this half-wooden city from ruinous conflagrations. Say, you heroic dare-devils who man the engines, how often have you been balked and dismayed, less by the furious flames than by the absence of water to put them out? I have still more to say another time.[2]

LETTERS FROM PAUMANOK
[No. 3][3]

Brooklyn, August 11.

THE hot day[4] was over at last; though the opera at Castle Garden did not commence till eight; and even had it not been leisure enough and to spare, was there any escape from those imperial commands in the west? So with wool-hat crushed in my hand behind me, for the sundown breezes felt good, there on old "Clover Hill," (modernized Brooklyn Heights,) I took my time, and expanded to the glory spread over heaven and earth.

Sails of sloops bellied gracefully upon the river, with mellower light and deepened shadows. And the dark and glistening water formed an undertone to the play of vehement color above.

-----

[1] Unfortunately, Whitman does not explain how this feat is to be accomplished.

[2] I can find no other signed articles on the subject in the *Advertizer*, nor any other that is clearly Whitman's; but the subject was frequently aired during his editorship of the Brooklyn *Daily Times*.

From the New York *Evening Post*, August 14, 1851.

It was reprinted, in part, in my article "Walt Whitman at Thirty-One" in the New York *Evening Post* Book Review, Saturday, June 26, 1920.

[4] "*La Favorita*" was produced at the Castle Garden on Friday evening, August 8.

Rapidly, an insatiable greediness grew within me for brighter and stronger hues; oh, brighter and stronger still. It seemed as if all that the eye could bear, were unequal to the fierce voracity of my soul for intense, glowing color.

And yet there were the most choice and fervid fires of the sunset, in their brilliancy and richness almost terrible.

Have not you, too, at such a time, known this thirst of the eye? Have not you, in like manner, while listening to the well-played music of some band like Maretzek's,[1] felt an overwhelming desire for measureless sound—a sublime orchestra of a myriad orchestras—a colossal volume of harmony, in which the thunder might roll in its proper place; and above it, the vast, pure Tenor,—identity of the Creative Power itself—rising through the universe, until the boundless and unspeakable capacities of that mystery, the human soul, should be filled to the uttermost, and the problem of human cravingness be satisfied and destroyed?[2]

Of this sort are the promptings of good music upon me. How is it possible, that among the performers there, with their instruments, are some who can jest, and giggle, and look flippantly over the house meanwhile? And even good singers upon the stage beyond them, you may see presently, who will mar their parts with quizzing and ill-timed smiles, and looks of curiosity at the amount of their audience.

Come, I will not talk to you as to one of the superficial crowd who saunter here because it is a fashion; who take opera glasses with them, and make you sick with shallow words, upon the sublimest and most spiritual of the arts. I will trust you with confidence; I will divulge secrets.

The delicious music of "the Favorite," is upon us. Gradually, we see not this huge ampitheatre, nor the cropped heads and shaved faces of the men; nor coal-skuttle bonnets; nor hear the rattle of fans, nor even the ill-bred chatter. We see the groves of a Spanish convent, and the procession of monks; we hear the chant, now dim and faint, then swelling loudly, and then again dying away among the trees. The aged Superior and the young Fernando, we see. In answer to the old man's rebukes and questions, we hear the story of love.

---

[1] Max Maretzek, manager of the Opera House in New York, and author of "Crotchets and Quavers, or Revelations of an Opera Manager in America," 1855.

[2] *Cf. post*, II, p. 85.

Those fresh vigorous tones of Bettini!—I have often wished to know this man, for a minute, that I might tell him how much of the highest order of pleasure he has conferred upon me. His voice has often affected me to tears. Its clear, firm, wonderfully exalting notes, filling and expanding away; dwelling like a poised lark up in heaven; have made my very soul tremble.— Critics talk of others who are more perfectly artistical—yes, as the well-shaped marble is artistical. But the singing of this man has breathing blood within it; the living soul, of which the lower stage they call art, is but the shell and sham.[1]

Yes, let me dwell a moment here. After travelling through the fifteen years' display in this city, of musical celebrities, from Mrs. Austin[2] up to Jenny Lind,[3] from Old Bull[4] on to conductor Benedict,[5] with much fair enjoyment of the talent of all; none have thoroughly satisfied, overwhelmed me, but this man. Never before did I realize what an indescribable volume of delight the recesses of the soul can bear from the sound of the honied perfection of the human voice. The *manly* voice it must be, too. The female organ, however curious and high, is but as the pleasant moonlight.

The Swedish Swan,[6] with all her blandishments, never touched my heart in the least. I wondered at so much vocal dexterity; and indeed they were all very pretty, those leaps and double somersets. But even in the grandest religious airs, genuine masterpieces as they are, of the German composers, executed by this strangely overpraised woman in perfect scientific style, let critics say what they like, it was a failure; for there was a vacuum in the head of the performance. Beauty pervaded it no doubt, and that of a high order. It was the beauty of Adam before God breathed into his nostrils.

Let us return to Balthazar, and his prophetic announcements. "Ah, Fernando," we hear him say, "this magnificent world, which allures you, is deceptive and false. The angel you now

---

[1] *Cf. infra*, pp. 104–106.

[2] A grand opera singer of the early 1830's.

[3] Jenny Lind took New York by storm with her singing at the Castle Garden in 1850, under the management of P. T. Barnum.

[4] Ole Bornemann Bull (1810–1880), a Norwegian violinist famous for his technical skill, who came to America five times, and who, for a short period in 1855, managed the New York Academy of Music.

[5] Sir Julius Benedict (1804–1885), a prominent operatic conductor from London, who conducted for Jenny Lind on her American tours.

[6] The "Swedish nightingale," Jenny Lind. (*Cf.* "Complete Prose," p. 516.)

love may prove treacherous. Yes, tossed by tempests, you will gladly seek again this haven of peace."

I always thought the plot of the "Favorite" a peculiarly well-proportioned and charming story. It is a type of the experience of the human kind, and, like Shakspeare's dramas, its moral is world-wide.

Fernando, young, enthusiastic, full of manly vigor, and at the same time of tenderness, trusted and loved a beautiful unknown woman. She, Leonara [Leonora], though the favorite and mistress of the king, returned the young man's love. Thus, he would not complete the burial of himself among the priesthood. He left the convent, and having received from Leonara a commission of rank in the army, joined the camp, and rendered such important services, that the king, in person, thanked him before the court. He, however, abruptly discovered the amour between his favorite and the young officer.

The king's own love was faithful, but the Papal court interfered, and Leonara confessing her genuine attachment to Fernando, the royal consent sealed their marriage. Previously to this, the disgraced woman had sent her lover a true account of herself; but it was intercepted, and Fernando immediately afterwards found that his idol was the cast-off mistress of the king.

All the indignant passions of his soul then broke forth. He upbraided the king with such perfidy, tore the golden order from his neck, broke his sword, and cast it at the monarch's feet, and retired in a fury of sorrow and disappointment, back into the shadows from which he had sallied forth into the world.

Now we approach the close of the legend. We see again the dark groves of the convent. Up through the venerable trees peal the strains of the chanting voices. Oh, sweet music of Donizetti, how can men hesitate what rank to give you!

With his pale face at the foot of the cross kneels the returned novice, his breast filled with a devouring anguish, his eyes showing the death that has fallen upon his soul. The strains of death, too, come plaintively from his lips. Never before did you hear such wonderful gushing sorrow, poured forth like ebbing blood, from a murdered heart. Is it for peace he prays with that appealing passion? Is it the story of his own sad wreck he utters?

Listen. Pure and vast, that voice now rises, as on clouds, to the heaven where it claims audience. Now, firm and unbroken, it spreads like an ocean around us.   Ah, welcome that I know not the mere language of the earthly words in which the melody is embodied; as all words are mean before the language of true music.

Thanks, great artist.   For one, at least, it is no extravagance to say, you have justified his ideal of the loftiest of the arts. Thanks, limner of the spirit of life, and hope and peace; of the red fire of passion, the cavernous vacancy of despair, and the black pall of the grave.

. I write as I feel; and I feel that there are not a few who will pronounce a Yes to my own confession.

SUNDAY RESTRICTIONS[1]

MEMORIAL IN BEHALF OF A FREER MUNICIPAL GOVERNMENT, AND AGAINST SUNDAY RESTRICTIONS

To the Common Council and Mayor of the City of Brooklyn:

With great respect, I present you the following considerations on the subject of Sunday Restrictions, and Municipal Policy; and ask, in behalf of myself and many other citizens, the permanent suspension of the clause against running the City Railcars every seventh day; and that all ordinances and movements to compel, by arrests, imprisonments and fines, the religious observance of the Sabbath, be repealed and desisted from; and, in general terms, that the government of Brooklyn take a more expanded scale and more uniformity and spirit.

[1] From the Brooklyn *Evening Star*, October 20, 1854.   Reprinted in the *Conservator*, November, 1903, Vol. XIV, p. 135.

The editor of the *Star* prefaced the memorial with these remarks: "We have received from their author, Walter Whitman, a copy of his memorial to the Common Council and Mayor, on some general and some special topics.   As this is a time when the matters it treats of are attracting considerable attention, and this paper desires to give a full field for discussion, we lay the memorial before our readers, for them to judge for themselves."

The memorial itself was presented to the Council on October 16 by Alderman Fowler. Apparently no action was taken on it.

The present memorial records no particular development in Whitman's conception of the proper function of government, being rather an application of political theories set forth some seven years before (see *infra*, pp. 166–168); but, appearing in 1854, it has a special significance in proving that its author was not so intent upon the creation of the poetry of democracy to be published the following year as himself to neglect what he considered the rights and duties of a citizen of a democratic country. *Cf.* "Song of the Broad-Axe," 1856, "Leaves of Grass," 1917, I, 228–230.

It is highly probable that an article in the Brooklyn *Daily Times* (March 14, 1857) arguing for Sunday cars and signed "W. W." was also written by Whitman.   But in such a collection as this, one essay must stand for both.

The security, peace, and decorum of the City are in charge of the authorities at all times, and are never to be intermitted any day of the week or year. It is likewise proper that they protect to every individual and religious congregation his or its right to worship, reasonably free from any noise or molestation.

The mere shutting off from the general body of the citizens the popular and cheap conveyance of the City Railroads, the very day when experience proves they want it most, and the obstinate direction of the whole executive and police force of Brooklyn into a contest with the keepers of public houses, news depots, cigar shops, bakeries, confectionary and eating saloons, and other places, whether they shall open or close on Sunday, are not in themselves matters of all engrossing importance. The stoppage of the Railcars causes much vexation and weariness to many families, especially in any communication to and from East Brooklyn, Williamsburg, Greenpoint, Bushwick, New Brooklyn, Bedford and Greenwood; and both stoppages do no earthly good. But beneath this the blunder rises from something deeper.—These restrictions are part of a radical mistake about the policy and lawful power of an American City Government.

No attempts of the sort can be so trivial, but they lead to the discussion of principles. The true American doctrine is not that the legislative assemblage of the City or State or Nation is possessed of total wisdom and guardianship over the people, and can entertain any proposition, and try it on just when and how they like. The office of Alderman or Mayor or Legislator is strictly the office of an agent. This agent is faithfully and industriously to perform a few plainly written and specified duties. He is not so continually to go meddling with the master's personal affairs or morals. Such is the American doctrine, and the doctrine of common sense.[1]

Shallow people, possessed with zeal for any particular cause, make it a great merit to run to and fro after special prohibitions that shall fix the case, and emasculate sin out of our houses and streets. Alas, gentlemen, the civilized world has been overwhelmed with prohibitions for many hundred years. We do not want prohibitions. What is always wanted, is a few strong-

[1] This is an early statement of the doctrine "Resist much, obey little" which Whitman shared with Emerson and, of course, with the States' Rights party as well. *Cf.* his utterances on slavery and free-soil. *Cf.* also the poems "Poem of Remembrance for a Girl or a Boy of These States" (in McKay Edition, 1900, pp. 510–511; first published in 1856) and "To the States" (1917 Edition, I, p. 10).

handed, big-brained, practical, honest men, at the head of affairs.

The true friends of the Sabbath and of its purifying and elevating influences, and of the many excellent physical and other reforms that mark the present age, are not necessarily those who complacently put themselves forward, and seek to carry the good through by penalties and stoppages, and arrests and fines.

The true friends of elevation and reform are the friends of the fullest rational liberty. For there is this vital and antiseptic power in liberty, that it tends forever and ever to strengthen what is good and erase what is bad.

For the City or State to become the overseer and dry nurse of a man, and coerce him, any further than before mentioned, into how he must behave himself, and when and whither he must travel, and by what conveyance, or what he shall be permitted to use or dispose of on certain days of the week, and what forced to disuse, would be to make a poor thing of a man. In such matters, the American sign-posts turn in the same direction for all grades of our government. The citizen must have room. He must learn to be so muscular and self-possessed; to rely more on the restrictions of himself than any restrictions of statute books, or city ordinances, or police. This is the feeling that will make live men and superior women. This will make a great, athletic, spirited city, of noble and marked character, with a reputation for itself wherever railroads run, and ships sail, and newspapers and books are read.

The old landmarks of the law, established and needed to preserve life, liberty and property, are always good, and never denied by any body. Beyond them, what the people actually wish of those they commission in office is, the direct performance of a small number of distinct and incumbent duties, coming home to the necessity and benefit of all hands, and about which there is also no dispute. If those in office would do these duties, and do them well, it would take up their entire time, and give the public a satisfaction and pleasure they have never yet experienced.

I have also, gentlemen, with perfect respect, to remind you, and through you to remind others, including those, whoever they may be, who desire to be your successors, or to hold any office, prominent or subordinate, in the City Government, of the stern demand, in all parts of this Republic, for a better, purer, more generous and comprehensive administration of the affairs of cities; a demand in which I, in common with the quite entire body of my fellow-citizens and fellow tax-payers of Brooklyn, cordially join.—We believe the mighty interests of so many people, and so much life and wealth, should be far less at the sport or dictation of caucuses and cabals. We would have nothing hoggish or exclusive. We wish to see municipal legislation not so much stifled by little ideas and aims, or the absence of ideas and aims.[1]

I would suggest to no locality a reconstruction too far off. I do not think so highly of what is to be done at the Capitols of Washington or Albany. Here, it is enough for us to attend to Brooklyn. There is indeed nowhere any better scope for practically exhibiting the full-sized American idea, than in a great, free, proud, American City. Most of our cities are huge aggregates of people, riches, and enterprise. The avenues, edifices and furniture are splendid; but what is that to splendor of character? To encourage the growth of trade and property is commendable; but our politics might also encourage the forming of men of superior demeanor, and less shuffling and blowing.

Marked as the size, numbers, elegance, and respectability of Brooklyn have become, a more lasting and solid glory of this or any community must always be in personal, and might be, in municipal qualities. Out of these in ancient times, a few thousand men made the names of their cities immortal. The free and haughty democracies of some of those old towns, not one third our size of population, rated themselves on equal terms with powerful kingdoms, and are preserved in literature, and the admiration of the earth.

The Consolidated City of Brooklyn will commence well. Its start need not be clogged by anything embarrassing or lowering. Its beauty of site, cleanliness and health will never be surpassed by any city, old or new. Its historical reminiscences are more interesting than those on the Continent itself—the whole or any of them. Here was expended the keenest anguish, and the larger half of the blood and death of the American Revolution.

The citizens and government may well accept the spirit of its old days, and calculate our future on those large and patriotic premises. Early visited by the Dutch, our founders, who here planted their wholesome physical, political and

[1] *Cf. post*, II, pp. 252–253.

moral peculiarities—soon interfused with Anglo-Saxon mind and tendency to expansion—cheerfully receiving all honest and industrious comers, and resolving them into the general American type—the two ancient settlements of Brooklyn and Bushwick have sped onward, counting less than a hundred and fifty houses at the commencement of the present century, to what they now are, and to advance still faster under a combined impetus.

Every thing about the new phases of these old towns signifies their unavoidable and harmonious progress, merged into one, on the grandest scale. In the returns of inhabitants at the last authorized census, Brooklyn, Williamsburg, Greenpoint and Bushwick together contained as many as either one of the three States of California, Delaware, or Rhode Island, and considerably more than either one of the first two. The young men are now walking among us who will see consolidated Brooklyn a vast community of a million souls, and not merely one of the leading cities of this republic, but one of the greatest on the globe.[1] It is time that its municipal character and views should be big and progressive in proportion.

With its population of 200,000 as consolidated—with a stretch of eight miles between its northeastern and southwestern points, and six miles between its northwestern and southeastern ones—with its majestic river, unsurpassed by any that flows—its imposing heights, its shores, wharves, elevations, and the diversified surface of its eighteen roomy wards—its popular schools, and scores upon scores of churches, many of them of the grandest style of architecture and ornament—its solemn, ample, and appropriate cemeteries, confessedly the first either in this country or abroad—its massive National Dock, and workshops and enginery for constructing the heaviest metaled government ships—the Atlantic Docks and wharves also, with their long range of storehouses, and their sheltered artificial harbor—the busy ship yards of the shores of Williamsburg and Greenpoint, employing many hundreds of American mechanics, the choicest breed for the greatest city—the numerous ferries running night and day—Washington Park, embracing the breastworks of Fort Greene, and of the imperishable soil, the token of our dismal battle ground—the tracks of railroads, and their cars, and the interminable lines of conveniently laid out and flagged streets, lit

---

[1] A prophecy which was repeated seven years later in the "Brooklyniana" (see *post*, II, pp. 252, 292), and which has, of course, been more than fulfilled.

with gas at night—the hundreds and hundreds of first-class private dwellings, so rich in their display and sumptuousness, the thousands upon thousands of the comfortable homes of the free citizens and their families—and the wide spread fields of the outer wards, with our well ordered Public Institutions, Hospitals and Jails—and with the endless surroundings of the civilization of the nineteenth century in a land undisturbed by war or any threatening evil, Brooklyn may well be the choice and pride of her sons and daughters, and of all who are identified with the place in any public capacity.

I can think of hardly any office of a great city like consolidated Brooklyn but what is a dignified and responsible office, and no field for the narrowness of mere politicians or the endless hangers on of parties. Neither legislative, executive or judicial,—neither the duties of finance, police, law, fires, water, ferries, health, record, assessments, streets, schools, hospitals, repairs, lands and places, or what not, can ever be attended to by inferior men in any other than an inferior and mean manner. Especially for the first citizen, or Mayor—especially for Aldermen—especially for the Police, every member of that body, without a single exception, Brooklyn ought to show well-developed men, the best gentlemen, no cowards, always sober, wide-awake and civil, proud of the town and devoted to it and realizing in it and in themselves the supreme merit of a high and courteous independence. Every one should be possessed with the eternal American ideas of liberty, friendliness, amplitude and courage. It is nonsense to fancy such fine traits on a diffused and conspicuous scale, as President or Governor, and be without them for home consumption. The right sort of spirit will exemplify them just as much here directly at our doors, or the corners of the curbstones, or our City Hall.

After all is said, however, the work of establishing and raising the character of cities of course remains at last in their original capacity with the people themselves. Strictly speaking, when the proper time comes, it comes. Perhaps the citizens have no right to complain of being hampered and cheated and overtaxed and insulted; for they always hold the remedy in their own hands, and can apply it whenever they like. I am not the man to soft-soap the people, any more than I do office-holders; but this I say for them at all times that their very credulity and repeated confidence in others are organic signs of noble elements in the national character.

Printed in the United States
100773LV00001B/102/A